TAX
HANDBOOK
1994-95

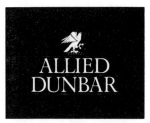

ALLIED
DUNBAR

TAX
HANDBOOK
1994-95

by

A Foreman

PANNELL
KERR
FORSTER

CHARTERED ACCOUNTANTS

LONGMAN

© Allied Dunbar Assurance plc 1994

ISBN 0 75200 0292

Published by

Longman Law, Tax and Finance
Longman Group UK Limited
21–27 Lamb's Conduit Street, London WC1N 3NJ

Associated Offices

Australia, Hong Kong, Malaysia, Singapore, USA

A CIP catalogue record for this book is available from the British Library.

Cover designed and illustrated by Sigmund Shalit, London.

Computerset by Kerrypress Ltd, Luton, Beds.
Printed in Great Britain by
Bath Press, Bath, Avon

Abbreviations

ACT	advance corporation tax
ADR	American depositary receipt
APPP	appropriate personal pension plan
AVC	additional voluntary contribution
BES	business expansion scheme
CAA	Capital Allowances Act 1990
CGT	capital gains tax
CGTA	Capital Gains Tax Act 1979
COMPS	contracted-out money purchase scheme
CPO	compulsory purchase order
CTO	Capital Taxes Office
DSS	Department of Social Security
EIS	enterprise investment scheme
ESC	extra-statutory concession
FA	Finance Act
F(No 2)A	Finance (No 2) Act
FPCS	fixed profit car scheme
FSAVC	free-standing additional voluntary contribution
FURBS	funded unapproved retirement benefit scheme
GCD	General Claims District
GMP	guaranteed minimum pension
HP	hire-purchase
IHT	inheritance tax
IHTA	Inheritance Tax Act 1984
IRC	Inland Revenue Commissioners
LAPR	life assurance premium relief
LIBOR	London inter-bank offer rate
LIFO	last in, first out
MIRAS	mortgage interest relief at source
NIC	national insurance contribution
NRE	net relevant earnings
NSB	National Savings Bank

para	paragraph
PAYE	pay as you earn
PEP	personal equity plan
PHI	permanent health insurance
PPP	personal pension plan
PRAS	pension relief at source
PRP	profit-related pay
PSO	Pension Schemes Office
PY	preceding year
reg	regulation
RPI	retail prices index
s(ss)	section (sections) of an Act
SAYE	save as you earn
Sched	Schedule of an Act
SDRT	stamp duty reserve tax
SERPS	State earnings-related pension scheme
SI	Statutory Instrument
SSAP	statement of standard accounting practice
SSAS	small self-administered scheme
STC	Simon's Tax Cases
TA	Income and Corporation Taxes Act
TC	Tax Cases
TCGA	Taxation of Chargeable Gains Act 1992
TESSA	tax-exempt special savings account
TMA	Taxes Management Act 1970
USM	Unlisted Securities Market
VAT	value added tax
VATA	Value Added Tax Act 1983

Preface

This book covers a wide field and is aimed at both the professional and non-professional reader. It deals with income tax, capital gains tax, inheritance tax, corporation tax and VAT. It also covers (in rather less detail) stamp duty and that other levy on our income, a tax in all but name, national insurance contributions.

The attempt to simplify our tax system seems to be a losing battle; this year's Finance Act is the longest ever (and by a margin of nearly 50 per cent). We are in a period of change and the Act introduces the self assessment regime which will come into force in 1997–98. There are also complex income tax and capital gains tax changes.

We have tried to make this Handbook 'user friendly', and at the same time provide a comprehensive analysis of the relevant legislation. The overall style of the book should help people from all walks of life who have to grapple with unfamiliar areas of taxation. The cross references will be especially useful to those whose daily work brings them face to face with our complex tax system—Accountants, Solicitors, and Company Secretaries.

If there is a complex problem requiring professional help, the comprehensive system of references will guide the reader to the precise point of the legislation that covers the matter in question. Nevertheless, because of the complex nature of the legislation, it would generally be advisable to seek professional guidance where substantial amounts are involved.

I have had invaluable assistance from Vince Jerrard and Stuart Reynolds of Allied Dunbar, my colleagues at Pannell Kerr Forster, Peter Jun Tai, Mark Francis, Peter Swash and Tim Buss who each contributed chapters, and from Kenneth Crofton Martin, Paul Clarke, Jon Hills and Julie Evans who conducted a 'Peer Review'. I must also acknowledge the enormous contribution made by David Vessey of Allied Dunbar and Jilli Smith of Longman who have devoted endless effort to making the material contained in this book more accessible and useful.

A Foreman

Contents

12 Life assurance and pensions

by Vince Jerrard and Stuart Reynolds

13 Capital gains tax

14 The calculation of capital gains

23 National insurance contributions and social security benefits

24 Tax and companies

by Peter Swash

25 Outline of VAT

by Tim Buss

Finance Act 1994—Checklist

Main Subject	Sections	Schedules	References
Customs & Excise			
Rates	1–6	1–3	Chapter 25
Appeals and Penalties			
and powers	7–27	4–5	
Air passenger duty	28–44	6	
VAT, insurance premium tax	45–74	7	
Income tax			
Rates	75		27.1.1
Allowances	76–78		27.1.2
Relief for maintenance payments	79		Chapter 8
Mortgage interest relief	81–81	8	Chapter 9
Relief for blind persons	82		7.10
Medical insurance	83	9	10.5
Relief for vocational training	84		10.4
Corporation tax rates	85–86		Chapter 24
Benefits in kind	87–89		3.4
Capital gains			
Annual exemption	90		27.2.1
Reinvestment and retirement relief	91–92	11	Chapter 15
Indexation allowance			
(restriction for losses)	93		14.5
Futures, options and settlements	95–97		
Profit related pay	98–101		3.10
Pension schemes	103–108		Chapter 12
Annuities (proposals for PAYE rather than basic rate deducted at source)	109–110		
Unit trusts, rates and distributions	111–112	14	
Exchange gains and losses	114–116		
Capital allowances	117–121		2.5
Manufactured dividends	122–124		

The UK 'tax system'—and you

In this chapter, the following areas of tax and tax planning are covered:

(1) Introduction and outline of the major taxes.
(2) Completing your tax return.
(3) Understanding your responsibilities and rights.

Introduction

> . . . No man in this country is under the smallest obligation, moral or other, so to arrange his legal relations to his business or to his property as to enable the Inland Revenue to put the largest possible shovel into his stores. The Inland Revenue is not slow . . . to take every advantage which is open to it under the taxing statutes for the purpose of depleting the taxpayer's pocket. And the taxpayer is, in like manner, entitled to be astute to prevent, so far as he honestly can, the depletion of his means by the Revenue.
>
> Lord Clyde in *Ayrshire Pullman Motor Services and Ritchie v IRC*.

Some people might take the view that we have never had it so good—the present 40 per cent top rate seems quite reasonable when compared with the rates of 83–98 per cent which applied in the 1970s. On the other hand, many feel that the combined consequences of income tax, capital gains tax, VAT, corporation tax and inheritance tax still enable the Inland Revenue to take an unreasonably large share of our income and savings.

One thing is clear: despite a succession of Chancellors who undertook to simplify the tax 'system', personal taxation is still a complex matter on which professional advice is often required. The structures of individual taxes may have been simplified, but difficulties still arise from the interaction and overlap of various taxes. Even a simplified tax does not always stay simple. New reliefs and anti-avoidance provisions may be added in each year's Finance Act or Acts.

The taxes that affect us

The three major taxes with which this book is concerned are income tax, capital gains tax and, to a lesser extent, inheritance tax (previously known as estate duty and capital transfer tax).

(1) Income tax is a tax on *income*. Capital receipts are not taxed as income unless they fall within certain very specific provisions which deem them to be income.

(2) Capital gains tax is a tax on gains realised from the disposal of a capital asset. Usually the dividing line is fairly clear, but sometimes it is uncertain as to whether a lump sum receipt is income or capital. The normal way of telling is to ask yourself whether you still own the asset which has produced the receipt, but this is not an infallible rule.

(3) Inheritance tax is a capital tax levied on a person's net wealth when he dies, and can also apply to certain lifetime gifts.

There is a range of other taxes (such as stamp duty, VAT, corporation tax etc). Another potential claim on your income is national insurance contributions which, whilst not strictly a tax, are an increasingly important source of revenue to the Government. You should also bear in mind that a single transaction may give rise to more than one tax. A transfer of property, for instance, may attract stamp duty and inheritance tax as well as capital gains tax.

Husband and wife

The tax legislation which applied before 6 April 1990 generally treated a married couple as one person for income and capital gains tax purposes. The incomes of the husband and wife were added together (subject to exemptions) and tax was charged on the combined amount.

From 1990–91 and subsequent tax years, husband and wife have been treated as separate taxpayers for both income tax and capital gains tax (this is called 'independent taxation'). They have always been assessed separately in relation to inheritance tax.

The schedular system of income tax

When Lord Addington re-introduced income tax in 1801, it was not thought to be proper or appropriate for a civil servant to be supplied with full details of an individual's total income. Consequently, income tax was made payable under several schedules, each with its own system of assessment. This made it possible for a taxpayer to report the income taxable under each schedule to a separate Inspector and so avoid the full extent of his income being known by any one official. This legacy remains with us today. Over the past two centuries, a great number of different rules have grown up so that the way in which income is assessed under each different schedule varies and different payment dates apply.

Income tax is collected under six schedules as follows.

Schedule A

Schedule A applies to income from property (ie land and buildings) and includes rent and certain lease premiums. It does not include rents from furnished lettings as these will normally be assessed under Schedule D Case VI.

Schedule B

This schedule applied to the taxation of woodlands managed on a commercial basis with a view to making a profit. It was abolished with effect from 6 April 1988.

Schedule C

This covers paying agents (eg bankers) who have the responsibility for handling the income from UK gilt-edged securities and any public revenue organisations based overseas.

Schedule D

This schedule is itself sub-divided into six cases as follows:

Cases I and II cover the profits or gains arising from trades (Case I) or professions or vocations (Case II), ie income from self-employment.

Case III is primarily concerned with the taxation of interest and annual payments but a whole range of related items has been included over the years.

Cases IV and V cover the overseas income of UK resident individuals. Case IV is concerned with interest on overseas securities (unless already covered by Schedule C); Case V covers income from overseas possessions.

Case VI covers miscellaneous profits which do not fall into other Cases of Schedule D and are not taxed through any of the other schedules.

Schedule E

Schedule E covers the taxation of all wages, salaries, benefits etc resulting from employments (including directorships). It is divided into three cases as follows:

Case I applies to earnings received by UK resident and ordinarily resident individuals.

Case II applies to earnings received by individuals who are resident but not ordinarily resident in the United Kingdom.

Case III applies to work carried out abroad.

Schedule F

This schedule covers dividends and other distributions by companies.

Income tax an annual tax

Income tax is an annual tax in that it arises on an individual's income for a tax year (which ends on 5 April). Capital gains tax is also an annual tax in this sense. In contrast, inheritance tax may be levied by reference to a person's chargeable transfers during a seven year period.

There is one other way in which income tax is an annual tax. It is an obligation imposed by each year's Finance Act (unlike capital gains tax which is imposed by the Taxation of Chargeable Gains Act 1992). This can have some surprising consequences. For example, where an individual is made bankrupt after the Finance Act for the current year has received Royal Assent, his liability for that year comes to an end and is recoverable only out of the assets held by the individual's trustee in bankruptcy. At the end of the tax year concerned, the individual loses this exemption from income tax since a fresh liability for the following year is imposed by that year's Finance Act.

The Budget and Finance Bill

Each year, the Chancellor of the Exchequer introduces his Budget. Things sometimes move slowly in this country and it was only in November 1993, after over 200 years, that the concept of a 'unified Budget' was introduced so that the Government's spending plans could be looked at together with its proposals to raise revenue by taxation.

Shortly after the Budget (usually during the same week) the Chancellor introduces the Finance Bill and it is said to have a 'first reading'. However, this is somewhat misleading since the Bill is not actually printed for a further three weeks.

It is then read in Committee, at which time points of detail are considered and amendments are made.

It is then brought back for a 'third reading'—in this case a formal vote of approval by the House of Commons. It is then approved by the House of Lords (actually their Lordships cannot amend it because it is a 'Money Bill' and since 1911 the House of Lords has been debarred from making changes to such Bills). It then receives the Royal Assent and becomes an Act. This last stage must happen by 5 May as otherwise the Provisional Collection of Income Tax Act would cease to apply and there would no longer be a legal requirement to deduct tax at source (eg under PAYE).

The whole period during which the Chancellor's proposals move from being a Finance Bill to becoming an Act is less than 100 working days for Parliament. The draft legislation is often complex (the 1993 Finance Act was the longest ever seen until the Finance Act 1994 which was nearly a third longer) and it is not surprising when it subsequently emerges that the legislation is ambiguous or uncertain. Hence the need for statements of practice and extra statutory concessions (see page 9).

Completing your tax return

You may well have noticed that the tax return form has changed considerably. It now asks a great many more direct questions. As you work through it and go through the Revenue's notes, you may like to refer to the relevant section of this book which looks at matters more from a taxpayer's perspective. Bear in mind that the sometimes rather arbitrary order of items on the Revenue's form largely reflects our present system of tax schedules, each having a different set of rules for determining the taxable amount. We have arranged this book slightly differently so as to cover various broad categories of income in more depth with a view to bringing out the salient points.

Income from self-employment—See Chapter 2

Details of the way that taxable profits are computed (see 2.3–2.4).
Capital allowances (see 2.5).
Enterprise allowance (see 2.4.2).
National Insurance Class 4 (see 23.4 and 2.9.2).

Income from employment—See Chapter 3

Main principles (see 3.1).
Lump sum and compensation payments (see 3.18).
Profit-related pay and profit sharing (see 3.10–3.11).
Cars and car fuel (see 3.5).
Other benefits in kind (see 3.4–3.9).
Allowable expenses (see 3.3).
Earnings from work abroad (see 3.19).

Pensions

State pensions (see 12.14 and 23.5).
Other pensions (see 12.11–12.13 and 12.15 and 5.16 (pensions from overseas)).
Surpluses repaid from an FSAVC scheme (see 12.12.4).

National insurance and social security benefits (see 22.5)

Pension contributions

Retirement annuity payments (see 12.10).
Personal pension contributions (see 12.9).
FSAVC schemes (see 12.12).
Trade Union or friendly society death benefit schemes (see 10.6).

Income from property

Rent-a-room scheme (see 4.8).
Property abroad (see 5.11).
Other rentals in the UK (see 4.1–4.5 and 4.7).

Income from your savings and investments

National Savings (see 5.1 and 11.1).
Income from UK banks, building societies and deposit takers (see 5.1 and 6.2).
Other interest received in the United Kingdom (see 5.2).
Dividends from shares in UK companies (see 6.3).
Stock dividends (see 6.3.5).
Income from UK unit trusts (see 6.3.2).
Accrued income (see 5.5).
Income from savings and investments abroad (see 5.10 and 6.5).
Other income from savings and investments (see 5.17).

Other income

Income from trusts funded by others (see 6.6.3).
Income and capital from settlements for which you have provided funds (see 19.5).
Income from estates (see 6.6.4).

Maintenance and alimony (see Chapter 8)

All other income and profits (see 5.17, 12.3 and 20.1–20.6)

Deductions and outgoings

Mortgage interest (see 9.1).
Other qualifying loans (see 9.2–9.4).
Vocational training (see 10.4).
Private medical insurance for people aged 60 or over (see 10.5).
Gift aid donations (see 10.3).
Covenants to charity (see 10.2).
Other covenants (see 10.1).
Maintenance or alimony payments (see Chapter 8).

Capital gains

Chargeable gains (see Chapters 13–15).
Benefits from a non-resident settlement (see 20.12).

Payments abroad (see 21.6.8)

Personal allowances

Allowances for those born before 6 April 1929 (see 7.6).
Allowances to be claimed by married men (see 7.5 and 7.9).
Allowances for widows (see 7.7).
If you have a child and are single, separated, divorced or widowed (see 7.8).
Blind person's allowance (see 7.10).

Understanding your responsibilities and rights

The Inland Revenue is now increasingly run more like a business. At the same time, the Government requires it to operate quality management and to assess its efficiency in terms of 'satisfied customers'. This has led to the Revenue issuing the Taxpayer's Charter, which reads as follows:

The Taxpayer's Charter

You are entitled to expect the Inland Revenue

To be fair
- By settling your tax affairs impartially
- By expecting you to pay only what is due under the law
- By treating everyone with equal fairness

To help you
- To get your tax affairs right
- To understand your rights and obligations
- By providing clear leaflets and forms
- By giving you information and assistance at our enquiry offices
- By being courteous at all times

To provide an efficient service
- By settling your tax affairs promptly and accurately
- By keeping your private affairs strictly confidential
- By using the information you give us only as allowed by the law
- By keeping to a minimum your costs of complying with the law
- By keeping our costs down

To be accountable for what we do
- By setting standards for ourselves and publishing how well we live up to them

If you are not satisfied
- We will tell you exactly how to complain
- You can ask for your tax affairs to be looked at again
- You can appeal to an independent tribunal
- Your MP can refer your complaint to the Ombudsman

In return, we need you
- To be honest
- To give us accurate information
- To pay your tax on time'

All we ask is that you keep us up to date with your tax affairs. When we send you a tax return (which probably won't be very often) do fill it in and send it back promptly.

And please don't wait for us to send you a return if you find your income is not being properly taxed—or changes take place in your life which could affect your tax position. Just let your Tax Office know.

It's not simply that the law says you should do so, it's in your interests anyway. Because if you don't contact us early enough, you may pay more than you should—or worse still, find that you actually owe tax.

What this means in practice

In practice, this means that a taxpayer should attend promptly to correspondence from the Inland Revenue and complete tax returns within a reasonable period, If you find that there are some aspects of your tax return which are complex and which prevent you from completing the entire form, you should contact the Inspector and explain the reason for the difficulty. You would also be well advised to report certain income and gains by 31 October following the end of the tax year in order to avoid potential interest charges (and penalties).

In future, the responsibilities for taxpayers to make returns are likely to be even more onerous. The Government is planning to introduce a form of self assessment which will come into operation from 1996-97. As from that year, an individual will have to make a decision whether or not to calculate his or her own tax liability. If he decides to calculate his own tax, the tax return and calculation will need to be submitted to the Inland Revenue by 31 January following the end of the tax year. Taxpayers who choose to ask the Revenue to work out their liability will need to submit their tax returns by 30 September following the end of the tax year. Interest will be charged where returns are submitted late, or tax is not paid on time.

Statements of Practice and Extra Statutory Concessions

It is extremely important that the Inland Revenue operates a uniform interpretation of the tax legislation. This is all part of the Taxpayer's Charter which requires the Revenue to deal with two taxpayers in the same way if their circumstances are identical.

In cases where the legislation is obscure, or its precise implication is uncertain, the Inland Revenue publish Statements of Practice. These operate as a shield rather than a sword for the taxpayer. You can rely upon the Revenue applying these statements of practice but they do not affect your statutory rights and, if you believe that the Revenue interpretation is wrong, it is still open to you to appeal to the Commissioners.

The Inland Revenue also publish Extra Statutory Concessions. These apply in cases where the legislation is quite clear, but the letter of the law produces an unreasonable result. In effect, the Inland Revenue recognises that Parliament could never have intended to impose certain tax liabilities, and Extra Statutory Concessions are commonsense rules which the Revenue applies so as to avoid an unreasonable result. Once again, the Revenue publishes these Extra Statutory Concessions because it recognises the need to treat all taxpayers alike. In general, and unless your circumstances are special, or you are seeking to apply an Extra Statutory Concession so as to avoid tax, you can rely on the Inspector of Taxes applying a published Extra Statutory Concession if it covers your particular circumstances.

If you and the Revenue cannot reach agreement

There will be cases from time to time where an Inspector of Taxes and a taxpayer (or his professional adviser) form different conclusions as to whether, or how, tax should apply to a particular transaction. In such cases where there is an honest difference of opinion, or even in cases where there is an argument as to the actual facts, the Revenue do *not* have the last word. The procedure for resolving such disputes is to require an appeal to be heard by the Commissioners.

There are two types of Commissioners, General Commissioners and Special Commissioners (see 19.2), but the difference lies mainly in the type of disputes that each type of Commissioner is best equipped to deal with. Questions of fact, requiring local knowledge, are best heard by General Commissioners. Special Commissioners are generally lawyers and are normally regarded as more competent to deal with technical issues arising from the interpretation of the legislation.

The Commissioners are an independent body and are not connected with the Inspector of Taxes or the Inland Revenue. Their findings on matters of fact are normally final, but if a taxpayer (or the Inland Revenue) is dissatisfied with their decision on a point of law, an appeal may be made to the Courts. Normally, the appeal is heard by the High Court (or the Court of Session in Scotland). It is even possible to appeal against decisions by the Courts and ultimately the matter may go right up to the House of Lords for a decision.

1 Managing your tax affairs— and saving tax

Managing your tax affairs and planning ahead are really inextricably connected with one another: you can't really plan in an effective way unless you are on top of your responsibility to file returns and you are aware of key deadlines.

In this chapter we cover:

General strategy

(1) Key points to bear in mind.

Some specific situations where you need to plan ahead

(2) If you are thinking of becoming self-employed.
(3) If you're already in business.
(4) If you are employed.
(5) Managing your investments.
(6) Tax deductible investments.
(7) Your family affairs and personal financial planning.

Managing your tax affairs

(8) Ensure that all important deadlines are kept.

1.1 Key points to bear in mind

There is no simple solution to the question of how to pay less tax— if only there were! And there are plenty of ways of going wrong and increasing your tax problems. However, you will almost certainly do well to adopt the following basic principles of effective tax management and planning:

Do carry out some background research

Your tax affairs need to be taken seriously. It is important to fill out your tax return in a meticulous way. You should carefully read the notes issued with the tax return and, if there are areas on which you are not quite sure, you should seek advice, either from the Inland Revenue itself or from a practising accountant.

Don't let your tax returns get into arrears

When you receive a tax return, you are enjoined to fill it out and return it within 30 days. In practice, no-one pays much attention to this particular time limit unless the Revenue issues the tax return after 30 September. However, it is important to complete your tax return and get it in to the Inland Revenue by 31 October following the end of the tax year—otherwise you may be liable for interest and penalties.

Self-assessment is being introduced over the next few years. Once that system comes into force, you will need to submit your tax return, together with a cheque covering your outstanding tax, by 31 January following the tax year. If you fail to do this, you will automatically become liable for interest and penalties. Whilst self-assessment is still two or three years away, it makes sense to bring your affairs up to date now so that you will be well placed to cope with the demands of the new tax regime.

Don't get involved in evasion

Before you take any action, ask yourself whether you would be happy for all the documentation to be put before the Inspector of Taxes. If in fact a scheme relies upon non-disclosure, you may be getting involved in evasion. If you are found out you will become liable for interest and penalties and you might be subject to prosecution.

Do carry out an annual review or 'audit' of your tax affairs

Income tax and national insurance contributions probably eat up nearly one-third of your total income. Unless your circumstances are very straightforward and you have only one source of income, you may well receive communications from two or more tax districts, various Collectors of Taxes and the Department of Social Security. Don't take it as read that all the Civil Servants concerned will liaise amongst themselves, it is quite possible that you may have overpaid tax on one type of income at the very time that you are receiving demands for payment of tax in relation to other income or capital gains.

Mistakes do happen, and in the past you may have failed to claim all the allowances to which you were entitled. You should therefore carry out a periodic check or 'audit' to ensure that you (and members of your family such as your minor children or your elderly dependent relatives) have claimed all the tax allowances and reliefs to which you are entitled. If you find that mistakes have occurred, you need to file a repayment claim within the six year time limit or the overpaid tax will be lost to you forever.

Do plan ahead

Part of practical tax planning is to anticipate things which could change in the future. For example, it may be that you are likely to sell your present home in two or three years' time when you reach retirement. If you have let a property in the past, you need to look into the position now to see whether there could be a capital gains tax charge when you sell the property and, if there is a potential problem, what steps you might take to avoid the problem. If you are going to sell your business when you retire in a few years' time, you need to find out what tax may be payable and what you can do to reduce this.

Do take all taxes into account

It is important to be aware that steps you might take to avoid income tax may have capital gains tax consequences, or *vice versa*. For example, you may be able to get a tax deduction if you set aside part of your home for work. However, if a couple of rooms are set aside exclusively for business purposes, this may affect your main residence exemption and could result in a capital gains tax charge when you sell the property. There may well be ways in which you could both have your cake and eat it, but you need to look into the fine detail of the rules concerning the main residence exemption.

Do be flexible

It makes no sense to invest in a savings plan because the return is free of tax if the plan is not suited to your personal requirements and the capital is tied up for (say) ten years. You should bear in mind that circumstances may change and it may therefore be unwise to put all your spare investments into a trust for the benefit of your children if your own situation might change. In recent years, many individuals have suffered unexpected demands on their capital (spare a thought for members of Lloyd's) and some people are now regretting that they gave away capital which is no longer surplus to their requirements.

Don't forget the law may change

Tax legislation is subject to a review at least once a year in the Chancellor's Budget. Moreover, decisions by the Courts are constantly resulting in changed interpretations. This is another area where you need to be flexible rather than lean too heavily upon a favourable tax situation afforded by the present rules.

At one time, it was possible to obtain income tax relief for all interest payments. When the law was changed, individuals were given relief for a transitional period on existing borrowings. Nevertheless, the withdrawal of interest relief came as a serious blow to those who had come to depend upon it. So before you carry out any tax planning which will affect your situation in future years, ask yourself how much various tax reliefs are worth to you and how you could rearrange your affairs if the law were changed and the reliefs curtailed or abolished.

Don't be fooled by G & T tax advice

One of the things that all professional advisers complain of is that clients invariably know someone who assures them that, quite legitimately, he is paying virtually no tax at all. Be wary of advice given over a Gin and Tonic: very often, the individual himself does not understand all the ramifications of his own affairs. Worse still, some of the schemes put forward often turn out to involve evasion (which is illegal) rather than avoidance. Even where there is some substance to what is being said, your friend's or colleague's situation may be quite different from yours. For example, someone who advises you that he pays no tax on his earnings from work carried out outside this country may have a foreign domicile (see Chapter 22) and so be entitled to reliefs which are not available to you as a UK national.

Do take professional advice

Unless your affairs are extremely straightforward, you could probably do with a financial 'health check' from time to time, ie a discussion with an accountant or tax adviser to go over your affairs and look for ways in which you might improve your situation and pay less tax. A good accountant should be able to more than cover the fees that he charges by pointing out ways in which you can reduce personal taxes.

If your affairs are more complex, you probably need to take professional advice on a regular basis. It will also make sense for a tax accountant or adviser to take over the detailed work of preparing your tax return, agreeing assessments and making sure that deadlines are not missed.

Do bear in mind the anti-avoidance provisions

The tax legislation contains extensive anti-avoidance provisions intended to make sure that you cannot save tax by carrying out transactions in a roundabout way. In particular, much legislation is aimed at preventing a person from converting interest income into capital gain. There are also provisions aimed against the use (or, to be more specific, the *abuse*) of settlements. In the main, you will be assessed on income arising to trustees of a settlement if you created that settlement and there is any way in which you, or your spouse, may benefit under the settlement.

If you are considering taking steps for tax planning which you hope will help you to escape tax, but which are contrary to the spirit of the legislation, you will need to take a particularly close look at the anti-avoidance provisions. This is a situation where it is normally necessary to take professional advice.

1.2 If you are thinking of becoming self-employed

1.2.1 Will the Revenue accept that you are self-employed?

The first question to address is whether the Revenue is likely to accept that you are self-employed. If the main thing that you have to sell is your time, and you are subject to supervision in the way in which you carry out your work, the Revenue may well regard you as an employee. It cuts no ice that your contract may state that you are self-employed.

One reason why the Revenue will look into this so closely is that, if you are self-employed, you will be able to claim certain expenses which are not allowable deductions for employees. So you should take all possible steps to ensure that your claim for self-employed status can stand up to scrutiny by the Inland Revenue (see 2.2).

In theory, the risk of the Revenue's reclassifying a self-employed person as an employee lies with the employer. If the Revenue view is eventually upheld, the employer will be liable to pay Class I national insurance contributions and the Revenue may well require him to pay over the tax that he ought to have withheld under PAYE. Where this happens, the consequences can be disastrous. In law, an employer is precluded from collecting arrears of Class I national insurance contributions by deducting them from subsequent payments to the individual concerned. In other words, if the employer does not get it right first time round, he cannot correct his mistake later on. Similarly, the primary responsibility for deducting tax under PAYE and paying it over to the Revenue lies with the employer. The Collector of Taxes will normally be reluctant to get into time consuming disputes with the employee and will simply demand the tax from the employer, leaving him to make any adjustment by agreement with the employee. Nevertheless, most self-employed individuals also have a vested interest in the Revenue's accepting that they are genuinely self-employed. If a dispute arises with someone to whom you provide services, he is unlikely to want to deal with you again in the future, certainly not on a self-employed basis.

1.2.2   Keep the Revenue informed

Once you start to be self-employed, your best interests are safeguarded by keeping the Revenue advised as to what you are doing. Make your existence known to your local tax district and advise them as to when they may expect to receive accounts. An Inspector of Taxes is like anyone else, he is likely to be more reasonable if he is handled properly rather than irritated by the fact that he constantly has to chase you for information.

There are various other practical matters. You should make enquiries of your local VAT Office to see if you will need to be registered for VAT (see 25.4.1). You should also advise the Department of Social Security that you are self-employed and start to pay Class 2 national insurance contributions as a self-employed person.

1.2.3   Should you employ your spouse?

Depending upon the type of business you carry on, it may be appropriate for you to employ your spouse, or even to have your spouse as a partner (see 1.3.4 below). This may be a particularly good idea if your spouse would otherwise have little or no taxable income. However, if you employ your spouse, do not pay an unrealistic salary. The Revenue is almost bound to challenge a situation where the salary is disproportionate. The Revenue's argument is that you will be due a deduction only for a reasonable rate of remuneration paid to your spouse in return for services and expertise provided.

Do be careful on this; in principle you could suffer double taxation if you get it wrong since your spouse will still be taxed on his or her full salary even if only part of that salary is allowed as a deduction in arriving at your business profits for tax purposes.

Finally, when you commence self-employment, do think ahead and make provision for the tax payments that you will need to make over the next 18 months to two years. Get into the habit of setting aside part of your earnings each month so that you will have something in hand to pay the Inland Revenue when the assessments are eventually issued.

1.3 If you're already in business

1.3.1 Keep good records

Much of what has already been said applies to the same extent if you have been in business for a number of years already. In many businesses, some figures have to be estimated (for example, the extent to which a trader's telephone bill relates to business calls as opposed to private calls). There is nothing wrong with estimates, but do try to keep some sort of record so that the estimate can be supported if the Revenue challenges it.

Your accountant should avoid situations where estimated figures are included in accounts without any indication to the Revenue that the figures are estimates. The Inspector of Taxes may well want to go back to previous years if he looks into the position later on and decides that an estimate is unreasonable. The main defence against this would be where the Inspector was already on notice that the figures reported for earlier years' accounts were estimates.

1.3.2 Don't cut corners on PAYE

Beware of situations where you should withhold tax, especially where you are paying casual workers or freelance workers whom the Revenue may regard as employees. The Revenue has teams of investigators who carry out regular reviews of PAYE compliance.

1.3.3 Take VAT seriously

VAT is a constant source of problems. Whenever you carry out a major transaction you should ask a VAT specialist for advice. Also, bear in mind that Customs and Excise make regular control visits to examine accounting records. Penalties can be levied if mistakes are uncovered at such control visits so it is well worth having a review carried out in good time for errors to be corrected before such a control visit.

1.3.4 Remunerating your spouse

Think carefully about the salary that you pay your spouse. If the salary is less than you have to pay to an ordinary employee, increase the amount. Perhaps you should set up a pension scheme for your spouse as your contributions will be tax deductible.

Think also about bringing your spouse into partnership. This is a complex matter on which it is probably best to seek professional advice which will take account of the nature of your business, and the time, expertise or capital brought to the business by your spouse.

1.3.5 Taking a new partner or buying out an existing partner

In general, you ought to take professional advice whenever you bring in a new partner or, indeed, when you buy out an existing partner. There are a number of traps for the unwary here. For example, tax payable on the profits earned by a partnership is a 'joint and several' liability. This means that you could be asked to pay tax on all the profits of the business, and not just your share. It follows that if a partner leaves a firm, you should reach some agreement as to the cash which should be set aside to settle the firm's outstanding tax liabilities.

1.3.6 Relief for losses

If your business has not been going so well, and you have been suffering losses, look into the best way in which you can get relief. In some cases, you may be able to carry the losses back and set them against your other income (see 2.10). In other situations, the choice that is open to you will be to set your losses against your income for the year of the loss, or against your income of the following year, or carry the losses forward to be set against trading income received in later years. Obviously, it is going to make a great deal of difference if you take relief in a year in which you are otherwise going to be subject to 40 per cent tax rather than in a year in which your other income is relatively low and tax relief will be obtained at only 20 per cent or 25 per cent.

1.3.7 Plan ahead—changes in the Schedule D rules

Some of the longest and most complicated sections in this year's Finance Act relate to the way in which self-employed individuals are to be taxed in future. We are in the midst of a major upheaval as the existing 'preceding year' basis of assessment is to be superseded by the 'current year' basis (see 2.3.3).

The new rules will not come into full effect until 1997–98 but there are some complex transitional provisions. These offer opportunities for tax planning (as well as headaches to tax specialists!). If you are well advised you may be able to achieve substantial tax savings between now and 5 April 1997.

1.3.8   Reorganise partnership borrowings

There is one very important point for partners as we approach the change to the current year basis of assessment. If the firm has an overdraft, or other bank borrowings, the interest will normally be allowed as a deduction in arriving at the firm's profits. However, the assessment for 1996–97 may be based on the firm's average profits for a period of two years (or more) ending in 1996–97. This means that in effect only 50 per cent of interest payments made by the firm will qualify for tax relief.

It is possible to get round this and at the same time bring forward the relief. If individual partners raise personal loans and use the money that they have borrowed to contribute partnership capital, or to make loans to their own firm, they will be entitled to tax relief for the interest (see 9.3). The interest on such loans is allowed as a charge against the individual's income rather than as a deduction in arriving at the firm's profits. This means that relief is due for the year in which the partner pays the interest.

You should discuss with your accountant the possibility of you and your partners raising personal loans to put money into your firm to enable it to clear part or all of its existing borrowings. As far as the bank is concerned, there should be no overall effect, the money really goes round in a circle and at the end the total exposure of the bank will be much the same as it was to begin with. Restructuring borrowings in this way may enable you to secure more relief for interest payments.

1.3.9   Personal pension schemes (see 12.9)

It is particularly important for self-employed individuals to provide for their retirement since they qualify only for the basic State pension and not for SERPS. The Government has played its part in recent years in improving matters and the maximum contributions which may be paid to a personal pension scheme are now much greater than in earlier years—unless you are caught by the earnings cap because your profits exceed £76,800.

Contributions to a personal pension scheme are tax deductible. Furthermore, the pension scheme is not subject to tax of any kind and so the fund is likely to grow at a far faster rate than personal investments which are subject to tax.

It is possible to take the benefits from a personal pension sheme at any time after you reach age 50. Up to 25 per cent of the fund may be taken as a tax-free lump sum. The balance must be used to purchase an annuity.

1.3.10   Should you transfer your business to a company?

If your business is going really well, you should consider whether you should incorporate your business, ie transfer your business to a company. There are some general principles set out in 24.12 but once again this is a matter where you would probably be best advised to consult an accountant or tax adviser.

1.3.11   Plan for retirement and handing the business on to the next generation

Finally, do plan ahead, both for retirement and for passing on your business in due course to your family. There are key questions to be addressed in relation to capital gains tax planning (make sure that any gains that you realise on disposing of your business are going to be covered be retirement relief—see 15.8). Will inheritance tax be payable on your death or can matters be arranged so that 100 per cent business property relief will be due? See 17.8 on this.

1.4   If you are employed

Whether you are a company director, a senior executive, a manager or an ordinary employee, there are all manner of ways you may be able to reduce your tax liabilities.

1.4.1   Claim expenses

It is important to claim all allowable expenses (see 3.3). If you have to belong to a professional institute, the subscription should normally be an allowable expense. There are fixed deductions for workers in certain industries. If you are required to provide certain equipment yourself (for example, a fax machine at home) make sure that you put in a claim for the expenses associated with it, and claim capital allowances.

1.4.2   Keep records

If you are provided with a mobile phone, keep a note of the calls that you make and be prepared to demonstrate to the Revenue that you reimburse your employer for the full cost of any private calls. Otherwise, you may be charged tax on the standard scale benefit of £200.

If you are required to travel extensively, especially overseas, keep a note of your itinerary and the main types of expense that you incur. By doing this, you will be well placed to answer any queries from the

Inspector of Taxes and you should be able to demonstrate that there
is no benefit in kind if all the expenses were business related.

If you need to use your own car in the course of your employment,
find out whether the Fixed Profit Car Scheme applies (see 3.4.9). If
it does not, or the mileage payments exceed the FPCS rates, you need
to keep a detailed note of your business and private mileage so that
any benefit in kind can be calculated. Even if the mileage paid to you
by your employer is within the FPCS scale, do let the Revenue know
if you have taken a bank or HP loan to buy your car, as part of the
interest that you pay should be allowable.

1.4.3   Reduce car scale benefits

If you have a company car, bear in mind that the scale benefit is
increased by 50 per cent if your business mileage is less than 2,500
miles per annum and the scale benefit is halved if you have business
mileage of 18,000 miles or more per annum (see 3.5). If you are close
to either of these margins, it may be worthwhile bringing forward
some business trips to make sure that you qualify.

If you made a capital contribution towards the cost of your company
car, this should be deducted in arriving at your benefit in kind for
1994–95 and future years. The scale benefit will normally be 35 per
cent of the list price of your company car as reduced by any capital
contribution made by you up to a limit of £5,000 (whether this
contribution was made before or after 6 April 1994).

1.4.4   Tax efficient benefits

If you have any influence over the way in which your remuneration
package is made up, take account of the fact that some benefits are
more tax efficient than others. For example, it is well worth having
an interest free loan of £5,000 since no benefit in kind is assessed
whatsoever. The benefit of having the right to occupy a company flat
is often taxed on a favourable basis, especially where it originally cost
your company £75,000 or less (see 3.8 on this).

1.4.5   Pension schemes (see 12.11)

Pension benefits are particularly attractive as they are not normally
taxable. If you do not need all your salary to cover your living costs,
it may well be attractive if you can reach a 'deal' with your employer
so that he makes contributions towards your pension instead of giving
you a larger annual pay rise.

Quite separately from this, do carefully consider the merits of making
additional volutary contributions. If you are not in a company pension
scheme, you are most strongly advised to start a personal pension scheme.

1.4.6   Share incentives

Company directors and senior executives are often offered an opportunity to acquire shares in their company. However, there are various pitfalls which can apply if you acquire shares through an unapproved scheme (see 3.12) and this is an area where you need professional advice. Also plan ahead. If you have been given approved share options in the past (see 3.13), give some thought as to how you will reap the benefit. Don't forget that capital gains tax may be payable when you exercise your share options if you go on to sell the shares that you have acquired.

1.5   Managing your investments

It is important to keep tax planning in perspective. In general, investment considerations should dictate your investment policy. These will naturally vary according to an individual's perspective ie his age, need for short term and medium term liquidity, income requirements, the degree of risk that is acceptable, expectations as to future levels of inflation and perception of the economic climate etc. Tax planning has to be fitted in around these investment considerations. Having said all that, there are some quite simple steps which should be considered and which may help you to reduce the tax payable on your investment income and gains.

1.5.1   Use all your family's allowances

A married couple both have their own personal allowances and their income is taxed completely separately. If your spouse has little or no income, or is liable only at 25 per cent whereas you have to pay 40 per cent tax, there may be advantages in transferring income to him or her. There is a fairly straightforward way of doing this, ie hold bank deposit accounts, and other investments in your joint names. The basic rule is that where investments are held in this way, half of the resulting income is taxed on each spouse.

You should also bear in mind that your spouse will have his or her own £5,800 capital gains tax annual exemption. You should look for ways of using this each year, possibly by transferring investments (transfers between spouses are deemed to take place on a no gain/no loss basis) in order to put your spouse in a position to realise a gain on a sale to a third party. This will often be appropriate where a gain has built up on quoted securities. A judicious transfer to your spouse of stocks and shares which show a paper gain can save significant amounts of tax even if the transfer takes place shortly before the securities are sold. However, take care. The Revenue will often look very closely at the paperwork on such inter-spouse transfers and you will need to show that beneficial ownership of the securities actually passed to your spouse before a firm of stockbrokers was instructed to sell the shares. All other things being equal (which they seldom are) it is generally best to allow a few days to elapse between the transfer of the shares to your spouse and the sale by her (or him).

Sometimes there may be scope for using your children's annual capital gains tax exemption. This is more difficult since a gift of shares etc to anyone other than your spouse will normally be treated as a disposal which is deemed to take place for capital gains tax purposes at market value. However, if you hold shares in *unquoted* trading companies, and you can see an opportunity coming up whereby you will be able to realise those shares at a large gain, it may be worth transferring part of your shareholding to your children. Because the shares are in unquoted trading companies, it may be possible to 'hold over' any capital gain so that your child (or other relation or friend) takes over the shares at your original acquisition value (see 16.6). This means that you will have no capital gain. The recipient of the gift will have a gain on disposal of the difference between your acquisition value (as adjusted for inflation) and the sale proceeds. However, if you plan carefully you can probably ensure that the child etc realises a gain which is just within his or her £5,800 annual exemption—so no one pays tax on the capital gains.

For capital gains tax planning generally see Chapter 16.

1.5.2 Take full advantage of tax efficient investments

If you can afford to set aside a total of £9,000 over the next five years, you should have a Tax Exempt Special Savings Account (a 'Tessa'). Your spouse should do likewise. The income from a Tessa is totally exempt provided that any withdrawals during the period of five years do not exceed the amount of interest credited to your account less the 25 per cent tax which would be withheld at source by the bank, building society etc if it were not for the Tessa's tax exempt status. For further details see 11.2.

Another tax efficient investment is a personal equity plan. You and your spouse can both take out PEPs in each tax year. You can invest up to £6,000 each, and you can also both invest a further £3,000 in a single company PEP. Income and capital gains earned within a personal equity plan are totally free of tax and there is no tax charge on an investor winding up a PEP and withdrawing his capital. For further details see 11.3.

National Savings Certificates also offer a safe and tax free return, albeit at a relatively low rate of interest.

For longer term investments, qualifying life insurance policies are often attractive. Once a policy has been in force for ten years, there will normally be no tax charge whatsoever on the policy being cashed in.

1.5.3 Planning for some special situations

If you have suffered Case VI losses in the past on 'one off' transactions which are dealt with under Schedule D Case VI (see 5.17) look out for ways of realising Case VI gains. The point is that Case VI profits may generally be set against Case VI losses brought forward from previous years, and the profits do not have to arise from the same source. It follows that if, for example, you suffered some losses on furnished lettings, you can use up those losses, even if you have disposed of the property concerned, by selling gilts shortly before they go ex-div. The point is that the sale of gilts cum-interest will normally give rise to a Case VI charge on notional income by virtue of the 'Accrued Income Scheme' (see 5.5). Another alternative way of generating Case VI profits is to invest in offshore roll-up funds. In many cases, such investments are very similar to having money on a bank deposit overseas. The point is that no income is deemed to arise until the investor realises the investment. When this happens, the profit is charged under Schedule D Case VI.

Your circumstances may be special in another way. It may be that you plan to work overseas for a few years and will therefore cease to be resident in the United Kingdom. In such a case, it will obviously make sense to defer taxable income until after you have ceased to be resident as this will mean that no tax will arise. Once again, a possible way of doing this is to invest in offshore roll-up funds, rather than bank deposit accounts, with a view to cashing in the offshore roll-up investments after you have ceased to be a resident.

1.5.4 Property investments

Investments in real estate tend to be longer term investments. For that reason, the tax planning considerations also tend to be long term in nature.

One planning point is relevant at the time that you acquire an investment property. As explained at 9.2, interest on a qualifying loan may be set against any rental income which is taxable under Schedule A, ie any rental income from properties in the United Kingdom which are let (otherwise than on a furnished basis). However, it is not normally possible for a person who already owns a property to take a qualifying loan later on. The planning point is therefore very simple; you should normally borrow at the outset unless you are quite sure that you will not need to borrow money to finance your property investments later on. Even if you do have sufficient capital, it may be best to borrow to make property investments and use your spare capital for other purposes. For example, it would not be good tax planning to use your capital to purchase an investment property and at the same time take a long term non-qualifying loan to finance (for example) school fees.

Don't plan for one tax in isolation. If you let part of your home, or if you let your home for a period whilst you are living elsewhere, check on the capital gains tax implications (see 14.12). There are a number of reliefs and extra statutory concessions, but you need to be very careful not to put your extremely valuable main residence exemption into jeopardy.

If you do let part of your home, bear in mind the special rent-a-room relief (see 4.8) which may mean that rental income of up to £3,250 is totally exempt from tax.

1.5.5 Qualifying loans for company directors

If you work full time for a close company (see 9.4) or if you hold more than five per cent of the shares, and you wish to purchase further shares, you may be able to raise a qualifying loan. Remember that there is no £30,000 limit. Moreover, interest on a qualifying loan of this nature ranks for relief at your top rate of tax rather than 20 per cent relief as applies for MIRAS.

1.5.6 Plan ahead when buying a private company

If you purchase the whole of the share capital of a private trading company, and things do not go to plan, you will not normally be due income tax relief for any loss. Of course, you may be able to get a loss allowed for capital gains tax purposes, but capital losses may be set only against capital gains, not against income and therefore it may be some years before you get effective relief.

There may be a way around this. You should speak with your accountant, but basically what will be involved is for you to form a new company, subscribe cash for new shares in that company and have the company acquire the shares in the private trading company. At the end of the day, your position will be almost exactly the same, except that you will hold shares in a company with a wholly-owned subsidiary rather than hold shares in the subsidiary itself. What is important is that by dealing with matters in this way, you will be entitled to s 574 relief on any capital loss (see 15.2), ie you will be able to set the loss against your income for the year of loss or the preceding tax year.

1.6 Tax deductible investments

There are basically three types of investment which attract income tax relief when you make the investment:

- Pension contributions.
- Investment in enterprise zone properties.
- Investments under the enterprise investment scheme.

1.6.1 Pension contributions

We keep coming back to pension contributions because the tax situation is so attractive. There is no other type of investment where you can get tax relief when you pay money in, enjoy the benefits of a gross fund which pays no tax on its income and gains, *and* take part of the fund as a lump sum which is not taxable. The last aspect is one of the most important; contributions to pension schemes allow a person to effectively convert taxable income into a tax free capital sum.

It is precisely because the tax treatment is so beneficial that restrictions have been introduced in recent years. For example, there is the 'cap' on pensionable earnings (presently £76,800) which means that you cannot make personal pension contributions based on your actual earnings if they exceed this amount. On the other hand, the percentage limits which vary according to your age have been improved, so it is now possible to make larger contributions on the first £76,800 of your annual earnings. Furthermore, if you have not made the maximum contributions in earlier years, you can pick up the relief now by paying a one-off contribution which covers all or part of the unused relief for the last six years.

It is worth noting that if you make payments into a retirement annuity policy, ie a policy similar to a personal pension plan which was taken out before 1 July 1988, the earnings cap does not apply. This means that if your earnings for 1994–95 are £200,000, you can get income tax relief for retirement annuity premiums based on £200,000 and not on £76,800. However, be careful: the tax situation is quite complicated where an individual pays a mixture of retirement annuity and personal pension plan contributions and this is an area where you need advice from a specialist.

1.6.2 Investment in enterprise zone properties

A 100 per cent allowance is available where a person invests in a commercial building located in an enterprise zone. Basically, the building must be unused or you must make your investment within two years of it having first been let.

The enterprise zones were designated for a period of ten years and this period has now run out for many of the zones. Nevertheless, there are still a number of enterprise zone property investments available.

Many people prefer to invest via a syndicate or fund. These funds are often called enterprise zone property trusts. Basically, a person who invests in such a trust is entitled to relief for the corresponding proportion of the trust's investments in enterprise zone properties.

1.6.3 Investments under the enterprise investment scheme

The enterprise investment scheme is really the original business expansion scheme in disguise. However, in some ways it is less attractive. It is not possible to invest in a company which uses the money to purchase properties which are let under assured tenancies. Indeed, a major feature of the EIS legislation is that a company does not qualify if more than 50 per cent of its net assets consists of land and buildings.

Another way in which the enterprise investment scheme is less attractive than BES investments is that relief is initially due only at 20 per cent (more relief may be due later if the investment has to be written off).

Despite all this, wealthy individuals should consider making selective investments under the enterprise investment scheme. It is now possible to invest up to £100,000 per annum under the scheme. The investor can become a paid director. Most important of all, any capital gain on a disposal of the EIS shares after five years is totally tax free.

1.7 Your family affairs and personal financial planning

So far in this review of ways in which you may save tax, we have concentrated mainly on the income side. There are other important areas for tax and personal financial planning, ie house purchase, tax implications of marriage (and, sadly, separation and divorce), life assurance, funding school fees, providing help to elderly dependent relatives, assisting your children in buying their first home etc. Looking further ahead, there are issues which need to be addressed such as the way in which your Will should be drawn up, and possibly the way in which your spouse's Will should be drawn up. Inheritance tax also needs to be borne in mind.

1.7.1   House purchase

Although the rate of relief has now been reduced (and will be further reduced in 1995–96), it is still important to secure MIRAS relief when you take out a mortgage to purchase a property. MIRAS relief is like a discount or subsidy on the mortgage payments that you would otherwise be required to pay.

When you purchase your home, there are several different types of mortgage available. You should take advice as to whether an ordinary repayment mortgage, an endowment mortgage, or a pension mortgage is the most appropriate for you.

Incidentally, if you purchased your home before 31 July 1988 and you and your partner were not married, it was possible for you both to have £30,000 MIRAS loans (the legislation has since been changed). However, you should bear in mind that when you married your partner, the MIRAS relief should have been reduced as a married couple may have only one £30,000 qualifying loan between them. In many cases, the building society do not pick up the change in the couple's marital status, but this leads to problems later on when the Revenue eventually finds out what has happened. So, in many cases, the building society is faced with a demand from the Inland Revenue and will ask the couple to refund several years' excess MIRAS relief in one lump sum. Obviously, this will often be extremely painful and the best course of action is to try to ensure that things are dealt with properly as they go along so that a major problem does not build up in this way.

1.7.2   Life insurance

Income tax relief is no longer given for life insurance premiums although life assurance premium relief (LAPR) may still be due on a policy taken out by you prior to 13 March 1984.

If you are self-employed, it is possible to obtain income tax relief at your top rate for life insurance premiums paid under a personal pension plan. You should consult your adviser about the possibility of taking out a 'section 621' policy. However, bear in mind that if you use up part of your relief for personal pension contributions in this way, it may limit the amount which you can pay into a personal pension plan in order to secure pension benefits.

1.7.3 Marriage

Many of the tax planning issues which arise in connection with marriage concern capital gains tax or inheritance tax.

1.7.4 Capital gains tax

Bear in mind that if you transfer shares or other chargeable assets to your intended spouse before your marriage, you will be deemed to have made a disposal at market value and a capital gain may therefore arise. From this point of view, it may be better to delay matters until after you are married as no capital gain arises on transfers between spouses who are living together.

Of course, if you are thinking of transferring an asset on which a capital loss would arise, it may be best to crystallise this loss by making the transfer before you get married.

Something else to bear in mind is the position if both of you already own your own home. Basically, you will have three years grace to resolve the position, but at the end of that time only one property can qualify as your main residence (see 14.15.4). The property concerned may be a new home or one of you may move into the other's existing home.

1.7.5 Separation and divorce

Full income tax relief is no longer available on payments under Court Orders issued after 14 March 1988. The basic idea is that a man who is required to maintain his former wife will qualify only for the married person's allowance and will not be due relief on the actual amount of his maintenance payments.

It is still possible to have relief of up to 40 per cent on maintenance payments under pre-14 March 1988 Court Orders. However, there are a number of conditions which need to be watched carefully if this relief is to be preserved (see 8.2).

So far as capital gains tax is concerned, you may find yourself in a Catch 22 situation. The legislation provides that a man and his wife are connected persons for capital gains tax purposes until the marriage comes to an end. The marriage comes to an end when there is a decree absolute, not a decree nisi. However, the exemption for transfers between spouses applies only if you are living together. You may therefore find yourself in a situation where a capital gains tax charge may arise because you are required to transfer assets to your spouse as part of your divorce settlement.

As so often, it is possible to get round this problem if you plan ahead. The basic rule that transfers between spouses are not subject to capital gains tax applies to transfers made during a tax year in which you have been living together at some time. Thus, if you and your wife separate on (say) 10 April 1994, a transfer of assets between you will not give rise to a capital gains tax charge provided the transfer is made before 6 April 1995.

1.7.6 Funding school fees

If grandparents or other relatives are able to help, advantage could be taken of your children's tax allowances. One way of doing this is for your relatives to set up trusts and for the trustees to distribute income to your children. This money could then be used to pay school fees.

Bear in mind that this will not work if you make a trust for your own children as any income which is paid out before they attain age 18 will be treated as if it were your income.

Where grandparents etc cannot assist, things are more difficult but not necessarily impossible. You should start saving as early as possible and take full advantage of privileged investments such as TESSAs, PEPs and qualifying insurance policies. Take advice from a specialist.

1.7.7 Providing for elderly dependants

Many readers will be making a contribution towards the support of elderly parents or other relatives. Unfortunately, recent Chancellors of the Exchequer have significantly reduced the scope for obtaining assistance towards these costs through tax relief. In particular, it is no longer possible to transfer income by means of a deed of covenant and the income tax allowance for dependent relatives has been abolished altogether.

One area where it may be possible to secure tax relief is where it is necessary to purchase a property which is used by the relative as his or her home. There is no tax relief for a mortgage taken out for this purpose, but it may be possible to secure capital gains tax exemption in due course if you follow a fairly involved route.

The capital gains tax exemption is not available if you own the property yourself (unless you owned the property prior to 5 April 1988). However, if you form a trust and put money into the trust to enable the trustees to buy the dependant's home, the trustees may be entitled to an exemption as and when they eventually sell the property. Furthermore, this exemption is not affected by your being a beneficiary under the trust yourself. So the answer may be to set up a trust under which your elderly father or mother is entitled to occupy the property during their lifetime, with the trust coming to an end on their death and the property passing to you as a beneficiary of your own trust.

There are other aspects to be considered, not least the inheritance tax position if the property has a value in excess of £150,000. You therefore need to talk this through with a specialist tax adviser to see whether this solution would work in your particular circumstances.

1.7.8 Assisting your children in buying their first homes

There will be no relief if you take out a mortgage in your own name. However, if you guarantee a mortgage granted to your child, MIRAS should apply. So the answer may be for your child to take out his own mortgage and for you to make cash payments on a monthly basis to enable the child to make his own mortgage payments.

1.7.9 Inheritance tax

This is a highly specialised area, but in general a person should:

(1)   Make use of the annual exemptions.
(2)   Preserve (and maximise) business property and agricultural reliefs.
(3)   Consider making exempt transfers by a deed of variation.
(4)   Make potentially exempt transfers which escape IHT after the donor has survived seven years.
(5)   Fund insurance policies so as to provide cash to meet IHT payable on death.

See chapter 17.

1.8   Ensure that all important deadlines are kept

It is pointless trying to arrange your affairs tax efficiently unless you do the basics right and keep your affairs tidy. This means watching deadlines for action (eg paying tax) and making elections.

This is particularly important as we approach a time when self-assessment will be introduced. If you are not on top of your tax affairs in 1994–95 and 1995–96 you may find it almost impossibly difficult to catch up when the new regime comes into force.

The most important tax planning deadlines are listed below. This section should, however, be read subject to three cautions:

(1) Most of the deadlines are dates by which a return, claim or election must be received by the Inspector of Taxes, or a payment received by the Collector. Obviously, a document or payment must be posted at least one working day before the deadline and, because of the danger of postal delays, ideally at least a week.

(2) To keep this checklist to a manageable size, only those deadlines likely to apply to the majority of people have been included. The checklist is not, therefore, fully comprehensive.

(3) Many deadlines cannot be included because they are fixed by reference to the facts of the individual case. For example, partnership 'continuation basis' elections (see 2.8.4) must be made within two years of the date a partner joined or left the firm. Similarly, most corporation tax deadlines are fixed by reference to the end of the company's accounting period.

1.8.1   1994 deadlines

May 19   (Thursday): Employers who do not file end-of-year returns (on Forms P14, P35 and P38/P38A) by today may be fined (see 19.13.4).

June 3   (Friday): Substantial fines may be imposed on employers who do not submit Forms P11D (returns of benefits, etc provided for employees) by today (see 19.13.4).

Today is also the last day for electing to pay by instalments the tax on certain share options granted in 1983–84 or earlier years and exercised during 1994–95 (see 3.12.3).

June 17   (Friday): Due date for payment of 1994–95 Class 1A national insurance contributions (company cars and fuel) (see 23.1.9).

July 1   (Friday): Second instalment of Schedule D tax for 1994–95 due.

July 5   (Tuesday): Last day to elect that relief for a personal pension or retirement annuity contribution paid in 1994–95 be given in 1993–94 (see 12.9.4).

July 19   (Tuesday): PAYE quarterly payment date for small employers.

October 5   (Wednesday): Last day for making an Enterprise Investment Scheme investment which can be related back to the 1993–94 tax year (see 11.7).

October 19   (Wednesday): PAYE quarterly payment date for small employers.

October 31   (Monday): To avoid the danger of incurring an interest charge, personal tax returns must be filed by 4 pm today (see 19.7).

December 1   (Thursday): Due date for payment of higher-rate tax on taxed income received in 1994–95 and for payment of 1994–95 capital gains tax.

December 30 (Friday): Last day for claiming a reduction in a 1994–95 Schedule A assessment on the grounds that one or more properties are no longer owned (see 4.6).

The due date for payment of the first instalment of 1994–95 Schedule D income tax is 1 January 1995. However, the first business day of 1995 is Tuesday, 3 January in England, Wales and Northern Ireland and Wednesday, 4 January in Scotland. Therefore, tax not paid by 31 December cannot in practice be paid until 3 or 4 January and the Collector is entitled to charge interest for non-business days. To avoid an interest charge, it may, therefore, be worthwhile making payment on 30 December.

Closing date for claiming, on grounds of low income, repayment of Class 2 national insurance contributions paid in 1993–94 (see 23.2.3).

1.8.2   5 April 1995 deadlines

A large number of claims and elections must be made within a certain number of years of the end of the tax year in question. For example, claims to personal allowances have to be made within six years, so that claims for 1988–89 must be made by 5 April 1995.

The list below shows, for each year of assessment, the claims or elections which must be made by 5 April 1994. It must be emphasised that, owing to the complexity of the legislation, this table is not comprehensive.

Deadlines in relation to the tax year 1988–89

Personal tax

(1)   Claiming personal allowances for 1988–89 (see 7.2.1).

(2)   Claiming relief for interest paid in 1988–89.

(3)   Claiming relief for pension contributions paid in 1988–89.

(4)   Claiming 'top-slicing' relief in respect of life assurance policy gains arising in 1988–89 (see 12.3.6).

(5)   Claiming relief to correct an error or mistake made by the taxpayer which resulted in an excessive assessment being made in the year to 1988–89 (see 19.12).

(6)   Electing to have a Case III source of income assessed on the current-year basis for 1988–89 where that is the third year (see 5.1.2).

(7)   Claiming to exclude from assessment rent due in 1988–89 which was never in fact received (see 4.1.6).

Capital gains tax   Claiming roll-over and hold-over relief in respect of disposals which took place in 1988–89 (see 15.3 and 15.5).

Deadline in relation to the tax year 1989–90

Personal tax   Requesting the Inspector formally to assess 1989–90 Schedule E liabilities.

Deadlines in relation to the tax year 1992–93

Personal tax

(1)   Submitting Form BES3 in respect of Business Expansion Scheme investments made in 1992–93 (see 11.4.3). If this deadline is missed, BES relief will be lost.

(2)   Claiming a set-off for industrial buildings allowances on enterprise zone investments made in 1992–93 (see 11.8 and 4.5.3–4.5.4).

(3)   Electing to split rents received from a furnished letting in 1992–93 between Schedule A and Case VI assessments (see 4.7.1).

(4)   Claiming relief against income tax for 1991–92 for a loss on the disposal (in 1991–92 or 1992–93) of shares in a qualifying trading company (see 15.2).

Capital gains tax

(1)   Electing to compute all gains and losses on assets acquired before 31 March 1982 by reference to values on that day (possible only where the first relevant disposal took place after 5 April 1992) (see 14.3.2).

(2) Claiming that an asset became of negligible value during 1992–93 (see 13.4.11).
(3) Claiming relief in respect of a rolled-over or held-over gain which crystallised in 1992–93 (see 14.4.1).
(4) Electing to calculate the gain or loss on an asset, acquired on or before 6 April 1965, by reference to its market value on that date (see 14.3.4).
(5) Claiming a set-off against capital gains assessed for 1992–93 in respect of a loss incurred on a qualifying loan to a trader (see 15.1).

Business tax

(1) Claiming that a trading loss incurred in 1991–92 or 1992–93 should be set against other income of 1992–93 (see 2.10.2).
(2) Claiming that a trading loss incurred in 1992–93 should be set against a capital gain realised in 1992–93 (see 2.10.13).
(3) Claiming that a trading loss incurred in 1992–93 be carried back, where this is permitted under the 'new business' rules (see 2.10.11).
(4) Claiming capital gains tax retirement relief in respect of a disposal made in 1992–93, where that claim is based on ill health (see 15.8.3).
(5) Electing to treat plant or machinery purchased in 1992–93 as a short-life asset for capital allowance purposes (see 2.4.8).
(6) Electing for post-cessation receipts received in 1992–93 to be taxed for the year the trade was discontinued (see 2.7).

Deadline in relation to the tax year 1993–94

Personal tax

Paying a personal pension or retirement annuity contribution for which relief is to be given against income of 1993–94 (see 12.9.4).

Deadline in relation to the tax year 1994–95

Personal tax

(1) A couple who married during 1994–95 electing to transfer half or the whole of the married couple's allowance for that year to the wife (see 7.5.5).
(2) Paying an additional voluntary contribution (to an employer's pension scheme or under 'free-standing' arrangements) for which relief is to be given against income of 1994–95 (see 12.11–12.12).

2 Tax and self-employment

This chapter deals with income which is charged to income tax under Schedule D Case I (trades) or Case II (professions and vocations). This income may arise from a business carried on by an individual (a 'sole trader' or 'sole practitioner') or by a partnership. The rules governing Schedule D Cases I and II are identical and therefore all references in this chapter to a person carrying on a trade apply equally to a person who is engaged in a profession.

The following matters are covered:

(1) How self-employed individuals pay tax.
(2) Are you really self-employed?
(3) Basis of assessment.
(4) How taxable profits are computed.
(5) Capital allowances.
(6) Pre-trading expenditure.
(7) Post-cessation receipts.
(8) Partnerships.
(9) Administrative aspects and payment of tax.
(10) Relief for trading losses.
(11) Lloyd's underwriters ('Names').

2.1 How self-employed individuals pay tax

2.1.1 Taxation by assessment

Unlike employees who suffer deduction of tax from their earnings under PAYE, self-employed individuals pay tax by assessment. The Inspector of Taxes will normally issue an assessment each year, either based on the accounts of the business or on the Inspector's estimates of the profits of the year. The tax assessed in this way is generally payable in two instalments, in January and July (see 2.9.4 for further details).

2.1.2 Assessment based on accounts

A self-employed trader must therefore keep books and records so that accounts can be drawn up and submitted to the Inland Revenue. Very often, accounts are drawn up for other reasons as well, eg for production to banks and other lenders and it is important to bear in mind that there may need to be some specific adjustments for tax purposes—the main rules are covered in 2.4–2.5 below. There are also specific rules which govern the amount of 'capital allowances' that a trader may claim—in broad terms, capital allowances are an adjustment for depreciation or wear and tear on equipment etc used in the business.

A self-employed person's assessment will normally take the following form:

Profits assessable under Schedule D	A
Less capital allowances	B
	C
Less personal allowances (see Chapter 7) and deduction for Class 4 NIC (see 2.9.2)	D
Taxable income	E

2.2 Are you really self-employed?

2.2.1 Introduction

It is not possible to elect to be self-employed; whether you are self-employed is a matter of fact. However, since the Taxes Acts do not define self-employment the rules have evolved through decisions handed down by the Courts.

The real distinction between being self-employed and an employee is that there is no 'master-servant' relationship. However, in practice it is often difficult to discern the dividing line and the Revenue may take a different view from the parties concerned. For example, freelance workers may not necessarily be recognised as being self-employed and salaried partners may be classified as employees. The position can be further complicated in that the Department of Social Security may be involved in assessing liability for national insurance contributions and the criteria applied by the DSS Inspectors do not always coincide with those used by the Revenue.

These grey areas can result in companies treating freelance workers as if they were employees and deducting tax and NIC under PAYE accordingly. This reflects the Revenue's practice of seeking unpaid tax from employers in cases where a company has not operated PAYE. As a result, it is very difficult, for example, for workers in the computer field to secure payment on a self-employed basis. Similar problems are often experienced by workers in the TV industry, actors and artistes, journalists and many other industries where freelance workers are required to work 'on-site'.

2.2.2   The Inland Revenue's criteria

Guidelines issued by the Revenue in conjunction with the DSS to clarify employment status (leaflet IR56 *Employed or self-employed?*) included the following points:

(1)   An *employee* generally does the work in person (and does not hire someone else to do it) working at times and places and in the way specified by the firm for whom the work is done and normally paid at hourly, weekly or monthly rates, possibly including overtime.

(2)   A *self-employed* person may hire and pay others to do the work, or do it personally, in either case specifying the time and the way it is done, providing major items of equipment, being responsible for losses as well as profits and correcting unsatisfactory work in his own time and at his own expense.

These criteria, however, are for guidance only and in some cases the Courts have held that a person who did not fulfil those in (2) above was nevertheless self-employed. In *Hall v Lorimer* [1994] STC 23, the Court of Appeal held that a TV vision mixer was self-employed even though the extremely expensive equipment he used was provided by the companies concerned and his work was rigorously controlled.

The moral is to take professional advice if you are a borderline case rather than simply accept a 'ruling' from the Revenue.

2.3   Basis of assessment

The way in which the profits are ascertained relates to the profits *before* capital allowances (see 2.5).

The same rules apply for both Schedule D Case I and Case II. A self-employed person may draw up accounts to any date that he chooses, there is no requirement that accounts be made up to 5 April in order to fit in with the fiscal year.

2.3.1 Preceding year basis
(TA 1988, s 60)

The profits on which an individual is taxed are normally determined on the 'preceding year' basis so that a self-employed person's assessment on profits for 1993–94 is determined by his profits for an accounting year which ends some time between 6 April 1992 and 5 April 1993. However, a different rule applies for new businesses which commence after 5 April 1994.

2.3.2 Businesses which start to trade after 5 April 1994

The assessable profits of such a business will be dealt with on the 'current year' basis so that the assessment will be determined by the profits for the accounting year which ends in the year of assessment. There are special rules which govern the first tax year since there will normally be no accounts which end in that tax year (see 2.3.4 below).

2.3.3 Changes in the future

The preceding year basis will be abolished altogether from 5 April 1996. The 1995–96 assessment on a trader who was in business before 6 April 1994 will be on the preceding year basis (unless there is a cessation) during 1995–96. The 1996–97 assessment will be based on the average profits for the two years' accounts which end in the tax year 1996–97. The 1997–98 assessment will be on the current year basis.

2.3.4 Opening years of a business
(TA 1988, ss 61–62)

Where a person starts up in business, he clearly cannot be assessed on his profits for the preceding year. The legislation therefore sets out rules for determining taxable profits for the first three years of assessment. These rules vary according to whether the business started before 6 April 1994.

Business commenced prior to 6 April 1994

(1) The first tax year's assessment is made by reference to profits actually earned during that year.

(2) The second tax year's assessment is determined by the actual profits of the first 12 months of the business, subject to an option for the taxpayer to choose to be taxed on actual profits (see 2.3.6).

(3) The third tax year's assessment is normally determined by the preceding year basis but, if there were no accounts ending in the

previous year, the profits for the first 12 months are taken instead. Again this is subject to an option to be taxed on actual profits.

Business commenced after 5 April 1994

(1)   The first tax year's assessment is made by reference to profits actually earned during that year.

(2)   The second tax year's assessment is normally determined by the profits of the first 12 months, with no option.

(3)   The third tax year's assessment will be on the current year basis— see 2.3.2 above.

2.3.5   Examples of the opening years' rules

The following examples show how the above rules operate in relation to a business which started before 6 April 1994:

(1) B starts a business on 5 January 1993. She makes up accounts to 5 January 1994 which show profits of £24,000.

Under the above rules, her assessments for 1992–93–1994–95 will be:

		£
1992–93	$\frac{3^1}{12}$ × £24,000 =	6,000
1993–94	First 12 months	24,000
1994–95	Preceding year basis	24,000

$$^1\text{ie} \quad \frac{\text{Period from commencement to 5 April 1993}}{12 \text{ months}}$$

(2) C starts a business on 5 July 1992 and decides to make up accounts to 5 October 1993 (this is because the business is seasonal and 5 October 1993 brings him to the end of his first full season). Profits amount to £45,000 for the 15 months ended 5 October 1993, and £38,000 for the year ended 5 October 1994.

C's tax assessments will be:

		£
1992–93	$\frac{9}{15}$ × £45,000 =	27,000
1993–94	$\frac{12}{15}$ × £45,000 =	36,000
1994–95	$\frac{12}{15}$ × £45,000 =	36,000
1995–96	(preceding year basis)	38,000

2.3.6 Taxpayer's option
(TA 1988, s 62)

A taxpayer who was already in business at 5 April 1994 may elect that his assessments for the second and third tax years should be based on his actual profits for those years. The election must be made for *both* the second and third years: it is not possible to take one year in isolation.

2.3.7 Example—Electing for actual profits

Assume that in example (1) in 2.3.5 above, B's profits for the year ended 5 January 1995 amounted to £12,000 and her profits for the year ended 5 January 1996 were £48,000.

If B made the election under s 62, the position would be:

			Assessable Profits £
1992–93	As before		6,000
1993–94	$\frac{9}{12}$	x £24,000[1]	18,000
	$\frac{3}{12}$	x £12,000[2]	3,000
			21,000
1994–95	$\frac{9}{12}$	x £12,000	9,000
	$\frac{3}{12}$	x £48,000	12,000
			21,000

[1] Profits for year ended 5 January 1994
[2] Profits for year ended 5 January 1995

2.3.8 Closing years of a business
(TA 1988, s 63)

Under the present system the assessable profits for the last tax year will always be the actual profits earned during that period. This will not be so for a business which ceases after 5 April 1997, but, as this is still some time away, the following examples reflect the current position.

2.3.9   Example—Closing years

If C has been in business for many years and his accounts for his year ended 31 December 1994 are his last year of business, the assessment for 1994–95 will be based on a proportion of the profits for that year. If the accounts to 31 December 1994 show a profit of, say, £36,500, the Schedule D Case I assessment will be:

£36,500 x $\dfrac{\text{Period from 6 April 1994–31 December 1994 (270 days)}}{\text{12 months (365 days)}}$

Thus, the figure will be $\dfrac{270}{365}$ x £36,500, ie £27,000

Just as the taxpayer had an option in the early years, the Revenue also has the right to choose to adjust the assessments for the two previous years to make them equal to the actual profits earned during those tax years. The Revenue must also either adjust both years or neither: the Revenue cannot pick and choose.

2.3.10   Example—Adjustment by Revenue

A has always made up accounts for his business to 31 December. His profits have been:

	£
Year ended 31 December 1991	9,125
Year ended 31 December 1992	27,375
Year ended 31 December 1993	73,000
Year ended 31 December 1994	36,500

He ceases business on 31 December 1994.

As shown in 2.3.9, the 1994–95 assessable figure would be £27,000.

The existing assessments for the two preceding tax years would be:

1992–93	Preceding year basis	£ 9,125
1993–94	Preceding year basis	£27,375

The Revenue could adjust the assessments as follows:

1992–93:

		£
$\dfrac{270}{365}$ x £27,375	=	20,250
$\dfrac{95}{365}$ x £73,000	=	19,000
		39,250

1993–94:

		£
$\dfrac{270}{365}$ x £73,000	=	54,000
$\dfrac{95}{365}$ x £36,500	=	9,500
		63,500

Note: For simplicity, we have ignored the fact that 1992 was a Leap Year.

2.4   How taxable profits are computed

This section covers the rules which govern the tax treatment of income and expenses and deals with some of the more common adjustments to accounts which are required for tax purposes. For example, a set of accounts prepared for commercial reasons may include a provision for wear and tear to a building. Such a provision needs to be 'added back' (as no relief is available for depreciation as such, relief is due only via the capital allowances system).

2.4.1   Accounts should be on the 'earnings basis'

The Revenue's view is that accounts should normally be prepared to reflect a trader's earnings for a year rather than just the cash received. For example, the accounts should include debtors, ie bills which have been issued but which have not been paid by the year end. Similarly, the accounts should include work in progress.

Barristers are an exception. A barrister's accounts will normally be prepared on a cash basis as the Revenue acknowledges the special feature of that profession which prevents barristers from suing for unpaid fees (see Inland Revenue Statement of Practice A3).

The Revenue will require accounts to be prepared on the earnings basis for the first three years of a business. However, the Revenue will allow a trader to switch to a cash basis thereafter, provided the trader gives an undertaking that bills for work which has been completed will be issued at regular and frequent intervals (see Inland Revenue Statement of Practice A 27).

Where accounts are prepared on the cash basis, this treatment applies to expenses as well as income.

2.4.2   Enterprise allowance should not be included
(TA 1988, s 127)

Where a trader has received an enterprise allowance, this should not be included in the computation of profits assessable for Schedule D Case I purposes. The allowance is taxable income, but is charged to tax under Schedule D Case VI rather than Case I (see 5.17).

2.4.3   Expenditure which is specifically disallowed
(TA 1988, ss 74 and 577)

Certain types of expenditure are disallowed even though it may be sound accounting practice to deduct such costs in a trader's accounts.

Capital expenditure
(TA 1988, s 74)

The acquisition of a capital asset is not a cost which may be deducted in arriving at profits for tax purposes. This may seem obvious where an asset such as a building is acquired, but the definition of capital expenditure goes a long way beyond the acquisition of tangible assets. The generally accepted definition was given by Lord Cave in *British Insulated and Helsby Cables Ltd v Atherton* (1925)10 TC 155 where he stated:

> . . . when an expenditure is made . . . with a view to bringing into existence an asset or an advantage for the enduring benefit of a trade . . . there is very good reason (in the absence of special circumstances leading to the opposite conclusion) for treating such expenditure as properly attributable not to revenue but to capital.

The acquisition of goodwill, for example, would be capital expenditure. Less obviously, a lump sum payment to secure release from an onerous liability such as a lease at a high rent or a fixed rate loan would also be regarded as capital expenditure.

Entertaining
(TA 1988, s 577)

Any expenses relating to entertaining customers or suppliers which are included in a set of accounts normally need to be added back. There is a modest exemption which may apply where the entertaining is provided by a hotelier, restaurateur or by someone else who provides entertainment in the ordinary course of his trade. Staff entertainment is also an allowable expense but the individual employee may be assessed on a benefit in kind.

Gifts to customers etc
(TA 1988, s 577)

The cost of gifts to customers, potential customers and to potential introducers is also disallowed by s 577 unless the gift carries a conspicuous advertisement and is neither food, drink, tobacco or a voucher exchangeable for such goods; nor an item which costs more than £10 per recipient per year.

Illegal payments

A specific provision disallowing illegal payments such as bribes came into force on 11 June 1993 (this was the date that the relevant clause was introduced in the committee stage of the 1993 Finance Bill). Prior to 11 June 1993, it was open to a business to claim a deduction for such payments where they were incurred wholly and exclusively for the purposes of the trade—although this will often have been difficult to prove in practice.

The disallowance was extended by the Finance Act 1994 to cover payments made on or after 30 November 1993 in response to threats, menaces, blackmail and other forms of extortion.

Lease rentals on expensive cars
(CAA 1990, s 35)

Where a trader uses a leased car or provides a motor car to an employee and the original cost was £12,000 or more (£8,000 prior to 10 March 1992), part of the lease rentals must be added back as a disallowable expense. The amount disallowed is the following proportion of the lease rental:

$$\frac{1}{2} \times \frac{(\text{Cost of car} - £12,000)}{\text{Cost of car}}$$

Thus, if a car which cost £16,000 is leased for a rental of £2,400 per annum, the amount disallowed is:

$$\frac{1}{2} \times \frac{(£16,000 - 12,000)}{16,000} \times £2,400 \text{ ie } £300$$

This treatment does not apply to maintenance costs included in the lease rentals provided they are identified separately under the terms of the leasing agreement.

Amounts paid under an HP agreement are dealt with differently (see 2.4.4).

Provisions for bad debts
(TA 1988, s 74(j))

A general provision against bad debts is not allowable, but provisions against specific debts are a proper deduction for tax purposes provided that it can be shown that the amount is a reasonable provision.

Remuneration not paid within nine months of the year end
(FA 1989, s 43)

Bonus payments to employees may be made after the end of a year. If they clearly relate to a period of account, it would be normal for the trader's accounts to include a provision. However, this provision is allowable only if the remuneration is paid within nine months of the year end.

Pension contributions for employees
(FA 1993, s 112)

A deduction is due only if the contribution is paid during the course of the trader's year. This applies whether the contribution is paid to an approved or unapproved scheme.

Pension contributions for the trader himself are not an allowable deduction in computing profits although relief is available as a deduction from taxable profits (see 12.9–12.10 for details of the method of dealing with personal pension contributions).

Expenditure not wholly for the purposes of the trade
(TA 1988, s 74(a))

The legislation requires the expenditure to be incurred 'wholly and exclusively' for the purposes of the trade. Consequently, expenses which are incurred partly for trade purposes and partly for personal reasons are not allowable.

The Revenue has invoked s 74(a) to disallow the cost of black dresses worn in Court by a female barrister on the grounds that the expenditure had a dual purpose (warmth and decency as well as the need to dress in a particular way when appearing in Court). The Revenue has also relied upon s 74(a) to disallow the cost of meals incurred by a self-employed carpenter when he was working away from home. Where an expense is incurred for mixed purposes the whole amount is disallowed. However, where it can be shown that an *additional* cost was incurred wholly for business reasons, a deduction may be due for this. Consequently, if a trader paid his wife a salary which exceeded the real value of her services as an employee, it would normally be only the excess which would be disallowed.

Sums recoverable from an insurance policy etc
(TA 1988, s 74(c))

Where a trader can get back from an insurance company the money that he has paid out, there is no deduction due for the expenditure. The same treatment applies where a trader has been indemnified against a particular cost.

Annual payments
(TA 1988, s 74(p) and (q))

Certain annual payments (for example, patent royalties) generally need to be paid net of tax at the basic rate. The payments are not deductible in arriving at profits which are assessable under Schedule D Case I or Case II, although they are allowed as a deduction for higher rate purposes.

2.4.4 Other expenditure where adjustments may be required

Interest

Interest payments on loans taken by partners will be allowable (if at all) against the partner's general income, (see 9.3). Interest paid by a sole trader or by a partnership may be deducted in arriving at the taxable profits of the business provided it passes the 'wholly and exclusively' test (see above).

Problems may arise where overdraft interest is charged in a set of accounts and the proprietor's capital account is overdrawn. The Revenue is likely to argue that the interest (or, at any rate, part of the interest) was incurred not for the purposes of the business but in order to finance drawings. If you find yourself in this situation you should take advice from an accountant.

Cost of raising business finance
(TA 1988, s 77)

There will often be certain costs in raising long term finance and for many years these costs were regarded as capital expenditure by the Revenue. A statutory deduction is now available provided certain conditions are satisfied:

(1)   The costs must be wholly and exclusively incurred for the purposes of obtaining loan finance, providing security or repaying a loan.

(2)   The costs must represent expenditure on professional fees, commissions, advertising, printing or other incidental expenses in relation to raising finance.

In some cases a deduction will be available even though the expenditure failed and the loan finance was not in fact obtained.

Lease rentals

The way in which lease rentals are treated depends upon the type of the lease. If the lease is an 'operating lease', ie a lease for a period which is less than the asset's anticipated useful life, it is normal for rentals to be deducted in arriving at the profits for the period to which the rentals refer. In practice, most leasing agreements provide for rentals to be payable in advance. For example, if a trader pays lease rentals of £12,000 on 1 December which cover a period of six months, and he makes up accounts to the following 31 March, the amount deducted in arriving at the profits for the year ended 31 March would be:

$$\frac{4 \text{ months}}{6 \text{ months}} \times £12,000 = £8,000$$

A different treatment is required where a trader pays rentals under a 'finance lease', ie a lease agreement under which the trader acquires almost all the benefits of outright ownership. There is a special accounting standard which governs the accounting treatment of such leases, and the Revenue's view is that the amount which should be deducted is the amount charged in the trader's accounts in accordance with SSAP 21 (ie the relevant Statement of Standard Accounting Practice issued by the Institute of Chartered Accountants).

Hire purchase

Where equipment is acquired under an HP contract, the cost of the equipment counts as capital expenditure (in most cases capital allowances will be available). The 'interest' element is apportioned over the term of the contract and relief is given for the amount of interest which relates to the accounting period concerned.

2.4.5   Example—Adjustments for HP contracts

A trader acquires a computer under a three year HP agreement. The cost of the computer was £12,000, but the trader pays 36 monthly HP payments of £420.

The interest payable over the three years totals £3,120. This would normally be allocated roughly as follows:

Year one — £1,715
Year two — £1,040
Year three — £365

This type of allocation reflects the amount of the HP 'loan' which is outstanding during each year.

Legal and professional expenses

Where an Inspector of Taxes examines a trader's business accounts, he will normally ask for an analysis of any substantial amounts relating to legal and professional expenses. Legal costs in connection with the *acquisition* of capital assets are disallowable as capital expenditure as are legal costs in connection with renewing a lease of more than 50 years. In contrast, legal costs which are incurred in order to *protect* a capital asset are generally allowable as a revenue expense.

Professional costs incurred in connection with tax appeals are not allowable on the grounds that such costs relate to tax on profits rather than an expense incurred in earning profits. However, in practice the costs of preparing and agreeing tax computations are usually allowed.

2.4.6   Relief for premiums
(TA 1988, s 87)

A trader may be required to make a lump sum payment to a landlord in order to obtain a lease. In cases where the lease is for a period of less than 50 years, part of the lump sum may be treated as income in the landlord's hands (see 4.4) and the trader may claim a deduction for this amount as if it were rent payable over the period of his lease.

There is no relief if the lease is for more than 50 years or if the premium is paid to someone other than the landlord since such a third party (for example, an outgoing tenant) is not subject to income tax under Schedule A.

Sometimes the lease will require a tenant to have certain building work carried out which will increase the value of the landlord's interest in the property. The landlord may be assessed under Schedule A on a *notional* premium (see 4.4.3). Where this applies, the trader will be able to claim a deduction just as if he had been required to pay a premium in cash. However, the notional premium will generally be far less than the actual cost of carrying out the work concerned.

2.4.7   Example—Treatment of premiums

B pays a premium for a lease of ten years of which £40,000 is treated as income of the landlord for Schedule A purposes. The whole of this is taxed in the landlord's hands as income for the year in which the premium is payable.

B can claim a deduction in his accounts for the ten years as if he had paid rent of £4,000 per annum.

If it were not for s 87, the expenditure would be treated as capital expenditure and would attract no relief.

2.4.8   Provisions against liability to pay sums after the year end

This is an aspect of accounts to which Inspectors of Taxes pay particular attention. The Revenue will need to be satisfied that relief is not sought for expenditure which will be incurred only in the future. Consequently, an Inspector will almost certainly withhold relief unless he is satisfied that a trader became liable to make the payment concerned before the year-end. For example, it will not be possible to secure a deduction for redundancy costs unless the necessary redundancy notices were served by the end of the trader's accounting period. Similarly, the Revenue will argue that a provision for an amount which may be due to a client for professional negligence is not allowable unless the client's claim has been admitted by the year end.

This interpretation is not free from doubt, but the difficulty of persuading an Inspector of Taxes to adopt a more favourable interpretation should not be underestimated. Again this is a situation where professional advice is required if sizable amounts of tax are at issue.

There are sometimes circumstances where a payment will almost certainly be required in the future although the precise amount has yet to be ascertained. An example contained in a recent Revenue publication concerns an insurance broker who may be required to refund commission to an insurance company if clients allow policies to lapse. The Revenue has accepted that a provision may be allowable in these circumstances provided it is arrived at scientifically by reference to past experience. A 'rough and ready' general provision is not allowable.

2.4.9   Valuation of stock and work in progress

A trader's accounts should include his stock in hand at his year end (unless the cash basis applies). Individual items of stock should be valued at the *lower* of cost or realisable value. Cost should normally include a proportion of overheads.

Similarly, work in progress should be valued at the year end on the same basis. Where the accounts relate to a profession, it is not necessary to include in cost the time value of work put in by the sole proprietor or partner since this represents the proprietor's profit rather than a cost incurred in carrying on the profession.

The treatment of long-term work in progress can involve complex issues and should be discussed with the firm's accountant.

2.5   Capital allowances

2.5.1   Introduction

A trader is entitled to capital allowances on plant and machinery which is used in the trade. Capital allowances are also available on commercial buildings located in an enterprise zone, agricultural buildings, industrial buildings and hotels. Allowances may also be claimed for expenditure on know-how and scientific research expenditure. All these are dealt with differently, and various rates of initial and annual allowances are given.

Capital allowances are treated as a separate deduction from the individual's (or partnership's) Schedule D   Case I or Case II assessment. At present they are given on the preceding year basis, subject to special rules for the opening and closing years (see 2.5.20). Where a new business starts after 5 April 1994, the allowances are given on the current year basis, but once again with special rules for the first tax year.

2.5.2   Allowances for plant and machinery
(CAA 1990, s 24; FA 1993, s 115)

A 40 per cent first year allowance was available for expenditure on assets other than motor cars during the year ended 31 October 1993. Expenditure is deemed to fall within this period if it is incurred under a contract entered into during this 12 month period and either the invoice was paid by 31 October 1993 or the period of credit (if any) allowed by the supplier did not exceed four months.

Plant and machinery purchased outside this period attracts only a 25 per cent writing-down allowance. Once again, expenditure is deemed to be incurred when a trader enters into an unconditional contract; it is not necessary that the trader should have actually paid for it or have brought it into use by his year end (there is an exception for plant and machinery acquired under an HP contract (see 2.5.7)).

Writing-down allowances are computed on the balance of the 'pool' at the year-end. The opening balance of the pool represents the cost of plant and machinery brought forward from previous years, less the capital allowances already received. A trader receives writing-down allowances based on the opening balance plus the cost of additional plant and machinery acquired during the year less any disposal proceeds.

2.5.3   Example—Writing-down allowances

A and B are in partnership. In their year to 31 March 1993 they had acquired plant and machinery at a cost of £30,000 (all before 1 November 1992) and received capital allowances of £7,500.

During their year ended 31 March 1994, they sell some of this plant for £2,000 and buy new plant for £20,000, all after 31 October 1993. Their pool would be as follows:

	£
Written-down value brought forward at 1 April 1993	22,500
Additions during year ended 31 March 1994	20,000
	42,500
Less disposal proceeds	2,000
	40,500
Writing-down allowances (25 per cent)	10,125
Written-down value carried forward	30,375

Assets acquired during the year ended 31 October 1993 and which qualify for the 40 per cent first year allowance do not also attract writing-down allowances as part of the pool for the year, although they will count as part of the pool for subsequent years.

2.5.4   Assets which are kept separate from the pool
(CAA 1990, ss 34 and 79)

Motor cars which cost more than £12,000 (£8,000 prior to 10 March 1992) need to be kept separate. The maximum writing-down allowance for such a car is £3,000, but a balancing allowance (or charge) arises on disposal.

2.5.5   Example—Writing-down allowances for motor cars

A operates an advertising business. He makes up his accounts to 30 April. On 1 May 1992 he acquires a car which costs £30,000 and this is used by an employee. After two years, the car is sold for £10,000.
The car is deemed to be in a separate pool and the position is as follows:

		£	
Year one —	Cost	30,000	
	writing-down allowance for 1994–95	3,000	(PY basis)
		27,000	
Year two —	writing-down allowances for 1995–96	3,000	(PY basis)
		24,000	
Year three —	disposal proceeds	10,000	
Balancing allowance for 1996–97		14,000	(PY basis)

Under s 79 certain other assets are kept separate from the pool. One particular category is assets which are used partly for the purposes of the trade and partly for other purposes. For example, a van used by a sole trader as to 40 per cent for business, 60 per cent for private motoring, would be deemed to form a separate pool. The trader would be entitled to 'scaled down' allowances, ie he would receive 40 per cent of the full writing-down allowance and 40 per cent of any balancing allowance.

'Short life' assets are also kept separate (see 2.5.8).

2.5.6 Assets brought into use part way through a year
(CAA 1990, ss 24(2) and 60)

An asset which is acquired towards the end of a trader's accounting period still attracts the full 25 per cent allowance *unless* the trade has not been going for 12 months. In such a case, under s 24(2), the 25 per cent allowance may be scaled down.

2.5.7 Example—Assets bought in year trade is commenced

B commenced trading on 5 October 1993. On 5 April 1994 he acquired plant and machinery for £60,000.

The capital allowances due to him for 1993–94 are:

$\frac{6}{12}$ x 25 per cent x £60,000 ie £7,500

Allowances will normally be due where a trader incurred qualifying expenditure by his year end by entering into an unconditional contract to purchase the plant and machinery. He does not need actually to have brought it into use by his year end.

There is one exception to this. If the plant and machinery is acquired under an HP contract, the entitlement to allowances arises only when the plant and machinery is actually brought into use.

2.5.8   'Short life' assets
(CAA 1990, ss 37-38)

Where expenditure is added to the pool, the trader receives writing down allowances which are likely to get smaller and smaller. For example, a trader invests expenditure of £100,000 on plant in year one. He does not acquire any other plant and machinery for five years. His writing down allowance in year one will be £25,000 (ie 25 per cent of £100,000), £18,750 in year two (ie 25 per cent of the residual £75,000) and so on. By the end of year five, the written-down value will be just under £24,000 but the equipment itself may be worn out and have a scrap value of only, say, £2,000.

To cover this type of situation, the legislation allows for a trader to designate certain assets as short life assets. The cost of these assets is kept in a separate pool and a balancing allowance (or charge) arises on a sale within five years, or on the assets being scrapped by then. If an asset is not sold within that period, the written-down value of the asset is transferred to the pool.

(1)   In the above example, if the plant and machinery were actually scrapped at the start of year five and the trader received no scrap value at all, he would receive a balancing allowance of £31,640.

(2)   Again using the same basic facts, if the plant and machinery were still in use at the end of year five, the written down value of £23,730 would be transferred to the trader's pool of other plant and machinery.

The following cannot be short life assets:

(1)   Motor cars.
(2)   Assets used partly for non-trade purposes.
(3)   Assets originally acquired for non-trade purposes (for example, assets acquired prior to the trade being commenced).
(4)   Ships.
(5)   Certain assets leased-out in the course of a trade.

An election needs to be made for an asset to be treated as a short life asset. This needs to be submitted to the Inspector of Taxes within two years of the accounting period in whch the short life asset is acquired. The Inspector will require sufficient information to be able to identify the assets at a later stage (see Inland Revenue Statement of Practice SP1/86).

2.5.9   What is plant and machinery?

Until this year there was no definition of 'plant and machinery' within the Taxes Acts. Even after the introduction of specific legislation, in FA 1994, the position remains unclear. The statutory definition focuses mainly on what is *not* plant as it forms part of a building and the Revenue's practice and interpretation are still largely based on decisions handed down by the Courts.

The earliest judicial definition was provided in *Yarmouth v France* (1887) 19 QBD 647, in which Lindley LJ stated:

> . . . in its ordinary sense, it includes whatever apparatus is used by a businessman for carrying on his business—not his stock-in-trade, which he buys or makes for sale, but all goods or chattels, fixed or movable, live or dead, which he keeps for permanent employment in his business . . .

Some items are clearly within this definition, for example, typewriters, dictating machines, telephone equipment, computers, manufacturing equipment, vans and other motor vehicles.

What is less obvious is that a building may contain items which are plant and machinery. In some cases the plant will have become part of the building, for example a lift. Also, there may be structures which are items of plant, for example a dry dock or a grain silo, or a mezzanine floor put into a factory in order to create storage space. Capital allowances are also due on building work which is needed to enable plant and machinery to be installed—this would apply if a floor had to be strengthened in order to install a computer.

You should take professional advice if you acquire a building or adapt premises to meet the requirements of your trade in order to ensure that you obtain the Inspector of Taxes' agreement on the full amount which is eligible for capital allowances.

2.5.10   Expenditure on landlord's fixtures
(CAA 1990, s 52)

The decision of the Court of Appeal in *Stokes v Costain Property Investments Ltd* [1984] STC 204 established that capital allowances were not due on expenditure on plant by a tenant where the plant became part of a building and therefore became a landlord's fixture. The reason for this was that the items of plant did not 'belong' to the tenant. This was clearly unsatisfactory as tenants are often required to install plant within a building such as lifts, air conditioning and so on. Accordingly, the legislation was amended and now specifically provides that a tenant who incurs expenditure in these circumstances can receive allowances but a balancing charge may be made on the expiry or surrender of the lease, according to the market value of the plant at that time. There are complex provisions dealing with situations where more than one person incurs expenditure on the same fixture or where expenditure is incurred by an equipment lessor.

2.5.11 Buildings located in an enterprise zone
(CAA 1990, s 1)

Qualifying expenditure on a commercial building which is located in an enterprise zone can qualify for a 100 per cent initial allowance. A commercial building is defined as a building or structure, other than an industrial building or hotel, which is used for the purposes of a trade, profession or vocation or is used as an office. The definition specifically excludes a building which is wholly or partly used as a dwellinghouse. Certain conditions must be fulfilled:

(1) The building must have been constructed under an unconditional contract entered into before the enterprise zone came to the end of its designated life.

(2) The building must be acquired unused or within two years of its having been let for the first time.

The part of the purchase price which relates to the cost of the land does not qualify for capital allowances.

Plant and machinery contained in the building which have become an integral part of the building may also qualify for the 100 per cent allowance.

The initial allowance can be disclaimed, in whole or in part, and the remaining amount of qualifying expenditure is then available as 25 per cent. The 25 per cent writing-down allowances are given on a straight line basis over four years rather than on the reducing basis which applies for plant and machinery.

2.5.12 Example—Capital allowances on buildings in an enterprise zone

An enterprise zone building is acquired for £200,000. The land cost is £20,000, so £180,000 qualifies for capital allowances. The purchaser disclaims the whole of the initial allowance. He will then receive annual allowances as follows:

	£
Year of expenditure	45,000
Year two	45,000
Year three	45,000
Year four	45,000

If the purchaser had disclaimed only £80,000, the position would have been:

	£
Year of expenditure	
Initial allowance	100,000
Annual allowance	45,000
	145,000
Year two annual allowance	35,000
Year three annual allowance	nil
Year four annual allowance	nil

The point to note is that the annual allowances are based on the total qualifying costs, not on the balance left over after deducting the initial allowance.

2.5.13 Example—Disposal of a building in an enterprise zone

A disposal of an enterprise zone building within 25 years of acquisition gives rise to a balancing charge.

An individual acquires an enterprise zone building in year one and takes the full 100 per cent initial allowance on the qualifying expenditure of £95,000. In year four he disposes of the building.

If he receives disposal proceeds of £75,000, there will be a balancing charge of £75,000. If he receives £120,000 (ie more than the trader's qualifying expenditure) the balancing charge is limited to £95,000.

2.5.14 Agricultural buildings allowances
(CAA 1990, s 123)

The term 'agricultural buildings allowances' is slightly misleading in that the expenditure does not need to be on a building. The allowances are given in respect of expenditure on farmhouses, farm or forestry buildings, cottages, fences, ditches, drainage and sewerage works. The *land* must, of course, be used for agricultural purposes.

Expenditure on agricultural buildings which is incurred during the year ending 31 October 1993 qualifies for an initial allowance of 20 per cent. If the buildings etc are brought into use during the trader's accounting period, he will also qualify for a four per cent annual allowance. Expenditure outside this period qualifies only for a four per cent annual allowance. A balancing allowance or charge may arise on a disposal taking place within a period of 25 years.

2.5.15 Industrial buildings
(CAA 1990, ss 3 and 18)

An industrial building is a building or structure which is used for the purpose of a trade consisting of:

(1) the manufacture or processing of goods or materials; or
(2) the maintaining or repairing of goods or materials for customers; or
(3) the maintaining or repairing of goods or materials owned by the trader himself provided that the relevant trade consists of the manufacture or processing of goods or materials; or
(4) the storage of:
  (a) raw materials for manufacture;
  (b) goods to be processed;
  (c) goods manufactured or processed, but not yet delivered to any purchaser;
  (d) goods on arrival by sea or air into the United Kingdom; or
(5) the working of mines, oil wells etc or foreign plantations.

In addition, a sports pavilion provided for the welfare of workers employed in any trade qualifies for industrial buildings allowances. Qualifying expenditure once again excludes the land element in the purchase price.

Qualifying expenditure on an unused industrial building which was incurred during the year ended 31 October 1993 qualified for an initial allowance of 20 per cent. If the building is brought into use, a four per cent annual allowance is also due. Expenditure on a building which has already been brought into use for a trade normally qualifies only for four per cent annual allowances. Expenditure incurred after 31 October 1993 will also attract only the four per cent annual allowances.

A balancing charge or allowance may arise on a disposal within 25 years.

2.5.16 Example—Disposal of industrial buildings

An industrial building was acquired in November 1992 for a cost of £250,000. The land element was £20,000. If the purchaser brought the building into use immediately, allowances would be due as follows:

			£
	Qualifying Cost		230,000
Year one	–	initial allowance	46,000
			184,000
Year one	–	annual allowance	9,200
Residue			174,800
Year two	–	annual allowance	9,200
Residue			£165,600

If the building is sold in year three, a balancing allowance or charge will arise according to whether the proceeds exceed £165,600. If the proceeds were £175,000 there would be a balancing charge of £9,400. If the proceeds were £150,000 there would be a balancing allowance of £15,600. The maximum balancing charge would be £64,400, ie, the allowance received in year one and year two.

2.5.17   Hotels
(CAA 1990, ss 7 and 19)

A qualifying hotel attracts industrial buildings allowances (see 2.5.15–2.5.16). A qualifying hotel must fulfil the following conditions:

(1)   Accommodation must be provided in a building of a permanent nature.

(2)   The hotel must be open for at least four months during April–October.

(3)   There must be at least ten bedrooms available for letting to the public in general which must not normally be in the same occupation for more than a month.

(4)   The services provided must normally include the provision of breakfast and evening meals, making beds and cleaning rooms.

2.5.18   Expenditure on 'know-how'
(TA 1988, s 530)

Expenditure on acquiring know-how for use in a trade attracts capital allowances.

'Know-how' means any industrial information and techniques of assistance in manufacturing or processing goods or materials, or working or searching for mineral deposits, or which may be relevant to agricultural, forestry or fishing operations. Allowances are given on 'qualifying expenditure' which is the aggregate of any capital expenditure on know-how during the basis period, together with any unused balance of expenditure brought forward from the previous basis period and less any disposal value for know-how which has been sold.

Writing down allowances are given at the rate of 25 per cent.

2.5.19   Expenditure on scientific research
(CAA 1990, ss 136–139)

'Scientific research' is defined as activities in the fields of natural or applied science for the extension of knowledge. Any capital expenditure incurred by a trader on scientific research related to the trade attracts a 100 per cent allowance.

2.5.20 Capital allowance basis periods for unincorporated businesses
(CAA 1990, s 160)

The basis period for an unincorporated business will usually be the same as the period which is taken in arriving at the profit (ie in general the preceding year). However, where basis periods overlap, expenditure in the common period is normally treated as incurred only in the earlier period. Expenditure incurred in a gap between two periods is treated as incurred in the later period.

2.5.21 Example—Basis periods for unincorporated businesses

In the case of a new business which started on 1 January 1993, the position would be as follows:

Basis period for capital allowances

1992–93	1 January–5 April 1993
1993–94	6 April–31 December 1993 (assuming the assessment is based on the first 12 months of profits)
1994–95	No basis period

The treatment where a business ceases is slightly different in that expenditure in an interval between two basis periods is treated as incurred in the earlier basis period. For example, if a business made up accounts to 31 May and a cessation occurred on 31 May 1994, there might be a gap between the basis period for 1993–94 (year ended 31 May 1992 on the preceding year basis) and the basis period for 1994–95, 6 April–31 May 1994. Expenditure in this gap would be treated as if it had been incurred in the basis period for 1993–94.

2.6 Pre-trading expenditure
(TA 1988, s 401 as amended by FA 1989, s 114 and FA 1993, s 109), CAA 1990, s 83 (2))

A person may incur expenditure before he starts to trade such as:

(1)   Rent for business premises
(2)   Rates, insurance, heating and lighting

(3)   Advertising wages or other payments to employees
(4)   Bank charges and interest
(5)   Lease rentals on plant and machinery and office equipment
(6)   Accountancy fees.

Pre-trading expenditure may not be deducted in arriving at the profits of
the trade but can be allowed as if it were a loss incurred at the date that
the trade actually commences (see 2.10 on relief for trading losses).

Expenditure can be relieved in this way only if it is incurred within seven
years of the date that the trade is commenced (five years for traders who
commenced business before 1 April 1993).

Pre-trading capital expenditure which qualifies for capital allowances is
dealt with slightly differently in that the expenditure is normally treated
as having been incurred at the date the trade is commenced.

2.7   Post-cessation receipts
(TA 1988, ss 103–104)

Where a person has been assessed on the cash basis (see 2.4.1) special
rules apply if the trade or profession is discontinued. Subsequent receipts
are normally taxed under Schedule D Case VI as income for the year in
which they come in, although an election may be made for the post-
cessation receipts to be treated as arising in the year of discontinuance.

Expenses may be deducted in so far as they were incurred wholly and
exclusively for business and are not otherwise allowable. For example,
a solicitor who had post-cessation receipts would be able to deduct
premiums paid on a professional indemnity policy where the cover
related to the period after the solicitor had ceased to carry on his
profession.

A similar charge may arise where a change occurs in the treatment of a
trader's profits so that the cash basis ceases to apply and his profits are
assessed on the earnings basis. Amounts received from customers after
the change which relate to invoices issued when the business was dealt
with on the cash basis are treated as post-cessation receipts.

Relief may be due under TA 1988, s 109 where the person was carrying
on the trade or profession at 18 March 1968 and his earnings from that
trade or profession had not been assessed on the earnings basis at any
time. The amount assessed under s 104 (but not s 103) is reduced by five
per cent for every year, or part year, by which his age at 18 March 1968
exceeded 51. The maximum reduction under this provision is 75 per cent
and there may be a further restriction where the person was in business
as a partner rather than a sole trader.

2.8   Partnerships

A partnership's profits are computed in the same way as a sole trader's profits (see 2.4–2.5). However, there are a number of additional complications.

2.8.1   Salaried partners

A salaried partner is engaged under a contract of employment. He will normally be taxed under Schedule E rather than under Schedule D. His remuneration will be treated as a normal employee cost in arriving at the firm's profits. Sometimes partners have a fixed share of profits. It will not always be easy to determine whether they are Schedule D or salaried partners. The key indicators that a partner is assessable under Schedule D are that the individual has capital at risk and that he is not subject to the control and direction of the Schedule D partners.

2.8.2   How partnership profits are taxed

A partnership's assessable profits for a year are generally assessed in one amount payable by the firm as a whole and each partner is jointly and severally liable. The assessment reflects the way in which income is divided amongst the partners, their allowances etc. This will come to an end in 1997–98 and thereafter partners will be assessed separately.

Partners are taxed as they share profits for the year of assessment

For tax purposes, a partner's share of the partnership assessment is determined by the way in which the partners share out the profits for the tax year. This may give rise to anomalies since the assessment will generally be made on the preceding year basis and the basis on which profits are shared in the year of assessment may differ from the basis which applied during the preceding year.

Where a firm starts business after 5 April 1994 or is deemed to start a new business, the new rules will come into operation immediately. Assessments will be made on the individual partners and there will be no joint and several liability for taxation.

2.8.3   Example—Assessment of partners' profits

A, B and C shared profits equally during the partnership year ended 31 March 1994 when the firm made profits of £90,000. The assessment for 1993–94 on the preceding year basis is £82,500. During 1994–95 the basis on which profits are shared changes to:

A—50 per cent
B—30 per cent
C—20 per cent

The 1994–95 assessment on profits of £90,000 will be divided for tax purposes between:

A's share	£45,000
B's share	£27,000
C's share	£18,000

The actual profits for the year ended 31 March 1995 may be only £75,000 which means that A will have actually enjoyed profits of £67,500 (one-third of £90,000 plus one-half of £75,000), but will have been taxed on a total of £72,500 (one-third of £82,500 plus one-half of £90,000).

2.8.4 Changes in partners
(TA 1988, s 113)

The strict position is that every time a partner joins or leaves a firm there is a cessation (see 2.3.8) of the trade or profession carried on by the 'old' firm and the trade or profession is recommenced by the new firm. However, the partners may elect for the change in partners to be ignored so that no cessation is deemed to have occurred. This election must be made by all the parties concerned, ie all those who were partners before the change and all those who were partners after the change. The election is generally referred to as a 'continuation election' and has to be made within two years of the change in partners.

There may be circumstances where the consequences of a change in partners giving rise to a cessation are favourable to some partners but not to others. A properly drawn-up partnership agreement will make provision for this so that, if the overall position is that tax will be saved by a continuation election being made, the partners who suffer any disadvantage are indemnified by the partners who benefit. Sometimes a partner who has retired dies before the election is made (or his death may have been the event which caused the change in partners). In such situations, the election under s 113 will need to be signed by his personal representatives.

An election can be submitted to the Inspector of Taxes on a provisional basis and will then cease to be effective if it is formally withdrawn during the two year period.

The current effect of the preceding year basis, and of a change in profit sharing, often becomes even more marked where a partner leaves the firm. Consequently, in the example in 2.8.3, if C had retired on 31 March 1994, leaving A and B sharing profits equally, they would both end up being taxed for 1993–94 and 1994–95 on profits which exceeded their annual share of the profits received in the two years ended 31 March 1994. On the other hand, if the change were the admission of a new partner into the firm, the fact that assessable profits are determined on the preceding year basis may well work in the partners' favour as profits are likely to rise and there will be more individuals to share the assessable profits.

2.8.5 Extended commencement provisions where a partnership has a deemed cessation
(TA 1988, ss 61–62)

The Public Accounts Committee's concern about the loss of tax due to large professional partnerships taking full advantage of the rules which apply where partners join or leave the firm prompted special legislation introduced in 1985 which extends the normal rules which apply where a new unincorporated business is commenced.

The legislation applies where a deemed cessation has taken place, and a continuation election could have been, but was not, made. In this case, the assessable profits for the new firm are based on its actual profits for the first four years. The preceding year basis then applies for the fifth and subsequent years, unless an election is made by the firm for profits to be assessed on an actual basis for years five and six.

This special rule applies *only* where a partnership is involved both before and after the cessation. It does not apply where a partner or partners retire from a firm leaving one partner to continue as a sole trader, nor does it apply in the converse situation where a sole trader admits a partner.

2.8.6 Partnerships controlled outside the United Kingdom
(TA 1988, s 112)

A UK-resident individual may be a partner in a partnership which is controlled outside the United Kingdom. His earnings from such a partnership are normally assessable under Schedule D Case V rather than under Schedule D Case I or Case II (however profits which are earned by a UK branch are taxed under Schedule D Case I or II).

An individual who is UK-domiciled will normally be taxed on the full amount of his profits for the preceding year (computed as if the partnership were resident in the United Kingdom). A foreign-domiciled individual will be charged tax on the profits which he remitted to the United Kingdom during the preceding year.

Special rules apply for the opening and closing years.

Opening years

First year—actual income is assessable.

Second year—normally the actual income for the year is assessable, unless the source was held at 5 April in the first year of assessment (see below).

Third year—this is assessed on the preceding year basis unless the taxpayer elects for the actual income of the year to be assessed instead.

Where the first year's income is a full year's income (ie the source was held at 6 April in year one) the assessable income for the second year is the preceding year's income, with the taxpayer having an option to have his actual income assessed instead. The third year's assessment is determined on the preceding year basis (with no right of election on the part of the taxpayer).

Closing years

The income of the final tax year is ascertained by reference to the actual income for the year. The income of the penultimate year will normally be assessable on the preceding year basis but the Revenue has the option of substituting the actual income for the year if that is greater.

2.9 Administrative aspects and payment of tax

2.9.1 Introduction

The Inspector of Taxes will issue a Schedule D assessment which charges income tax on the profits of the business, less the capital allowances due for the year. The assessment may be estimated or based on accounts and computations submitted by the trader or his accountant. Estimated assessments are normally adjusted to agree with tax computations once they have been agreed.

The Revenue, however, only requires three entries (sales, expenses and net profit) on a tax return where a trader's turnover (sales) does not exceed £15,000, although the Revenue reserves the right to call for a more detailed analysis.

2.9.2 Class 4 NIC

A deduction is available for half of the trader's liability for National Insurance Class 4 contributions (see 23.4) in arriving at the trader's income tax liability.

2.9.3   Double tax relief
(TA 1988, ss 497–498)

Double taxation relief may be available where a business has an overseas branch which is subject to foreign tax. Relief may be given as a credit against the UK tax payable on the profits of the business. Where there is no UK liability (ie the business is running at a loss) the foreign tax may be deducted as if it were an expense.

2.9.4   Payment of tax
(TA 1988, s 5)

Tax is normally payable under Schedule D Case I and II by two instalments. The first instalment is due for payment on 1 January in the year of assessment concerned, and the second instalment falls due for payment six months later, on 1 July. Where a Schedule D assessment is issued between 1 December and 31 May, the first instalment is due for payment 30 days later. Where an assessment is issued after 31 May following the end of the tax year, the full amount of tax is payable in one instalment.

In all the above situations, deferment or 'postponement' of tax may be secured where the Inspector is satisfied that the assessment over-charges tax or it may exceed the true liability (see 19.2).

In 1996–97 the payment dates are to be changed to 31 January and 31 July.

2.9.5   Annual payments
(TA 1988, ss 349 and 387)

These include any annuity or other annual payment (other than interest) and any royalty or other sum paid in respect of the use of a patent.

These payments will normally be made out of profits or gains chargeable to income tax (see 6.6). However, where a trader makes losses or has insufficient profits to cover the annual payments, a liability to account for basic rate tax may arise under s 349. In such a case, the trader can add the gross amounts of the annual payments to his trading loss.

2.10   Relief for trading losses

Relief may be available for a loss incurred by an individual in a trade or profession. Relief may also be due for pre-trading expenditure which is treated as a loss incurred when the trade was commenced (see 2.6 above). The provisions which govern the relief for trading losses are complex and there are several ways in which losses may be utilised.

2.10.1 Carry forward relief against subsequent assessments
(TA 1988, s 385)

A loss incurred by a sole trader or a partner's share of his firm's trading loss may be carried forward and deducted in assessments for later years in respect of the same trade or profession. Where losses are carried forward in this way, they must be used against the assessable profits for the first subsequent year in which profits arise. The loss which is carried forward in this way may also be relieved against certain income which is connected with the trade even though it is assessed under a different schedule (for example, interest earned on temporary investment of trade receipts and dividends from trade investments). There is no limit on the number of years for which a loss may be carried forward provided that the same trade is carried on.

2.10.2 Relief against general income
(TA 1988, s 380)

Where a sole trader or partner incurs a loss and the trade was carried on with a view to profit, the loss may be relieved against his general income for the year of assessment in which it was incurred (ie his total income for the year). Relief may also be claimed against the individual's general income for the following tax year provided that the relevant trade, profession or vocation is carried on by the individual at some time during that year.

The claim for a loss to be set against an individual's general income for the following tax year is an alternative to the claim for the loss to be relieved against income of the year of loss. In other words, either the loss may be set against income of the current year (with any balance being set against income of the following year) or the individual may forgo the chance to set the loss against his income for the current year and set the full amount against income of the following year.

Where an individual takes relief for trading losses against his general income, he must use up the losses to the extent to which he has taxable income. It is not possible for a claim to be made to restrict the amount of losses so as to enable sufficient income to be left to make use of the individual's personal allowances. On the other hand, the legislation permits the individual to deduct certain items before arriving at his general income against which trading losses can be offset. These items include relief for allowable expenses for Schedule E purposes, retirement annuity and personal pension contributions, interest relief and relief for donations to charities by deed of covenant or gift aid.

Prior to 1990–91, the loss had to be set against earned income first unless the trade would produce profits which were taxed as investment income, in which case the loss had to be set against investment income first. The current rules permit an individual to choose what type of income is covered by loss relief.

Relief under s 380 must be claimed within two years from the end of the tax year for which relief is claimed. For example, the claim for a 1992–93 loss to be set against the individual's general income for 1992–93 needs to be submitted by 5 April 1995. However, if relief is taken against the individual's general income for the following tax year (1993–94), the individual has until 5 April 1996 to make a claim.

2.10.3 Relief by aggregation

Where the profits of different accounting periods are time apportioned (eg on commencement of a business) a loss may be relieved by aggregation with a profit. This situation could arise if a first period of trading were less than 12 months.

2.10.4 Example—Loss relief by aggregation

A started business on 1 January 1993. He made a loss of £9,000 for the period ended 30 September 1993 and a profit of £24,000 for the year ended 30 September 1994. Relief by aggregation would produce the following result:

Profits assessable 1992–93	NIL
Profits assessable 1993–94	NIL
Profits assessable 1994–95	NIL

The reason for this is that the first 12 months' trading would be deemed to produce a net loss computed as follows:

	£
Loss for period 1 Jan–30 Sept 1993	(9,000)
3/12 of profit for year ended 30 Sept 1994	6,000
	(3,000)

Relief for the same loss may be obtained more than once when the loss is used by aggregation and this can produce effective relief which exceeds the loss actually incurred.

If a loss is set against other income, it cannot also be relieved by aggregation. Thus, if A had claimed relief for the loss that he had incurred in 1992–93, only part of the loss for the period ended 30 September 1993 which relates to the period 6 April–30 September 1993 could be taken into account in arriving at the profits of the first 12 months' trading.

2.10.5 Example—Loss set against other income

B commenced trading on 1 August 1993. He has a loss during the nine months ended 30 April 1994 of £36,000. He has profits for the year ended 30 April 1995 of £60,000.

If the 1993–94 loss is used by its being set against B's other income, the position is as follows:

1993–94	NIL
1994–95	
Profits of first 12 months:	
nine months ended 30 April 1994	NIL
3/12 x profits for year ended 30 April 1995	15,000
	15,000
1995–96	
Profits of first 12 months	
	15,000

Contrast this with the situation where relief for the loss is obtained by aggregation.

1993–94	NIL
1994–95	
Profits of first 12 months	NIL
1995–96	
Profits of first 12 months	NIL

2.10.6 Computation of loss

Normally, for a trader who has been carrying on business for a number of years, a trading loss incurred in an accounting year which ends in a year of assessment is treated as a loss for that year. Consequently, if a trader makes up accounts to 31 July 1994, and the accounts for that year show a loss, this will normally be treated as a 1994–95 trading loss. However, this is largely a matter of practice and convention and strictly speaking the loss which qualifies for relief under s 380 is the loss incurred in a year of assessment ie the results of two accounting periods should really be apportioned to arrive at the loss (if any) incurred in a tax year.

2.10.7 Example—Computation of loss

If A has a profit for the year ended 31 July 1993 of £12,000, a loss for the year ended 31 July 1994 of £48,000, and a loss to July 1995 of £6,000, the strict position should be as follows:

1993–94	£
3/12 x profits for year ended 31 July 1993	3,000
9/12 x loss for year ended 31 July 1994	(36,000)
	(33,000)

1994–95	£
3/12 x loss for year ended 31 July 1994	(12,000)
9/12 x loss for year ended 31 July 1995	(4,500)
	(16,500)

The Revenue insists on the loss being calculated on the strict basis in certain circumstances, ie

(1)   where the year of the loss is one of the first three years of assessment of a new business;

(2)   where the year of loss is the fourth year that a new business has been carried on and the taxpayer has elected for his profits for years two and three to be assessed by reference to actual profits;

(3)   where the year of assessment immediately follows a year for which a loss has been ascertained on the strict basis;

(4)   in the tax year in which the business is permanently discontinued;

(5)   in any other year of assessment if the individual so chooses.

2.10.8 Capital allowances and loss claims
(TA 1988, s 383)

The general principle is that where capital allowances cannot be given because there are insufficient profits, the allowances must be carried forward and given in subsequent years. However, it is possible for an individual to claim for capital allowances to be treated as a deduction in arriving at the loss for the year of assessment. Capital allowances which are claimed in this way may either increase a loss or convert a profit into a loss.

The capital allowances to be taken into account are those of the normal basis period which relates to the tax year. This still applies even though the loss itself may be arrived at on the strict basis by apportioning the results of the accounting periods which overlap the relevant tax year.

2.10.9 Example—Capital allowances and loss claims

A commences trading on 6 October. His results are as follows:

Year ended 5 October 1993—profit £4,000
Year ended 5 October 1994—profit £12,000
Year ended 5 October 1995—profit £50,000

Assume that capital allowances are as follows:

| 1992–93 | £30,000 |
| 1993–94 | £38,000 |

If A claims that his capital allowances for 1992–93 should be deducted and the resultant loss relieved under s 380, the position is as follows:

1992–93	£
6/12 x profits for year ended 5 October 1993	2,000
Capital allowances for 1992–93	(30,000)
Loss after deducting capital allowances	(28,000)

1993–94	£
6/12 x profits for year ended 5 October 1993	2,000
6/12 x profits for year ended 5 October 1994	6,000
	8,000
Capital allowances for 1993–94	(38,000)
Loss after deducting capital allowances	(30,000)

The £28,000 loss for 1992–93 may be set against A's other income for 1992–93 or 1993–94. The £30,000 loss for 1993–94 is available to be set against A's other income for 1993–94 or 1994–95.

2.10.10 Loss relief for partners

Each individual partner may decide how to utilise his share of a firm's loss, ie whether to carry it forward against future profits or to set it against other income. When a partner retires, any unused losses carried forward by him go to waste and they are not available to cover profits subsequently earned by other partners.

There is one exception to the principle that each partner may choose how to relieve his loss. A claim may be made under s 383 for capital allowances to be added to the trading loss only with the written consent of all the partners concerned. In fact, the Revenue also requires written consent to be given by individuals who have subsequently become partners even though they were not involved during the year itself.

2.10.11   Losses in early years of a trade
(TA 1988, s 381)

In certain circumstances, relief may be claimed against an individual's general income for the three years of assessment preceding the year in which the loss is incurred. Relief is given against income for the earliest year first. The loss may be computed in the normal way, or it may be augmented by capital allowances as described in 2.10.8.

There are certain preconditions for a loss to be claimed in this way.

(1)   The loss must arise during the first four tax years in which the business is carried on.

(2)   Where a trade is acquired from a spouse, the four years run from the date that the spouse first commenced trading (unless the trade is taken over on the death of the spouse).

(3)   The trade must be carried on on a commercial basis *and with a reasonable expectation of profits.*

A claim for a loss to be relieved in this way must be made within two years of the end of the tax year in which the loss was incurred.

2.10.12   Consequences of carrying back losses

Where a loss is carried back, the following order of set-off applies:

1990–91 and subsequent years

The loss must be set against the individual's total income.

1989–90 and prior years

The loss may be set off in the following ways:

(1)   earned income;
(2)   investment income;
(3)   spouse's earned income;
(4)   spouse's investment income.

However, the individual may elect not to allow the loss to be relieved against his spouse's income under (3) and (4).

Where a loss is carried back in this way, any repayment will normally produce an entitlement to repayment supplement (see 19.11).

2.10.13 Relief for trading losses against capital gains
(FA 1991, s 52)

An individual who has incurred a trading loss during 1991–92 or a subsequent year may have the loss set against any capital gains which arise in the same year.

It is not possible to claim relief for trading losses in this way without first having made a claim for relief under s 380 for the loss to be set against the individual's general income for the year.

It is also possible for a trading loss to be set against an individual's capital gains for the following year provided that a claim is first made under s 380(2) for the trading loss to be set against the individual's general income for that year. A precondition for a loss to be relieved in this way is that the individual has carried on the relevant trade at some time during the following tax year.

2.10.14 Terminal loss relief
(TA 1988, s 388)

Where a trade, profession or vocation is permanently discontinued, a loss incurred during the last twelve months can be deducted from the profits charged to tax in the three tax years before the final year. The relief can include a claim for the loss arising in the tax year in which the cessation takes place, and a proportion of the loss for the previous tax year.

Capital allowances for the final tax year may also be claimed, as can an appropriate proportion of the preceding year's capital allowances, representing the allowances due for the period beginning twelve months prior to the cessation.

The terminal loss may be carried back against profits from the same trade for the three tax years preceding the year of cessation. The relief is given against the latest year's profits first.

If interest and dividends would have been included as trading profits, (except that they were subject to deduction of tax at source), the terminal loss may be set against such income.

Partnership changes

A deemed cessation does not count for terminal loss relief. On the other hand, outgoing partners can claim terminal loss relief even though the business continues.

2.10.15 Anti-avoidance provisions

Farming losses
(TA 1988, s 397)

Restrictions may apply to losses suffered by farmers. The legislation may prevent a farming loss being set against the individual's other income where he has suffered losses for each of the preceding five tax years. The only way of avoiding this restriction is for the individual to show that no reasonably competent farmer would have expected to have made a profit during the period in question.

Losses from limited partnerships
(TA 1988, s 117)

Limited partnerships were widely used in tax avoidance arrangements. The House of Lords decided in *Reed v Young* [1986] STC 285 that a limited partner could be entitled to loss relief for an amount which exceeded his actual liability under the Limited Partnership Act. This led to specific legislation to limit the amount of loss relief to the capital which is 'at risk'. Any losses incurred beyond this amount have to be carried forward to be set against any future share of profits received by the limited partner from the firm.

The provisions of s 117 apply to individuals who are limited partners or members of a joint venture arrangement under which their liability is limited to a contract, agreement, guarantee etc.

2.10.16   Loss relief where a business has been transferred to a company
(TA 1988, s 386)

Where a business has been carried on by an individual (either as a sole trader or in partnership) and the business is transferred to a company, it is possible for any unused trading losses to be relieved against the individual's income from the company in subsequent years.

This relief is available only if the business is transferred to a company in return for an allotment of shares and then only if the individual has retained ownership of those shares throughout the tax year concerned. In practice, the Revenue does not withhold relief provided the individual has retained at least 80 per cent of the shares.

2.10.17   Schedule D Case V losses
(TA 1988, s 391)

Profits from a trade managed or controlled abroad are taxed under Schedule D Case V. Loss relief is calculated in the same way as for a loss incurred in a trade, profession or vocation taxed under Schedule D Case I or Case II.

Relief for such losses is given in the same way as relief is given for UK trading losses, except that where a loss is to be set against other income, a Case V loss can be deducted only from:

(1) profits from other foreign trades assessable under Schedule D Case V,
(2) foreign pensions and annuities where a ten per cent deduction is available;
(3) foreign emoluments assessable under Schedule E.

2.11 Lloyd's underwriters ('Names')

An individual who is a Name at Lloyd's is deemed to carry on a trade whose profits are charged to tax under Schedule D Case I. For years up to 1992, profits from Lloyd's are treated as earned income only if the Name spends 75 per cent of his time working at Lloyd's but, with effect from the 1993 underwriting year, all underwriting profits (including syndicate and other Lloyd's investment income and syndicate capital appreciation) will be treated as earned income. However, the DSS has confirmed that any profits will not be liable to Class 2 or Class 4 national insurance contributions where the individuals have previously been regarded as non-working Names.

There is a time lag in that Lloyd's syndicates make up their accounts only after a period of two years has elapsed. This means that the results for Lloyd's account 1991 (ie the year ended 31 December 1991) will be known only in the spring of 1994. Nevertheless, the income is taxable for the year 1991–92.

The basis of assessment of individual Names is to change for the 1994 and subsequent accounts. The profits of 1994 will be assessed for the year of assessment in which the profits are declared and not for the year in which they arose. Thus, profits of 1994 will be assessed for 1997–98 and not for 1994–95.

There will be transitional arrangements but these are complicated and outside the scope of this book.

2.11.1 Allowable deductions

A deduction may be claimed for the following expenses borne by the Name:

(1) Premiums for insurance policies (known as Personal Stop Loss policies) paid to minimise a Name's exposure to underwriting

losses. The premiums are allowable as a deduction for the underwriting year to which they relate. Any recovery from the insurance company will in turn be treated as additional underwriting income.

(2)   The annual cost of maintaining a letter of credit for bank guarantee.

(3)   Interest on a loan raised to finance an underwriting loss and, with effect from 1 January 1990, on money borrowed to fund Lloyd's deposit and reserves (see Lloyd's Market Bulletin 13 January 1992).

(4)   Personal accountancy fees. The Inland Revenue takes the view that only fees relating to the agreement of income tax assessments or to the earning or calculation of profits for the Name are allowable (and, therefore, those relating to the computation of transfers to the special reserve fund or the submission of loss claims are not). Each year, the Inland Revenue publishes guidelines as to the maximum fees which will normally be allowed, though higher or lower figures may be charged in appropriate cases. The figures allowed are normally related to the number of syndicates of which the Name is a member. The amounts for the 1990 account are as follows:

	£
First syndicate	400
Second to sixth syndicates (each)	120
Seventh to twenty-sixth syndicate (each)	50
Any further syndicates	NIL

(5)   Premiums paid to an estate protection plan (an insurance arrangement intended to facilitate the winding-up of a Name's estate following death).

(6)   Subscriptions to the Association of Lloyd's Members and certain expenses of attending meetings.

(7)   Purchase of Lloyd's 'blue book' (annual listing of syndicate members), Chatset tables (Lloyd's league tables) and certain other publications.

(8)   Subscriptions to Names' Action Groups, eg Outhwaite.

2.11.2   The special reserve fund
(TA 1988, s 452)

The purpose of the special reserve fund is to enable Names to set aside some of their Lloyd's income, free of higher rate tax, as a reserve against future liabilities. Subject to the rules set out below, the amount transferred (if any) is entirely at the discretion of the Name.

For the 1992 and subsequent accounts, a new and more generous form of special reserve fund applies and the old fund is to be wound up.

Transfers to the existing fund

Transfers to the existing special reserve fund are made up of two elements:

(1) the 'basic' transfer, which is limited to 35 per cent of the Name's 'Lloyd's income' for the year (subject to a maximum of £5,000);

(2) the 'additional' transfer, which is 15 per cent of the Name's Lloyd's income for the year (subject to a maximum of £2,000).

The total of the basic and additional transfers cannot exceed £7,000 in any year.

Where a Name suffers a loss for a year, he must withdraw a corresponding amount from the special reserve fund. The withdrawal is treated as income which has borne tax at the basic rate.

New special reserve fund

The new fund will operate as follows:

(1) Transfers into and withdrawals from the fund will be made gross rather than net of tax at basic rate.

(2) Payments into the fund will be deducted as a trading expense and withdrawals will be taxed as trading receipts.

(3) A transfer into the fund will be permitted of up to 50 per cent of the profits for an underwriting year provided the value of the fund at the end of the year does not exceed 50 per cent of the Name's overall premium limit.

(4) Transfers will be voluntary and time limits will be prescribed.

(5) Income and gains on the investments in the fund will be exempt from income tax and capital gains tax.

(6) If an underwriting loss is sustained, a withdrawal must be made from the fund of the lower of the loss and the amount of the fund.

(7) If a cash call is made, a withdrawal has to be made of the lower of the cash call and the amount of the fund and, if the cash call is greater than the ultimate loss, the excess must be transferred back.

(8) Starting at 31 December 1994, the fund will be valued each year at 31 December and if the value of the fund exceeds 50 per cent of the premium limit for that year, the excess must be withdrawn.

(9) When a Name ceases to underwrite, the balance of the fund will be repaid to him or his estate. This repayment may take the form of money or money's worth. Where assets are transferred, the Name (or his personal representatives) will acquire the assets at market value for capital gains tax purposes.

(10) Because the fund is a gross fund, the managers will be able to claim repayment of tax suffered by deduction and payment of tax credit.

(11) Although funds accumulate tax free in the fund, there will be a potential tax liability on withdrawal and this will be on the full value of the fund.

(12) If a withdrawal is made when a Name ceases to underwrite, the payment will be treated as a trading receipt received immediately after the end of the year preceding the one in which his Lloyd's deposit is repaid to him, ie normally it will be a receipt of his final year.

2.11.3 Payment of tax

As stated above, the new rules are to be applied to the 1994 account, and once again there are to be transitional arrangements. However, the treatment in respect of underwriting accounts up to and including the 1993 account is as follows.

Income tax at the basic rate will be deducted at source by the member's underwriting agent based on the underwriting profits/losses and will be paid over to the Inland Revenue one year and one day after the close of the year of account, (so that tax for the 1991 year of account will be paid on 1 January 1995). Any higher rate tax and any further basic rate tax liability is payable by the Name personally on the following 1 July, before which date an assessment should have been issued by the Inland Revenue showing the tax payable (giving credit for the basic rate tax paid on his behalf by the underwriting agent). The assessment will also take into account not only the allowable expenses as indicated above, but also any adjustments agreed with the Inspector of Taxes (estimated figures being used if necessary). Any excess basic or higher rate tax paid by or on behalf of the Name is repayable directly to the individual.

2.11.4 Investment income on special reserve and personal reserve funds

Interest and dividends on the investments comprised in a Name's Lloyd's deposit, personal reserve and special reserve funds are normally mandated direct to the Name and assessed personally on him.

Most such income will have suffered basic rate tax (or its equivalent) at source, in which case, any higher rate tax is payable by the Name on 1 December in the following year of assessment. Where the income is received gross, both basic and higher rate tax are payable by the Name on 1 January in the year of assessment.

This is to change with effect from 6 April 1993. Thereafter, Lloyd's investment income will be included in the Schedule D Case I underwriting result.

2.11.5   The treatment of underwriting losses for UK taxation purposes
(TA 1988, ss 380–381, 385 and 450)

Underwriting losses arise where the net claims and expenses of a syndicate for an underwriting year (including reinsurance costs and personal stop loss recoveries) exceed the syndicate's income from premiums and investments. A formal claim for the relief of such losses must be made by the Name to the Inspector of Taxes.

Order of set-off

Such losses are set off against the claimant Name's income in the following order:

(1)   The mandatory withdrawal from the Name's special reserve fund (see 2.11.2). Income tax at the basic rate on the gross amount of the withdrawal is recoverable by the Name.

(2)   Other income of the same year of assessment. For years up to and including 1989–90 non-working Names had to set off losses against investment income first. Working Names similarly had to set off losses against earned income first.

(3)   Any balance of loss may be set against the individual's other income (of whatever description) for the previous year of assessment under TA 1988, s 450 (3), *provided* that the individual was a Name in that year. For years up to and including 1989–90, the order of set-off was as in (2) above.

(4)   Whereas (2) and (3) are options, any unused losses can only be carried forward under TA 1988, s 385 against future underwriting income, and investment income from the Lloyd's deposit, special reserve fund and personal reserves (but not capital gains). Consequently, if beneficial, a Name can choose to carry forward all losses with the exception of the mandatory special reserve fund withdrawal, against future Lloyd's income.

(5)   From the 1991 account, underwriting losses can be set-off against a Name's capital gains in certain circumstances (see 2.10.13).

New Names have the option, in any of their first four years of underwriting, to carry back any loss under TA 1988, s 381(1) against any income of the three years immediately preceding that in which the loss arose (taking the earlier year first) (see 2.10.11). The order of set-off for 1989–90 and earlier years is as in 2.10.12 above.

3 Employment income

This chapter deals with the following matters:

(1) Basis of assessment.
(2) How tax is collected.
(3) Allowable expenses.
(4) Benefits in kind in general.
(5) Company cars.
(6) Free use of assets.
(7) Beneficial loans.
(8) Living accommodation.
(9) Miscellaneous benefits.
(10) Profit related pay.
(11) Profit sharing schemes.
(12) Non-approved options and employee share schemes.
(13) Approved share option schemes.
(14) Options to acquire company assets.
(15) Golden hallos.
(16) Restrictive covenants.
(17) Redundancy payments.
(18) Golden handshakes and other termination payments.
(19) Special rules for working outside the United Kingdom.
(20) Designing a 'tax efficient' remuneration package.

3.1 Basis of assessment

3.1.1. Introduction
(TA 1988, s 19)

An individual who holds an office or employment is taxed under Schedule E. There are three different cases of Schedule E which depend upon the residence, ordinary residence and domicile of the individual and where the duties of the employment are carried out:

Table 3.1—Schedule E

Case I	—	Individual resident and ordinarily resident in the United Kingdom. Tax due on total remuneration received.
Case II	—	Individual resident but not ordinarily resident in the United Kingdom. Tax due on total remuneration received (subject to special treatment of foreign emoluments—see 22.2 and remuneration taxed under Case III—see below).
		Individual not resident in the United Kingdom. Tax due on total remuneration received for duties performed in the United Kingdom.
Case III	—	Individual resident but not ordinarily resident in the United Kingdom where the duties are performed outside the United Kingdom. Case III may also apply to foreign domiciled individuals' earnings from duties performed outside the United Kingdom.

The remainder of this chapter concentrates on employees who are taxed under Schedule E Case I.

Chapter 22 deals with foreign domiciled individuals in so far as they are taxed under Schedule E Case III.

3.1.2 Receipts basis
(TA 1988, s 202A)

The amount which is assessable for a tax year is the amount of earnings received in that year. Prior to 1988–89, Schedule E income was assessable on the earnings basis.

3.1.3 Date remuneration is deemed to be received
(TA 1988, s 202B)

Special provisions define the date that an individual is deemed to receive remuneration as the earlier of:

(1) the date when payment is actually made; and
(2) the time when the employee becomes entitled to payment.

In the case of directors, the date can be earlier than above, in that payment is deemed to take place on the earliest of (1) and (2) and

(3) the date that income is credited to the director in the company's accounts or records;
(4) the date when the amount of income for a period is determined;

(5)   the end of a period if the director's remuneration for a period is determined before the period has expired.

The employer is required to operate PAYE when payment is deemed to take place (see 19.13).

3.1.4   Amounts deducted in arriving at pay
(TA 1988, s 202)

Contributions made by an employee to an approved retirement benefit scheme and contributions of up to £900 to a payroll giving scheme ('give as you earn') are deducted from an individual's salary in arriving at taxable pay for the purposes of both PAYE and Schedule E. Profit-related pay must also be left out of account provided that it does not exceed the limits which are set out in 3.10.

It should be noted that national insurance contributions are based on pay *before* such amounts are deducted (see 23.1).

3.2   How tax is collected

3.2.1   Tax deductions under PAYE

All payments of 'emoluments' by a UK-resident employer to directors and employees are subject to PAYE. The following are listed in the *Employer's Guide to PAYE* as payments from which PAYE should be deducted:

Salary
Wages
Fees
Overtime
Bonus
Commission
Pension
Honoraria
Pay during sickness or other absence from work
Holiday pay
Christmas boxes in cash
Employee's income tax borne by the employer
Payments in respect of the cost of travelling between the employee's home and his normal place of employment
Payments for time spent in travelling
Cash payments for meals
Payments in lieu of benefits in kind
Certain lump sum payments made on retirement or removal from employment

Certain sums received from the trustees of approved profit sharing schemes
Gratuities or service charges paid out by the employer.

On the other hand, PAYE cannot be deducted from certain benefits even though they are assessable income for Schedule E purposes. The *Employer's Guide* states that the following are income from which tax cannot be deducted:

Living accommodation provided rent-free or at a reduced rent
Gifts in kind such as Christmas hampers
Luncheon vouchers up to 15p per day
Employee's liabilities borne by the employer
Income in the form of company shares.

The scope of PAYE has been extended by FA 1994, s 127 which came into force on the Finance Bill receiving Royal Assent. Employers are now required to account for PAYE when they pay their staff in 'marketable assets' such as gold bars or commodities, or with non-marketable assets where the employer has made arrangements for the employee to convert them into cash.

PAYE code numbers

The Inland Revenue issues code numbers which determine the amount of PAYE deductions. Such code numbers are based on the latest information available to the Revenue and are intended to ensure that the amounts withheld under PAYE approximate closely to the individual's actual liability. Nevertheless, deduction of tax under PAYE is provisional in that if the actual liability exceeds the amount withheld under PAYE, the Revenue may collect the balance either by increased PAYE deductions in subsequent years or by raising an assessment.

Although the top rate of tax is 40 per cent, the Revenue may issue 'K' codes under which increased deductions may be made of up to 50 per cent of an individual's pay. The principle behind K codes is that notional pay is added to an employee's actual pay, and PAYE is operated accordingly. This is intended to cover the situation where the benefits in kind which are taxable exceed a person's allowances.

3.2.2 Foreign employers who are unable to operate PAYE

Where a person is employed by a foreign employer which has no place of business in the United Kingdom, PAYE is not normally operated. The employee is assessed (by the 'direct collection method') and the tax and national insurance contributions are normally collected by four equal instalments over the course of a year.

3.2.3   Schedule E assessments

A Schedule E assessment may be made after the end of a tax year. Tax becomes payable as and when the actual liability is determined, either by the Inspector issuing an agreed assessment or by an appeal being determined under the Taxes Management Act (TMA)1970, s 54 or by the appeal being determined by the Commissioners.

Tax equal to the underpayment may be demanded by the Collector of Taxes and the due date for payment (and for interest) is 14 days after the Collector issues a demand for the Schedule E unpaid tax.

In practice, employees and directors who enjoy substantial benefits in kind should complete their tax return by 31 October 1993 or should supply sufficient information to the Inspector of Taxes by that date in order for the Inspector to issue a Schedule E assessment which is correct. Failure to observe this deadline may result in the Revenue seeking interest under TMA 1970, s 88 (see 19.7).

3.3   Allowable expenses

3.3.1   Schedule E expenses
(TA 1988, s 198)

The rules governing the amounts which may be deducted for tax purposes from remuneration which is subject to Schedule E tax are extremely strict. The legislation provides for a deduction to be made only in respect of expenses which are wholly, exclusively *and necessarily* incurred in the performance of the duties of the employment or office.

Wholly, exclusively ...

The Courts have held that the following expenses are not deductible for Schedule E purposes because they were not deemed to have been incurred *wholly and exclusively* in the performance of the duties of the employment:

(1)   Meal expenses paid out of meal allowances
(2)   Rent of telephone installed for business reasons but not used wholly and exclusively in the performance of duties
(3)   Cost of domestic assistance where the taxpayer's wife was employed
(4)   Cost of looking after a widower's children
(5)   Cost of ordinary clothing.

... and necessarily ...

The situation often arises that the employer has reimbursed the expense because it is regarded as essential. This is helpful, but not conclusive. The Revenue will assess the amount paid to a director or P11D employee (see 3.4.1) but may then seek to disallow the claim by the individual in respect of the expenditure on the grounds that it is not *necessary*. Two recent cases involved reimbursed expenditure by journalists on newspapers and other periodicals and the point at issue was whether reading such newspapers was part of, or inherent in the performance of the journalists' duties. (It is fairly typical that in one case the journalists succeeded, in the other case the Revenue won). The key point here is that it is not the employer's decision which determines the case. The employer may be fully prepared to reimburse the expenditure but the Revenue may still argue that the expenditure fails to meet the very strict guidelines on what constitutes 'necessary'.

... in the performance of the duties

Other expenses were rejected on the grounds that they were not incurred *in the performance* of the duties of the relevant employment:

(1) Employment agency fees (although entertainers are now specifically entitled to claim a deduction for such expenses up to 17½ per cent of their earnings)
(2) Headmaster's course to improve background knowledge
(3) Articled clerk's examination fees
(4) Travelling costs from home to the place where the duties of the employment were performed
(5) Living expenses paid out of living allowances paid to an employee when working away from home.

Cases where the taxpayer has succeeded

There have been cases where travelling expenses have been allowed because the Courts were satisfied that a person's duties started as soon as he left home. For example, in *Gilbert v Hemsley* [1981] STC 703, the duties of a director of a plant-hire company involved his using his home as a base and travelling to various sites. The Court therefore held that once he left home he was travelling in the course of his duties. Similarly, in *Pook v Owen* (1969) 45 TC 571, a doctor was 'on call' and his duties started once he was telephoned by the hospital to ask him to attend.

3.3.2 Expenses which are allowable
(TA 1988, s 201)

There are certain expenses which are specifically allowable, such as the cost of professional subscriptions to an approved body which is relevant to the individual's employment (eg the annual subscription to the Institute of Chartered Accountants or the Law Society). Also, flat rate expenses are given to employees in certain industries to cover expenditure on tools, overalls, special clothing etc.

Despite the very restrictive rules outlined in 3.3.1, you may be able to secure a deduction under s 198 if you pay interest on a loan used to purchase equipment used by you in the course of your employment (for example, a car or a fax machine at your home which you use for business purposes).

In addition to claiming a deduction for loan interest, relief may be due for expenses such as running costs and (in the case of a fax machine) the line rental. Capital allowances may also be due, subject to a restriction if the equipment is used for private purposes as well as for your employment.

3.4. Benefits in kind in general

3.4.1 Directors and 'higher paid employees'
(TA 1988, ss 153–168)

The legislation distinguishes P11D employees (ie employees and directors earning at the rate of £8,500 or more per annum) from other employees. An employer is required to submit form P11D in respect of each P11D employee who may then be assessed on the cost to the employer of benefits in kind received by them. Other employees are normally taxed on benefits only if they are convertible into cash.

An employee will fall within the P11D category where remuneration, *together with benefits and reimbursed expenses*, is £8,500 per annum or more. Such employees were formerly called 'higher paid' employees. The threshold of £8,500 was set in 1979 and, in accordance with the Government's intentions that all employees should pay income tax on the whole of their earnings whether received in cash or in kind, this limit has not been increased. By 1989 the term 'higher paid' had become inappropriate and consequently, while there was no change made in the level of the threshold, references to higher paid employees were deleted from the legislation.

All reimbursed expenses and other benefits have to be reported on form P11D and count towards the £8,500 limit, even though they may be justified as being for business purposes and no taxable benefit in kind ultimately arises. Employees are treated as earning £8,500 or more if they are remunerated *at the rate* of £8,500 per annum or more. For example, a person whose employment began on 1 January 1993 and who had received a salary of £2,000 and reimbursed expenses of £200 by 6 April 1993 would be within the P11D category as the total amount of £2,200 would give an annual rate greater than £8,500.

Directors are normally within the P11D regime, regardless of whether their remuneration reaches or exceeds the £8,500 limit (subject to one exception—see below).

Furthermore, individuals who control a company's affairs and who take management decisions may be treated as directors even if they do not hold a formal position with the company and even though they may have another title or job description within the company.

A person remunerated at a rate below £8,500 by a particular company is still within the P11D category if a directorship is held with another company in the same group, or if the total remuneration from group companies amounts to £8,500 per annum whether or not any directorships are held. Certain directors are exempt from the above rules by virtue of s 168 and are therefore excluded from the definition. To qualify for this favourable treatment, certain conditions need to be satisfied. The director:

(1) must not hold more than five per cent of the company's ordinary share capital (holdings by his 'associates' may need to be included as if he held the shares); and

(2) must be employed on a full-time basis (or the company must be a non-profit making organisation); and

(3) must be receiving remuneration and benefits which in aggregate are *less* than £8,500 per annum.

3.4.2 Dispensations

The Revenue may grant a dispensation so that certain reimbursed expenses need not be reported on form P11D. This is clearly useful in reducing administration and accounting work and, wherever possible, employers should apply for a dispensation. The expenses covered by it will be set out by the Revenue and any expenses not covered must still be reported. Any changes in the method of reimbursing expenses or scales of allowances must be notified to the Revenue.

3.4.3   Benefits in kind provided by third parties
(Extra-statutory concession A70, TA 1988, s 155(7))

It is not uncommon for wholesalers and distributors to offer benefits in kind to the employees of retailers with whom they do business. Subject to certain *de minimis* rules, such benefits are taxable just as if they had been provided by the retailer himself. A non-monetary gift costing no more than £100 in any tax year, which an employee or his family receives from someone other than the employer, will generally be exempt from income tax. Likewise, no income tax liability will usually arise on entertainment which an employee receives from a third party. These concessions only apply, however, where the gift or entertainment is not provided directly or indirectly by the employer and, furthermore, it is not provided as a reward for, or in recognition of, specific services done or to be done by the employee.

3.4.4   Benefits for director's family
(TA 1988, s 154 (1))

A fundamental point is that an assessment may arise even though the director or employee has not *personally* received a benefit in kind. A tax liability may arise if the benefit was made available to a member of the director's or employee's household by reason of his employment. The Revenue may argue that substantial benefits in kind enjoyed by a director's family are provided by reason of that person's employment even though the recipient may also be a company employee. The Revenue is especially likely to argue this where a director's spouse is employed by the company and receives abnormally large benefits in kind for employees of that category.

3.4.5   Scholarships
(TA 1988, s 331 and s 165 (1))

There is a general exemption for scholarships although the provision of scholarships to children by reason of their parents' employment may give rise to a Schedule E charge for the parents. In 1983, a test case involving an employee of ICI came before the House of Lords who held that the employee was not taxable on the value of scholarships awarded to his children under an ICI-sponsored scheme. It was held that even though the scholarships were provided by reason of the parent's employment, no taxable benefit in kind arose because of a specific statutory exemption. That exemption was then removed by specific legislation. This legislation preserved the exemption for certain scholarships already in existence at the time of the change but it means that scholarships awarded after 14 March 1983 generally give rise to a taxable benefit in kind, unless the employee is himself the holder of the scholarship.

The position can therefore be summarised as follows:

(1) If the scholarship was awarded before 15 March 1983 and the first payment made before 6 April 1984 then the scholarship will remain exempt so long as the student remains at the same educational establishment he was attending at 6 April 1984. The exemption is generally lost where the student changes educational establishments after 5 April 1989.

(2) Scholarships awarded after 14 March 1983 give rise to a benefit in kind for the parent unless it can be shown that the scholarship was not awarded by reason of the employment and 75 per cent of the scholarships awarded by the fund are awarded to children whose parents are not employed by the company.

3.4.6 Benefits which may result in a tax charge for non-P11D employees

The general rule is that employees who are not within the P11D category are assessable only on benefits capable of being converted into cash or on any benefits provided through an employer meeting an employee's own personal liability. This principle has been modified to some extent so that, for instance, credit vouchers are an assessable benefit even if the employee is not within the P11D category. However, the principle continues to hold good with regard to benefits such as the provision of a company car, free use of assets, beneficial loans etc.

Table 3.2 below sets out the position.

3.4.7 Tax treatment of specific benefits where received by a non-P11D employee

Benefits capable of being converted into cash

Where the benefit is convertible into cash, the measure of assessable benefit is the amount of cash which could be realised. For example, an employee provided with a new suit by the employer would be taxable on its second-hand value.

Luncheon vouchers

These are dealt with at 3.4.8.

Table 3.2—Treatment of benefits received by non-P11D employees

	Taxable	Non-Taxable
Benefits capable of being turned to pecuniary account ie convertible to cash	✓	
Luncheon vouchers in excess of 15p per working day	✓	
Credit tokens and vouchers	✓	
Transport vouchers (ie any ticket, pass or other document or token intended to enable a person to obtain passenger transport services)	✓	
Living accommodation	✓	
Payment of employees' personal liabilities	✓	
Company cars		✓
Free use of assets		✓
Beneficial loans		✓
Medical insurance		✓

Credit tokens and vouchers
(TA 1988, s 142)

The taxable amount in respect of credit tokens and vouchers is the cost to the employer of providing them. Vouchers other than cheque vouchers are deemed to be taxable emoluments as and when they are *allocated* to a particular employee, not when they are *used* by that employee.

Transport vouchers
(TA 1988, s 141)

Specific legislation was introduced in 1976 in order to ensure that season tickets provided by employers should be taxable. Once again, the measure of the assessable benefit is the cost to the employer of providing the voucher.

Living accommodation
(TA 1988, s 145)

The assessable amount is the greater of the gross rateable value of the property or the rent payable by the employer, less any amount made good by the employee. Following the abolition of domestic rates, estimated values are used for new or substantially altered properties. No assessable benefit arises where the employee occupies representative accommodation (see 3.4.8).

Payment of employee's personal liabilities

A liability arises where the employer pays a personal liability of the employee. This would include such items as home heating and lighting bills and water rates, but special rules apply where the employee is in representative accommodation (see 3.4.8).

3.4.8 Benefits which are not taxable for any category of employees

There are certain benefits that are not usually taxable even when the employee is within the P11D category. The most widely used tax-free benefits are:

> Retirement benefits
> Luncheon vouchers
> Staff canteen and dining facilities
> Sports facilities
> Workplace nurseries and creches
> Removal expenses
> Long service awards
> Awards under suggestion schemes
> Use of a pooled car
> The provision of representative accommodation
> Retraining

Retirement benefits

Payments by an employer to an *approved* occupational pension scheme to secure retirement benefits for an employee do not give rise to an income tax liability for that employee. Payments into a non-approved scheme are taxable as additional remuneration for the year that the employer makes the relevant contribution. To secure approval, a pension scheme must be established for the sole purpose of providing 'relevant benefits' (ie pensions, death-in-service payments, and widow's and dependants' pensions). In addition, an employee's contributions must not exceed 15 per cent of his remuneration. The pension benefits payable by an approved scheme must not exceed certain limits. Pension schemes are covered in more detail in chapter 12.

Luncheon vouchers

Non-transferable luncheon vouchers (ie vouchers which are not capable of being exchanged for cash) are exempt from income tax up to a limit of 15p per working day. Vouchers for larger amounts are partly exempt, with the excess over 15p being taxable in full, whether or not the employee is within the P11D category.

Staff canteen and dining facilities

No taxable benefit in kind arises where the canteen etc is used by all staff. Furthermore, the use of a separate room by directors and more senior staff does not prejudice this exemption, unless the meals provided are superior. The Revenue may also accept, in certain cases, that facilities provided by the employer for staff to use a local restaurant may come within the definition of a 'canteen', provided that *all* staff are eligible to use these facilities on the same terms.

There are requirements which need to be strictly observed. For example, there must be no voucher or form of identification which employees need to produce on entering the restaurant. Furthermore, the Inland Revenue may try to withhold exemption from directors and employees earning £8,500 or more who use such a restaurant facility.

Sports facilities
(FA 1993, s 75)

No taxable benefit arises in respect of the use or availability of sports facilities owned by the employer. Similarly, no taxable benefit generally arises where an employer takes out corporate membership of an outside sports club so that *all* the employees are able to use the club's facilities. An assessment will, however, be made if the employer takes out a subscription for a particular director or employee earning £8,500 or more, or if the subscription covers a small group of such employees and directors.

Workplace nurseries and creches

Since 6 April 1990, employees have been exempt from income tax on the benefit derived from the use of a workplace nursery provided by the employer. The exemption applies only to nurseries run by employers alone or jointly with other employers or bodies, either at the workplace or elsewhere. The provision by an employer of cash allowances to employees for childcare, or the direct meeting of an employee's childcare bills by an employer are taxable benefits.

Relocation expenses
(FA 1993, s 76)

For some years, the treatment of relocation expenses was governed by two extra-statutory concessions. Extra-statutory concession A67 exempted certain payments made to existing employees in order to meet the additional costs incurred because they were required to move to a higher cost area. Relief was available only for a limited period and was restricted to the amount paid to Civil Servants as an additional housing cost allowance which varied from time to time. This concession was withdrawn from 6 April 1993 unless the employee had been relocated before the date or there was a commitment to move at that time and the employee started work at the new location by 1 August 1993.

Extra-statutory concession A5 provided that an employee should not be taxed on certain removal expenses borne by his employer when he had to change his residence to take up a new job within the same organisation, or to take up completely new employment. The relief was available only where it would be unreasonable to expect the employee to work at the new location without moving closer to it. Furthermore, the Revenue view was that the terms of the concession required the sale of the employee's old residence and the Revenue withheld relief where the employee retained his old home, even in cases where it was needed for occupation by his spouse and children.

The concession was replaced by a statutory provision in FA 1993, s 76 in respect of all job relocations after 5 April 1993. The new rules provide for a ceiling of £8,000 for the amount which may be paid tax free in respect of any one move. On the other hand, it will no longer be necessary for the individual to dispose of his former residence in order to qualify for the exemption. The Revenue also decided to change its practice on compensation payments with effect from 6 April 1993 and payments made to compensate employees for losses on the sale of their old houses are now regarded as taxable. Many practitioners still regard this as debatable and base their arguments on a 1959 decision by the House of Lords, *Hochstrasser v Mayes* [1960] AC 376; 38 TC 673.

Long service awards

Awards to directors and employees to mark long service are exempt provided the period of service is at least 20 years and no similar award has been given to the employee within the previous ten years. The gift must not consist of cash and the cost should not exceed £20 per year of service. An Inland Revenue concession has extended the exemption to gifts of shares in the company which employs the individual or in another group company.

Awards under suggestion schemes

Provided the employee concerned is not engaged in research work, he may receive a tax-free payment under a firm's suggestion scheme. The making of suggestions should not, however, be regarded as part of the employee's job. The size of the award should also be within certain limits, ie £25 or less where the suggestion, although not implemented, has intrinsic value. Where the suggestion *is* implemented, the amount should be related to the expected net financial benefit to the employer.

Pool cars
(TA 1988, s 159)

No tax charge arises by reason of the use of a pooled car. A car qualifies as a pooled car only if *all* the following conditions are satisfied:

(1)   It is available for, and used by, more than one employee and is not ordinarily used by any one of them to the exclusion of the others.
(2)   Any private use of the car by an employee is merely incidental to its business use.
(3)   It is not normally kept overnight at or near the residence of any of the employees unless it is kept on premises occupied by the employer.

The above requirements are strictly interpreted. It should be noted that a car only qualifies as a pooled car *for a tax year*. There is a danger therefore in a car being taken out of pooled use and allotted to a specific employee towards the end of a tax year. As the car now no longer qualifies as a pooled car, any employee who has had the car available for private use during the same tax year may be assessed. Therefore, if the car is ordinarily parked overnight near the home of one of the users, it will not qualify as a pooled car and will create a tax problem for any other employees who use it.

Representative accommodation
(TA 1988, s 145(4))

Living accommodation qualifies as representative accommodation if *any one* of the following conditions is satisfied:

(1)   It is necessary for the performance of the employee's duties that he should reside in the accommodation.
(2)   The accommodation is provided for the better performance of the employee's duties and it is customary to provide accommodation for such employees.
(3)   The employee has to live in the accommodation because of a special threat to his security.

The exemption under the first two conditions is usually only available to directors who (together with their associates) hold five per cent or less of the company's ordinary share capital and are full-time working directors. Where the employer pays for heating, lighting, repairs, maintenance etc, the representative occupiers cannot be assessed in respect of such benefits on more then ten per cent of their emoluments of the employment.

Re-training
(TA 1988, s 588–589)

Where an employer pays the cost of a course undertaken by an employee (or former employee) for the purpose of providing him with skills for future employment elsewhere, the cost of the course can be a deductible expense of the employer, and may not be a taxable benefit of the employee.

Sandwich courses
(Statement of Practice SP4/86 re-issued November 1992)

Where an employee is released by his employer to take a full-time educational course at a university, technical college or similar educational institution which is open to the public at large, payments for periods of attendance may be treated as exempt from income tax. There are various conditions which attach to this exemption ie:

(1) The course must last for at least one academic year with an average of at least 20 weeks of full time attendance.
(2) The rate of payment must not exceed the greater of £7,000 and the rate of payment that an individual would have received had he been granted a public grant.

Where the rate of payment exceeds the above limits, the full amount is taxable but where the amount of payment is increased during a course, only subsequent payments are taxable.

3.4.9 Expenses relating to directors and P11D employees

This section deals with problem areas which regularly arise in practice with regard to expenses paid on behalf of directors or reimbursed to them.

Travelling, subsistence and entertaining
(TA 1988, s 153)

Fares and incidental travelling expenses are not treated as a benefit in kind so long as the individual has a 'normal place of work' which he attends the majority of the time. Where an employee performs incidental duties of the employment at another location and travels there directly to or from his home, the allowable expense is the lesser of the travel and subsistence expenses actually incurred, and the expenses which would have been incurred if the journey had started and finished at the normal place of work.

In order to secure tax relief on reimbursed travelling expenses, the employee must keep adequate records so as to distinguish business from non-business travel. Ideally, expenses claims to the employer should show the actual cost of such travel and, if the employer is to obtain a dispensation, the Revenue will need to be satisfied that such internal controls exist.

Mileage allowances should not be so large as to create a 'profit' element which would of course be taxable. The Revenue have been especially concerned about high business mileage drivers who are paid the standard AA and RAC rates. Maximum rates have been introduced which are *reduced* when the business mileage exceeds 4,000 miles per annum. The rates from 6 April 1994 are:

	Amount per Mile	
Engine Size	*Up to 4,000 miles*	*Over 4,000 miles*
Up to 1000cc	27p	15p
1001–1500cc	33p	19p
1501–2000cc	41p	23p
Over 2000cc	56p	31p

Where reimbursement is not linked to engine size, the rates are 36p up to 4,000 miles per annum and 20p thereafter. Provided these rates are not exceeded and mileage is for business purposes, no benefit in kind will arise. Interest paid on a loan taken out for the purchase of a car used for business purposes may qualify for tax relief. Relief for interest is not included in Fixed Profit Car Scheme (FPCS) rates. It needs to be claimed separately.

Travel between home and the ordinary place of work does not rank as business travel. Where an individual is 'on call' and assumes the responsibilities of the employment upon leaving home, it may be possible to argue that home to work travel is business and not private travel, but this will usually apply only in exceptional cases.

Overseas travelling expenses
(TA 1988, ss 192–193)

Where some or all of the duties of an employment are performed abroad, the expenses of travelling to and from the United Kingdom to carry out these duties are specifically regarded as having been necessarily incurred in the performance of the overseas employment. It follows, therefore, that if those expenses are reimbursed by the employer, no benefit in kind arises. Recent legislative changes have relaxed the rules further, so that, while the employee is serving abroad, the employer may pay for an unlimited number of journeys made by the employee to and from the United Kingdom without any tax charge arising. However, these journeys must be made wholly and exclusively for the purpose of performing the duties of the employment.

Moreover, where an employee travels between places where different jobs are performed, and one or more of these jobs is performed wholly or partly overseas, the expenses incurred in travelling overseas are also deemed to be necessarily incurred in performing the duties carried out overseas, so that once again no benefit in kind arises. In many cases, there is dual purpose in travelling and a taxable benefit in kind arises on the private element. Consequently, where travel expenses relate partly to a foreign holiday taken at the end of the business trip, there would be a taxable benefit in kind.

Similarly, a benefit in kind may be assessed on some or all of the expense where a spouse accompanies a director or employee and where this is not necessary for business purposes.

Subsistence

The Revenue's view is that it is strictly only the extra costs of living away from home which are allowable. If there are continuing financial commitments at home, the whole cost of living away from home is normally allowed. This concession is not available if the employee has no permanent residence, for example an unmarried person who normally lives in a hotel or club and who gives up that accommodation when away on a business trip. There is a specific exemption where an employee performs his duties wholly overseas and needs board and lodging abroad in order to do so.

Maintenance of records

A director or employee who travels overseas should be able to substantiate a claim that expenses were necessarily incurred for business purposes by producing details of the expenses and the time spent away from home. A brief itinerary should be available where travel is undertaken within the overseas country or countries. Inspectors of Taxes will normally expect that an employer will properly control expenditure but in certain cases they may wish to see receipted bills or other vouchers.

3.4.10 Spouse's travelling and subsistence expenses

Where a spouse or other member of the family accompanies the director or employee abroad on a business trip, it will be helpful in satisfying the Revenue that no benefit in kind arises if the board of directors minute their decision that the director should be so accompanied. However, this will not generally be sufficient in itself and it will be necessary to show that the spouse or other relative was able to perform certain tasks which could not be performed by the director.

It may be possible to show this if the spouse has some practical qualification, for example an ability to speak the foreign language concerned. A relative's expenses might also be allowable where the director or employee is in poor health and to travel alone would be impracticable or unreasonable. Where the individual's presence is for the purpose of accompanying his or her spouse at business entertainment functions, the expenses of the trip may be disallowed in calculating the employer's tax liability under the entertainment legislation, even though the expenses may be allowable in determining the employee's tax liability.

3.4.11 Employees working overseas—family visits
(TA 1988, s 194)

Where an employee is abroad for a continuous period of 60 days or more, there is an exemption for amounts borne by the employer in respect of the travelling expenses for visits by the employee's spouse and minor children. The exemption is only available for two journeys by the same person in each direction in a tax year. There is no relief if the employee ultimately bears the expense personally.

3.4.12 Entertaining expenses and round-sum allowances

It is not uncommon for directors or employees to have a round-sum allowance to cover such things as travelling, subsistence and entertaining. In the case of travelling and subsistence, the allowance counts as the taxable income of the director or employee, but a tax deduction may be claimed in respect of any part of the allowance which can be shown to have been spent for business purposes. It is very important to have a record-keeping system which enables such claims to be substantiated. It may be better for the employer to dispense with round-sum allowances and reimburse the director or employee for properly substantiated expenditure. In this way, no benefit in kind should arise.

In the case of entertaining expenditure, the situation is rather more complex. If an employer reimburses a director's or employee's entertaining expenditure or pays a round-sum allowance which is specifically intended for entertaining, the expense to the employer is disallowed for tax purposes. The reimbursement or allowance will be entered on the director's or employee's P11D but a deduction may be claimed for all the expenditure which is for genuine business purposes. If, on the other hand, the director or employee is given a round-sum allowance not specifically designated as being for entertaining, there is no question of the allowance being disallowed in the employer's tax computation. However, the director or employee would only escape liability on any part of the allowance which could be shown to have been used for business expenditure *other than* entertainment.

3.5 Company cars
(TA 1988, s 157)

3.5.1 Tax treatment for 1993–94 and earlier years

The most widespread benefit is the company car made available for private use. The assessable benefit for 1993–94 was generally determined by the following scales, according to the cost, size and age of the car (unless the car was a pool car, see 3.4.8 above).

Retail Price when new	Age of car at end of tax year			
	Under 4 Years		4 Years or more	
	1992–93	*1993–94*	*1992–93*	*1993–94*
(1) Up to £19,250;	£	£	£	£
Up to 1400cc	2,140	2,310	1,460	1,580
1401cc to 2000cc	2,770	2,990	1,880	2,030
More than 2000cc	4,440	4,800	2,980	3,220
(2) £19,251–£29,000	5,750	6,210	3,870	4,180
(3) More than £29,000	9,300	10,040	6,170	6,660

All these figures were halved if the car was used for 18,000 or more business miles per annum. On the other hand, the scale figures were increased by 50 per cent where the employee had insubstantial business use, ie 2,500 miles or less per annum. Travel from home to office does not normally count as business mileage.

The scale figures were reduced where an employee was provided with a company car part way through the tax year, or where he ceased to have a company car. However, there was no reduction where the car was not available for use because of the need for repairs, unless it was incapable of being used for at least 30 consecutive days.

3.5.2 1993–94 tax treatment of second cars

Where a company provided a director or employee with more than one car, the scale benefit for the second car was increased by 50 per cent. It was a matter of fact as to which car was most used for business; it was not strictly open to the employee to elect that the more expensive car be treated as the main car.

3.5.3 Contribution by employee in 1993–94 and earlier years

An employee could claim a reduction of the annual scale to the extent that he was required by the employer to make a contribution towards the cost of making the car available for private use. At least an exchange of letters between the company and the employee was advisable as evidence that the payment was required to be made so that the car could be available for personal use. Other contributions were not deductible up to 5 April 1994; in particular, there was no deduction for a lump sum payment made to the employer to enable a car above the allotted price range to be acquired.

A contribution by an employee was generally regarded as inclusive of VAT, so that if an employee had paid £300 to the employer, it was treated as a taxable supply by the employer of £255.32 and VAT of £44.68.

3.5.4 Car benefits for 1994–95 and subsequent years

The taxable benefit for 1994–95 and subsequent years will be based on the list price of the car at the time that it was first registered, and not on the cost of the car. The taxable benefit will be 35 per cent of the list price which includes delivery charges, standard accessories and optional accessories fitted when the car was first made available to the employee. A separate addition to the list price is also made where accessories are fitted after the car has been made available, but accessories with a list price of less than £100 and accessories installed before 1 August 1993 are left out of account. Where the car is at least four years old at the end of the tax year the benefit is reduced by one-third.

Where the list price of a vehicle exceeds £80,000, the excess is not taken into account.

Where a car is more than 15 years old at the end of the tax year, the car has a market value of at least £15,000 and the market value exceeds the list price, the benefit in kind is calculated by reference to the market value rather than original list price.

The assessable benefit is reduced by one-third where there is at least 2,500 business miles per annum. There is a reduction of a further one-third where the business mileage is at least 18,000 miles per annum.

3.5.5　Tax treatment of employee contributions in 1994–95 and subsequent years

Contributions made by an employee towards the cost of the car can be deducted from the list price, subject to a maximum deduction of £5,000. Capital contributions made before 6 April 1994 may be deducted in this way, even though there was no deduction prior to 1994–95.

3.5.6　Example—Employee contributions to company cars

Two employees are entitled to company cars. One contributes £4,000 towards the car which has a list price of £18,000 while the other contributes £11,000 towards a car with a list price of £25,000. Their assessable benefits in kind for 1994–95 are:

		A	B
		£	£
List price		18,000	25,000
Less capital contribution income of:			
(A) amount contributed	(4,000)		
(B) deduction for capital contribution limited to			(5,000)
		14,000	20,000
35% thereof		4,900	7,000
Assessable benefits		4,900	7,000

Annual payments made by employees in respect of private use of a car may still reduce the assessable benefit on a £1 for £1 basis. In the above example, B would be better off to reduce his initial capital contribution and make annual payments in return for being allowed to use the vehicle for private purposes.

3.5.7　Private petrol
(TA 1988, s 158)

An additional scale benefit applies where an employer provides private petrol for use in a car to which a scale benefit charge arises. The scale charge depends entirely on engine size (for cars with a recognised cylinder capacity) as follows:

	1993–94		1994–95	
	Petrol	*diesel*	*Petrol*	*diesel*
	£	£	£	£
Up to 1400cc	600	550	640	580
1401 to 2000cc	760	550	810	580
More than 2000cc	1,130	710	1,200	750

For 1992–93 and earlier years, all these figures were halved if the car was used for 18,000 business miles per annum, but this reduction was abolished by FA 1993 with effect from 6 April 1993.

The scale figures apply regardless of the amount of private fuel provided. If *any* is provided, the fuel scale charge will always apply unless the employee reimburses his employer for the full cost. In some cases it may be cost effective for an employee to do this and the position should therefore be reviewed before the start of each new tax year.

3.5.8   Other related costs

The scale benefit does not cover the salary of a chauffeur. If a director is allocated a chauffeur, the full cost to the employer of providing the chauffeur should be included on the director's form P11D and will therefore be potentially assessable as a benefit in kind (subject to a claim for business mileage).

3.5.9 Car parking spaces
(FA 1988, s 46)

For 1988–89 and subsequent years, the provision of a car parking space at or near the employee's place of work is not a taxable benefit. Where, however, an employee pays for car parking himself, he will not be able to claim a deduction for those charges.

3.5.10   Private use of company vans
(FA 1993, s 73)

The 1993 Finance Act introduced a new scale charge for employees who have private use of company vans. From 6 April 1993 the employee may be assessed on a standard amount of £500 per year in respect of private use of the van. The amount will be reduced to £350 for vans which are four or more years old at the end of the tax year. Any vehicles in excess of 3.5 tons are exempt from tax altogether (unless the vehicle is used wholly or mainly for the employee's private purposes). Where an employee has two or more vans made available for private use at the same time, tax is charged on the scale figure for each van. The standard amount will be reduced *pro rata* where the van is only available part of the year. As for company cars a pound for pound reduction is made for any contributions made by the employee towards the private use. Where a van is shared amongst several employees the standard amount is apportioned among the employees.

3.6 Free use of assets
(TA 1988, s 156)

A taxable benefit arises where an asset is made available by an employer for use by a director or P11D employee. The annual amount is 20 per cent of the asset's market value when it was *first* made available for use by the employee, unless the asset was made available before 6 April 1980, in which case the annual value is ten per cent. Assets which may be involved include yachts, furniture, television sets, stereo equipment, company vans etc ie virtually any asset apart from living accommodation and company cars. If the employer rents or hires the item concerned for a sum in excess of 20 per cent of the asset's original market value, the higher rental charge is substituted as the assessable benefit. A deduction is allowed for any contribution or rental payable by the employee.

A further charge may arise if the ownership of assets is eventually transferred to the employee. The amount may be determined either by the market value of the asset at the time of transfer of ownership, or, where a higher figure results, by the original cost of the asset at the time it was first made available as a benefit for *any* person, less any amounts already charged as benefits in connection with the availability of the asset.

The second alternative does not apply to cars.

3.6.1 Example—Transfer of assets

A company provides an employee with the use of a yacht which costs £40,000 with the employee paying a rental of £2,000 per annum. After two years the yacht is sold to the employee for its second-hand market value of £20,000. The assessable benefit would be:

	Benefit
Year one	
£40,000 x 20 per cent	£8,000
Less rental paid	£2,000
	£6,000

Year two	
£40,000 x 20 per cent	£8,000
Less rental paid	£2,000
	£6,000
Year three	
Cost of yacht	£40,000
Less benefits assessed in years one and two	(£12,000)
Amounts paid by employee	(£24,000)
	£4,000

Where an asset, previously made available to an individual, is transferred at no cost to him (or to another employee), at a time when its market value is still high, it is possible that the overall effect will be that the total cost of the benefit for tax purposes exceeds the original cost. In other cases, the rules may operate to impose a high benefit charge upon the transfer of an asset despite the value of the asset having rapidly depreciated during the period of use.

Such rules must therefore be carefully considered when planning the provision of an asset for use by an employee or arranging for its transfer to the employee. It may be that transfer of ownership should be avoided where assets have a relatively short useful life if a tax-efficient remuneration package is desired.

3.6.2   Example—Ownership of assets

A company provides employees with the use of suits which remain the property of the company. The suits cost £200 and have a useful life of two years, after which they are scrapped.

An employee could therefore have an effective benefit of £200 but would be charged tax on only £40 for each of the two tax years.

3.7   Beneficial loans
(TA 1988, s 160)

3.7.1   Type of loans which are caught

A charge generally arises for directors and P11D employees on the annual value of beneficial loan arrangements. The annual value of a loan is taken as interest at the 'official rate' less the amount of interest (if any) paid by the employee. The official rate is revised regularly but is 7.5 per cent at the time of publication. An additional taxable benefit arises if the loan is subsequently written off or forgiven.

The beneficial loan provisions can also apply if a loan is made to a member of an employee's family.

Moreover, the Inland Revenue is able to assess benefits even though there may be no formal loan, where credit has been involved. In particular, a director who overdraws his current account with the company will be regarded as having obtained a loan and be subject to an assessment.

Almost all loans by employers (and persons connected with them) will be caught as the legislation deems such loans to have been given by reason of the employment. Until 6 April 1994, there was only a single exception in that this rule did not apply where the employee was related to the employer and it could be shown that the loan was given for family reasons. There were no other exceptions and there have been cases where bank employees etc have paid a normal commercial rate of interest on money lent to them, but have been assessed on a benefit because the interest they have paid has been less than the official rate.

For 1994–95 and subsequent years, loans made by an employer whose business includes the lending of money to the general public will not give rise to a charge on the employees provided the loans are made on similar terms to the public.

3.7.2 Beneficial loans used for a qualifying purpose

No charge arises in respect of a cheap loan where the money which has been borrowed has been applied for a qualifying purpose, eg for the purchase of shares in a close company in which the individual has a material interest or where he is employed full time in the conduct and management of the company's business.

3.7.3 *De minimis* exemption

Once again, with effect from 1994–95, there is an exemption for all cheap or interest free loans made to an individual employee which do not exceed £5,000. This figure excludes loans which qualify for tax relief such as loans of up to £30,000 for house purchase.

For 1993–94 and earlier years, there was a *de minimis* rule so that no benefit was assessed where the interest forgone was less than £300.

3.7.4 Employee loans written off

If the loan is written-off, the amount forgiven is treated as assessable income for that year even if the person concerned is no longer employed by that company. The only exception here is if the loan is forgiven on the death of the employee.

Some care needs to be taken if it is decided to clear a loan by making an *ex gratia* or compensation payment to an employee upon the termination of the employment. An income tax liability will arise if the loan is formally written off. On the other hand, no liability normally arises if the employee receives a cheque as an *ex gratia* or compensation payment and uses that sum to clear his outstanding loan. It is recommended that professional advice be taken in such circumstances.

3.8   Living accommodation
(TA 1988, ss 145–146)

3.8.1   Introduction

The income tax charge which generally applies where an employee is provided with accommodation (unless it is representative accommodation—see 3.4.8), depends upon whether the property is owned or rented by the employer. In the past, where the employer owned the property, the assessable amount was usually the gross annual value for rating purposes. Despite the abolition of domestic rates, this treatment continued to apply for properties on existing rating lists (see 3.4.7). For new properties, and those where there have been major improvements, the Revenue makes an estimate of what the gross annual value would have been had rates continued.

Where the property is rented by the employer, the assessable amount is the greater of the rent paid and the annual value as above. In addition a charge may arise on the annual value of any furniture and fixtures, and on any occupier's expenses borne by the company such as water rates, decorations, gardener's wages etc.

An additional charge may arise where the employer paid more than £75,000 to acquire the property. The amount assessable is a percentage of the excess of the cost of the property over £75,000. The percentage to be applied is the official rate of interest used for beneficial loans (see 3.7) as at the *beginning* of the tax year.

3.8.2   Example—Charge on living accommodation in excess of £75,000

A company director occupies a property owned by the company which has a gross annual value of £2,000. The cost of the property in 1989 was £100,000.

The director will be assessed on the following amount for 1993–94:

Gross annual value		£2,000
Additional charge:		
Cost in 1989	£100,000	
Less	£ 75,000	
Total	£ 25,000	
Assessment on £25,000 at		
the official rate of 7.75%		£1,937
Total		£3,937

3.8.3 Properties owned for more than six years

Where the property is made available to an employee after 31 March 1983, and it has been owned by the company for at least six years, the figure taken into account in computing the additional charge is the market value at the time it was made available rather than the cost. The actual cost (including improvements) to the employer is still used to determine whether or not the provisions will apply. Consequently, properties whose actual cost was less than £75,000 (including the cost of any improvements) are not within the scope of this additional charge even if their market value exceeds £75,000. Where the actual cost exceeded £75,000, the additional charge will be based on the market value.

3.8.4 Example—Charge on living accommodation purchased over six years ago

In example 3.8.2, assume that the company has owned the property for more than six years and that in May 1992, when the director first occupies it, the market value is £200,000. As the original cost of the property exceeded £75,000, the director will be assessed on the following amount for 1993–94:

Gross annual value		£2,000
Additional charge:		
Market value in 1992	£200,000	
Less	£75,000	
Total	£125,000	
Assessment on £125,000		
at the official rate of 7.75 per cent		£9,687
Total		£11,687

3.8.5 Possible reduction in assessable amount

It may be possible to reduce the assessable amount where the employee is required to occupy a property which is larger than would normally be needed for his or her own purposes. In the case of *Westcott v Bryan* (1969) 45 TC 476 a director was required to live in a large house so that he could entertain customers. He was allowed a reduction in the assessable amount to cover the relevant proportion of the annual value and the running expenses.

Some care is needed if it is intended to claim relief in this way. This claim succeeded because the house was larger than needed for the director and his family. It would not have succeeded had the property merely been more expensive than he would have chosen. It was also helpful that the directors of the company had approved board minutes setting out their requirement and the business reason for it.

Holiday accommodation and foreign properties

Some employers buy holiday flats or cottages etc for use by staff. In practice, the Revenue generally apportion the assessable amount for the year amongst those employees who have occupied the property. The assessment can be reduced by letting the accommodation to third parties when it is not required by directors and employees.

A practical problem arises with regard to overseas properties. Because there is no rateable value, the benefit is the annual rent which the property would normally command on the open market.

3.9   Miscellaneous benefits

Council tax

Where an employer pays the council tax on behalf of an employee, this will normally be chargeable as part of the employee's remuneration package, resulting in a charge to both income tax and NICs. The one exception to this is where the employee is a representative occupier (see 3.4.8).

Mobile telephones
(FA 1991, s 30)

Tax is charged on a standard amount of £200 per year per telephone unless the employee is required to make good the whole cost of any private use. The Revenue interprets these provisions so that the requirement to make good the full costs of private calls must exist throughout the year. It is therefore wise to ensure that the internal arrangements are sufficient to meet this requirement.

Medical insurance
(TA 1988, s 155(6))

The cost of medical insurance is normally assessable on P11D employees. Where the employer has a group scheme, a proportion of the total premiums is related to individual employees. There is an exception in that the premiums are exempt to the extent that they provide cover for an employee working outside the United Kingdom.

Telephone rental

The Revenue treats the full amount of the rental paid by the employer as a taxable benefit in kind even though the telephone may be partly (or mainly) used for business calls. The decision in *Lucas v Cattell* (1972) 48 TC 353 was that the expenditure on rental had a dual purpose (ie that a telephone is intended to be used for both business and personal use) and therefore no part of it was allowable.

Club subscriptions

A benefit in kind is deemed to arise where an employer pays or reimburses an employee's subscription to a club, even though the employee may only belong to the club in order to entertain the employer's customers.

In-house tax and financial advice

This is a type of expenditure which the Inland Revenue has ignored in the past, but certain Inspectors of Taxes are now treating this as a benefit in kind where the cost can clearly be allocated to particular employees. Similarly the Revenue will seek to assess directors on a benefit in kind where work on their personal taxation affairs has been carried out by the company's auditors, the cost being recovered in whole or in part from the company.

Christmas parties

The Revenue has said that it will not assess a benefit in respect of 'modest' expenditure on a Christmas party for staff, provided the party is open to all staff. The limit for expenditure to be regarded as modest in this context is currently £50 per head. Although this rule is generally attributed to Christmas parties, it may apply to a function at another time of year, but only *one* function will qualify. The exemption may not be used to cover more than one party even if the combined costs fall below the rate of £50 per head.

Legal fees

There may be expenditure which is incurred for the benefit of the company's business but nevertheless is deemed to give rise to a benefit in kind. A leading case in this connection concerned a director of a company who was accused of dangerous driving. It was necessary for the company's business that he should not be imprisoned and the company paid his legal expenses. Although the lawyers engaged by the company were more expensive than the director would have used himself, the expenditure by the company was treated as a benefit in kind.

Outplacement counselling
(FA 1993, s 108)

The value of outplacement services provided to employees made redundant after 15 March 1993, or incurred after 15 March in respect of employees made redundant before 16 March 1993, is exempt from income tax. Such services may include assistance with CVs, job searches, office equipment provisions and advice on interview skills. Prior to 16 March 1993, these types of costs could be treated as part of a termination payment (see 3.18).

Goods and services provided at a discount to the normal price ('In-house benefits')

Where employees are allowed to purchase goods or services from their employer, no tax charge arises provided they pay an amount equal to the employer's cost. The House of Lords decided in November of 1992 that 'cost' meant marginal cost not average cost (*Pepper v Hart* [1992] STC 898). This will normally produce a significantly lower benefit.

Following this, the Revenue published a statement in January 1993 setting out its practice for the future with regard to teachers, employees within the transport industry and other employees who receive goods or services from their employer. The relevant press release stated that Treasury Ministers had the matter under review but, in the event, the decision has not been disturbed.

The Revenue has stated that the decision in *Pepper v Hart* means that:

(1)   rail or bus travel by employees on terms which do not displace fare-paying passengers involves no or negligible additional costs;

(2)   goods sold at a discount which leave employees paying at least the wholesale price involve no or negligible net benefit;

(3)   where teachers pay 15 per cent or more of a school's normal fees, there is no net benefit;

(4)   professional services which do not require additional employees or partners (eg legal and financial services) have no or negligible cost to the employer (provided the employee meets the cost of any disbursements).

Where individuals have been taxed on the average cost basis for past years, they may be entitled to a repayment. A formal claim for 1988–89 will need to be submitted by 5 April 1995.

FURBS
(TA 1988, s 595)

Some employers make contributions to unapproved pension schemes or FURBS (Funded Unapproved Retirement Benefit Schemes). The creation of the scheme has to be reported to the company's Inspector of Taxes within three months. The employer's contributions also need to be reported on Form P11D and the employee is treated as if he had received a benefit whose cost is equal to the amount paid into the FURBS. For further details on FURBS, see 12.13.

Making good benefits in kind for previous years

The cash equivalent of any benefit chargeable to tax under TA 1988, s 156 is the cost of the benefit 'less so much (if any) of it as is made good by the employee to those providing the benefit'. The Revenue accepts that there is no time limit for making good and, provided the relevant year's assessment has not been determined, there could be some merit in the person concerned taking further remuneration now and and using the net cash left to him after PAYE to make good benefits provided for earlier years. This could be a particularly good idea where a director of a family company is faced with a Schedule E assessment plus penalties and interest in respect of prior year incorrect returns because benefits have not been reported properly in the past.

Where beneficial loans are concerned, however, the Revenue's view is that the cash equivalent can only be reduced by a payment in a later year if the interest is paid under an obligation which existed at the time of the loan. Also, the scale benefit on a mobile phone can be reduced by a payment from the employee only if he was required to make the contribution and paid it during the tax year concerned.

3.10   Profit-related pay
(TA 1988, ss 169–171)

The rules on profit-related pay schemes are complex in so far as they concern the companies which set up a scheme. They are relatively straightforward from the point of view of the employee.

3.10.1   PRP exempt from income tax

Where an individual receives profit-related pay under a registered scheme, all or part of the PRP is exempt from income tax. The exemption is available on the lowest of:

(1)   20 per cent of total remuneration for the year;
(2)   £4,000;
(3)   the actual PRP received in the tax year.

Where an individual participates in more than one PRP scheme, the £4,000 exemption has to be divided between the amounts payable under each PRP scheme.

Profit-related pay forms part of a director or employee's earnings for national insurance contributions.

3.10.2   Conditions required for a PRP scheme to be registered

The following conditions need to be satisfied before the Revenue will register a profit-related pay scheme:

(1)   The scheme rules should provide for at least 80 per cent of relevant employees to participate. Relevant employees are those who are in the pay unit concerned (these need not necessarily be the company as a whole but could, for example, be a division within the company).
(2)   The PRP legislation requires that employees must participate 'on similar terms'. This does not necessarily mean that all employees should receive the same amount (although a scheme could be established on such a basis). Instead, the scheme rules may provide for payments to vary in order to reflect the following factors:
    (a)   levels of remuneration;
    (b)   length of service;
    (c)   hours worked;
    (d)   other similar objective factors.
(3)   Individuals who have more than a 25 per cent shareholding in a company (either alone or taken together with associates) cannot participate in a PRP scheme.

3.11   Profit sharing schemes
(TA 1988, ss 186–187)

These operate by means of a trust, with the trustees receiving payments from the company's profits to enable them to buy shares on behalf of the employees. In computing its profits, the company should get a deduction for the sums paid so long as the trustees apply the money in accordance with the approved scheme rules. The amount which may be appropriated to an employee under the scheme cannot exceed £3,000 or, if greater, ten per cent of the employee's remuneration for PAYE purposes, with an overall limit of £8,000.

The employee will be entitled to dividends paid on the shares during the period of retention by the trustees. The trustees *must* retain the shares for a period of two years; if the shares are then retained by the trustees for a further three years, there will be no income tax charge on him. If they are sold by the employee within five years of appropriation, an income tax charge will arise based on the percentage of the 'locked-in value' ie the lower of the market value of the shares when they were appropriated by the trust fund or the sale proceeds. The percentages are as follows:

Disposals within four years   100 per cent

Disposals during the fifth year   75 per cent

This charge is reduced to 50 per cent where the individual is no longer an employee because of his leaving through injury, disability, redundancy or reaching pensionable age.

Provided that the shares are held in trust for five years, normally the only liability arising to the employee will be to capital gains tax when he disposes of the shares appropriated to him. The capital gains liability will arise on the difference between the disposal proceeds of these shares less their open market value on the day on which they were appropriated to him. The growth in value from the date of acquisition by the trust to the date of appropriation is tax free.

3.11.1 Examples—Disposals of shares in a profit sharing scheme

(1)   In March 1989, the trustees of an approved scheme appropriated 500 £1 shares to an employee at a time when the market value was £1.25 each. The locked-in value is therefore £500 at £1.25 = £625.

In June 1993 the shares are sold for £2.35 each. The sale was made between years four and five and consequently an income tax liability will arise based on 75 per cent of the locked-in value, ie £468.75.

(2)   The facts are as in example (1) but the sale is delayed until June 1994. The sale is after the end of year five therefore there is no schedule E liability. A capital gains tax charge could arise on a disposal of the shares. The gain is the difference between £2.35 per share and £1.25 as adjusted for indexation.

3.12 Non-approved options and employee share schemes
(TA 1988, ss 135 and 162; FA 1988, ss 77–87)

3.12.1 Introduction

A Schedule E income tax charge may arise on the exercise of a share option or on the growth in value of shares which have been acquired by reason of the individual's office or employment (and, in particular, shares in dependent subsidiaries). The legislation was introduced on a piecemeal basis and it is often difficult to discern any clear or logical structure or principles which underlie the legislation.

3.12.2 Non-approved share options
(TA 1988, s 135)

A tax charge may arise either on the grant of the option or on the exercise of the option.

Grant of the option

A charge may arise only if the option has a potential life of more than seven years. Even if the option is capable of being exercised more than seven years later, the Revenue is unlikely to assess a value greater than the difference between the value of the shares at the time the option is granted and the aggregate of the amount (if any) paid for the grant of option and the amount payable under the option.

Exercise of the option

A person who is subject to tax under Case I of Schedule E may be subject to an income tax charge when he exercises a non-approved share option which has been granted to him by reason of his office or employment. The charge is not dependent upon his selling the shares but arises on any profit or gain that he is deemed to have made by exercising the option. Normally the profit will simply be the difference between the market value of the shares at the time that he exercises his option and the price payable under the option.

3.12.3 Example—Exercise of share options

A was granted an option to acquire 1,000 shares in XYZ Ltd at a price of £2 per share. After five years have elapsed, he exercises the option and pays £2,000 to acquire the 1,000 shares. By this time the shares have grown in value to £5 per share.

A will be assessed for the year in which he exercises the option. His profit will be assessed as £3,000, ie:

	£
Market value of 1,000 shares	5,000
Less amount paid	2,000
	3,000

Where the option was granted before 6 April 1984, the tax payable may be paid by instalments over five years provided the individual makes a formal election under TA 1988, s 137. The election must be made within 60 days of the end of the tax year in which the option is exercised.

3.12.4 Residence status of the employee

No charge arises under these provisions if the employee was not resident and ordinarily resident in the United Kingdom at the date that the option was granted. This is because the individual has to be UK-resident and ordinarily resident if he is to be chargeable to tax under Case I of Schedule E.

The charge will, however, still arise where an individual who was resident and ordinarily resident when the option was *granted* ceases to be UK-resident before the option is *exercised.*

3.12.5 Other employee share options
(TA 1988, s 162)

Where an individual exercises an option which was granted to him as an employee, but at a time when he was not chargeable to tax under Case I of Schedule E, and he retains the shares, an income tax charge may arise on the eventual disposal of the shares. The legislation on beneficial loans contains deeming provisions which treat the difference between the market value of the shares at the time that the option is exercised and the amount payable to exercise the option as if it were a loan. On a subsequent sale or disposal of the shares the loan is deemed to be written off and a Schedule E charge arises if the individual is resident in the United Kingdom at that time.

3.12.6 Schedule E charge on employee shares
(FA 1988, ss 77–87)

FA 1988 contains provisions which may apply to any shares acquired by reason of an individual's employment which is charged under Schedule E Case I. The legislation may apply to any shares acquired in this way whether by exercise of an option, subscription for new shares or purchase of existing shares.

Liability to tax under Schedule E may arise:

(1)   when any restrictions affecting the employee's shares are removed; or
(2)   when the shareholder receives any special benefit by virtue of ownership; or
(3)   where the shares are in a 'dependent subsidiary'.

Shares in a dependent subsidiary

A company which is a subsidiary is deemed to be a dependent subsidiary unless the directors certify each year that it is not a dependent subsidiary and the auditors confirm their agreement to this. A company will be regarded as a dependent subsidiary if there is any significant amount of trading with the parent company or another member of the group.

Where an employee holds shares in a dependent subsidiary, a tax charge may arise on the growth in the value which takes place at the earliest of the following times:

(1)   the time when he actually disposes of the shares;
(2)   the date that the company ceases to be a dependent subsidiary;
(3)   the expiry of seven years from the date of acquisition.

A charge may arise even though the company was not a dependent subsidiary when the person acquired his shares if it subsequently becomes a dependent subsidiary.

3.13   Approved share options
(TA 1988, s 185 and Schedule 9)

3.13.1   Introduction

There are two main types of approved share option schemes for employees: save as you earn (SAYE) linked share option schemes and executive share option schemes.

Approved SAYE linked share option schemes were introduced in 1980. The main features of these schemes are that there is a limit on the value of the shares which may be allocated to an employee and that participation in the scheme must be open to all full-time employees who have completed five years' service.

In 1984 the Government introduced a further category of approved share options intended to cover special arrangements for senior executives. The maximum amounts involved are much more generous and there is no requirement that the option be granted to all employees.

It is possible for an employer to establish both types of scheme and, indeed, to grant non-approved share options as well.

3.13.2 Approved SAYE linked share option schemes

These schemes entail the grant of an option for employees to purchase company shares at a price which must not be 'manifestly less' than 80 per cent of their market value at the time that the options are granted. The employee is required to take out a SAYE linked savings scheme (maximum £250 per month) and may use the proceeds to exercise the share option either five or seven years later, depending upon the rules of the particular scheme. No income tax liability arises on the grant of the options or upon their exercise. Capital gains tax is charged on an eventual disposal of the shares.

3.13.3 Executive share option schemes

The general principle is that an income tax charge may arise on the exercise of a share option, but certain approved share option schemes may be established which avoid such an income tax liability. Capital gains tax may still apply but only on a subsequent disposal of the shares concerned.

3.13.4 Conditions for approval

In order to receive Revenue approval, the following conditions must be satisfied:

(1) Participation in the scheme must be open only to full-time directors or employees or to part-time employees working at least 20 hours a week. Part-time directors may not participate in this scheme. The Inland Revenue has indicated that it regards a director who works 25 hours per week as full-time. The employer may choose which of the employees are to be permitted to participate in the scheme.

(2) Where the employer is a close company, no participant must own (or be entitled to acquire as a result of the grant of the option) more than ten per cent of the company's shares. Furthermore no individual who has owned more than ten per cent of the company's shares within the previous 12 months is able to participate.

(3) The price at which the option is to be exercised must not be 'manifestly less' than the value of the shares at the time that the option is granted. With effect from 1 January 1992, it became possible for options to be granted at a discount of up to 15 per cent of the market value of shares at the time of granting where the company also operates an approved profit sharing scheme or savings related share option scheme.

(4)   There is a limit on the number of shares over which a particular employee may be granted options. The scheme must limit the employee's options to shares with a market value at the time that the options are granted which does not exceed the greater of £100,000 or four times that person's current or preceding year's remuneration for PAYE purposes. Remuneration for PAYE purposes excludes benefits in kind and reimbursed expenses and is after deducting contributions to an approved pensions scheme.

(5)   The shares issued under the scheme must be fully paid ordinary shares of the company or its parent company. They must either be shares quoted on a recognised stock exchange or shares in a non-close company which is controlled by a quoted company or shares in a company not under the control of another company.

(6)   Options must not be transferable and must be exercisable only between three and ten years after they are granted. There is an income tax charge on individuals who exercise options under the scheme more than once every three years. This three year time limit is waived if a director or employee dies, in which case the option must be exercised by the personal representatives within one year of death.

3.13.5   Example—Grant of options

A director is granted options under an approved scheme as follows:

2,000 £1 ordinary shares 1 January 1993 valued at £19 each.
2,000 £1 ordinary shares 1 January 1994 valued at £20 each.

It is proposed to grant further options on 1 January 1995.

His remuneration for 1994–95 will be:

	£
Salary	£22,000
Fees	£ 5,000
Benefits	£ 2,000
Total	£29,000

Benefits are excluded and remuneration for share option purposes is £27,000 (which is greater than for 1993–94).

Limit = 4 x £27,000 = £108,000

Value of options granted:

	£
2,000 at £19	£38,000
2,000 at £20	£40,000
	£78,000
Value remaining	£30,000

On 1 January 1995 it will be possible to grant options over shares with a value of up to £30,000.

3.14 Options to acquire company assets

3.14.1. Introduction

The treatment of non-approved employee share options can be disadvantageous but this is due to specific legislation on *share* options; the rules governing options involving other assets are quite different. An income tax charge may arise at the time that an option is granted if the option has a market value. However, if the price at which the option may be exercised is higher than the asset's present market value, it is arguable that the option has little or no value at the time that it is granted.

No Schedule E income tax charge would normally arise upon the exercise of the option. Furthermore, on a subsequent disposal of the asset there would normally be liability only for capital gains tax on the profit over the amount paid. Although special care needs to be taken where the director or employee is connected (perhaps as a shareholder) with the company which grants the option, this type of option can provide substantial benefits.

3.14.2 Example—Option to acquire assets

A company director, who is not a shareholder, is granted the option to purchase surplus development land owned by the company for £150,000 at any time during a period of ten years. The land has a market value of only £125,000 at the time the option is granted and the option, therefore, has only a small value at that time. When the option is exercised the land has a market value of £250,000 and the director has in effect acquired a capital asset at a discount of £100,000 on its current market value. This discount would not normally be subject to income tax.

3.15 Golden hallos

These are payments made to induce a prospective employee to take up employment with the company and are occasionally not taxable. A case involving a chartered accountant, *Pritchard v Arundale* (1971) 47 TC 680, concerned the senior partner in a firm of chartered accountants who was approached by a client to leave his practice and become a director of that client's company. In order to induce him to do this, he was given shares in the company which were held to be not a reward for services to be rendered in the future but an inducement to leave his practice and take up the employment. It was therefore not taxable.

Another case, *Vaughan-Neil v IRC* [1979] STC 644, concerned a barrister who received £40,000 to induce him to give up practising as a barrister and join a company as its 'in-house adviser'. Once again it was held that the payment was not taxable. By contrast, in *Glantre Engineering Ltd v Goodhand* [1983] STC 1, a payment by an engineering company to induce an employee of a firm of accountants to join them was held to be taxable.

The principles which emerge from these three cases are as follows:

(1)   It must be clear from the facts that the payment is an inducement and not a reward for future services;

(2)   The payment must not be returnable if the person does not take up the employment; and

(3)   It is probably more likely that the payment will be accepted as non-taxable if the recipient has previously been in practice or self-employed rather than an employee of another company.

The case of *Shilton v Wilmshurst* [1991] STC 88 extended these principles by deciding that a payment made by a football club to a footballer about to transfer as an inducement to him to join his new club, was taxable. The House of Lords held that an emolument for an employment meant an emolument for being *or becoming* an employee and therefore would include a sum paid by a third party as an inducement to enter into a contract of employment to perform services in the future. It was not necessary for the payer to have any interest in the performance of those services.

3.16   Restrictive covenants
(FA 1988, s 73)

Where the present, past or future holder of an office or employment gives an undertaking which restricts his conduct or activities, any sum paid in respect of that restrictive covenant is treated as remuneration from the office or employment for the year in which the payment is received. This rule applies even where the restrictive covenant is not legally valid. In some cases, valuable consideration other than money is given for the restrictive covenant and in such a situation a sum equal to the value of that consideration is treated as having been paid. The payment may not *necessarily* come from the employer and so a payment to an employee which was made by a major shareholder in a family company might well be caught under these provisions.

3.17   Redundancy payments
(TA 1988, s 579)

A statutory redundancy payment made under the Employment Protection (Consolidation) Act 1978 is exempt from tax although it may need to be taken into account in computing the tax payable on a termination payment (see 3.18).

Payment to an employee under a non-statutory redundancy scheme will generally be treated by the Revenue as exempt under Statement of Practice SP1/81 where the following conditions are satisfied:

(1)   Payments are made only on accounts of redundancy as defined in Employment Protection (Consolidation) Act 1978, s 81.
(2)   The individual has at least two years' continuous service.
(3)   Payments are made to all relevant employees and not merely to a selected group of employees.
(4)   The payments are not excessively large in relation to earnings and length of service.

In the recent case of *Mairs v Haughey* [1993] STC 569, the Inland Revenue sought to tax a payment made to an employee for giving up contingent redundancy rights. The Revenue argued that the payment constituted an emolument of the employment, but it was held that a redundancy payment is not an emolument and a lump sum paid in lieu of a right to receive such a redundancy payment is equally not an emolument.

This case has also cast doubt on the view generally held within the Inland Revenue that a termination payment is always taxable where the employee is contractually entitled to it.

Statement of Practice SP1/81 has recently been replaced by an expanded version SP1/94.

3.18   Golden handshakes and other termination payments
(TA 1988, s 148)

3.18.1   Introduction

Where a director's or employee's contract of service is terminated, it may be possible for a compensation payment or *ex gratia* payment to be made which is either wholly or partly tax-free *provided* the employee is not entitled to the compensation under a contract of service and the payment is not deemed to be a benefit under a retirement benefit scheme. Where the individual receives compensation, under a term of his contract of employment, the Revenue's view is that it is taxable under Schedule E in the usual way. A payment made to a director as compensation for accepting a reduced salary or any other variation of his service contract is not regarded as a termination payment, and the amount received is normally taxable in full.

3.18.2   Exemptions from the charge under s 148

There are various types of termination payment which are exempt:

Payments made because of death or disability
(TA 1988, s 188)

A termination payment which arises where an employment is terminated because of death, injury or disability is exempt. Disability covers not only a condition arising from a sudden affliction but also covers a continuing incapacity to perform the duties of an office or employment because of the culmination of a process of deterioration of physical or mental health caused by chronic illness (see Statement of Practice SP10/81).

Terminal grants and gratuities to members of HM forces

Payments to members of HM forces are exempt from the charge under s 148.

Payments from Commonwealth government superannuation schemes

Lump sum payments from Commonwealth government superannuation schemes or compensation for loss of career due to constitutional changes in Commonwealth countries are exempt from tax under s 148.

Contributions to an approved retirement benefit scheme

A special contribution by an employer into an approved retirement benefit scheme is not taxable as a termination payment.

Foreign service
(TA 1988, s 188(3))

A lump sum termination payment is not taxable where the employment has constituted foreign service which exceeds the following limits:

(1)   three-quarters of the whole period of service;
(2)   the last ten years;
(3)   one half of the period of service provided that this amounted to at least 20 years and subject to at least ten of the last 20 years of service being foreign service.

'Foreign' service is defined as meaning a period of service during which the earnings were not assessable under Schedule E Case I either because the individual was not resident in the United Kingdom or because the 100 per cent deduction was available because the period spent working overseas exceeded 365 days (see 3.19).

3.18.3   Basic £30,000 exemption
(TA 1988, s 188(4))

Where a termination payment is not wholly exempt, the first £30,000 is normally free from tax and only the balance is chargeable. Where an individual receives both statutory redundancy payments and a termination payment, the amount of the statutory redundancy payments uses up part of the £30,000 exemption and only the balance is available to cover part of the termination payment.

3.18.4 Employment includes a period of foreign service

The £30,000 exemption may be increased where the employment has included 'foreign service'.

3.18.5 Example—Increased exemption due to foreign service

B was non-resident in the United Kingdom from 1972 to 1980. He then qualified for the 100 per cent deduction from 1980 until 1982, so that he was not subject to UK tax on his salary even though he was resident. In December 1993 he retires and receives compensation of £80,000.

The exemption is found by using the fraction:

$$\frac{\text{Foreign service}}{\text{Total period of employment}} \quad \text{ie in this case} \quad \frac{10 \text{ years}}{21 \text{ years}}$$

This fraction is applied to the amount of the golden handshake after deduction of the £30,000 exemption.

The taxable amount would be arrived at as follows:-

Compensation	80,000
Less: 'normal exemption'	30,000
	50,000
$\frac{10}{21}$ thereof	23,809
Taxable amount	£26,191

3.18.6 Year for which a termination payment may be taxed

The time when a termination payment is made does not affect the tax liability as it is treated as taxable income for the year in which the employment is terminated.

3.18.7 *Ex gratia* payments

There has been concern that *ex gratia* payments may be subject to tax under Schedule E as unapproved retirement benefits taxable under TA 1988, s 596A. If this charge arises, the £30,000 exemption is not available. The Revenue issued a statement of practice in October 1991 (SP 13/91) and has subsequently clarified the position. An *ex gratia* payment will normally be regarded as a retirement benefit taxable under s 596A only where it is paid in connection with an individual's retirement. The Revenue has also given the following guidelines on hypothetical situations:

(1)   A person who has worked for a company for 20 years leaves at age 54 to take a senior executive position in another company—'golden handshake'.

(2)   A long-service employee leaves to take a senior executive position in another company at the age of 60—borderline, probably retirement.

(3)   A division of a company is sold and the 55 year old manager responsible for running it leaves to take a job with the purchaser—'golden handshake'.

(4)   A person in his 50s has a heart attack and is advised by his doctor to leave and seek a less stressful position—'golden handshake'.

(5)   An employee aged 35 is involved in an accident and suffers disabilities that make him unable to continue with his job—'golden handshake'.

(6)   An employee aged 50 leaves to take a job nearer home to be able to nurse her aged parents—borderline, 'golden handshake'. If the employee did not take a new job, or was nearer normal retirement age, this situation would be treated as retirement.

3.19   Special rules for working outside the United Kingdom
(TA 1988, s 193 and Sched 12)

3.19.1   Introduction

Where a person is resident and ordinarily resident in the United Kingdom but works overseas for a continuous period of at least 365 qualifying days, a 100 per cent deduction may be available. There will then be no UK tax payable on the earnings concerned.

A qualifying day is a day when the individual is absent from the United Kingdom at midnight and the following conditions are fulfilled:

(1)   the individual has spent that day working abroad under his contract of employment; or

(2)   the individual has spent part of that day travelling overseas in order to perform duties under his contracts of employment; or

(3)   the day is one of at least seven consecutive days which (taken as a whole) are substantially devoted to performing duties overseas.

There are specific rules on what counts as a qualifying day for people working on board ship or on board aircraft and travelling to a foreign destination.

Shorter periods may be aggregated to make up the 365 day period provided the periods are not separated by more than 62 consecutive days spent in the United Kingdom, or by a total period greater than one sixth of the periods being aggregated.

3.19.2   Example—Working outside the United Kingdom

B works overseas for the following periods:

1 January 1994	–	30 April 1994
1 June 1994	–	31 October 1994
1 December 1994	–	24 December 1994
1 January 1995	–	10 January 1995

(1)   The period 1 January 1994–31 October 1994 may form a qualifying period because the days spent in the United Kingdom are less than one sixth of the total.

(2)   Similarly, the period 1 December–24 December 1994 is not separated from the earlier period by 62 days and the one sixth limit is not breached. Consequently, a combined period of 1 January 1994–24 December 1994 can be built up.

(3)   In turn, this can be combined with the subsequent period spent working overseas of 1 January–10 January 1995 and the total period 1 January 1994–10 January 1995 therefore constitutes a qualifying period which exceeds 365 days.

The position would have been different if the days spent overseas were the same in total, but the initial period was

1 January–31 March 1994	working overseas
1 April–30 April 1994	in the United Kingdom
1 May–31 May 1994	working overseas

The period 1 January to 31 May 1993 would have contained non-qualifying days which were more than one sixth of the total and so the qualifying period could only start from 1 May. The period 1 May 1994–10 January 1995 would be insufficient in itself to qualify for the 100 per cent deduction as it is less than 365 days.

3.19.3   Periods of non-residence

The Inland Revenue changed its practice with effect from 6 April 1992 so that a period of non-residence may no longer be taken into account when calculating the qualifying period for the purposes of the 100 per cent deduction. This practice applies to anyone who became resident in the United Kingdom on or after 6 April 1992.

3.19.4   Computation of the deduction

If you are entitled to the 100 per cent deduction, it may be that you should review the way in which your earnings were assessed for 1990–91 and 1991–92. Until the legislation was amended, provisions which governed the way in which the 100 per cent deduction should be calculated had an unforeseen consequence. The former legislation permitted the 100 per cent deduction to be calculated on an individual's earnings before allowable deductions such as pension contributions, expenses payments and capital allowances. For 1992–93 and subsequent years, the deduction is based on the individual's earnings *after* such deductions.

3.19.5   Unapproved share options

The Revenue now takes the view that profits realised on the exercise of non-approved options do not constitute 'emoluments' and are therefore not to be taken into account in computing the 100 per cent deduction. In effect, the profit on the option may attract UK tax even though the individual's other earnings are covered by the 100 per cent deduction. This treatment applies to options exercised after 5 April 1994.

3.19.6   Double tax relief

Where an individual works abroad, he may be liable for foreign tax. If the 100 per cent deduction is not available, there will also be a UK tax liability. The foreign tax may be allowed as a credit against the UK tax.

3.20   Designing a 'tax efficient' remuneration package

Where an individual has a real degree of influence over the way in which his total remuneration package of salary and benefits is made up, the following should be borne in mind.

(1)   Pension schemes are very tax efficient.
(2)   Approved share options are treated more favourably than non approved options.
(3)   The legislation on benefits in kind still leaves some scope for manoeuvre.
(4)   Golden handshakes are not always taxable.

3.20.1 Advantages of pension funds in general

There can be no better medium to long-term investment than a pension scheme. The fact that pension schemes are not subject to tax internally because of the funds' exemption from UK income tax and CGT, combined with the facility to take a tax-free lump sum at retirement means that the overall return will almost certainly beat any comparable investment.

3.20.2 Pension schemes which are not subject to the earnings cap

Some individuals may be in a company pension scheme which they had joined prior to 17 March 1987. If there is any element of choice, and the individual can afford to do so, it may well be better to forego salary in return for an increased level of funding for the company pension. The fact that there is no ceiling on the tax-free lump sum of one and a half times final remuneration is obviously extremely attractive.

In practice, even if the company operates a first class pension scheme, there is likely to be some scope for augmenting the individual's pension entitlement. For example, many company pension schemes do not define final remuneration so as to include the maximum amount which the Revenue would permit. In these cases, it may be possible for an individual to have his pension entitlement increased to take account of 'fluctuating emoluments' such as benefits in kind, etc.

3.20.3 Schemes where the individual is subject to the earnings cap

Where an individual is subject to the earnings cap (see 12.11.4), because he has taken up employment after 31 May 1989, or has become a member of a company pension scheme only after that date, there may still be considerable scope for increasing the level of benefits. If the individual can afford it, he should pay the maximum additional voluntary contributions and he should arrange matters so that his employer funds the scheme to the maximum extent permitted. In most cases, the individual will not receive the full pension if he accrues benefits at the standard rate of 1/60th final remuneration for each year of service, whereas the Revenue will permit a scheme to be funded so that the full pension is due after 20 years' service (see 12.11.5).

In the case of a family company, where both spouses are active in the business, it may well be possible for each to have the maximum permitted pension benefits.

3.20.4   Approved share option schemes

The tax treatment of an individual who exercises an approved share option or who receives shares via an approved profit-sharing scheme is significantly better off than someone who benefits via an unapproved arrangement. Basically, no tax charge arises on the exercise of an approved share option provided that the necessary conditions have been observed (see 3.13).

The conclusion must be that wherever an individual has a choice, he should normally participate via an approved rather than a non-approved scheme.

3.20.5   Tax efficient benefits in kind

Despite the Government's long-term intention to remove any discrimination between the tax treatment of benefits in kind and cash remuneration, there are still certain benefits in kind which are favourably treated for tax purposes. If a person is a company director, or someone else who has a degree of say in the way in which his remuneration package is made up, significant tax benefits can be secured by a judicious choice of benefits in kind.

Company cars

Because of the high rate of depreciation in the first year, it may well be advantageous for a director to arrange for his company to purchase a car with a view to its being sold to him after it has been used for a period. Provided that he pays the full market value for the car in its second-hand condition, there will be no Schedule E charge on the difference between the cost of the car to the company and the amount at which the director purchases it. Admittedly, there will be a scale benefit for the period the company owns the car, but this will often be significantly less than the depreciation of the vehicle during the period concerned.

Car fuel

It is clearly beneficial that an individual should have as much free petrol as possible as the scale benefit does not vary according to how much private petrol is provided to an employee.

Interest free loans

There is a *de minimis* limit so that, if an individual has a beneficial loan from his company, no Schedule E charge arises unless the loan exceeds £5,000.

Company accommodation

It may be possible to secure a reduction in the taxable benefit which arises where a director or employee occupies a company property. This is a complex area where you should take professional advice.

3.20.6 Golden handshakes are not always taxable

Despite the rules being tightened up, a termination payment can still be favourably treated, either because of the £30,000 exemption or because it qualifies for total exemption (see 3.18).

4 Income from UK property

This chapter deals with rental income from land or property in the United Kingdom. Such income is taxable under Schedule A unless the property is let as furnished accommodation, in which case tax is charged under Schedule D Case VI.

The following matters are covered in this chapter:

(1) Computation of Schedule A income.
(2) Permitted deductions.
(3) Relief for deficiencies.
(4) Lump sums deemed to be rent (premiums).
(5) Capital allowances on investment properties.
(6) Administration of Schedule A.
(7) Furnished lettings.
(8) 'Rent-a-room' relief.
(9) Furnished holiday accommodation.
(10) Woodlands.
(11) Mineral royalties.

Rents received from letting an overseas property are taxed under Schedule D Case V and the tax treatment of such income is covered in Chapter 5.

4.1 Computation of Schedule A income
(TA 1988, ss 15, 21–24)

4.1.1 Introduction

Schedule A applies to profits or gains arising in respect of:

(1) rents from UK land or property;
(2) rent charges, ground annuals, feu duties and other annual payments arising from UK land;
(3) any other receipts from an estate in UK land or from an interest in or right over such land;

(4)   lump sum premiums deemed to be rent (see 4.4).

There are certain stated exceptions, so that tax is not charged under Schedule A in respect of:

(1)   woodlands;
(2)   payments from which tax is deducted at source in respect of mines, quarries and other similar concerns;
(3)   furnished lettings.

4.1.2   Basis of assessment
(TA 1988, s 15(1) and (2))

A person is charged to tax under Schedule A by reference to the rents or receipts to which he becomes entitled in the tax year concerned. Payments which are actually made during the chargeable period may be deducted if they fall within the definition of 'permitted deductions'.

4.1.3   Example—Basis of assessment

A lets a property under a lease which provides for rent of £2,500 to be payable on the normal quarter days. The tenant is late in paying the rent due on 25 March 1993 and the actual amount of rent received in 1993–94 is therefore only £7,500.

A incurs certain expenses of which £2,200 were paid in 1993–94 and £300 were incurred by 5 April 1994, but were paid only during 1994–95.

A is assessable under Schedule A on an amount of £7,800

	£
ie rents *receivable*	10,000
less expenses *paid*	2,200
	7,800

4.1.4   Exceptional circumstances where expenses may be related to the period in which they were incurred
(TA 1988, s 25(3))

If an expense was incurred before the end of a tax year, but was paid only after the tax year, it may be allowed against rents for the year in which it was incurred only where it cannot be relieved against rental income for the year of payment. This is also subject to the overriding requirement that the liability was incurred by reason of dilapidation attributable to the period when the property was let.

4.1.5   Different types of rental income

Rental income for Schedule A purposes includes ground rents. It also includes 'other receipts from an estate' in land such as charges levied by a landlord in return for maintaining a block of flats and payments made to a land owner for sporting rights.

Rental income does not include admission charges made by hotels, boarding houses, theatres etc since the profits of such businesses are chargeable to tax under Schedule D Case I.

The income from taking in lodgers is generally treated as trading income rather than rental income assessable under Schedule A. However, see 4.8 on 'rent-a-room' relief.

4.1.6   Relief where rents are not received
(TA 1988, s 41)

Where rent (or any other payment falling within Schedule A) is not received by the end of the tax year in which it falls due, this does not by itself affect the amount of the landlord's income for Schedule A purposes, since the statutory basis of assessment is the rent *receivable* for the year. However, in certain circumstances a landlord who does not receive rents due to him can claim appropriate relief for Schedule A purposes.

He must be able to show that *either* the tenant has defaulted and he has not been able to recover the rent in question although he has taken all reasonable steps to enforce payment; *or* he has waived payment to avoid hardship to the tenant and has not received any consideration in return for doing this.

The claim for relief must be made in writing to the Inspector of Taxes within six years from the end of the tax year in which the lost rents fell due.

4.1.7   Example—Relief where rents are not received

B lets a property at a rent of £9,000 per annum. The tenant has had a bad year in 1993–94 because his major customer went into liquidation and B therefore agrees to accept £1,000 in full and final satisfaction of the rent falling due in 1993–94 so as not to cause hardship.

On proof of these facts, B can have his liability under Schedule A for 1993–94 adjusted on the basis that the rent receivable was £1,000 instead of £9,000.

If the lost rent is subsequently recovered, the landlord must notify the Inspector of Taxes within six months. The assessment for the year in which the rent was due will then need to be adjusted.

4.1.8 Rent receivable from a connected person carrying on a trade
(F(No 2)A 1992, s 57)

There is an exception to the general rule that rent is income for the year in which it is due for payment. Where rent is payable in arrears, and the tenant is both a connected person and a trader, the landlord may be assessable on rent which has accrued during a tax year even though it is not due for payment until after the end of the year.

The intention behind the legislation is to ensure that a deduction in the trader's accounts for accruals of rent is matched by assessable income for the landlord.

An individual is a connected person if he is married to the other person, or is a relative or the spouse of a relative. A trustee of a settlement is connected with the settlor. A company is connected with a person who controls it, either on his own or together with other connected persons.

These provisions apply only to rent which accrued after 9 March 1992. Rent which relates to a period before 10 March 1992 is taxable income for the year in which it fell due.

4.2 Permitted deductions
(TA 1988, ss 25–33)

4.2.1 General rules

A person may deduct the following types of payment:

(1) Maintenance or repairs, insurance or management.
(2) Other services that he as the landlord was obliged to provide and for which he receives no separate payment.
(3) Rates or other charges on the occupier which the landlord was obliged to defray.
(4) Any rent, rent charge, ground annual, feu duty or other periodical payment reserved in respect of, or charged on, or issuing out of, land.

However, there are certain tests which need to be satisfied before a payment under one of the above headings may be deducted:

(1) No deduction is due for any sum which is recoverable from an insurance policy or from some other person.
(2) The maintenance and repairs must arise from 'dilapidations' (ie wear and tear) during the currency of a lease and must not, for example, be attributable to the state of the property when it was acquired. There is a concession here which applies where the

property was acquired from the taxpayer's spouse (or a trustee for the spouse) and the property had previously been let.

The following are types of expenditure which are normally allowable as maintenance or repairs:

Interior repairs and redecorations
Exterior repairs and redecorations
Maintenance of common parts of a building
Cost of cleaning and other similar services
Upkeep of gardens
Premiums for buildings insurance
Valuation fees incurred for insurance purposes
Costs of rent collection
Legal costs in connection with lettings, provided the lease is for a period not exceeding 21 years.

A landlord of a large estate may also be able to claim for the upkeep of estate offices, salaries, wages and pensions for employees and former employees engaged in estate management, but the Revenue will strongly resist any claim for travelling expenses incurred in visiting the property to collect rents or supervise repair work etc. It is known that a taxpayer recently succeeded before the Commissioners on a claim for travel costs incurred in travelling from London to Sheffield to collect rents, but it would be unwise to rely upon this as a precedent.

In addition, part of the cost of alterations or improvements may be allowed where it can be shown that the alteration obviated the need to carry out repairs. This is subject to the Revenue's being satisfied that the repairs were not so substantial as to amount to reconstruction of the property and no change in the use of the property had rendered it unnecessary to carry out the repairs (see extra-statutory concession B4).

Capital allowances may also be claimed in respect of plant and machinery belonging to the landlord, whether this be equipment in his office, such as typewriters, or a computer, or plant which has become an integral part of the building such as a lift.

4.2.2   Expenditure on a property whilst it is vacant
(TA 1988, s 25)

Expenditure on repairs whilst property is vacant (a 'void period') is allowable only if the dilapidations which necessitated the repairs occurred during a period when the premises were let at a full rent by the landlord, or at the time when the premises were kept for letting at a full rent. Furthermore, even where this condition is satisfied, relief may still be denied where the landlord has taken up occupation of the premises before the repair work was carried out or where the premises are let at less than a full rent before the work is undertaken.

On the other hand, where a property has been let by the owner at a full rent, expenditure relating to the period of the letting or on repairs which are to make good dilapidations which occurred during that period, is an allowable expense *provided* that the expenditure is incurred before the owner takes up occupation.

4.2.3   Dilapidations attributable to previous years
(TA 1988, s 25(3))

Even where a property is let by the owner, expenditure relating to earlier periods may not always be allowable. Where the expenditure was incurred in respect of a period of owner occupation, or any void period which followed such a period of owner occupation and preceded the property being let, it cannot be set against the rents from the letting. A similar rule applies where the property was previously let at less than a full rent (see 4.3.1).

4.2.4   Interest

Interest is not deductible in arriving at Schedule A income, although qualifying interest on a loan used to purchase a property or carry out improvements may be set against Schedule A income (whether from that property or another property).

Where the qualifying interest exceeds the amount of the Schedule A income, the excess may be carried forward and set against the individual's Schedule A income for subsequent years until such time as the individual disposes of the property.

For further details on qualifying loan interest, see 9.2.

4.3   Relief for deficiencies
(TA 1988, ss 25, 31, 37(9))

4.3.1   Introduction

A deficiency is said to occur where a landlord's expenses on a property exceed the rent due for that year.

TA 1988, s 24 distinguishes between three types of property:

(1)   Properties let at a rent which is not a full rent.
(2)   Properties let at a full rent on a landlord's repairing lease.
(3)   Properties let at a full rent on a tenant's repairing lease.

A property is regarded as let at a full rent where the rents are sufficient (taking one year with another) to cover the landlord's obligations, maintenance, repairs etc. Contributions payable by the tenant under the terms of the lease are taken into account in determining whether the rent is sufficient for this purpose. Where a rent cannot be increased because of legal reasons, it will nevertheless be treated as a 'full rent' if it was a full rent at the time that it was fixed.

A landlord's repairing lease is one where the landlord is responsible for repairs. A tenant's repairing lease is one where the tenant is under an obligation to repair the whole, or substantially the whole, of the premises. A lease under which the tenant is liable for repairs, fair wear and tear excepted, is not a tenant's repairing lease within this definition.

The scheme of the legislation reflects the fact that a deficiency is most likely to arise in the case of (1) and least likely to arise on properties which are in category (3), ie properties let under a tenant's repairing lease.

4.3.2   Deficiencies on properties not let at a full rent

Where a landlord has a deficiency on a property which is not let at a full rent, the deficiency cannot be set against any other Schedule A income. Furthermore, the deficiency can be set against future income from that property only whilst it is let under that particular lease. For example, if a man lets a flat to his grandmother for an inclusive rent of £200 per annum and in 1993–94 he has a deficiency of £1,500, this can be carried forward only until the grandmother's lease comes to an end. It cannot be set against income from subsequent lettings.

4.3.3   Deficiencies on properties let under landlord's repairing lease

A deficiency can be set against rents of other properties which are let at a full rent on a landlord's repairing lease. Consequently, rents and expenses of properties let at full rents are pooled and tax is payable on the balance of aggregate receipts after deducting aggregate allowable expenditure. If the allowable expenditure exceeds the receipts, the excess may be carried forward against the pool income for the following year, and so on.

For this purpose, a lease at a full rent is treated as continuous with previous leases by the same landlord of the same property at a full rent, provided that the property has been continuously in his ownership and there has been no intervening period when it was owner occupied or let at less than a full rent. A period during which the property was unoccupied does not affect the entitlement to carry forward expenses.

A deficiency on a property cannot be carried forward to a tax year after the property has been disposed of, or after the property has been occupied by the owner, or let for less than a full rent. When one of these events takes place, the unrelieved deficit on that property must be taken out of the pool.

4.3.4   Deficiencies on properties let under tenant's repairing leases

Any deficiency can be set against rents from properties which are let at a full rent under landlord's repairing leases. The deficiency may not be set against rents from other properties which are let under tenant's repairing leases.

4.3.5   Deficiency on an agricultural property
(TA 1988, s 33)

Where an estate consists of, or includes, agricultural land, a deficiency may be set against any Schedule A income. Any balance which cannot be relieved in this way may be set against the individual's other income for the year, or the following tax year.

Agricultural land is defined as land, houses or other buildings in the United Kingdom occupied wholly or mainly for the purposes of husbandry. An estate means any land and buildings managed as one estate. Where only part of the estate is used for husbandry, only a proportion of any deficiency can be relieved in this way.

4.4   Lump sums deemed to be rent (premiums)
(TA 1988, ss 34–39)

4.4.1   Introduction

A landlord faced with the choice of letting a property for five years at £10,000 per annum, or taking a lump sum in return for granting a lease for five years at an annual rent of £100 would regard the two transactions as very similar in their overall consequences. The purpose behind the tax legislation which deals with such lump sums (or 'premiums') is to ensure that the tax treatment of the two types of transaction is also similar in nature. The principle is that a proportion of a premium received by a landlord for granting a lease of less than 50 years should be taxed as if it were rent.

The following sections apply only where the person who receives the premium is the landlord, ie a person who continues to hold a superior interest in the property. An outgoing tenant who assigns the whole of his interest in the property is not regarded as receiving a premium for Schedule A purposes.

4.4.2 How premiums are apportioned between income and capital
(TA 1988, s 34)

The rule is that the full amount of the premium is treated as rent except for two per cent for every complete year of the lease after the first year. For example, if a ten year lease is granted for a premium of £25,000, the amount which is subject to tax under Schedule A is 82 per cent of £25,000, ie £20,500.

4.4.3 Payments in kind
(TA 1988, s 34(2))

It is provided that if a tenant is required to carry out work as a term of his lease, the whole of the benefit accruing to the landlord is deemed to be a premium receivable at the commencement of the lease.

4.4.4 Deemed premiums
(TA 1988, s 34(5))

Any lump sum paid by a tenant in order to vary the lease can be treated as a premium receivable at the time that the contract for the variation is entered into.

4.4.5 Example—Deemed premium

A is the landlord of a property used as offices and let on a 15 year lease. It is a term of the lease that the tenant should not use the premises for any other purpose.

The tenant secures planning consent to use the property for light industrial use. He makes a payment to A of £12,000 in year four in order to induce him to vary the lease so that the property can be used for industrial purposes.

A is deemed to receive a premium in year four. The taxable amount is:

	£
	12,000
less (10 x 2 per cent)	2,400
	9,600

Similarly, if A had received a lump sum to induce him to waive the relevant term in the lease, the lump sum would be treated as a premium.

4.4.6 Sale with right to repurchase the property
(TA 1988, s 36)

Where the freehold or leasehold of a property is sold subject to a condition that at a future date the purchaser may be required to sell the property back to the vendor at a lower price, the vendor is liable to tax under Schedule D Case VI on the excess of the sale price over the repurchase price. The difference is treated as a premium so that the amount charged is reduced by two per cent for each complete year between the date of sale and the date of resale less one year. A similar rule applies where a vendor sells a property, but retains an option to repurchase it.

4.5 Capital allowances on investment properties

4.5.1 Introduction

Capital allowances are usually given when the Revenue assesses the profits of a trade. However, it is possible to qualify for capital allowances in respect of expenditure on investment properties. The allowances must first be set against the income of a defined class (see below) but any surplus of allowances may be set against the individual's other income. The legislation states that such allowances may be given by way of 'discharge or repayment of tax'.

4.5.2 Agricultural buildings allowances
(CAA 1990, ss 132(3) and 141)

Agricultural buildings allowances (see 2.5.14) are available for relief by 'discharge or repayment of tax' if the landlord does not carry on a trade of farming. The allowances must first be set against agricultural or forestry rental income.

It is necessary to make a claim under CAA 1990, s 141 within two years of the end of the year of assessment in order that agricultural buildings allowances may be set against other income rather than carried forward. If the individual wishes, the surplus allowances may be set against income of the following tax year.

4.5.3 Industrial buildings allowances
(CAA 1990, ss 9 and 141)

An individual who owns the relevant interest in an industrial building may qualify for industrial buildings allowances (see 2.5.15) because the property is occupied and used for a qualifying trade. Similarly, an individual who owns a property in an enterprise zone will generally qualify for allowances where the building is occupied for commercial purposes.

The allowances on such buildings must first be set against rental income from the industrial buildings and then against any balancing charge which arises on the disposal of an interest in an industrial building. If there is a surplus of allowances, these allowances may then be set against the individual's income for the year, or the following tax year. Once again, a formal claim is required under CAA 1990, s 141.

4.5.4 Enterprise zone trust

It is possible to invest in properties in enterprise zones through a syndicate or 'enterprise zone property trust'. An individual who invests in the enterprise zone property trust is treated as if he had incurred a proportion of the trust's expenditure on enterprise zone properties and the allowances may be set against his other income in the same way as described at 4.5.3 above. In some cases, there may be a delay in that an individual invests in a trust at the end of one tax year and becomes entitled to allowances only for the following year (because that is the year in which the trust acquires the relevant properties).

4.5.5 Relief for loan interest

Where an individual has borrowed to acquire a property in the United Kingdom which is let for at least 26 weeks of a year, relief is available for the interest paid (see 9.2).

An individual may be able to claim relief for such interest either where he has acquired a direct interest in an industrial building or enterprise zone building, or where he has done so indirectly through investing in an enterprise zone property trust.

The Revenue's practice is to deduct qualifying interest from rental income first and then to look at the individual's capital allowances. In general, this should be favourable in that it will mean that the individual has a larger surplus of capital allowances which is available to be set against other income.

4.5.6 Example—Relief for loan interest

A invests £100,000 in an enterprise zone property trust on 1 July 1993. He raises a loan of £80,000 for this purpose.

In 1993–94, the position is:

	£
rents receivable	9,000
interest paid	8,000
capital allowances (say)	95,000

The Revenue interpretation produces the following result:

	£
Schedule A income	9,000
less qualifying interest	8,000
	1,000
capital allowances	(95,000)
available for offset against other income	(94,000)

4.6. Administration of Schedule A
(TA 1988, ss 22–23)

Schedule A tax is due for payment on 1 January in the year of assessment, or 30 days after an assessment is issued if later.

The legislation enables the Revenue to issue an initial assessment which is determined by the actual amount of assessable income for the preceding tax year. The only grounds of appeal against such an assessment is that the individual no longer owns the property concerned. It is not normally possible to have the tax postponed simply because the property is vacant or the rents receivable are likely to be less than in the preceding year. Once the actual figures for the year are known, the initial assessment is adjusted and either tax is repaid or additional tax is payable.

4.7 Furnished lettings

4.7.1 Income normally assessed under Schedule D Case VI
(TA 1988, s 15(1) and (4)(c))

Income from furnished lettings is normally assessable under Schedule D Case VI unless the services provided by the landlord amount to his carrying on a trade for the purposes of Schedule D Case I. This condition will be satisfied only where a landlord lets premises on a furnished basis, and he provides additional services such as cooking, cleaning etc.

Taxpayer's option
(TA 1988, s 15(2))

A person who receives income from furnished lettings can elect that the income attributable to the use of the property should be assessed under Schedule A instead of Schedule D Case VI. This may be advantageous if the individual has other property assessed under Schedule A and relief for excess expenditure on the other property can be set against Schedule A income from the furnished lettings (see 4.3 above).

The election needs to be given under s 15(2) within two years of the end of the tax year concerned.

4.7.2   Basis of assessment under Schedule D Case VI

The basis of assessment is slightly different from that which applies for Schedule A purposes in that it is rents *received* rather than rents *receivable* which need to be taken into account.

Expenses of the type which are allowable under Schedule A are also allowable for Schedule D Case VI purposes. In addition, a person may deduct interest on money borrowed to purchase the property in computing his income from furnished lettings. Wear and tear allowances may be claimed in respect of furniture and furnishings. Relief may be claimed on the so called 'renewals basis', but this requires complicated records and in practice most individuals adopt the alternative permitted by the Revenue whereby an amount equal to ten per cent of rents received may be claimed in respect of depreciation.

Case VI assessments on furnished lettings are normally due for payment on 1 January in the year of assessment. The procedure on Schedule A initial assessments does not apply to Case VI assessments.

4.8   'Rent-a-room' relief
(F(No 2)A 1992, s 59 and Sched 10)

There is a special relief which is available to an individual who receives payment for letting furnished accommodation in a qualifying residence. The relief provides total exemption from income of £3,250 unless sums accrue to another person in respect of lettings of furnished accommodation in the same property, in which case the exemption is reduced to £1,625.

A qualifying residence is a residence which is the individual's only or main residence at sometime in the basis period for the year of assessment in relation to the lettings. Residence means a building (or part of a building) occupied or intended to be occupied as a separate residence.

Rent-a-room relief is available automatically unless the taxpayer elects otherwise or the gross sums received exceed the £3,250 limit.

Where the gross sums received exceed the £3,250 limit for the year of assessment (or the £1,625 limit where some other person receives income from furnished lettings within the same property), the taxpayer may elect for his profits or gains for the basis period to be treated as equal to the excess. For example, if a taxpayer has gross rent of £4,000, he may compute his taxable income as £750 or he can compute it in the normal way by reference to the expenses that he actually incurred.

4.9   Furnished holiday accommodation
(TA 1988, ss 503–504)

4.9.1   Definition of furnished holiday accommodation

Where a person lets furnished holiday accommodation (this includes caravans), it may be treated as a trade provided the following conditions are satisfied:

(1)   The property must be situated in the United Kingdom.
(2)   It must be let on a commercial basis.
(3)   It must be let as furnished accommodation.
(4)   It must be available for commercial letting to the public as holiday accommodation for at least 140 days in a 12-month period.
(5)   It must be let for at least 70 such days.
(6)   It must not normally be occupied by the same person for more than 31 consecutive days at any time during a period of seven months within the 12 month period.

Where a person has more than one property let as furnished holiday accommodation, the 70 day test may be satisfied by averaging any or all of the accommodation let by that person. A claim for averaging must be made within two years of the end of the year of assessment to which it is to apply.

4.9.2   Consequences where lettings are classified as furnished holiday lettings

The following consequences will follow if a property is treated as being let as furnished holiday accommodation.

Relief for interest

Interest on loans used to purchase the property, and to finance the lettings, should qualify as an expense incurred in the trade. In some cases, the inclusion of such interest will give rise to a loss for tax purposes.

Capital allowances for plant and machinery

Equipment and furniture and furnishings may attract allowances for the capital allowances system.

Relief for pre-trading expenditure

Expenditure incurred before the business of letting the properties as furnished holiday accommodation actually commences may be allowed as a loss incurred at the point in time when the lettings commence as pre-trading expenditure (see 2.6).

Relief for losses

Because the activity of letting property as furnished holiday accommodation is regarded as a trade for the purposes of Schedule D, it will be possible to obtain relief for losses against the individual's other income (see 2.10). This will apply whether the loss arises from interest, capital allowances or pre-trading expenditure or for other reasons *provided* that it can be shown that the activity was carried on on a commercial basis.

Profits classified as earned income

The legislation provides that profits arising from letting furnished holiday accommodation should be treated as earned income. This is not dependent on the owner taking any active involvement in the lettings, the whole activity can be dealt with by an agent where this is desired. Because the profits are regarded as earned income, any tax can be paid by equal instalments on 1 January in the year of assessment and 1 July following the end of the tax year. Furthermore, profits from furnished holiday lettings may qualify as 'relevant earnings' for the purposes of personal pension contributions and retirement annuity premiums (see 12.9 and 12.10).

Capital gains tax

Roll-over and retirement reliefs may be available—see 15.3 and 15.8.

4.10   Woodlands
(FA 1988, s 65 and Sched 6)

At one time, profits arising from the occupation of woodlands in the United Kingdom were taxed under Schedule B. This charge was abolished with effect from 6 April 1988. Profits or gains arising from the occupation of woodlands are now exempt and woodlands are not chargeable under Schedule A.

In some cases, woodlands were owned prior to 15 March 1988 and an election was made for profit or losses to be taxed under Schedule D. Such an election ceases to have effect at 6 April 1993 and profits which arise after that date are not taxed under Schedule D and are therefore exempt income.

4.11   Mineral royalties
(TA 1988, s 122 and Sched 6)

Mineral royalties will normally be received net of tax at the basic rate. However, only part of the royalties is taxable as income.

Where the recipient is resident or ordinarily resident in the United Kingdom, one half of the mineral royalties is treated as capital gains rather than income. Similarly, only 50 per cent of any management expenses or other sums deductible for Schedule A purposes may be set against the part of the mineral royalties treated as income.

When the mineral lease comes to an end, the person may claim a capital loss as if he had disposed of the land at its market value at that time. The loss may be set against capital gains for the year in which the mineral lease expires or against capital gains taxed on mineral royalties during the preceding 15 years.

'Mineral royalties' are defined so as to include rents, tolls, royalties and other periodic payments which relate to the winning and working of minerals (other than water, peat and topsoil) under a lease, licence or other agreement.

5 The taxation of other income received gross

This chapter deals with various types of investment and other income which are not subject to deduction of UK tax at source. Such income may be taxed under Schedule D Case III, IV, V or VI, according to the circumstances.

The following are dealt with:

Income taxed under Schedule D Case III

(1) Bank and building society interest
(2) Other interest income
(3) Loans to individuals and other private loans
(4) Gilts and loan stocks

Other interest and discounts taxed under Schedule D Case VI

(5) Accrued income scheme
(6) Deep discount securities
(7) Deep gain securities
(8) Sale of certificates of deposit
(9) Gains from roll-up funds and other offshore funds

Schedule D Cases IV and V: Untaxed income from abroad

(10) Foreign interest and dividends
(11) Foreign real estate income
(12) Alimony and maintenance payments
(13) Investment in overseas partnerships
(14) Case IV and V assessments
(15) Double tax relief
(16) Pensions taxable under Schedule D, Case V

Other income taxed under Schedule D Case VI

(17) Sundry income which may be assessed under Case VI
(18) Tax planning in relation to investment income.

Individuals who are resident in the United Kingdom but domiciled abroad are taxed under Schedule D Case IV and V on a different basis— readers should refer to Chapter 22 on this.

5.1   Bank and building society interest

5.1.1   Circumstances in which interest may be received without deduction of tax at source

The National Savings Bank (NSB) always pays interest without deduction of tax. The first £70 interest paid on an ordinary NSB account is exempt (see 11.1) but interest on an NSB investment account or from deposit bonds, income bonds or capital bonds is taxable in full.

Interest payments by UK banks or building societies on deposit accounts are normally subject to deduction of tax at source unless the depositor completes form R85. This form requires the depositor's full name, address, date of birth and national insurance number and contains a declaration that the depositor is unlikely to be liable for income tax.

Banks are permitted to pay interest without deduction on non-transferable fixed deposits for amounts of £50,000 or more and where the deposit is for a fixed period of at least seven days.

Interest payments may be made without deduction of tax on certificates of deposit provided the deposit is for at least £50,000 and the bank or building society takes the deposit for a fixed period (the period must not exceed five years). Interest may also be paid without deduction of tax on deposits where no certificate of deposit has been issued, but the depositor would be entitled to a certificate if he called for one to be issued.

Interest may also be received without tax being deducted at source from loans to individuals, deposits held by a solicitor and on certificates of tax deposit (see 5.2).

5.1.2   Basis of assessment
(TA 1988, ss 64 and 66–67)

Interest which is chargeable to tax under Schedule D Case III is normally assessed on the preceding year basis so an individual who receives interest of £2,000 during the tax year 1993–94 will normally be assessed on that amount for 1994–95. However, there are special rules for the year in which the taxpayer acquires the source and the following two years (the 'opening years') and the last two tax years in which he has the source (the 'closing years').

The assessable income for the first year is the actual amount of interest received. The assessable income for the second year is the actual interest received in that year unless the source was acquired on 6 April of year one (in which case the taxpayer has the option to be taxed on the preceding year basis). The assessable income for the third year is the amount of income received in the second year or (at the taxpayer's option) the actual interest received in year three.

The assessable income for the final year is the actual amount of interest received for that year. The assessable income for the penultimate year is the actual interest received during that year or the amount assessable on the preceding year basis, with the Revenue having the right to choose the higher amount.

Where a new source of Case III income first comes into existence after 5 April 1994, the above rules will not apply. Such income will always be assessed according to the actual income which arises during the year.

5.1.3   What is a source of Case III income?

In practice, the Inland Revenue regards each deposit account as a separate source so that the opening and closing years rules apply as an account is opened and closed. Nevertheless, it is not unusual for an individual who regularly receives interest from large deposits for (say) one month at a time to be assessed on the preceding year basis. In some cases where the amounts involved are small, the Revenue may treat all deposit accounts as a single source.

Bank account inherited from spouse

Where an individual dies and a source of Schedule D Case III passes to the surviving spouse, the closing year and opening year rules are not applied unless the Revenue receives a specific request from the deceased's personal representatives or the surviving spouse (see extra-statutory concession A7).

5.1.4   Date of receipt

Interest is regarded as received when it is credited to the account. From time to time, cases arise where an individual is required to make a deposit with a bank as a condition of the bank advancing money to a company. In some situations, the individual is precluded from making withdrawals from the deposit account as long as the company's borrowings are outstanding.

The Courts have held that an individual who has a deposit account which is subject to such a block may nevertheless be taxed on interest credited to that account. Furthermore, there is no relief if the individual never receives the interest because the company goes into liquidation and the bank appropriates the money outstanding to his credit on the deposit account.

5.1.5   Minor children's accounts

An individual will generally be charged tax on interest credited to an unmarried minor child's account where he is a parent and the person who provided the capital, unless the total income from such parental gifts does not exceed £100, (see 20.5.3 on aggregation of minor children's income in general).

5.2   Other interest income

5.2.1   Interest payable by a solicitor

Interest may be received without deduction of tax from client's accounts held by a firm of solicitors or accountants. Such income is taxable under Schedule D Case III but, because such deposits are generally short term in nature, the opening years rules apply so that the income assessable is generally the actual interest received in the tax year.

5.2.2   Interest receivable on compulsory purchase monies

Where a property is the subject of a compulsory purchase order which goes to appeal, and the amount payable is increased, interest will generally be payable on the increase. This is regarded as income for the year in which the entitlement arises, ie, when the CPO appeal is settled by agreement or on appeal and the interest is received. The principle is not affected by the fact that the interest may have accrued over several years and may be calculated using six monthly rests.

5.2.3   Certificates of tax deposit

Interest is credited to an individual where he has invested in certificates of tax deposit which are either applied to cover tax payable by assessments or are encashed. The interest is taxable and is income for the year of receipt.

5.2.4   Exempt interest

Interest paid by the Inland Revenue or Customs and Excise on over-payments of tax is not itself subject to tax. This type of interest is called 'repayment supplement' (see 19.11). However, interest paid by Customs in respect of official error is taxable.

5.2.5. Interest awarded by the Courts

This may be exempt. The treatment turns on whether the Court order or arbitration award provides for payment of interest as such (taxable) or is merely an element which is taken into account in arriving at the amount to be awarded (in which case it is capital and not income taxable under Schedule D Case III).

5.3 Loans to individuals and other private loans

Interest on a private loan to an individual or trust will generally be received without deduction of tax. Interest paid by cheque is received when the sum is credited to the recipient's account, not when the cheque is received.

Where the rate fluctuates, the preceding year basis may give rise to problems.

5.3.1 Example—Private loans

A made a private loan of £200,000 in 1988 to his nephew B to enable him to buy a house. Interest is payable at a rate equivalent to the average LIBOR for the half year.

In 1990–91, 1991–92 and 1992–93 A receives interest of £13,000, £12,500 and £9,500 respectively. In 1993–94 interest rates fall and A receives only £7,000. A's assessable income under Schedule D Case III will be as follows:

	Assessable	Actual income
	£	£
1992–93	12,500	9,500
1993–94	9,500	7,000
	22,000	16,500

5.3.2 Position where no income arises for six consecutive years

The preceding year basis continues to operate where a person has a source of income even though no interest is actually received. However, where no income has arisen for six consecutive years of assessment, the taxpayer may claim to be treated as if he had ceased to possess the source at the end of those six years. Also, where a taxpayer ceases to have a source of Case III income and no income arose during the last two years of ownership, the taxpayer may elect for the cessation provisions to apply as if he had ceased to possess the source in the year in which income last arose.

Interest is not assessable where an individual waives the interest before it falls due for payment provided he receives no consideration for such a waiver. However, the fact that interest has been waived for a year of assessment does not affect the preceding year basis.

5.4 Gilts and loan stocks

Interest payments on British Government Securities ('gilts') and loan stocks issued by companies are normally subject to deduction of tax at source. There are two exceptions:

(1)   Interest on 3½% War Loan is always paid without deduction.
(2)   Where interest is paid on gilts which are held on the National Savings Bank register, interest is also paid without deduction.

5.5 Accrued income scheme
(TA 1988, ss 710–728)

5.5.1 Introduction

An individual who sells a gilt or fixed interest loan stock may sell either cum-interest or ex-interest. In the former case, the buyer will receive the next interest payment; in the latter situation the seller receives the next interest payment even though it is paid after he has sold the gilt or loan stock. In practice, gilts etc are quoted on an ex-interest basis from six weeks or so before interest is due for payment.

The price at which a gilt or loan stock is sold will generally reflect an adjustment for accrued interest. For example, if a gilt pays interest every six months, a person who sells at the end of month four will receive a price which reflects four months' accrued interest. Conversely, a person who sells at the end of month five would normally sell on an ex-interest basis and the purchaser would take a deduction for one month's interest (as the seller would receive this).

5.5.2   Accrued income taxable

The accrued income scheme may apply where the nominal value of gilts or loan stocks held at any point in the year exceeds £5,000.

It brings into charge the interest credited to sellers of gilts and loan stocks. The interest which is deemed to accrue on a daily basis is treated for tax purposes as if it had been received by the vendor. The amount of any adjustments in the other direction (interest received but not earned over the period of ownership) is deducted and the net amount is charged to tax under Schedule D Case VI (see 5.17).

5.5.3   Example—Accrued income

A subscribes £30,000 for a new Government Stock, 10% Treasury Stock 2050 issued on 1 August 1994. He holds the stock for 43 days and then sells it to B who holds the stock at 1 February 1995 when the first six months' interest is payable.

A will be assessable for income tax purposes on £353,

ie $\frac{43}{183}$ x £1,500 (the half-yearly interest payable on stock).

B will be entitled to a deduction of the same amount in computing his taxable income. His position will therefore be as follows:

B receives six months interest of	£1,500
He deducts 'rebate interest'	£ 353
Taxable income	£1,147

5.5.4   Types of securities which are within the accrued income scheme
(TA 1988, s 710)

The scheme applies to acquisitions and disposals of virtually all types of fixed interest securities by UK-resident individuals. The securities must be loan stock not shares, but the scheme may apply to foreign securities as well as to UK loan stocks.

Savings certificates, certificates of deposit and zero coupon bonds are excluded. Bills of exchange and Treasury bills are not regarded as securities for this purpose because certificates of deposit are excluded and they are within the definition of certificates of deposit for the purposes of the accrued income scheme.

5.5.5 Types of disposal which may be caught
(TA 1988, s 710)

The scheme applies to transfers. This term is widely defined in TA 1988 and includes:

(1) a sale (s 710(5));
(2) an exchange (s 710(5)) or a conversion of securities (s 710(13));
(3) a gift (s 710(5));
(4) any transfer otherwise (s 710(5));
(5) death (s 721(1));
(6) a change in the true ownership where a person entitled to securities becomes a trustee in relation to them (s 720(4)).

5.5.6 Year of assessment
(TA 1988, s 714)

The assessment is under Schedule D Case VI. It is made for the tax year in which the interest period ends, ie, if a loan stock pays interest on 30 April, a disposal of the stock on a cum-interest basis on 5 April 1994 will produce taxable income for 1994–95.

5.5.7 Calculation of the accrued amount and the rebate amount
(TA 1988, ss 710, 713 and 714)

Where transactions go through the Stock Exchange, the accrued amount and the rebate amount are calculated by the broker and appear on the contract note. Where the transaction does not go through the market the calculation is made in the same way.

If there is more than one transaction in 'securities of the same kind', the accrued amounts and rebate amounts can be netted off. This term is interpreted strictly: £5,000 9% Treasury Stock 1994 is 'of the same kind' as £10,000 9% Treasury Stock 1994 but is not 'of the same kind' as some other issue of Treasury stock.

Separate calculation of all accrued amounts and rebate amounts is necessary. Relief is given for a rebate amount against the next interest received on that security or, if a transfer intervenes, against the accrued amount. Thus it is possible for a rebate amount in one tax year to be set against interest received in the next tax year.

5.6   Deep discount securities
(TA 1988, Sched 4)

5.6.1   Introduction

Schedule D Case III may also bring sums into charge which are deemed to be interest income.

A loan stock may be issued at a discount, or be redeemable at a premium. In either case, the borrower undertakes that when the loan is repaid the borrower will receive more than the amount originally paid on the issue of the stock. A typical situation is where a loan stock is issued at £80 for every £100 nominal and when the loan stock is redeemed the investor is entitled to receive £100.

The discount or premium is charged to tax under Schedule D Case III where the loan stock is within the definition of a deep discount bond and the company which issues the bond is a UK company. If the issuer is an overseas company, the discount is charged under Schedule D Case V.

5.6.2   Definition of deep discount bond
(TA 1988, Sched 4, para 1)

A loan stock will not be a deep discount bond just because it is issued at a discount. A discount is regarded as a deep discount only where it exceeds 0.5 per cent for every year of the intended life of the loan stock, or where the discount exceeds 15 per cent in total.

The following types of loan stock cannot be a deep discount bond:

(1)   an indexed security (this is a loan stock which pays interest and the principal is adjusted for inflation);
(2)   gilts issued prior to 14 March 1989;
(3)   a loan stock which is convertible into shares;
(4)   a 'deep gain' security (see 5.7).

5.6.3   Examples—Deep discount bonds

---

(1)   A five year loan stock is issued at £95 for every £100 nominal. This is a deep discount bond because the discount exceeds 0.5 per cent per annum.
(2)   A 35 year loan stock is issued at £80 for every £100 nominal. This is a deep discount bond, even though the discount is less than 0.5 per cent per annum, because it exceeds 15 per cent in total.

5.6.4   Events which give rise to a tax charge
(TA 1988, Sched 4, para 4)

A disposal of a deep discount security can give rise to a charge under Schedule D Case III. The discount which is attributable to the period of ownership is taxable as if it were interest.

5.6.5   Example—Disposal of deep discount security

A bond is issued at £82, redeemable at £100 after two years. This reflects a compound interest rate of approximately 10 per cent since $82 \times \left(\frac{110}{100}\right)^2 = 100$

If the holder sells after twelve months, he will be assessed on the difference between £82 and $\left(£82 \times \frac{110}{100}\right)$ ie £8.20

If the purchaser holds the bond until it is redeemed, he will be chargeable under Schedule D Case III on the discount which is deemed to accrue during his period of ownership, ie £100 minus $\left(£82 \times \frac{110}{100}\right)$

The charge on the accrued discount is not affected by the price actually obtained. Thus, if the seller had obtained only £86, he would still be deemed to have had income of £8.20 for Schedule D Case III purposes. He would also have a capital loss of £4. Similarly, if the purchaser paid only £86 this would not have had any bearing on the amounts on which he would be assessed under Schedule D Case III when the bond is redeemed, although it might mean that he would have a capital gain.

5.7   Deep gain securities
(FA 1989, Sched 11)

A deep gain security is similar to a deep discount security in that it is issued at a discount or is redeemable at a premium. It differs in that the terms of issue mean that the amount of the discount/premium cannot be allocated evenly over the life of the bond. Consequently, if a loan stock is redeemable on a defined event taking place, it will not be a deep discount bond unless it is known *when* that event will occur.

Where an investor holds a deep gain security, he may be charged tax under Schedule D Case III on a gain arising from a disposal of the security. Indexation relief is not available in computing this gain.

Qualifying convertible securities are not within the deep gain provisions. These are certain securities issued after 8 June 1989 which are convertible into the ordinary share capital of the issuing company. The following conditions need to be satisfied:

(1)   The security must be quoted on a recognised Stock Exchange.
(2)   The yield to redemption must not exceed a reasonable commercial return. The yield to redemption is measured over the period which ends on the day that the security falls for redemption.
(3)   The security must not be a deep discount security.

5.8   Sale of certificates of deposit
(TA 1988, s 56)

A certificate of deposit is a document which entitles the holder to receive the amount held on deposit. An owner of such a deposit can assign the deposit to someone else and where this is done for valuable consideration the profit is taxable under Schedule D Case VI.

At one time it was possible to avoid having taxable income by assigning ownership of a deposit without there being a certificate of deposit. However, profits on such transactions are now also caught as income which is taxable under Schedule D Case VI.

5.9   Gains from roll-up funds and other offshore funds
(TA 1988, ss 757–763)

A Case VI charge may arise on gains from disposals of certain offshore funds. The type of funds concerned are generally collective investment schemes similar to unit trusts. In many cases the fund earns bank interest which is accumulated within the fund rather than distributed as dividend. When the shareholder disposes of his investment he receives the benefit of this accumulated interest in the price that he obtains for his shares.

5.9.1   No charge on distributor funds
(TA 1988, s 760 and Sched 27)

Gains from distributor funds are generally exempt from the charge under s 757. Offshore funds qualify for distributor status where at least 85 per cent of investment income received by the fund is distributed as dividend. In the case of commodity funds, the 85 per cent distribution requirement is reduced to 42.5 per cent.

Where a fund does not qualify as a distributor fund, a Case VI charge is charged on a disposal. This includes certain disposals which are not taken into account for capital gains tax purposes such as a share exchange on a takeover of a fund. It also includes a deemed disposal on the death of the shareholder.

The charge arises on the gain as it would be computed for capital gains tax purposes, but with no allowance for indexation.

5.9.2 Example—Tax on offshore funds

A has held shares in an offshore fund since June 1990. The shares cost £14,000 and are worth £17,000 when sold in August 1992.

If the offshore fund does not have distributor status, the gain of £3,000 is Case VI income for 1992–93.

If the offshore fund had distributor status the gain would have been charged to capital gains tax rather than as income. The amount charged would have been less than £3,000 because of indexation allowance and the gain may have been covered by A's annual exemption for capital gains tax purposes (see 13.1.1).

5.9.3 Equalisation arrangements
(TA 1988, s 758)

Where an overseas fund has distributor status, and there are equalisation arrangements, any sum paid to a shareholder on the sale of his shares or units and which is treated as equalisation is income for the purposes of Schedule D Case VI. There is no income tax charge on the balance of the disposal proceeds.

5.9.4 Gains realised by foreign domiciliaries
(TA 1988, s 762)

A gain from a disposal of an offshore fund by a person of foreign domicile is taxed under Schedule D Case V rather than under Case VI, and the remittance basis applies (see 22.9).

5.10 Foreign interest and dividends

Debenture and Government bond interest and dividends paid by overseas companies will be taxed under Case IV or Case V only if they fall outside the paying agent procedures described in Chapter 7. Interest on overseas bank deposits and private loans will always be taxable under Case V.

If a UK resident lends money to an overseas resident, the interest arising may count either as United Kingdom or foreign income depending, largely, on the exact documentation used. However, as the rules for assessing UK interest under Case III of Schedule D are the same as those for assessing foreign interest under Case V, this is a technical point of no practical importance to the private investor.

Bank deposit interest counts as income of the year in which it is credited to the account (so that interest credited in, say, September 1993 counts as income of the year 1993–94 and will, unless the commencement or cessation provisions apply, be assessed for 1994–95).

A point to watch with all foreign investments is that income tax is charged on the interest credited or dividends received, without reference to any exchange gain or loss on the money deposited or invested.

5.10.1 Example—Foreign currency deposit account

In June 1992, F deposited £10,000 with a foreign bank. At the then exchange rate of £1 = 20 units of foreign currency, that sum was credited as 200,000 units. In June 1993, when the exchange rate was £1 = 25 units, interest of 30,000 units was credited to the account. In June 1994, F closed the account, receiving back his original capital, the interest credited in June 1993 and a further 20,000 foreign currency units as interest to close. However, by then the exchange rate was £1 = 30 units, so the sterling equivalent of the 250,000 units was only £8,333.

In commercial terms, F has suffered a loss of £1,667, but for tax purposes he received interest of £1,200 in June 1993 (30,000 units at £1 = 25) and £667 in June 1994 (20,000 units at £1 = 30) and income tax must be paid on that interest.

He has however also made a capital loss of £3,534, calculated as follows:

Proceeds of 250,000 units		£ 8,333
200,000 units cost (June 1992)	£10,000	
30,000 units cost (June 1993)	£ 1,200	
20,000 units cost (June 1994)	£ 667	
		£11,867
Capital loss		(£ 3,534)

Unfortunately, that capital loss may only be used by set-off against capital gains on the disposal of other assets. If F has no such gains, he cannot utilise the loss and so has paid tax on a profit of £1,867 when he has in fact made a loss of £1,667.

5.11 Foreign real estate income

It is not unusual for a UK resident to have bought—or inherited—a villa or flat abroad. It is less usual to own commercial premises, but the tax rules are the same. And the same rules also apply to properties bought under 'timeshare' arrangements.

The basic rule is that any rent paid by tenants is assessable to UK income tax. However, in calculating the assessable rent, the landlord may deduct expenses paid, such as repairs, redecoration, insurance, maid service, gardening, management fees and advertising. If the landlord sometimes uses the property himself, then an apportionment of these expenses must be made, in the same way as for a UK property (see 4.2).

However, there are four important differences between the tax treatment of rent from real property in the United Kingdom and rent from property abroad:

(1) The 'rent-a-room' scheme (see 4.8) applies only to properties in the United Kingdom. Therefore this exemption cannot be claimed against rents from an overseas property.

(2) Similarly, the special rules allowing the provision of furnished holiday accommodation to be treated as a trade (see 4.9) apply only where the relevant property is situated in the United Kingdom.

(3) Most significantly for the average landlord, although management expenses etc may be deducted in calculating the assessable rent, interest paid on any loan taken out to buy the property may not. This is so whether the loan is taken out in the United Kingdom or the country in which the property is situated. Therefore a property which in commercial terms is showing a loss (because interest paid exceeds net rental income) may still produce a substantial taxable profit.

(4) If the rental income statement for an overseas property shows a deficit for a year (that is to say, if expenses *excluding interest paid* exceed rent received), that deficit may be carried forward and deducted from the rent received in respect of the same property in the next year (and the deduction may be rolled forward indefinitely until there is rental income against which it can be set)—see extra-statutory concession B25. However, no other form of loss relief is available. In particular, the deficit may not be set against rents received from other properties, whether in the United Kingdom or abroad.

Rents from abroad are assessable under the usual Case V rules (and not on the current-year basis applicable to rents from UK properties).

Strictly speaking, rental income statements should be drawn up to 5 April annually but, in practice, the Inland Revenue will normally accept statements drawn up to any convenient date. For example, the rental statement for the calendar year 1993 will be taken as showing the income of the 1993–94 tax year, assessable (unless the commencement or cessation provisions apply) for 1994–95.

An added complication is that income may be received, and expenses may be incurred, in either UK or local currency. In practice, the Revenue will accept any reasonable basis of currency conversion. For example, if the rents are collected by a local agent, who disburses local expenses and remits a net sum to the landlord, that net amount may be converted at the spot rate for the day it was remitted. However, the Revenue will expect the same basis of conversion to be retained from one year to the next.

5.12   Alimony and maintenance payments
(TA 1988, s 347A(4))

A UK resident may receive maintenance or alimony payments from a spouse, former spouse or parent resident abroad. The tax treatment depends on whether that maintenance or alimony is paid under a United Kingdom or a foreign Court Order (or under a United Kingdom or foreign agreement). Payments under United Kingdom orders and agreements are taxed under Case III of Schedule D (as explained in 8.2.2). Payments under foreign orders and agreements are taxed under Case V of Schedule D. The significance of the distinction is that alimony and maintenance charged under Case III is always taxed on a current-year basis, whereas the usual preceding-year basis generally applies to alimony and maintenance charged under Case V.

However, this is subject to the overriding rule that payments under both United Kingdom and foreign Court Orders and agreements are not taxable unless the relevant order or agreement counts as an 'existing obligation'. Broadly, an existing obligation is one that was created by an order or agreement made before 15 March 1988 either in the United Kingdom or abroad (for further detail see 8.2).

If the order or agreement counts as an existing obligation, the first £1,720 received each year by a spouse or former spouse is exempt from tax, but the balance is taxable and the whole amount received by a child is taxable.

If the order or agreement does not constitute an existing obligation, payments under it are ignored for tax purposes and so do not constitute taxable income.

Whether an agreement is a United Kingdom or a foreign agreement is often a difficult legal question, on which expert advice may be needed. Furthermore, the tax position of payments to children under agreements can be very complex: for example, by a legal quirk, payments made by a parent resident abroad to a child resident in the United Kingdom may be taxed as if it was income received by that parent in the United Kingdom.

5.13 Investment in overseas partnerships
(TA 1988, s 391)

A UK resident may be a sleeping partner in a business carried on abroad. For example, a man might provide the finance for his son to set up in business abroad, in return for a share of the profits. He will then be a sleeping partner in the son's business. In some situations it may be difficult to tell whether the father has become a sleeping partner in the son's business or whether he has made a loan at interest to the son. If the father is entitled to a stated proportion of profits (say one-quarter), then he will certainly be a sleeping partner. However, if he is entitled to a fixed annual sum, he may be a sleeping partner or he may simply have made a loan. In practice, this will not be important, as both interest and a sleeping partner's profit share are taxed according to the usual Case IV/Case V rules.

The important question is whether the UK resident is a sleeping or an active partner. If he is an active partner the partnership business is likely to be carried on at least partly within the United Kingdom and complex questions arise, outside the scope of this book.

If the sleeping partner is entitled to a fixed sum, at annual or other intervals, and that sum is stated in a foreign currency, then each instalment must, for tax purposes, be converted into sterling at the spot rate for the date it falls due. If he is entitled to a stated proportion of profits, and the business accounts are prepared in a foreign currency, then the appropriate profit figure must be converted into sterling at the spot rate for the last day of the accounting period. If the sleeping partner is obliged to bear a share of a trading loss, that loss may be relieved against overseas trading and pension income, but not against overseas investment income or any UK income. In most cases therefore it will be relieved by deducting the amount of the loss from the partnership profit share assessable for a later year.

5.14 Case IV and Case V assessments
(TA 1988, ss 65–68)

As a general rule, income from abroad taxable under Case IV or Case V of Schedule D is assessed on the same 'preceding year' basis as UK income assessable under Case III (see 5.1.2) ie the 1994–95 assessment will normally be based on the income of 1993–94. The exception to this is where the individual acquires the source of Case IV or Case V income after 5 April 1994. The Finance Act 1994 provides that the assessable income should be computed according to the actual income arising in the tax year.

The same special rules apply when a new source of income is acquired or an existing source ceases:

New source of income

First year: assessment based on the income arising in the year of assessment itself ('current year basis').

Second year: current year basis *unless* the income first arose on 6 April in the first year of assessment, in which case the assessment for the second year is based on the income arising in the first year.

Third year (and subsequent years): assessment based on the income arising in the immediately preceding year.

Nevertheless, for the first year for which the preceding year basis would otherwise apply (usually the third year, but exceptionally the second) the taxpayer may elect to be taxed on a current year basis.

Ceasing to have a source of income

Penultimate year: assessment based on the income of that year or the immediately preceding year, whichever gives the *higher* figure.

Final year: assessment based on the income of the year of assessment itself.

5.14.1   Example—Assessments under Case IV or Case V of Schedule D

B opened a Channel Islands bank account in May 1988. Interest is credited on 31 December annually, as follows:

31 December 1988	£200
31 December 1989	£300
31 December 1990	£100
31 December 1991	£350
31 December 1992	£400
31 December 1993	£150

The account is closed on 31 December 1993.
The UK tax assessments will be:

1988–89	(First year[1]—current year basis)	£200
1989–90	(Second year—current year basis)	£300
1990–91	(Third year—preceding year basis would normally apply, but it will pay B to elect for the current year basis)	£100
1991–92	(Preceding year basis)	£100
1992–93	(Original assessment on preceding year basis was £350 but will be increased to current year figure)	£400

1993–94 (Final year–current year basis)   £150

[1] Although the account was opened in the 1987-88 tax year, the first year for assessment purposes is the first year in which interest is credited.

5.14.2   Income from the Republic of Ireland
(TA 1988, s 68)

Investment income arising in the Republic of Ireland is *always* taxed on a current year basis.

5.14.3   New residents

Where an individual comes to the United Kingdom, he may well retain overseas investments. Income from such investments is not chargeable to UK tax until he becomes UK resident, but the fact that the income then falls within the charge to UK tax for the first time does not make it a new source of income. Therefore the 'new source' rules set out in 5.14 do not apply and the new resident is immediately assessable on the preceding year basis. However, if the individual becomes resident during the tax year, only a proportion of the preceding year's income will be taxed.

5.14.4   Example—New residents

B came to the United Kingdom on 6 August 1993 and is deemed to be resident from that day. He retains an overseas bank account, to which interest of £1,200 was credited during 1992–93. As he is only resident in the United Kingdom for 8/12ths of 1993–94, his 1993–94 assessment will be based on 8/12ths of the interest credited in 1992–93—and so will be £800.

5.14.5   Those leaving the United Kingdom

The same principle also works in reverse. If an individual ceases to be UK resident, he is no longer liable to UK tax on overseas investment income, but the fact that his departure takes such income outside the UK tax net does not mean that the source itself has ceased. Therefore there can be no adjustment to the assessment for the penultimate year of UK residence and the assessment for the final year will be based on the appropriate proportion of the preceding year's assessment.

5.14.6   Example—Leaving the United Kingdom

C left the United Kingdom on 5 August 1994 and is deemed to be non-resident from that day. His 1994–95 assessment will be based on 4/12ths of his overseas investment income for 1993–94. By concession, the assessment will be reduced to the total overseas income arising in the period 6 April to 5 August, if that is a lower figure. (The taxpayer cannot choose to have some overseas investments dealt with on the 'income arising' and others on the 'proportion of preceding year' basis: he must choose one basis for all his investments.)

5.15   Double tax relief
(TA 1988, s 790)

The basic principles of double tax relief are explained in 2.9.3. Simply put, the foreign tax paid can be deducted from the UK tax charged on the same income.

5.15.1   Examples—Double tax relief

(1)   D, a basic rate taxpayer, receives an interest payment of £1,000 from abroad, on which the foreign tax is £100. The UK tax position is:

Gross interest	£1,000
Foreign tax deducted or paid	£ 100
Net receipt	£ 900
UK tax at 25 per cent of £1,000	£ 250
Less foreign tax paid	£ 100
UK tax to be paid	£ 150
After-tax income	£ 750

However, as was explained in 5.14 above, assessments under Case IV or Case V of Schedule D are usually made on the 'preceding year' basis—that is to say, the income received in 1993–94 will usually be assessed for 1994–95.

(2)   Suppose D received £1,000 interest in 1993–94, on which foreign tax of £100 was paid, and £1,200 in 1994–95, on which (following a change in the foreign country's laws) foreign tax of £180 was paid. On the 'preceding year' basis, the £1,000 received in 1993–94 will be assessed for 1994–95 and the basic rule is that foreign tax paid is linked to the receipt on which it was charged and is to be deducted from the UK tax charged on that same receipt. Therefore the foreign tax paid in 1993–94 is allowed against the UK tax charged on the 1994–95 assessment. Similarly, the £180 paid in 1994–95 will be allowed against the 1995–96 UK assessment.

5.15.2   New sources of income
(TA 1988, s 804)

Under the Case IV and Case V rules, when a new source of overseas income is acquired, the income of one year will be assessed twice.

5.15.3 Example—New source of income

In 1990–91, E inherited a flat in Spain. The position to date is:

1990–91	Net rents £5,000	Foreign tax £500
1991–92	Net rents £10,000	Foreign tax £1,000
1992–93	Net rents £12,000	Foreign tax £1,200

The Case V assessments will be:

1990–91	(Current year)	£5,000
1991–92	(Current year)	£10,000
1992–93	(Previous year)	£10,000
1993–94	(Previous year)	£12,000

Thus the £10,000 received in 1991–92 is assessed both for 1991–92 and 1992–93. However, equity is maintained by allowing the £1,000 foreign tax paid in 1991–92 to be deducted *both* against the 1991–92 *and* the 1992–93 assessments.

Conversely, when an overseas source ceases, a year will drop out of assessment and the foreign tax paid on that year's income will simply be lost. Moreover, if the foreign tax lost is less than the foreign tax allowed twice under the commencement provisions, the Inland Revenue will raise an assessment to collect the difference. However, there is no corresponding relief for the taxpayer if the foreign tax lost exceeds the tax allowed twice.

5.15.4 An important practical point

Relief for overseas tax will not be given unless the individual can prove that he has indeed paid the tax. It is not sufficient simply to demonstrate that tax is *payable* under foreign law: the claimant must be able to show that he has indeed *paid* that tax by producing an official receipt or tax deduction certificate.

5.16 Pensions taxable under Schedule D Case V
(TA 1988, s 58)

Certain pensions are charged to tax under Schedule D Case V rather than Schedule E.

(1) Pensions paid by a person outside the United Kingdom.
(2) Pensions paid on behalf of a person outside the United Kingdom.
(3) Voluntary pensions paid by a person outside the United Kingdom.

Pensions which are charged to tax under Schedule D Case V are assessed on the following basis:

(1)   Pensioner resident, ordinarily resident and domiciled in the United Kingdom—90 per cent of the pension is charged to tax.

(2)   Pensioner resident but not ordinarily resident in the United Kingdom—the pension is assessed on the remittance basis by reference to sums brought into the United Kingdom.

(3)   Pensioner resident and ordinarily resident in the United Kingdom but not domiciled in the United Kingdom—the pension is assessed on the remittance basis.

Pensions assessed under Schedule D Case V are taxed on the preceding year basis. Where an increase in pension is awarded in arrears, an individual may claim that the increase be related to the tax years for which the entitlement arose, rather than the year of receipt—see extra-statutory concession A55.

Nazi compensation pensions
(TA 1988, s 330)

Annuities and premiums paid under German or Austrian law to victims of Nazi persecution are exempt from income tax. These are pensions paid because of serious damage to the individual's health and are also exempt from tax in Germany and Austria.

5.17   Sundry income which may be assessed under Case VI
(TA 1988, s 15)

Tax may be charged under Schedule D Case VI in respect of any annual profits or gains which do not fall under any other case of Schedule D and which are not charged by virtue of any other schedule.

Post-cessation receipts (see 2.7) enterprise allowances (see 2.4.2) and income from furnished lettings (see 4.7) are charged under Case VI. In addition, Schedule D Case VI applies to gains from roll-up funds, profits under the accrued income scheme and gains on foreign life policies. Furthermore, where tax is charged under various anti-avoidance provisions (see Chapter 20) the charge is normally made under Case VI.

In addition, profits from certain 'one off' or isolated business activities in the nature of a trade have been charged under Case VI. Thus, the following have been held by the Courts to be Case VI income:

(1)   commission for guaranteeing overdrafts;

(2)   underwriting commission on share issues;

(3)   insurance commission;
(4)   receipts for the use of copyright material;
(5)   payments made to the wife of a train robber for their life story;
(6)   profits realised by an 'Angel', ie a person who sponsored a play and was entitled to a share of the profits.

Case VI income may be earned income or investment income. Where it is earned income, the tax is payable in two instalments in the same way as income which is chargeable under Schedule D Case I or II. Tax on Case VI investment income is normally due for payment on 1 January in the year of assessment.

5.17.1   Schedule D Case VI losses
(TA 1988, s 392)

Schedule D Case VI losses may be set against any profits assessable under Case VI, whether or not the profits arise from the same activity. However, they may not be set against income which is taxed under any other schedule.

Where an individual has suffered losses from an isolated transaction in the past, it may be sensible to arrange matters so that income arises which is taxable under Schedule D Case VI. For example an investment in an offshore roll-up fund (see 5.9) could be made with a view to producing a predictable level of Case VI profits which will be tax free because of the relief for Case VI losses.

5.18   Tax planning in relation to investment income

There are several ways of saving tax which are open to you if you are married and which are well worth considering, particularly in relation to income which is received without deduction of tax. It may also be possible to utilise your children's tax allowances.

5.18.1   Joint deposit accounts

The basic principle to bear in mind is that where a husband and wife receive interest on an joint bank deposit account, the normal rule is that 50 per cent of the interest is treated as the husband's income and 50 per cent as the wife's income. In cases where the husband has contributed most of the capital and he is subject to a higher rate of tax than his wife, the 50/50 treatment may be beneficial.

5.18.2 Example—Joint deposit accounts

A has put £240,000 into a bank deposit account in the joint names of A and B, his wife. Assume interest arises at 10 per cent per annum. £12,000 interest will be treated as B's income, and this will save significant amounts of tax if she has no other income.

Instead of A being charged 40 per cent tax on £24,000 (ie a total of £9,600), he will pay tax of £4,800. B will be charged tax calculated as follows:

	£
Taxable income	12,000.00
Less personal allowance (see chapter 6)	3,445.00
	8,555.00
20 per cent on £3,000	600.00
25 per cent on £5,555	1,388.75
	1,988.75

The total tax saving is therefore over £2,800.

5.18.3 Situations where the 50/50 treatment is not beneficial

There can be situations where the 50/50 treatment is not beneficial. In cases where the underlying capital is not owned equally, a married couple may jointly declare that the resulting interest should be taxed in the same way as the capital is owned. Thus, if the facts in the above example had been such that 70 per cent of the capital belonged to the wife, it could be tax-efficient for such a notice to be given. The broad effect would be that the amount which would be treated as her income, and which would therefore bear tax at a maximum of 25 per cent rather than her husband's 40 per cent rate, would be increased from £12,000 to £16,800. This could produce a further tax saving of £720.

Such a declaration may be made only where the underlying capital is *not* owned jointly. This may necessitate special instructions to the bank or building society concerned and a declaration of trust since the normal basis on which banks etc, operate is that the capital is owned jointly. Furthermore, the effect of making the declaration is that the income is treated as arising to each spouse in proportion to their ownership of the underlying capital and it is not possible for the married couple to claim that the income should be divided on any other basis, even though it might suit them from a tax point of view. You should also bear in mind that the declaration cannot be made retrospectively and thus it will only govern the tax treatment of income received after the declaration has been made.

5.18.4 Fine tuning the position

Some individuals may not wish to invest substantial sums in a joint deposit account. Other people may wish to transfer income into their spouse's name and the 50/50 treatment may only partially achieve that objective. One alternative is for an investment to be made in an offshore 'roll-up' fund. Many merchant banks and other financial institutions operate roll-up funds which operate like unit trusts except that the fund managers simply invest in bank deposits rather than equity investments. The normal practice is for the fund managers to accumulate all interest, rather than pay it out as dividends (hence the term 'roll-up' fund). The tax treatment of such funds allows considerable scope for tax planning. The profit realised when the investment is disposed of is treated as income rather than capital gain. Also, the investor may control the point at which taxable income arises since no taxable income will arise until a disposal takes place.

A transfer of such investments to a spouse does *not* count as a disposal. Consequently, it is possible for a husband to invest in a roll-up fund and, at a time when it suits him, transfer all or part of the investment to his wife for her to make the profit on sale.

5.18.5 Example—Taxation of roll-up fund

B has invested £100,000 in a roll-up fund. The investment is now worth £120,000. If B were to realise the investment he would be liable for income tax of £8,000 (40 per cent on his £20,000 profit). If he instead gives (or sells) the investment to his wife, he will not be taxed and the £20,000 profit will count as her income. Her tax might be calculated as follows:-

	£
Taxable income	20,000.00
less personal allowance	3,445.00
	16,555.00
Tax at 20 per cent on £3,000	600.00
Tax at 25 per cent on £13,555	3,388.75
	3,988.75

This is a tax saving of over £4,000

5.18.6 A word of caution

The Revenue's view is that a straightforward transfer of assets is a perfectly acceptable and sensible way of rearranging your affairs in view of independent taxation. However, the clear message is that the transfer must be intended to be a permanent one, ie it must be an outright gift with no strings attached. If there is any suggestion of impermanence, the original 'gift' could be regarded as a settlement with the income being treated as the donor's income for tax purposes. It may be advisable to consult an accountant on the implications of large transfers.

5.18.7   Children's tax reliefs

Where a person has surplus capital, it may well make sense to invest some of the surplus capital so as to utilise minor children's tax allowances.

Bare trusts

There is a gap in the legislation so that if a parent makes an outright gift of capital to a minor child, with the capital being held by a bare trustee, and the trustee does not pay out the income or pay it into a bank account in the child's own name, the income is not caught by the anti-avoidance legislation (see 20.5.3) and is treated as the child's own income for all income tax purposes. The same treatment applies where a parent creates a settlement under which a minor child has life interest or other interest in possession. Provided that the resulting income is not paid out to the child, or paid into a bank account in the child's own name, the income is not assessed on the parent.

Roll-up funds

Another way of achieving a tax saving may be for a parent to give capital to a minor child, with the money being invested in a roll-up fund or some other investment which does not produce taxable income. If the roll-up fund is cashed in shortly after the child's 18th birthday, the income will count as the child's income and not the parent's income. This may be a good strategy where a child is unlikely to have much income in his own right, perhaps because he will be in full time education during the year in which he attains age 18.

6 Taxation of net income

In this chapter, we examine the treatment of investment income which has borne tax at source.

When income tax was first introduced in 1799, the Government quickly found that many people were reluctant to declare their true incomes and even less willing to pay their assessed liabilities. Three years later, therefore, the principle of 'deduction at source' was established: namely that (wherever possible) a person paying money that was to count as income in the recipient's hands should deduct from it a sum equal to basic rate tax on that income. In the usual case, that sum was to be passed over to the Inland Revenue, but where the payment was deductible in computing the payer's taxable income, he was allowed to keep it for himself. This system was found to be a great success and so still exists today—though with a number of added complications.

This chapter deals with the following matters.

(1) Types of income from which tax is deducted.
(2) Interest received net of tax.
(3) Dividends from UK companies.
(4) Sundry receipts treated in the same way as dividends.
(5) Foreign interest and dividends received via UK paying agents.
(6) Other income received net of tax.
(7) Tax planning.

6.1 Types of income from which tax is deducted

The system of deduction is one under which tax is simply deducted at the basic rate. It is, of course, quite separate from the PAYE scheme, which aims to match deductions to the individual employee's personal circumstances.

The most common types of income from which tax is deducted at basic rate are:

- Bank and building society interest
- Debenture interest paid by UK companies
- Interest paid on British Government and local authority bonds
- Dividends paid by UK companies
- Foreign dividends and bond interest received via UK paying agents
- Annuities
- Payments under deeds of covenant
- Payments from family trusts and settlements
- Payments from the estates of deceased persons
- Sundry receipts treated as distributions

6.2   Interest received net of tax
(TA 1988, ss 480A–482)

Interest payments made by UK banks and building societies are normally subject to basic tax deduction at source (for exceptions see 5.1.1).

Interest paid on gilts will also be subject to tax except in the case of $3^1/_2\%$ War Loan and stocks held on the NSB register. Interest paid on local authority loan stocks and company loan stocks and debentures is subject to deduction of tax, as indeed is all interest paid by UK companies to persons other than group companies.

6.3   Dividends from UK companies

6.3.1   Dividends are taxable for the year in which they fall due for payment
(TA 1988, s 834(3))

The dividends which need to be reported on a tax return, and which are income for a tax year, are the dividends which were *due* for payment in the year. If you have shares in a company which declared a dividend which was payable on 5 April 1994, you will have to report the dividend as 1993–94 income. This is not affected by the fact that you may not have received the dividend cheque until early in the next tax year.

The period for which the dividend is paid is not relevant. A final dividend for a company's year which ended on 31 December 1992 would be income for 1993–94 if it was paid in (for example) June 1993.

A dividend from a UK company carries a tax credit (see 6.3.3).

6.3.2   Dividends paid by unit trusts

Dividends from unit trusts are treated in exactly the same way as dividends from companies except in regard to 'equalisation'. This is an amount paid to holders of units who have acquired them since the last dividend was paid. The equalisation payment is not taxable as income but is instead treated as a return of capital.

6.3.3   Tax credits
(TA 1988, 231; FA 1993, s 78)

When a UK company pays a dividend, it has to account for Advance Corporation Tax (see 24.5.3). The corollary of this is that the recipient is entitled to a tax credit.

For 1992–93 and earlier years this was equal to the basic rate of tax so that a dividend of £75 was treated as 'gross' income of £100 from which tax at 25 per cent has been withheld

From 1993–94 onwards the tax credit is restricted to 20 per cent. A dividend of £75 is therefore treated as gross income of £93.75.

Where the individual is liable for tax at 40 per cent, he has to pay additional tax at 20 per cent on his dividend income (ie 40 per cent less the 20 per cent tax credit). However, where an individual is not subject to higher rate tax, the tax credit is deemed to satisfy any liability to the basic rate.

6.3.4   Example—Tax treatment of a person who receives dividend income in 1993–94

A receives dividend income of £75,000 in 1993–94. The tax credits total £18,750 and the 'gross income' is therefore £93,750.

If A's other taxable income (after allowances and reliefs) is £20,000 he will be liable to tax:

- at 20 per cent on the first £2,500,
- at 25 per cent on the next £17,500,
- at 20 per cent on £3,700 (ie the balance of the basic rate band),
- at 40 per cent on £90,050.

He will therefore be liable for higher rate tax of £18,010 (ie 20 per cent of £90,050).

6.3.5   Stock dividends
(TA 1988, s 249)

A company may make a 'scrip' or bonus issue so that shareholders receive new shares in proportion to their existing shareholdings. This is not taxable income since in reality all that has happened is that the company has sub-divided its share capital by issuing new shares.

In contrast to this, a company may offer shareholders the choice between a cash dividend or additional shares to a similar value. This is called a 'stock dividend' and is taxable income. Sometimes, stock dividends are referred to as 'enhanced scrip dividends'.

The tax treatment is as set out below—enhanced scrip dividends are merely a special type of stock dividend where the company offers a premium to shareholders who take stock rather than cash

6.3.6   How stock dividends are assessed
(Statement of Practice A8)

A shareholder who accepts extra shares in lieu of a cash dividend is normally treated as if he had received a dividend equal to the cash that he could have taken. Tax is deemed to have been paid at the basic rate.

A slightly different treatment applies where the value of the shares taken as the stock dividend differs from the cash dividend by 15 per cent or more. In such a case, the shareholder is deemed to have received a dividend equal to the value of the shares at the date of issue.

The shareholder may therefore be required to pay higher rate tax on the 'grossed up' value of the dividend or the shares.

6.3.7   Example—Taxation of dividends

In 1993–94, A was entitled to a dividend of £2,100 or extra shares in X Plc. He took the shares. If the shares were worth £1,900, he will nevertheless be charged higher rate tax on £2,100 plus an amount equal to the tax credit ie the amount charged to higher rate tax for 1993–94 is £2,625 (£2,100 grossed up for the 20 per cent tax credit).

If the shares were worth £2,560 when they were issued, he would be charged higher rate tax on £2,560 'grossed up', ie £3,200.

6.3.8 No basic rate repayment
(TA 1988, s 249(4))

Although the stock dividend is treated as if it had borne 20 per cent tax at source, no repayment can be made to the shareholder if he was not liable for tax.

6.3.9 Consequences for capital gains tax of taking a stock dividend

In example 6.3.7, the shareholder's acquisition value for capital gains tax purposes of the shares that he acquires through the stock dividend is the amount on which he is assessed for higher rate purposes less basic rate tax.

6.3.10 Dividends which form part of a de-merger
(TA 1988, s 213)

A dividend may take the form of an issue of shares formerly held by the company in a subsidiary. Where the necessary Inland Revenue clearances have been obtained, such a dividend is treated as capital and not as taxable income. The documentation issued by the company will normally state that clearance has been obtained from the Revenue and that the de-merger is an exempt distribution.

6.3.11 Other dividend income

See 6.4 on sundry receipts from UK companies which are treated as distributions. See also 6.5.3 on dividends paid by foreign companies.

6.4 Sundry receipts treated in the same way as dividends

6.4.1 Deemed dividends
(TA 1988, s 209)

There are various transactions which can count as a distribution, particularly where a person holds shares in a close company (see 24.10). From the point of view of the recipient, a distribution is for all practical purposes the same as a dividend.

6.4.2   Interest at more than a commercial rate
(TA 1988, s 209)

Interest which is paid to a shareholder may constitute a distribution in so far as it exceeds a normal commercial rate.

6.4.3   Issue of redeemable shares
(TA 1988, 209(2)(c))

An issue to shareholders of redeemable preference shares (or other redeemable shares) counts as a distribution. The value of the redeemable shares at the date that they are issued is treated as if it were a dividend paid in cash at that time. This rule does not apply where the redeemable shares are issued for new consideration.

6.4.4   Bonus issue following repayment of share capital
(TA 1988, s 210)

Where a company has repaid share capital in the past, a subsequent bonus issue is treated as a dividend paid to the shareholders who receive the bonus shares. The shareholders who receive the bonus shares may not be the same people whose shares were previously bought back by the company, but this does not make any difference to the way in which the current shareholders are taxed on receipt of a bonus issue of shares in these circumstances.

6.4.5   Benefits in kind provided to shareholders
(TA 1988, s 418)

Where shareholders in a close company (see 24.10) are provided with benefits in kind, they may be assessed under Schedule E. However, if they are not employed by the company, it will not be possible for the Revenue to assess benefits in kind under Schedule E. In these circumstances, the company may be deemed to have made a distribution equal to the value of the benefits in kind concerned.

6.4.6   Assets transferred by a close company or to a close company
(TA 1988, s 209(4))

A deemed distribution may arise where assets are transferred from the members of a company to the company at a price which exceeds their market value, or company assets are transferred to shareholders at a price which is less than market value.

6.4.7   Purchase by a company of its own shares
(TA 1988, s 209)

The general rule is that where a company buys back its shares, the amount paid by the company is treated as a distribution in so far as it exceeds the original issue price of the shares.

The amount treated as a distribution is not affected by the value of the shares at the time when they were acquired by an individual. Consequently, where a person has acquired shares by inheritance, or bought them from an existing shareholder, his acquisition value may exceed the original issue price (ie the amount which was paid to the company in return for the shares being issued). In the event of a purchase of own shares by a company, it is the issue price which is important.

6.4.8   Example—Purchase by a company of its own shares

A acquires 1,000 shares in X Ltd for £10,000. The shares were originally issued at their par value of £1 per share. It subsequently transpires that A cannot get on with the directors of the company. If A's shares are bought back by the company at £9 per share A is deemed to have received a distribution of £8,000, even though he had actually made a capital loss.

6.4.9   Relief under TA 1988, s 219

In certain circumstances it may be possible for a company to purchase its own shares without the transaction being treated as giving rise to a distribution. Clearance needs to be obtained from the Inland Revenue that the purchase of own shares is for the benefit of the company's trade.

The conditions which must be satisfied are:

(1)   the company must be unquoted;
(2)   it must be a trading company or the holding company of a trading group;
(3)   the vendor must be resident and ordinarily resident in the UK;
(4)   the vendor must have owned the shares for at least five years;
(5)   the vendor's interest in the company must be 'substantially reduced';
(6)   the purchase must be undertaken in order to benefit the company's trade.

6.5 Foreign interest and dividends received via UK paying agents
(TA 1988, s 17, 44 and 123 & Sched 3; F(No 2)A 1992, Sched 11)

6.5.1 Foreign interest income

Interest on bonds issued by overseas Government or companies may be received via a 'paying agent'.

The paying or collecting agent receives from the overseas Government or company a remittance representing the interest due less the foreign tax payable on that interest. The rate at which foreign tax is deducted depends partly on the laws of the country concerned and partly on the terms of any Double Tax Treaty between the United Kingdom and that country. At worst, tax will be deducted at the full rate payable by residents of the overseas country. At best, no foreign tax at all will be deducted. More usually, however, tax will be deducted at a 'treaty' or 'withholding' rate of, typically, 10 per cent for interest and 15 per cent for dividends.

Before paying the interest over to the individual bondholders, the paying agent must deduct UK tax so that the total tax paid (foreign and United Kingdom) equals tax at the UK basic rate (currently 25 per cent).

6.5.2 Example—Tax deducted by paying agent

A has a holding of foreign Government bonds on which the interest, payable annually through a British bank, is 500 dinars, equivalent to £100 sterling. Foreign withholding tax is charged at ten per cent. The bank will send A a cheque for £75 (or will credit his account with that amount) and provide a voucher showing:

Gross income	£100
Less foreign withholding tax	£ 10
	£ 90
Less UK income tax	£ 15
Net payment	£ 75

The bank will, of course, pay the £15 UK income tax over to the Inland Revenue.

If A is a basic rate taxpayer, that is the end of the story: the deduction made by the paying agent clears his basic rate liability and gives him relief for overseas tax paid.

If he is a higher-rate taxpayer, he is in the same position as if he had received income on a British Government security: his total liability is £40 (40 per cent of £100) of which he has paid £25 by deduction. He must therefore pay a further £15, probably on his annual tax assessment.

However, if A is not a taxpayer at all, the Inland Revenue will repay only the £15 UK income tax deducted by the British bank—it will not repay the £10 foreign tax deducted by the foreign Government. In certain circumstances it may, theoretically, be possible to reclaim this money direct from the foreign authorities, but it is certain to be a difficult and time-consuming process, especially if correspondence in a foreign language is necessary. In almost all cases, it simply will not be worth the effort.

6.5.3 Foreign dividends

Until 5 April 1993, dividends paid by foreign companies and received via a UK paying agent were treated in an identical way to foreign interest (see 6.5.1–6.5.2 above).

From 6 April 1993, a UK paying agent deducts UK tax so as to bring the total of foreign tax and UK tax up to 20 per cent.

6.5.4 High overseas tax rate

In some instances, overseas tax may be deducted at a rate higher than the 20 per cent UK rate on dividends. In such a case, the UK paying agent will simply pass on whatever net payment is received from overseas.

6.5.5 Example—High overseas tax rate

B has a shareholding in a foreign company, on which a dividend equivalent to £100 is declared during 1993–94. However, the foreign authorities withhold tax at 35 per cent. The net remittance received by B will be £65.

If he is a basic rate taxpayer, no UK tax will be payable on the foreign dividend, because the UK tax is reduced to nil by relief for the £35 foreign tax paid. However, the excess foreign tax paid (£10 in this example) cannot be set against B's UK tax liability on other sources of income—it is simply lost.

If B is a higher rate taxpayer, his UK liability of £40 (40 per cent of £100) will be reduced to £5 by deducting the £35 foreign tax paid.

There are, therefore, two basic rules. First, the Inland Revenue will never refund tax paid to a foreign Government and second, foreign tax paid in respect of a particular source of income may only be set against UK tax charged on that same source.

6.5.6 Which year of assessment?
(TA 1988, s 835(6) & Sched 3 para 8; F(No 2)A 1992 Sched 11)

Until the end of September 1992, the rule was that interest and dividends within the 'paying or collecting agent' scheme were assessable as income of the tax year in which the funds became available in the United

Kingdom for credit to the individual bond or shareholders' accounts. An interest payment or dividend due, say, in March might not become available in the United Kingdom until the second or third week in April. Therefore a payment due, say, at the end of the 1991–92 tax year might not have become available for payment in the United Kingdom until the beginning of 1992–93. It was assessed as income of the later year.

The date funds became available in the United Kingdom was invariably shown on the paying or collecting agent's voucher and was usually described as the 'date of realisation'. This, then, was the operative date for tax purposes.

However, from 1 October 1992, a slightly different rule applies, namely that interest and dividends within the 'paying or collecting agent' scheme count, for tax purposes, as income of the year in which they are paid to the investor by the UK paying or collecting agent. Accordingly, the operative date will be the date the agent issues a cheque or authorises a credit transfer. This cannot be before, but may be a few days after, funds become available in the United Kingdom. Therefore it is still possible that a dividend or interest payment due, say, at the end of March 1993 will be assessable as income of the 1993–94 tax year. The payment date will of course be clearly shown on the paying or collecting agent's voucher, so no particular difficulty should arise.

6.5.7 Stock dividends and other peculiarities
(TA 1988, s 249)

As explained in 6.3, an investor who opts to take a stock dividend (that is to say, additional shares in lieu of a cash dividend) from a UK company is taxed as if he had received an equivalent amount in cash. This rule does not apply where a stock dividend is paid by a company not resident in the United Kingdom.

A higher-rate taxpayer offered the choice between a stock and a cash dividend would, therefore, usually be better off taking the stock dividend. However, this of course assumes that the additional shares offered are worth at least as much as the cash option and that they are readily saleable. As always, the 'tax-saving' tail must not be allowed to wag the 'sensible investment policy' dog. Moreover, in one Court case it was suggested that, if stock dividends are taken year after year, and the shares so obtained are sold to provide the shareholder with an income, then income tax may be charged on that income. However, the Inland Revenue is unlikely to take this point unless a substantial amount of money is at stake.

In a number of other cases, also, payments by an overseas company may escape tax where an equivalent payment by a UK company would be taxable as a dividend. Most often this will occur where a payment which under UK law would count as a distribution of profits counts, under the relevant foreign law, as a partial return of the shareholders' original investment. The correct position will usually be advised by the overseas company or the UK paying agent.

6.6 Other income received net of tax

6.6.1 Annuities
(TA 1988, ss 349 and 656–658)

Annuities which are paid by an insurance company are dealt with at 12.5. Where an annuity is payable by an individual or a private company, the payer must deduct tax.

6.6.2 Example—Annuity income received net of tax

A sells his business to B for a cash sum plus an annuity of £10,000 a year payable by B out of the profits of the business. Each year B will in fact pay A only £7,500 (£10,000 less tax at 25 per cent).

(1) A may set any available personal allowances against the annuity, so that if he is aged 67, is single, and has no other income, the position for 1993–94 will be:

Annuity (gross amount)	£10,000
Personal allowance (over-65 rate)	£ 4,200
Tax payable on	£ 5,800
£2,500 charged at 20%	£ 500
£3,300 charged at 25%	£ 825
Total tax due	£ 1,325
Tax paid by deduction	£ 2,500
Inland Revenue will repay	£ 1,175

(2) If A's other income is sufficient to utilise both his personal allowances and the lower rate band, there will of course be no repayment. If he is a higher-rate taxpayer, he will have to pay additional tax on the annuity, as follows:

Higher-rate tax on annuity (40% of £10,000)	£ 4,000
Less: Already paid by deduction	£ 2,500
Additional tax payable by assessment	£ 1,500

(3) The buyer, B, can obtain relief for the annuity paid to A, not as a trading expense but as a deduction in computing total taxable income.
   (a) If he is only a basic-rate taxpayer, he obtains the relief to which he is entitled by keeping for himself the £2,500 difference between the gross amount of the annuity and the £7,500 actually paid to A.
   (b) If he is a higher-rate taxpayer, additional relief is given by not

charging higher-rate tax on an amount equal to the gross annuity paid—a process usually referred to as 'extending the basic rate band'.

(4)   Suppose B's profits are £50,000, he has no other income and is entitled only to the basic personal allowance of £3,445. If he did not have to pay the annuity, his tax position would be:

Income	£50,000
Personal allowance	£ 3,445
Tax payable on	£46,555
£2,500 charged at 20%	£ 500
£21,200 charged at 25%	£ 5,300
£22,855 charged at 40%	£ 9,142
£46,555	£14,942

(5)   As he does have to pay the annuity, the basic rate band is extended by the gross amount of that annuity (£10,000), so the position becomes:

£2,500 charged at 20%	£ 500
£31,200 charged at 25%	£ 7,800
£12,855 charged at 40%	£ 5,142
£46,555	£13,442

This is a reduction of £1,500 and so overall the position is:

Gross annuity	£10,000
Net payment to A	£ 7,500
Basic rate tax relief	£ 2,500
Reduction in tax payable by assessment	£ 1,500
Total tax relief (40% of £10,000)	£ 4,000

6.6.3   Income from trusts

Income paid to a beneficiary of a trust will normally be taxed at source. For 1993–94, some income received by a life tenant or other beneficiary who has a fixed interest may carry a credit of only 20 per cent (see 18.4.4). Income payments to discretionary beneficiaries carry a credit for 35 per cent.

For 1992–93, tax was withheld at basic rate from all income unless the payment was made at the trustees' discretion, in which case tax was withheld at 35 per cent.

6.6.4   Estates of deceased persons
(TA 1988, ss 695–702)

When a man dies, it will take some time for his executors or personal representatives to identify all his assets, pay all his debts, settle any inheritance tax liability and work out the best way of dividing the estate between those entitled (for example, one beneficiary may want to take specific investments, another may prefer cash).

During this time, known as 'the administration period', it is quite likely that income will be received by the executors or personal representatives, both on the deceased's existing investments and, for example, as interest on a bank account into which the executors have paid money collected on behalf of the estate.

The executors or personal representatives must pay basic rate tax on all income received. Items such as share dividends and bond interest will, of course, be received net of tax, but assessments may be raised in respect of items such as rents received.

The executors or personal representatives will therefore have a pool of income on which basic rate tax has been paid. That pool must be divided between the beneficiaries in accordance with the terms of the deceased's Will, or of the laws of intestacy, if he left no Will.

6.6.5   Example—Tax treatment of estate income

The gross income from an estate is £200, on which the executors have paid tax of £50 (whether by deduction from interest etc received or by direct assessment). The deceased's son is, under the Will, entitled to half that income. He will receive a cheque for £75 plus a certificate, signed by the executors, confirming that tax of £25 has been paid to the Revenue. The son's income for tax purposes is £100, but he is treated as having already paid basic rate tax on that £100. If he has personal allowances or other reliefs available, he will be able to obtain (from the Revenue) a repayment of some or all of the £25 tax paid; if he is a higher-rate taxpayer, he will have to pay over to the Revenue the difference between basic and higher rate tax.

There are some complex rules for deciding the year for which a payment from an estate is to be taxed. *In the first instance*, if the beneficiary takes an absolute interest under the Will or intestacy (that is to say, is entitled to some part of the capital of the estate), a payment is treated as income of the year in which the underlying income arose. If the beneficiary has only a life interest, the payment is treated as income of the year in which the payment is made.

6.6.6   Example—Different treatments of beneficial interests

A left a life interest in half his estate to B, his wife, and everything else to C, his son. In January 1994, the executors receive rent of £2,000, on which they pay tax of £500. In June 1994 they send B and C cheques for £750 each.

B has a life interest—therefore the payment to her (grossed-up to the pre-tax figure of £1,000) will count as income of the year she received the cheque, namely 1994–95. However, as C has an absolute interest (he is entitled not only to the income from his half of the estate, but also to the capital) his £1,000 counts as income of the year it arose, namely 1993–94.

In practice, of course, the executors may be receiving income from a variety of different sources and making payments to those entitled either at regular intervals, as funds become available, or as the beneficiaries request. Those with life interests are, as already stated, taxable on a straightforward receipts basis. For those with absolute interests, the rule is that each payment is matched with the earliest hitherto unmatched item.

6.6.7   Example—Treatment of absolute interests

D has an absolute interest in half of E's estate. Counting the tax year in which E died as year one, the position has been:

	Estate income	D's share	Paid to D
Year one	£200	£100	Nil
Year two	£300	£150	£200
Year three	£400	£200	£100

Half of the £200 paid in year two will be treated as D's share of the income arising in year one and will be assessed for year one. The other half will be taken as part of the £150 arising in year two. £50 of the £100 paid in year three will be matched to the balance of the £150 arising in year two, so that the assessment for year two will become £150. The balance of £50 will be taxed as income of year three.

However, this is only half the story, because after administration of the estate is completed the figures are reworked so that:

(1)   A person entitled to a life interest is taxed on the basis of spreading his income from the estate evenly over the administration period. Therefore if the deceased died on 6 October 1993 and administration is completed on 5 April 1995, one-third of the income will be allocated to the 1993–94 tax year and two-thirds to 1994–95.

(2)   A person entitled to an absolute interest is taxed on his share of the income arising in each year of assessment (even if that income was not in fact paid to him until administration had been completed).

In practice, of course, if the beneficiary is subject to the same rate of tax for every year, it does not in fact matter if these adjustments are not made and, indeed, they very often are not made.

Moreover, in very straightforward cases—for example, where a man simply leaves his whole estate to his wife—the Revenue are usually agreeable to the 'payments from estates' rules being ignored altogether. All the income arising is then returned on the widow's or other beneficiary's tax return as if it were her own. If you take this course, however, it is essential that you tell the Inland Revenue what you have done. Preferably, you should obtain their prior agreement.

Finally, the executors of a Will are very often also appointed trustees of a family settlement established by that Will. It can then be a nice point to determine whether a particular payment has been made in the course of the administration of the estate or under the terms of the settlement. From a tax point of view, it may not matter, but if it does, you will need the advice of an experienced trust or probate lawyer.

6.7 Tax planning

The possibilities for saving tax which are described at 5.18 may be used to recover tax deducted at source from investment income in the same way as they can save tax on income received gross.

7 Personal allowances

This chapter looks in detail at the various personal allowances that may be claimed by individual taxpayers. The following topics are covered:

(1) What are personal allowances?
(2) Who may claim personal allowances?
(3) The basic personal allowance.
(4) Calculating 'total income'.
(5) Married couple's allowance.
(6) Pensioner couples.
(7) Widow's bereavement allowance.
(8) Additional personal allowance.
(9) Additional allowance for disabled wife.
(10) Blind persons.
(11) Withdrawn allowances and transitional reliefs.

7.1 What are personal allowances?
(TA 1988, ss 256–278)

Income tax is not charged on the whole of a person's income. In calculating the amount on which tax must be paid, an individual may deduct both relief for certain types of expenditure (for example, subscriptions to work-related professional bodies—see 3.3.2) and one or more 'personal allowances'. Entitlement to personal allowances depends on individual circumstances, as explained later in this chapter, but the following three examples illustrate the principles involved:

7.1.1 Examples—Principles of personal allowances

(1) A, a single man aged 35, earns an annual salary of £14,000, out of which he pays a qualifying professional subscription of £50. His tax bill for 1993–94 will be £2,501.25, calculated as follows:

Gross salary		£14,000
Professional subscription		£50
		£13,950
Basic personal allowance		£3,445
Tax payable on		£10,505

£2,500	charged at 20%	£500.00
£8,005	charged at 25%	£2,001.25
£10,505		£2,501.25

(2) B is a single mother, also earning £14,000 and paying a qualifying professional subscription of £50. Her tax bill for 1993–94 will be only £2,071.25, calculated as follows:

Gross salary		£14,000
Professional subscription		£50
		£13,950
Basic personal allowance	£3,445	
Additional personal allowance[1]	£1,720	
		£5,165
Tax payable on		£8,785
£2,500	charged at 20%	£500.00
£6,285	charged at 25%	£1,571.25
£8,785		£2,071.25

[1] See 7.8 below

(3) C, a widower, is aged 67 but is still in full-time employment. He also earns £14,000 a year and pays a qualifying professional subscription of £50. He is entitled to the higher personal allowance for the over-65s (see 7.3.2 below) and so his tax bill will be £2,312.50, calculated as follows:

Gross salary		£14,000
Professional subscription		£50
		£13,950
Higher personal allowance		£4,200
Tax payable on		£9,750
£2,500	charged at 20%	£500.00
£7,250	charged at 25%	£1,812.50
£9,750		£2,312.50

Consequently, it is possible for three people to earn exactly the same salary but, because of differing personal circumstances, to pay differing amounts of income tax.

7.2   Who may claim personal allowances?

(TA 1988, s 278 and British Nationality Act 1981, s 37)

Personal allowances may be claimed by anyone resident in the United Kingdom. There is no minimum age requirement so that, for example, a new-born baby is entitled to a personal allowance. Sometimes it is possible, through the use of trusts or settlements, to redirect part of a family's income to a child, so that it may (being covered by the child's personal allowance) be enjoyed tax-free (although the scope for transferring taxable income in this way has been whittled down by a succession of complex anti-avoidance provisions—see 20.5.3).

Personal allowances may also be claimed by British subjects and certain other categories of people not resident in the United Kingdom.

7.2.1   Time limit for claims

(TMA 1970, s 43)

A claim to any personal allowance must be made within six years of the end of the relevant year of assessment—ie a claim for the 1988–89 tax year may be made up to 5 April 1995. A claim is made on the day it is received by the Inspector, not the day it is posted.

Exceptionally, if you failed to claim a relief because you were misled by the Inland Revenue or any other Government Department, you may ask for the last twenty years to be re-opened.

Late claims should be avoided if possible, because they may cause difficulties. Although the Inland Revenue should in theory retain papers for at least the last six years, in practice the files for Schedule E taxpayers (those in employment, rather than in business on their own account) are often 'weeded out' after only two or three years. Therefore, unless you have yourself kept papers such as tax assessments and Forms P60 (employer's annual statement of pay and tax deducted), it may be impossible to determine how much tax was paid and how much is now repayable.

A final point is that the Revenue usually refuse to grant any relief (other than the basic personal allowance) until the claimant has submitted his tax returns for all relevant years. The Revenue argues that, until it has the returns, it cannot be sure that any relief claimed would not be cancelled out by the tax due on sources of income of which it is unaware.

7.3 The basic personal allowance
(TA 1988, s 257)

Every individual who is resident in the United Kingdom is entitled to the basic personal allowance. This is often called the 'single person's allowance'—a throwback to the days when there was also a 'married man's allowance'.

The basic personal allowance is £3,445. Although this is an allowance for a year, it is not scaled down if the individual is born, or dies, halfway through a year of assessment.

7.3.1 Example—Death during tax year

Suppose A (in example 7.1.1(1) above) died at the end of September 1993, by which time he had earned only half his annual salary. His tax bill for the 1993–94 year would be:

Salary	£7,000
Professional subscription paid	£50
	£6,950
Personal allowance	£3,445
Tax payable on	£3,505

£2,500	charged at 20%	£500.00
£1,005	charged at 25%	£251.25
£3,505		£751.25

Because the PAYE scheme assumes that personal allowances will be used in equal monthly (or weekly) instalments over the year, about £1,250 (half of £2,501.25) will have been deducted from A's salary while he was alive. On request, the Inland Revenue will therefore repay his executors the excess tax deducted (£1,250 less £751.25 = £498.75)

7.3.2 Higher allowances for the over-65s

Higher allowances are given to those who have attained the age of 65 *and who are of limited means*. The higher allowance is currently £4,200 for those between the ages of 65 and 74 and £4,370 for those aged 75 or more. If an individual attains the age of 65 (or 75) during a year of assessment, he is entitled to the appropriate allowance for the whole of that year. For example, a man born on 1 June 1929 will attain the age of 65 on 1 June 1994 and will be entitled to the higher allowance of £4,200 for the 1994–95 tax year.

The higher allowance is also given where the individual was alive on the first day of the tax year and would have achieved the age of 65 (or 75) within the tax year, had he not died.

However, the higher allowance is designed to assist only those of limited means. Therefore the allowance is reduced by £1 for every £2 by which the individual's 'total income' exceeds £14,200, until it falls back to the standard allowance for the under-65s.

7.3.3   Example—Reduced higher allowances

B, aged 70, receives a State pension of £3,000 a year, an occupational pension of £12,000 and building society interest of £300 (gross, before deduction of tax). His 'total income' will be £15,300 and his overall income tax liability will be:

Total income			£15,300
Higher personal allowance		£4,200	
Total income	£15,300		
Income limit	£14,200		
Excess	£1,100		
Half of excess		£550	
Reduced higher personal allowance[1]			£3,650
Tax payable on			£11,650

[1] This cannot be reduced below the standard personal allowance of £3,445.

£2,500	charged at 20 per cent	£500.00
£9,150	charged at 25 per cent	£2,287.50
£11,650		£2,787.50

The £1 for £2 reduction operates between 'total incomes' of £14,202 and £15,710 for those between the ages of 65 and 74 and between £14,202 and £16,050 for those aged 75 or more. Within this band, every £2 of income will cost 75p in tax (50p on the £2 itself, plus 25p on the £1 of allowances withdrawn). This is an effective rate of 37.5 per cent (although before 1989–90 the position was even worse: the 'clawback' was £2 in £3, giving an effective tax rate of 41.66 per cent).

The definition of 'total income' is, accordingly, very important, especially as in certain circumstances it is possible for an individual to re-arrange his investments so that his 'total income', as defined by the Taxes Acts, is less than his real income. This is explained in 7.4 below.

7.4 Calculating 'total income'
(TA 1988, s 835)

A person's 'total income', as defined by the Taxes Acts, differs from his real income, first because not all receipts count towards 'total income' and secondly because certain deductions can be made from real income in calculating 'total income'.

The first step in calculating 'total income' is to add together all the income *which is assessable to tax*. Income which is *not* assessable to tax is excluded. Examples include letting income exempt under the 'rent-a-room' scheme (see 4.8), the interest credited to a TESSA (see 11.2), the dividends earned by a PEP (see 11.3), the growth in value of National Savings Certificates (see 11.1.1) and amounts withdrawn from insurance bonds up to the five per cent limit (see 12.3.3). A person whose income falls within the 37.5 per cent band would, therefore, clearly do well to consider placing his money in tax-exempt investments.

The second step is to deduct, from the sum of assessable income, the following outgoings:

(1) Interest paid, insofar as it qualifies for tax relief under the usual rules (see Chapter 9).
(2) All of the 'other outgoings' listed in Chapter 10, insofar as each qualifies for tax relief under the normal rules. (The 'other outgoings' which may qualify are payments for vocational training, charitable donations, certain covenanted payments and certain maintenance and alimony payments.)
(3) Contributions paid to an occupational or personal pension plan.
(4) One-half of any Class 4 national insurance contributions paid.
(5) Any tax-allowable loss arising from investment in enterprise zone property (see 11.8).

7.4.1 Example—Total income

Suppose that B in the example 7.3.3(2) above receives a windfall of £5,000. He decides to invest £1,000 in an Enterprise Zone Property Trust and the balance in National Savings Certificates. To celebrate his good fortune, he signs a deed of covenant for £100 a year (gross) in favour of his local Church. Although B is now clearly better off, his tax liability for the year will in fact fall to £2,375, as follows:

Pension and interest received		£15,300
BES investment	£1,000	
Deed of covenant payment (gross)	£100	
		£1,100
'Total income'		£14,200
Higher personal allowance	£4,200	
Total income	£14,200	
Income limit	£14,200	
Excess	Nil	
Half of excess		Nil
		£4,200
Tax payable on		£10,000

£2,500	charged at 20 per cent	£500.00
£7,500	charged at 25 per cent	£1,875.00
£10,000		£2,375.00

7.5   Married couple's allowance
(TA 1988, s 257A)

7.5.1   Who may claim the allowance?

The basic rule is that a married man, whose wife is living with him, may claim the married couple's allowance. The couple must be legally married. Where the parties are domiciled abroad, the test is whether they are legally married according to the laws of their country of domicile.

If a man is domiciled in a country where polygamous marriage is allowed, he may claim the married couple's allowance if he has one or more wives. However, he is entitled to only one married couple's allowance, irrespective of the number of wives he has.

A married couple are taken as living together unless they have signed a separation agreement, are separated by order of the Court, or are living apart in such circumstances that the separation is likely to be permanent. Consequently, a couple will be treated as living together even if they are temporarily apart, for example because one is working abroad, or is in hospital or in prison. There have, however, been instances where an Inspector of Taxes has argued that a separation is permanent if one spouse is in hospital with a terminal illness, because there is then no prospect of the couple living together again.

Furthermore, in appropriate circumstances, it is possible for a man and his wife to be 'living apart' even though they are still under the same roof. For example, they may have divided up the available space, be preparing separate meals and communicating only by notes.

7.5.2   Amount of the allowance

The allowance has remained at £1,720 since 1990–91.

Until 1993–94, the allowance has been given as a deduction from the individual's total income, in the same way as the basic personal allowance (see 7.5.3 above). However, for 1994–95 the allowance is due only at the 20 per cent rate of tax. This means that whereas for 1993–94 and earlier years, married couple's allowance is simply deducted, in calculating the individual's taxable income, for 1994–95 it is necessary to calculate the liability without deducting the allowance and then to deduct 20 per cent of the allowance from the tax otherwise payable.

7.5.3   Example—Married couple's allowance in 1993–94 and 1994–95

A married man earns £10,000 a year. For 1993–94 his liability will be:

Earnings		£10,000
Personal allowance	£3,445	
Married couple's allowance	£1,720	
		£5,165
Tax payable on		£4,835
£2,500 charged at 20%		£500.00
£2,335 charged at 25%		£583.75
£4,835		£1,083.75

However, for 1994–95 it will be:

Earnings		£10,000
Personal allowance		£3,445
		£6,555
£3,000 charged at 20%		£600.00
£3,555 charged at 25%		£888.75
£6,555		£1,488.75
Less married couple's allowance (£1,720 at 20%)		£344.00
Tax payable		£1,144.75

In the November 1993 Budget, it was announced that the allowance will be further restricted in 1995–96 so that relief is given only at 15 per cent.

7.5.4   Year of marriage

The allowance is scaled down where marriage takes place during the tax year. It is reduced by one-twelfth (approximately £143) for every complete income tax month before the marriage. (An income tax month begins on the sixth day of one calendar month and ends on the fifth day of the next.)

7.5.5 Example—Married couple's allowance in the year of marriage

A married B on 19 June 1993. By then, the first two income tax months of 1993–94 had passed (the months ending 5 May and 5 June). A will therefore be entitled to a reduced married couple's allowance of £1,434, calculated as follows:

Full married couple's allowance	£1,720
Less 2/12ths	£286
Reduced allowance	£1,434

However, the allowance is not reduced if the parties cease to live together, or if the marriage comes to an end during the year of assessment, whether by divorce, annulment or death.

7.5.6 Transferring the married couple's allowance
(F(No2)A 1992, s 20 & Sched 5)

The basic rule is that the married couple's allowance is the husband's to claim. This was widely seen as unfair, so that in the 1992 Budget, the Chancellor introduced a new rule for the 1993–94 and subsequent years of assessment:

(1)   A wife may claim half the married couple's allowance for herself; and

(2)   Husband and wife may jointly elect for the whole of the married couple's allowance to be given to the wife.

A claim or election must be made on Inland Revenue Form 18 (available from your local tax office). The claim or election must be made before the beginning of the first year for which it is to have effect (so that the closing date for 1993–94 elections was 5 April 1993) except that:

(1)   Where a couple write to the Inspector, by the 5 April deadline, saying that they intend to make a claim or election, they have until 5 May to submit the Form 18 itself.

(2)   A claim or election for the year in which marriage takes place may be made during that year (so that if a couple marry in June 1993, they have until 5 April 1994 to submit Form 18).

Once made, a claim or election remains in force for future years, unless it is revoked. Where the couple have elected to transfer the whole of the allowance to the wife, the husband may, without his wife's consent, claim back half the allowance. Revocations or amended claims must be made before the beginning of the first year for which they are to have effect.

7.5.7 Husbands with excess allowances
(TA 1988, s 257B)

The new ability to transfer the married couple's allowance runs alongside an existing provision, in force since the introduction of independent taxation in 1990–91, under which the married couple's allowance (or part of it) may be transferred to the wife if the husband has insufficient income to utilise that allowance himself. The older provision will remain relevant because relief does not depend on a claim being made before the beginning of the year of assessment. Indeed, the usual time limit applies, namely that the relief may be claimed at any time up to the sixth anniversary of the end of the year of assessment.

Special rules apply when calculating the husband's available income (the income, that is, against which his personal allowances may be set).

7.5.8 Example—Special rules on husband's income

A earns only £5,000, out of which he pays mortgage interest of £1,000. However, the mortgage is within MIRAS (see 9.1), so he actually pays £750, with the building society reclaiming tax relief of £250 from the Inland Revenue.

As explained in 7.4 above, A's 'total income' will be £4,000 (£5,000 less mortgage interest of £1,000). It might be thought, therefore, that he could transfer £1,165 of the married couple's allowance to his wife, calculated as follows:

'Total income'		£4,000
Basic personal allowance	£3,445	
Married couple's allowance	£1,720	
		£5,165
Excess allowances		£1,165

However, if this were the case, A would in fact have to pay some tax, as follows:

Earnings		£5,000
Basic personal allowance	£3,445	
Married couple's allowance	£1,720	
	£5,165	
Transferred to wife	£1,165	
		£4,000
Tax payable on		£1,000

(No deduction may be made in respect of the mortgage interest paid, as relief has already been obtained under MIRAS.)

Therefore the rule is that mortgage interest within MIRAS may not be deducted in calculating available income for 'transfer of allowances' purposes. Accordingly, the transferable allowance in this example is £165 only, calculated as follows:

Earnings		£5,000
Basic personal allowance	£3,445	
Married couple's allowance	£1,720	
		£5,165
Transferable excess		£165

The same rule also applies to three other types of expenditure where tax relief is given by reducing the amount paid by the individual and paying a block grant to the provider:

(1)   Additional voluntary contributions to an occupational pension scheme and personal pension scheme contributions paid as an employee (see 12.11, 12.12 and 12.9.3).
(2)   Payments for vocational training (see 10.4).
(3)   Medical insurance premiums qualifying for tax relief (see 10.5).

There is also a fifth prohibited deduction—Business Expansion Scheme investments (see 11.4).

7.6   Pensioner couples
(TA 1988, s 257A)

A higher married couple's allowance is available if *either* spouse has attained the age of 65. The allowance is £2,465 if the elder spouse is aged between 65 and 74 and £2,505 if he or she is aged 75 or more. The same rules apply as for the age-related personal allowances (see 7.3.2 above), namely that the higher allowance is due if the relevant age is attained during the year of assessment, or if it would have been attained had the individual not died.

For example, suppose that a man was born on 1 January 1929 and his wife on 1 June 1929 (ie he will be 65 on 1 January 1994 and his wife on 1 June 1994). He may claim the higher (£2,465) married couple's allowance for 1993–94 and this will not be withdrawn should he in fact die before his birthday.

7.6.1   Pensioner couples—Transfer of excess allowances
(TA 1988, s 257B and F(No2)A 1992, s 20 & Sched 5)

Subject to the normal rules (as set out in 7.5.7 above), the whole of a higher, age-related married couple's allowance may be transferred to the wife if the husband has insufficient income to use it himself.

However, only the basic £1,720 married couple's allowance may be transferred under the general right to transfer the allowance, as set out in 7.5.6 above.

7.7   Widow's bereavement allowance
(TA 1988, s 262)

7.7.1   Introduction

Provided the couple were living together at the time the husband died, a widow may claim (in addition to her basic personal allowance) a 'widow's bereavement allowance' of £1,720. This allowance is given for the tax year in which her husband died and for the following year (except that it will not be given for the following year if she remarries before the beginning of that year).

Although the allowance is equal to the standard married couple's allowance, it is not increased if the widow has (or her late husband had) attained the age of 65.

Another important point is that it is the *widow's* bereavement allowance; there is no corresponding relief for widowers.

7.7.2   Rate of relief

As with the married couple's allowance (see 7.5.2) relief was given as a deduction from the widow's total income for years up to 1993–94, but is restricted to 20 per cent for 1994–95 and will be further restricted to 15 per cent in 1995–96.

7.8   Additional personal allowance
(TA 1988, ss 259–261A)

7.8.1   Introduction

The tax legislation recognises that single people with children have responsibilities equivalent to a married man. Therefore it provides the 'additional personal allowance' which may be claimed by a man or woman, who is either not married or is not living with his or her spouse, and who has care of a qualifying child. The allowance is £1,720 (and although this is equal to the married couple's allowance, it is not increased should the parent attain his or her 65th birthday).

A child, to qualify, must live with the claimant, but need not be the claimant's own son or daughter. For example, the allowance can be claimed by an unmarried aunt who is looking after her orphaned nephew. The detailed conditions are a little odd, however, in that they discriminate against natural children.

Any child will qualify for any year of assessment which begins before his sixteenth birthday, or eighteenth if still in full-time education. For this purpose, 'education' includes an apprenticeship or similar arrangement, provided it lasts for at least two years. However, a child who has attained the age of eighteen by the beginning of the year of assessment will qualify only if he is in full-time education *and* is the claimant's legitimate or legitimated child, or his adopted or stepchild.

The child does not have to reside with the claimant throughout the year— it will not affect entitlement to the relief if, for example, the child is sent away to school. Where a child's time is divided between two parents who are not living together, the additional personal allowance has to be divided between those parents either as they agree, or in default of agreement, by reference to the amount of time the child spends with each.

However many children a person is responsible for, he can only claim one additional personal allowance. However, if a separated couple have two children, and both children spend some time with each parent, each parent may claim half the allowance for both children (so that the result is the same as if each parent had claimed a single, full, additional personal allowance).

A household may consist of an unmarried couple and their children from previous marriages. If both the man and the woman were able to claim an additional personal allowance, they would in fact be better off than if they were married. Therefore the legislation provides that only one additional personal allowance may be claimed, and that it goes to the parent of the youngest qualifying child.

7.8.2   Rate of relief

The allowance has remained at £1,720 since 1990–91.

Until 1993–94, the allowance was given as a deduction from the individual's total income, in the same way as the basic personal allowance (see 7.5.3 above). However, for 1994–95 the allowance is due only at the 20 per cent rate of tax.

7.8.3 Year of separation

The introduction of the rule allowing a husband to transfer the married couple's allowance to his wife (see 7.5.6) has been accompanied by specific provisions for those separating after 5 April 1993. Whichever spouse takes the child will be able to claim the additional personal allowance for the year of separation, but from that allowance must be deducted any married couple's allowance already allocated to that spouse.

Where husband and wife separated during 1992–93 or an earlier year of assessment, and their child went to live with the husband, the husband could claim the married couple's allowance (but not the additional personal allowance) for the year of separation and the additional personal allowance for the following years. However, if the child went to live with the wife, she could claim the additional personal allowance from the year of separation.

7.8.4 Year of remarriage

If a 'single parent' father remarries, he may not claim both the additional personal allowance and the married man's allowance for the year of remarriage. As explained in 7.5 above, the married couple's allowance will be scaled down if marriage takes place after 5 May, so it will usually be better to disclaim the married couple's allowance and take the additional personal allowance.

However, if a 'single parent' mother remarries, she may claim the additional personal allowance for the year of remarriage without affecting her new husband's right to a married couple's allowance.

7.9 Additional allowance for disabled wife

There is one situation where a married man may claim both the full additional personal allowance *and* the full married couple's allowance. This is where his wife is 'totally incapacitated by physical or mental infirmity throughout the year [of assessment]'.

Five points should be noted:

(1) The allowance is (as is invariably the case with the additional personal allowance) available only where a 'qualifying child' (as defined in 7.8) is living with the claimant.
(2) The Revenue construes 'incapacitated' very strictly: simple blindness, for example, is not enough. The test is that the wife must

be quite unable to care for the child, in the sense of preparing his food and washing his clothes.

(3)   The allowance is not given unless the wife is incapacitated *throughout* the year of assessment. Therefore if a woman became paraplegic after a car accident in, say, May 1993, her husband could not claim the allowance until 1994–95.

(4)   The allowance is not due unless husband and wife are living together at least for part of the year of assessment. (Very often, by the time the wife is sufficiently ill to be 'incapacitated' under the Revenue's definition, she is so ill as to need the full-time care of a nursing home.)

(5)   The allowance is only given where the *wife* is incapacitated: there is no corresponding relief where the husband is incapacitated and the wife has become the family breadwinner.

7.10   Blind persons
(TA 1988, s 265)

A person who is blind may claim a special, additional, personal allowance of £1,200 for 1994–95 (£1,080 for 1993–94). A person counts as 'blind' if:

(1)   he lives in England or Wales and his name appears on the local authority's register of blind persons; or

(2)   he lives in Scotland or Northern Ireland and is so blind that he cannot perform any work for which eyesight is essential.

This definition means that a person resident abroad can never, for tax purposes, count as blind—an odd rule which is strictly enforced by the Inland Revenue.

A person who becomes blind during a year of assessment may claim the full blind person's allowance for that year.

7.10.1   Married couples

If husband and wife are both blind, each may claim a separate blind person's allowance.

A blind husband with insufficient income to use all his personal allowances may be able to transfer the whole, or part of, his blind person's allowance to his wife (whether or not she also is blind). However, the transfer of the married couple's allowance takes priority, so a transfer of blind person's allowance is only possible where the husband's income is insufficient to use his basic personal allowance and the blind person's allowance itself. Furthermore, the transfer of the blind person's allowance is subject to the same restrictions as a transfer of an unused married couple's allowance (see 7.5.7).

Similarly, a wife may transfer her unused blind person's allowance to her husband (whether or not he also is blind), but again subject to the point that she cannot, in calculating her income for this purpose, deduct the five prohibited items (see 7.5.8).

A claim to transfer a blind person's allowance to a spouse must be made, on Inland Revenue Form 575, within six years of the end of the relevant year of assessment.

7.10.2 Example—Blind married couple

A, who is sighted, earns £10,000 a year. His wife, B, who is blind, has a pension of £4,250. They live in a flat bought by B before their marriage, so the flat, and the mortgage, are in her sole name. The mortgage is within MIRAS and the gross interest payable for the current year is £2,000.

B's 'total income' (as defined by the Taxes Acts) is £2,250 (ie £4,250 less mortgage interest paid £2,000 as explained in 7.4 above). However, in calculating the allowance which may be transferred, the mortgage interest is to be ignored. Therefore the position is:

B

Pension		£4,250
Basic personal allowance	£3,445	
Blind person's allowance	£1,080	
		£4,525
Excess, transferable to husband		£275

A

Salary		£10,000
Basic personal allowance	£3,445	
Married couple's allowance	£1,720	
Blind person's allowance	£275	
		£5,440
Tax payable on		£4,560
£2,500 charged at 20 per cent		£500
£2,060 charged at 25 per cent		£515
£4,560		£1,015

However, the couple will also have enjoyed £500 of tax relief under the MIRAS scheme (although the gross mortgage interest was £2,000, they will actually have paid only £1,500). Therefore their net contribution to the Exchequer is only £515.

7.11   Withdrawn allowances and transitional reliefs

In recent years, a number of personal allowances have been withdrawn. However, they should not be overlooked as most were still available in the earliest of the six back years for which claims may yet be made. Also, in certain cases, transitional rules apply, ensuring that existing claimants were not disadvantaged by the introduction of new rules.

(1)   Allowances for children were abolished in 1979.

(2)   Three allowances were withdrawn at the end of 1987–88:

    (a)   The housekeeper allowance of £100, which could be claimed by a widow or widower who employed a resident housekeeper. This allowance could not be claimed in addition to the additional personal allowance.

    (b)   The dependent relative allowance of £100 (increased to £145 if the claimant was a single woman). However, the relief was reduced by £1 for every £1 the dependent relative's own income exceeded £2,054 (then the basic State retirement pension).

    (c)   The son's or daughter's services allowance of £55, available where the claimant, being incapacitated by old age or infirmity, was nursed by a son or daughter.

(3)   Until the end of 1989–90 husband and wife were assessed as a single entity. There was no 'married couple's allowance', but the husband was entitled to a 'married man's allowance'—effectively an amalgam of the basic personal allowance and what is now the married couple's allowance. The wife's personal allowance could be set only against her earned income and so was known as the 'wife's earned income allowance'.

Transitional reliefs

Generally speaking, a married couple will, under the 'independent taxation' rules introduced in 1990–91, pay either the same amount, or in some cases less, than they would under the 'taxed as one entity' rules applicable up to 1989–90. There are two exceptions. The first is where the husband has insufficient income of his own to use his basic personal allowance. Under the old rules, if the husband had no income, the whole of the married man's allowance could be set against his wife's income. Under the new rules, only the married couple's allowance may be transferred.

As a transitional measure, a husband was allowed to transfer his surplus basic personal allowance for 1990–91. For 1992–93 and future years, he is allowed to transfer an amount equal to the smaller of:

(1)   the amount transferred in the immediately preceding year less the amount by which his wife's own basic personal allowance and the relevant married couple's allowance has increased since that year (taking into account both Budget increases and any entitlement to higher, age-related, allowances); and

(2)   the amount of the husband's basic personal allowance which cannot be used against his own income for the year (calculated without deducting the five prohibited items, as in 7.5.8 above).

As this transitional relief works on a ratchet principle—in that the relief for any year will never be more than that given in the previous year—there are by now very few people entitled to claim. In fact, the current tax return does not even refer to the relief, so any claim would have to be made by letter.

The tax return does however refer to the other transitional relief, termed a 'special personal allowance'. Today, a man married to an older woman may claim only the basic personal allowance appropriate to his own age. Until 1989–90, however, the married man's allowance was based on the age of the elder spouse. Anyone whose basic personal allowance plus married couple's allowance for 1990–91 was less than his married man's allowance for 1989–90, was granted a special personal allowance. This was either £3,400 (if his wife was between 65 and 74 years of age on 5 April 1990) or £3,540 (if she was then aged 75 or more). This special allowance may be claimed every year until, by virtue of annual Budget increases in the personal allowance and/or his own increasing age, his ordinary personal allowance under the new rules equals or exceeds the special allowance.

In fact, for 1992–93 the only possible claimant would be a man, who had not achieved his 65th birthday by 5 April 1993, married to a woman who had attained her 78th birthday by that day. For 1993–94 the only possible claimant would be a man, who will not achieve his 65th birthday by 5 April 1994, married to a woman who will attain her 79th birthday by that day.

8 The taxation treatment of maintenance

(FA 1988, ss 36–40 and F(No2)A 1992, ss 61–62)

This chapter examines the tax treatment of maintenance payments, both from the standpoint of the payer and the recipient. The following aspects are covered:

(1) Definition of maintenance and alimony payments.
(2) Maintenance paid under an existing obligation.
(3) Maintenance under an existing obligation paid direct to a child.
(4) Increased payments under an existing obligation.
(5) 1988–89 and earlier years.
(6) Payer's relief for other maintenance payments.
(7) The Child Support Agency.

The Inland Revenue's booklet IR93 (*Separation, Divorce and Maintenance Payments*) outlines the tax positions when married couples separate or divorce and also deals with the tax treatment of maintenance payments.

8.1 Definition of maintenance and alimony payments

Maintenance payments (sometimes called 'alimony') may be received:

(1) by a woman from her husband or former husband and (in exceptional circumstances) by a man from his wife or former wife;
(2) by a child from a parent (including an adoptive or step-parent);
(3) by a woman from the father of her natural child;
(4) by any other person who has care of a child, from a parent of the child. (For example, if the child's mother is dead and the father is considered unfit to care for the child, the Court may grant custody to a grandparent but order the father to make a financial contribution.)

The tax treatment of such payments underwent a 'sea-change' on 15

March 1988 (Budget Day). For tax purposes, payments of maintenance or alimony to a wife or former wife (or exceptionally to a husband or former husband), and similar payments for the support of children, are divided into two categories: those which are, and those which are not, payments under an 'existing obligation'. As will be explained below, the tax treatment of payments under an existing obligation is far more generous than that of payments under later obligations.

Essentially, an existing obligation is one which existed at the time the 1988 Budget Statement was made, but the statutory definition is a little more complex.

A payment is made under an existing obligation if it is made:

(1)   under a Court Order made no later than 14 March 1988; or
(2)   under a Court Order made no later than 30 June 1988 in pursuance of an application made no later than 14 March 1988; or
(3)   under a written agreement signed by the parties no later than 14 March 1988 and produced to an Inspector of Taxes no later than 30 June 1988; or
(4)   under an oral agreement reached between the parties no later than 14 March 1988, written particulars of which were produced to an Inspector no later than 30 June 1988; or
(5)   subject to limitations (as explained below), under a Court Order or written agreement replacing, amending or varying a prior order or agreement qualifying under (1) to (4) above.

Any other payment is not made under an existing obligation

An order may qualify under (1), (2) or (5) whether it is made by a United Kingdom or a foreign Court. There is no requirement for the payer to be United Kingdom resident: and a payment for the maintenance of a child may be made to the child himself, to his parent or guardian, or to a third party (such as the school at which the child is educated).

8.2   Maintenance paid under an existing obligation

The following sections set out the rules as they apply for 1989–90 and subsequent tax years. Different rules applied in earlier years (see 8.5).

The current position depends partly on the identity of the recipient. Therefore, it is important to distinguish between an order (or agreement) under which an adult receives a payment earmarked for the support of a child and one under which a payment is made in theory direct to the child, but in practice to an adult as guardian of the child. For example, if the order says that payment is to be made *to* the mother *for* the child, then the mother is the recipient. However, if it says payment is to be made *to* the child, then the child is the recipient, even if the mother in fact receives the money on his behalf. If the documentation says anything else, it would be advisable to seek legal advice.

A payment to a wife or former wife (or to a husband or former husband) under an existing obligation is effectively treated as a transfer of taxable income from the payer to the recipient. This is so whether the payment is for the wife's (or husband's) own maintenance, or for the maintenance of a child. Similarly, a payment to the mother of the payer's natural child is treated as a transfer of taxable income to the mother. However, a payment direct to a child who has not yet attained his eighteenth birthday is treated as a transfer of income only if that payment is made under an existing obligation *arising under a Court Order.*

A payment to a child under the age of 18 made otherwise than under the terms of a Court Order was and is simply ignored for tax purposes. Payments to children aged 18 or more are considered separately, in 8.3.

At one time a 'net payment' system (similar to that used for charitable deeds of covenant) applied to most payments of maintenance but, from April 1989, virtually all maintenance and alimony has been payable gross (the sole exception relates to maintenance paid to children who have attained the age of 18 years—see 8.3).

8.2.1 Example—Payment under existing obligation

In 1987, A was ordered by the Court to pay his wife B maintenance of £300 a month and his son C (then aged thirteen) £200 a month. This will count as an existing obligation, so A may deduct, in computing his taxable income for the current year, £6,000 (twelve months at £500). Therefore the sum paid out will attract tax relief at the highest rate paid. That relief will be given in A's tax assessment or in his PAYE coding, as appropriate.

8.2.2 Maintenance paid under an existing obligation to a spouse or former spouse

Where the recipient is a spouse or former spouse of the payer, then the following rules apply (whether the payment is stated to be for the recipient's own support or for the support of a child living with him/her):

(1) Payment is made gross (ie the spouse making the payment should pay the full amount he/she agreed or was ordered to pay and should not, as was once the case, deduct an amount in respect of income tax on the payment).

(2)   Providing the recipient has not remarried, the first £1,720 received
      in each tax year is exempt from tax. (In fact the exemption is linked
      to the married couple's allowance and so was less before 1990–91.)
      Exemption is lost only if the recipient has remarried; cohabitation
      does not count. If the recipient remarries halfway through the tax
      year, the exemption may be claimed only against payments falling
      due before the date of marriage.

(3)   If the payment is made under a United Kingdom Court Order or
      agreement, the balance is taxable, under Case III of Schedule D,
      but on a current-year basis. However, if it is made under a foreign
      order or agreement, it is taxable under Case V on a preceding-year
      basis (see 5.12).

Wherever possible, this tax is collected by an adjustment to the
recipient's PAYE code but, where the recipient has no job, or the amounts
involved are too big to code out, a Schedule D assessment will be issued.
In principle, the whole of the tax is then payable on 1 January,
approximately three-quarters of the way through the tax year. However,
the Revenue will usually allow only three-quarters of the tax to be paid
on 1 January and the balance at the end of March.

Whether a Court Order payment is taxable under Case III (on a current-
year basis) or under Case V (on a preceding-year basis) depends on *where
the relevant Court Order was made*, not on whether the payer is resident
abroad or on whether payments come from abroad. Whether an
agreement counts as a United Kingdom or foreign agreement can be
difficult to tell. If both parties are domiciled in the United Kingdom and
the agreement was made here, then it will be a United Kingdom
agreement. In other cases, legal advice will be required.

8.2.3   Late payments

It is not unusual for maintenance payments to fall into arrears, or even
not to be paid at all. The recipient's assessment will be limited to the
amount actually received. If an amount due in one year is in fact paid in
a later year, it will still be assessed as income of the year in which it
should have been paid. (This avoids 'bunching' of income where
payments are not made regularly and will usually be to the recipient's
advantage.)

Suppose in example 8.2.1, that the husband had omitted to pay three
months' maintenance in the tax year 1993–94. In his tax assessment for
that year, he would be given relief only for the payments actually made
(9 x £500 = £4,500). However, if in, say, December 1994, he makes good
the payments omitted in 1993–94, the 1993–94 assessment may then be
re-opened to give relief for the late payments.

8.2.4   Maintenance paid under an existing obligation to a person (other than a spouse or former spouse) for the support of a child

A 'child' for this purpose is defined as a person under 21 years of age. Maintenance for a child may be payable by a parent, a step-parent or an adoptive parent.

Here we are concerned with payments other than to the child himself or to a spouse or former spouse. The payee may therefore be the child's natural mother or a relative, such as a grandparent, who has been given charge of the child.

Such payments must always be made gross and count in full as taxable income in the payee's hands. They will be taxed under Case III, if they are made under a United Kingdom Court Order or agreement, on a current-year basis, and under Case V, if made under a foreign order or agreement, on a preceding-year basis.

8.3   Maintenance under an existing obligation paid direct to a child

Payments 'direct to a child' can include to an adult as guardian of a child.

The tax treatment depends *both* on whether payment is made under a Court Order or under an agreement *and* on the age of the child (at the time of each payment, not at the time the order or agreement was made).

Payments under Court Order

Payments are to be made gross until the child reaches the age of 21; thereafter they are to be made under deduction of tax. Whilst payments are made gross, the parent may claim tax relief at 25 per cent or 40 per cent as appropriate. Once payments are made net, he may claim relief at the difference between 25 per cent and 40 per cent.

Payments count as the taxable income of the child throughout. Although they are taxable in full, they are unlikely to exceed the child's personal allowance, so in practice it is rare for tax to be payable.

For the position where a Court Order was amended between 15 March 1988 and the child's 21st Birthday, see 8.4.2.

Payments under an agreement

Such payments do not count as the child's taxable income until he attains the age of 18. Payment should be made gross until that age is attained. However, once age 18 is attained, such payments count as the child's taxable income (but for basic rate purposes only; by a quirk of the law, higher rate tax is never chargeable on maintenance received by a child under an agreement).

From age 18, payment should be made under deduction of tax. For example, if the gross payment due is £100, the parent should pay only £75. If the child is a taxpayer, that £25 covers his basic rate liability on the £100; if he is not a taxpayer (because his income does not exceed his personal allowance), he may reclaim the £25 from the Revenue.

In practice, of course, by the time a child starts work and so becomes a taxpayer, his parents' obligation to maintain him will usually have expired.

The distinction between payments made under a Court Order and those made under a written agreement may seem to be arbitrary and illogical. They arise as an unintended side-effect of legislation originally devised to counter tax avoidance by the (mis)use of family trusts and have, over the years, caused considerable difficulty to both lawyers and accountants—not to mention the actual participants in the divorce.

8.3.1 Example—Payments to children under existing obligations

In 1987, A was ordered by the Court to pay £250 a month to his daughter, B, until she completed her education. B was twenty-one on 1 June 1993, but will not complete her university course until 1994.

The May instalment is to be paid gross, but in June A should pay only £187.50 (£250 less basic rate tax). A keeps the £62.50 deducted as his own basic rate tax relief (and B may be able to re-claim the tax deducted from the Inland Revenue, as explained in 8.3). If A is a higher-rate taxpayer, the higher rate relief due (15 per cent of £250, or £37.50) will be given in his tax assessment or PAYE coding.

8.4 Increase of payments made under an existing obligation

An order or agreement which replaces an existing obligation will itself count as an existing obligation. For the exception, see 8.4.2.

However, payments made under a replacement order or agreement will only be treated as made under an existing obligation to the extent that they do not exceed the payments due to be made (as distinct from the payments actually made) in the 1988–89 tax year.

8.4.1 Example—Payments under an existing obligation increased

A divorced her husband in 1987. He was, at that time, ordered to pay her £300 a month. In 1993–94 she received £3,600 and so her position was:

Maintenance received	£3,600
Exempt (see 8.2.2)	£1,720
Taxable income	£1,880

In April 1994, the Court ordered her husband to increase the monthly payments to £400. The position for 1994–95 will be:

Maintenance received	£4,800
Increase over amount payable for 1988–89	£1,200
	£3,600
Exempt	£1,720
Taxable income	£1,880

In other words, the increase is simply left out of account.

Very occasionally, a pre-15 March 1988 Court Order or separation agreement will provide for the amount payable to increase automatically—perhaps in line with inflation. In such a case, tax relief is similarly limited to the amount payable in 1988–89.

8.4.2 Children who have attained 21 years

In one circumstance, an order or agreement which replaces an existing obligation will *not* itself count as an existing obligation. A 'replacement' order or agreement to pay maintenance to or for a child ceases to count as an existing obligation on that child's 21st birthday. Therefore, if a pre-15 March 1988 Order or agreement is varied, payments made on or after the child's 21st birthday are not deductible in computing the payer's taxable income and are not assessable as income of the child. Such payments, being outside the tax system altogether, should accordingly be made gross.

8.5 1988–89 and earlier years

Any payment made under an existing obligation in 1988–89 or an earlier tax year should have been paid under deduction of tax unless it did not exceed £208 a month (£48 a week) in the case of a payment to a spouse, former spouse or child, or £108 a month (£25 a week) in any other case.

The first £1,490 received by a spouse or former spouse in 1988–89 was exempt from tax. In earlier years, the whole was taxable.

8.6 Payer's relief for other maintenance payments

Payments under Court Orders and agreements which do not count as existing obligations qualify for tax relief *only* if they are made to a separated or former wife (or to a separated or former husband). Payments made direct to a child do not qualify, nor do payments to the mother of a natural child. However, payments made to a spouse or former spouse qualify even if they are earmarked for the maintenance of children.

Furthermore, a payment which is not an existing obligation will not qualify for relief unless it is due under a Court Order made in a Member State of the European Community or under a written agreement subject to the jurisdiction of the Courts of a Member State. Until 1992–93, relief was further limited to orders of the United Kingdom Courts and to agreements subject to their jurisdiction. (Whether an agreement is subject to the jurisdiction of a particular Court is a complex legal question outside the scope of this book. If you or your (ex)-spouse is domiciled abroad, or if the agreement was signed abroad, you should seek specialist advice on this point. Alternatively, you could submit your claim to the Inland Revenue, disclosing all the relevant facts, and seek specialist advice only if your claim is refused).

Tax relief for payments made otherwise than under an existing obligation is limited to an amount equal to the married couple's allowance (currently £1,720). Consequently, if a man is now ordered to pay his former wife £300 a month, he must pay that sum gross, but can claim relief for £1,720 only. However, if he remarries, he can claim the married couple's allowance in respect of his new wife in addition to the relief for maintenance payments made.

The man's entitlement to relief ends when his former wife remarries, even if the payments, being earmarked for the maintenance of children, continue.

The £1,720 limit is reduced, pound for pound, by any maintenance paid which qualifies under the existing obligation rules explained above, *except that* payments to children who have attained the age of 21 years may be ignored. (As mentioned above, these rules are not logical.)

Finally, the £1,720 limit is a global limit and is not increased even if a man is paying alimony to two or more ex-wives.

8.6.1 The payer's option
(FA 1988, s 39)

An individual paying maintenance under an existing obligation is entitled to disclaim existing obligation relief and elect instead to claim relief as if the relevant Order or agreement had been made after 14 March 1988. An election must be made, on Inland Revenue Form 142, within twelve months of the end of the first year of assessment for which it is to have effect (so that an election for 1992–93 must be made by 5 April 1994). Once made, an election is irrevocable and remains in force for all future years. In certain circumstances, an election can buy a short-term advantage at the expense of a long-term disadvantage (see example).

8.6.2 Example—Election to claim relief under new rules

In 1987 A was ordered to pay his former wife B maintenance of £100 a month. In 1993 that sum is increased to £150 a month. Under the existing obligation rules, relief is limited to £1,200 a year. However, under the later obligation rules, A may claim up to £1,720.

Suppose now that after A makes the election, his former wife remarries. If the payments were earmarked for the children, they will continue, but A will lose all his tax relief.

8.7 The Child Support Agency
F(No2)A 1992, s 62

In April 1993 responsibility for determining how much maintenance should be paid for a child was (in most cases) transferred from the Courts to the Child Support Agency. On request, the Agency will make a 'maintenance assessment' based on a published formula, taking into account factors such as the age(s) of the child(ren), the incomes of both parents, their housing costs and whether either has remarried or has responsibility for a 'second family'. The procedure is explained in some detail in a free booklet *For Parents Who Live Apart*, available from:

> Child Support Agency
> Freepost CL3349
> PO Box 1032
> Sudbury
> Suffolk
> CO10 6BR

Tel: 0435 830 830 (calls charged at local rates from anywhere in the United Kingdom).

This address and telephone number is only for booklet requests. The Child Support Agency also operates an enquiry line service on 0345 133 133 (9.00 am to 6 pm, Mondays to Fridays: calls charged at local rates from anywhere in the United Kingdom).

For tax purposes, a maintenance assessment made by the Child Support Agency is treated as if it were a Court Order. To the extent that it replaces a prior agreement or Court Order which was an existing obligation, the maintenance assessment may therefore count as an existing obligation, subject to the rules in 8.4.

9 Interest on qualifying loans

by PETER JUN TAI

Although at one time, tax relief was generally available on interest paid on borrowed money, there are now relatively few opportunities to claim relief for loan interest.

This chapter covers the following topics:

(1)   MIRAS.
(2)   Loans used to purchase investment properties.
(3)   Loans used to invest in partnerships.
(4)   Loans used to invest in close companies.

9.1   MIRAS
(TA 1988, ss 369–370)

MIRAS stands for Mortgage Interest Relief At Source and is the mechanism by which income tax relief is allowed to the borrower on the interest payable on the first £30,000 of a mortgage loan. From 6 April 1994 the relief was reduced from 25 to 20 per cent except for loans taken out in connection with the purchase of an annuity (see 9.1.2). From 1995–96, relief will be further reduced to 15 per cent.

The relief is not withdrawn where the individual is not liable to tax because his income is too low.

The availability of MIRAS on a home loan is not automatic. It is only allowed if all the following three conditions are satisfied:

(1)   The interest must be relevant loan interest.
(2)   The borrower must be a qualifying borrower.
(3)   The lender must be a qualifying lender.

Relevant loan interest

Relevant loan interest applies to loans used for the purchase of land, caravan or houseboat *in the United Kingdom* which is used wholly or substantially as the only or main residence of the borrower.

9.1.1 Negative equity
(FA 1993, s 56)

The legislation now allows a loan to qualify where the individual has ended up with negative equity and he has transferred his mortgage to a new property. Basically, a person may be treated as if he has raised a new eligible amount on the new property. The amount of the eligible loan will be the smaller of the purchase price of the new home and the amount of the outstanding loan. If relief on the old loan has been obtained on more than £30,000 (because the mortgage was taken out before 1 August 1988 by unmarried joint purchasers) this will be restricted to £30,000 when the borrowers move.

9.1.2 Loans used to purchase an annuity from an insurance company

The interest is also relevant loan interest if the borrower is aged 65 or more and at least 90 per cent of the loan on which the interest is payable is used to buy an annuity for the remainder of his life. Once again, the loan must be secured on the borrower's main residence.

Interest payable on these types of loan continues to attract 25 per cent relief despite the general reduction in MIRAS relief for 1994–95 (see 9.1).

9.1.3 Qualifying borrower
(TA 1988, s 376)

A qualifying borrower is any individual who pays relevant loan interest. However this does not include individuals who are employed in the United Kingdom but are exempt from UK income tax by virtue of some special exemption or immunity (eg diplomatic immunity).

9.1.4 Qualifying lender
(TA 1988, s 376)

This includes the building societies, local authorities, insurance companies authorised to carry on long-term business, etc. It does not automatically include the banks who have to be authorised by statutory instrument issued by the Treasury. To date, most of the larger banks and specialist mortgage companies have been authorised.

9.1.5 Administration

The application of MIRAS to a loan is not automatic. The procedure is for the borrower to complete a form, usually stocked and supplied by the lender, certifying that he is a qualifying borrower and that the interest is relevant loan interest. Alternatively, the Inland Revenue may, if asked, notify the lender and borrower that the interest may be paid under deduction of tax.

If at any time after the application of MIRAS to a loan has been established the borrower ceases to be a qualifying borrower or the interest is no longer relevant interest (eg because the borrower has bought another principal private residence), the borrower must inform the lender. Any excess MIRAS relief is recovered by direct assessment.

9.1.6   Loans pre-6 April 1988
(TA 1988, s 355 and FA 1988, s 43)

Interest on home improvement loans made on or after 6 April 1988 does not qualify for tax relief. Interest on loans arranged before 6 April 1988 continues to attract tax relief within the £30,000 limit. This relief is lost if the loan is replaced.

9.1.7   Joint borrowers
(TA 1988, s 356C)

Before 1 August 1988, joint borrowers other than husband and wife were each entitled to a £30,000 limit on their qualifying borrowings. For example, if a brother and sister jointly bought a house for £100,000 with a deposit of £20,000 and a joint loan of £80,000, MIRAS relief would be available on £60,000.

From 1 August 1988, the relief became residence-based so that only £30,000 is available per residence. This rule applies only to loans taken out after 31 July 1988 and pre-existing loans continue to attract full MIRAS relief.

Where a main residence is purchased jointly by two or more persons, the £30,000 is normally shared equally between the borrowers.

9.1.8   Example—Joint borrowers

A and B have a joint mortgage of £30,000 which is held as to £20,000 and £10,000 respectively. A would be entitled to a limit of £15,000 and so lose relief on £5,000. B on the other hand will also have a limit of £15,000 but will only obtain relief on £10,000 so wasting tax relief on £5,000. However, there is provision for the £5,000 to be transferred to A who will then obtain tax relief on £20,000. B will continue to obtain tax relief on £10,000 making a total of £30,000.

9.1.9 Husband and wife
(TA 1988, s 356B)

A married couple are only entitled to mortgage tax relief on £30,000 and effectively count as one person. This prevents the married couple obtaining excessive relief if there are other joint borrowers.

An election may be made so that the relief can be apportioned between husband and wife in whatever proportion they choose. This was especially valuable for tax years up to and including 1990–91 when tax relief at higher rate was available on mortgage interest.

9.1.10 Job-related accommodation
(TA 1988, s 356)

Where a person lives in job-related accommodation, he is entitled to claim MIRAS relief on a property which he owns provided that:

(1) the property is used as his main residence or is so used within 12 months after the loan is made, or
(2) the property is intended at that time to be used in due course as his only or main residence.

Living accommodation is job-related if it is provided to a person and is necessary for the proper performance of his duties or it is customary in that particular trade for employers to provide living accommodation or there is a special threat to security. Self-employed individuals may qualify in certain circumstances. Typical examples of people receiving job-related accommodation would be public school teachers, army personnel, school caretakers and publicans.

9.1.11 Temporary absences

Tax relief on mortgage interest is technically only available where, at the time the interest is paid, the property is used as the only or main residence. This relief can be denied where there are temporary absences from the property.

This can produce genuine hardship in many situations and the Revenue have confirmed that tax relief will not be denied or withdrawn in the following cases:

(1) Temporary absences of up to a year.
(2) Where the taxpayer is required to move to another place in the United Kingdom or abroad because of his employment, tax relief on a property used as his main residence before departure will be preserved provided that its use as a main residence is expected

to resume on return. This also applies where a property has been purchased and the person is prevented by his move from occupying it.

The relief will not be extended beyond four years. However, if the property is occupied as a main residence for at least three months after a four year absence, a further four year extension may be obtained.

Further details may be found in extra-statutory concession A27.

9.1.12   Part qualifying loan
(TA 1988, s 370)

MIRAS relief is available only where the whole loan would be eligible for tax relief if there were no £30,000 limit.

For example, if a loan of £50,000 is applied in full towards the purchase of a main residence, the whole £50,000 would be eligible for tax relief but would be restricted to £30,000.

Subsequently, if the loan is increased to £60,000 to provide £10,000 towards a new kitchen, MIRAS relief can be withdrawn because the loan (£60,000) has been used partly for qualifying purposes and partly for non-qualifying purposes (home improvement loans are not now eligible for tax relief).

The solution is to separate the £10,000 into a separate loan although the lender may charge a higher rate of interest for doing this.

9.1.13   Higher rate relief

Up to 5 April 1991, tax relief was available at higher rate on MIRAS interest paid.

Where the taxpayer was liable to basic rate tax only, no adjustment was required to the notice of coding as basic rate relief would already have been allowed under the MIRAS scheme.

Where the taxpayer was liable to higher rate tax, the relief was given by extending the basic rate band.

9.1.14   Example—Higher rate relief up to 5 April 1991

A is married and had an income of £35,000 in 1990–91. He has a mortgage and the interest paid in that year which qualified for MIRAS relief was £4,000 gross (£3,000 net). His assessment for 1990–91 would be as follows:

		£	£
	Income		35,000
Less:	Personal allowance	3,005	
	Married couple's allowance	1,720	
			4,725
			30,275

			£
24,700	(£20,700[1] + £4,000)	at 25%	6,175.00
5,575		at 40%	2,230.00
£30,275			£8,405.00

[1] The basic rate band for 1990–91 was £20,700.

For 1991–92 onwards, where the mortgage interest is paid under the MIRAS scheme, no adjustment is necessary in the notice of coding or the income tax assessment. However, people who qualify for the age allowance should take this into account in calculating their total income.

9.1.15 Death of borrower
(TA 1988, s 358)

If a borrower dies, any interest payable by the personal representatives on a loan previously taken out by the deceased to purchase his main residence will continue to qualify for tax relief provided that the property is used as a main residence by the deceased's widow/widower.

9.1.16 Year of marriage

A married couple is only entitled to one limit in respect of mortgage interest paid after the date of their marriage. However, where bride and groom each owned a qualifying property before marriage and one spouse goes to live in the other spouse's home, interest for the period in which the other property is vacant is allowed provided that it is sold within twelve months.

For further details, see extra-statutory concession A35.

9.1.17 MIRAS and let property

Where a person leaves his main residence to live elsewhere in circumstances where extra-statutory concession A27 applies (see 9.1.11) and the residence is let, problems arise because of the interaction of MIRAS and the computation of rental income.

The Revenue have said that the following will apply in such a situation:

(1)   Where the qualifying loan is less than £30,000, it will not be to the taxpayer's disadvantage to claim the benefit of ESC A27 unless he pays tax at higher rate (this may not be so now that MIRAS relief is given at only 20 per cent).

(2)   Where the loan exceeds £30,000 and the rent will clearly exceed the interest on the first £30,000 of the loan, ESC A27 would have the effect of restricting relief to £30,000. In such circumstances, it is not expected that the taxpayer will claim the benefit of ESC A27. MIRAS relief would be withdrawn and the computation of the rental profit would be as in 9.2.3.

Where the loan exceeds £30,000 and the rents fluctuate, it would be administratively inconvenient to claim and disclaim the benefit of ESC A27 and have the loan taken in and out of MIRAS. Where this situation occurs and the taxpayer stays within ESC A27, the Revenue is prepared to leave the loan in MIRAS but to grant any additional relief that would have been due on the statutory basis. This is done by setting the interest on the part of the loan over £30,000 against the rents but only to the extent that they exceed an amount equal to the interest on the first £30,000 of the loan.

9.1.18   Example—Tax relief on let property

A owns a property which is let whilst he is temporarily required to live elsewhere because of his employment. There is a £50,000 mortgage which is within MIRAS. In 1993–94, the position is as follows:

	£
rental income	9,000
interest	5,000

The Revenue's normal practice would be to leave the loan in MIRAS and restrict relief for the loan interest to $\frac{20,000}{50,000} \times £5,000$ ie £2,000. The result would therefore be:

	£
Interest relieved under MIRAS	£3,000

	£
rental income	9,000
less loan interest	2,000
taxable income	7,000

9.1.19   Bridging loans
(TA 1988 s 371)

If a bridging loan is taken out to fund the purchase of a property, interest payable on the borrower's former main residence may qualify for basic rate relief for a period of 12 months. Furthermore FA 1993, s 57 extends this relief to cover the situation where no new loan is taken out. It is therefore possible to move into rented property and still obtain relief, so long as the old home is on the market.

The 12 month period can be extended at the Inspector's discretion if there is difficulty in selling. Relief may be given at the higher rate in respect of interest where a bridging loan was taken out under a binding agreement in existence at that date.

9.2 Loans used to purchase investment properties
(TA 1988, ss 354–355)

9.2.1 Tax relief on investment properties

Tax relief is available on interest paid on a loan used to purchase an investment property provided the following conditions are satisfied:

(1) The property must be let at a commercial rent.
(2) In any period of 52 weeks, the property must be let for more than 26 weeks. When not being let, the property must either be available for letting or used as a main residence or prevented from being available because of construction work or repairs.
(3) The loan must be from a UK or Irish bank or the recipient of the interest must be taxable under Schedule D Case III (see 5.1.2)
(4) The property must be situated in the United Kingdom or the Republic of Ireland.

The form of the relief may differ according to whether the letting is furnished or unfurnished.

9.2.2 Unfurnished lettings
(TA 1988, s 355)

Provided that the conditions in 9.2.1 above are satisfied, tax relief is available on interest paid on a loan used to purchase the property or to carry out improvements to the property. The eligible purchase expenditure would include the cost of the property, solicitors' and surveyors' fees, stamp duty, land registry and other incidental fees associated with the purchase. It would also include the cost of repairs required to make good dilapidations which occurred before the commencement of ownership. The Revenue has issued a fairly lengthy list of what is considered to be improvement expenditure. This includes home extensions, new kitchen/bathroom/bedroom, swimming pool, sauna, rewiring, driveways, patios, etc.

The tax relief is granted by allowing the interest paid as a deduction from rents received from that property or other land or property similarly let.

9.2.3   Examples—Tax relief on unfurnished lettings

(1) C lets an unfurnished property in 1993–94 from which the rent receivable amounts to £2,500. The mortgage interest paid on the property is £3,500. Her assessment will be as follows:

Rental income	£2,500
Interest paid	£2,500
	£NIL

Unallowed interest £1,000 carried forward to 1994–95.

(2) C has a second property (on which there is no mortgage) which is also let unfurnished for a rental of £4,000. Her assessment is as follows:

Rental income—property No 1	£2,500
Rental income—property No 2	£4,000
	£6,500
Loan interest paid	£3,500
Net assessable	£3,000

(3) If the rental from property No 2 is only £500, the assessment would be as follows:

Rental income—property No 1	£2,500
Rental income—property No 2	£500
	£3,000
Loan interest paid	£3,500
Net assessable	£NIL

There will be unallowed interest of £500 carried forward to 1994–95 and future years for offset against rental income as long as property No 1 is commercially let.

9.2.4   Furnished lettings

The treatment of interest payable on a loan used to purchase a property which is let furnished is generally the same as that described for unfurnished lettings in 9.2.3 above, but in some situations loan interest is allowed as a deduction in arriving at the income assessable under Schedule D Case VI.

9.2.5   Furnished holiday lettings
(TA 1988, s 504)

There are special rules which apply when a furnished holiday lettings business is established. The activity is treated as a trade with all the advantages that flow from carrying on a trade eg offset of losses against general income, relevant earnings for pension purposes, roll-over relief, retirement relief, etc. It follows from this that interest payable on loans (or overdrafts) used to purchase the properties should be capable of being deducted from the income generated without restriction, as a trading expense. (For details of what constitutes furnished holiday lettings, see 4.9.)

9.2.6 Overdraft interest

Tax relief cannot be obtained on overdraft interest where the overdraft has been used to purchase a furnished or unfurnished property (except where the property is furnished and used for holiday letting as described in 9.2.5).

However, the Revenue will concessionally allow relief on a loan which replaces an overdraft used to purchase a qualifying property. The replacement must take place within twelve months of the overdraft being taken out (see leaflet IR11).

9.2.7 Investment property abroad

Loan relief is only available where the loan is from a UK lender and the property is situated in the United Kingdom or Republic of Ireland (see 9.2.1).

Consequently, an individual who borrows from a UK bank to acquire a property in, say, Portugal will be taxable on Portuguese rents receivable but will not obtain any relief on the interest paid in the United Kingdom. The situation is no different for UK tax purposes if the borrowing is from a bank in Portugal.

There is no easy way round this. However, if the acquisition of the property has to be financed with borrowings, there are two possible approaches:

(1) Re-arrange all existing loans so that all borrowings are for qualifying purposes
(2) Acquire the property via a limited company where loan interest relief may be available. This is a specialist area requiring professional advice.

9.2.8 Inward property investment

Investment by foreigners in property situated in the United Kingdom has many attractions not the least of which is freedom from capital gains tax (see 13.2).

Interest paid on a loan from a UK bank or UK branch of a foreign bank used by a foreigner to purchase a UK property is eligible for tax relief provided the other conditions contained in 9.2.1 are satisfied. Any non-resident with available cash who is considering purchasing an investment property in the United Kingdom should seriously consider investing the cash and borrowing to purchase the property.

9.3 Loans used to invest in partnerships
(TA 1988, s 362)

Tax relief may be obtained on loan interest where the money is to provide capital into a partnership. Relief is available where the loan is applied:

(1)   in purchasing a share in a partnership; or
(2)   in contributing capital to a partnership or advancing money to a partnership where the money advanced is used wholly for the purposes of the partnership's trade, profession or vocation; or
(3)   in paying off another loan the interest on which would have been eligible for tax relief.

In addition, the borrower must be a member of the partnership throughout the period (and not just as a limited partner) and he must not have recovered any capital from the partnership since rasing the qualifying loan.

9.3.1 Recovery of capital
(TA 1988, s 363)

If at any time after the application of the proceeds of the loan, the partner recovers any amount of capital from the partnership, he is deemed to have used the withdrawal to repay the qualifying loan on which he is claiming interest relief. This is so whether or not he actually uses the proceeds in this manner. It is therefore advisable to segregate the partners' capital and current accounts in the books of the partnership so that any withdrawal can be clearly identified.

9.3.2 Replacement capital

Where a partner has a surplus balance on either his current account or capital account with a partnership and he does not already have a qualifying loan, he may withdraw the balance due to him (with the consent of his partners), use the money to pay off non-qualifying borrowings and then borrow further funds to introduce capital into partnership with tax relief.

9.3.3   Example—Replacement capital

B is a partner in the XYZ partnership. He has a credit balance of £100,000 in his capital account. Outside the partnership, he has bought a yacht for his private use with the help of a £40,000 loan from his bank. In addition, he has a building society mortgage of £50,000 of which £30,000 is under MIRAS.

B would withdraw £60,000 from his capital account in the partnership and use the money to make the following repayments:

Yacht bank loan	£40,000
Building society	£20,000
	£60,000

This would leave B with outstanding borrowings of only £30,000 with his building society on which MIRAS relief is available.

Once these transactions have been completed, B would borrow £60,000 as a loan (not overdraft) and use the funds to re-introduce capital into the partnership with full tax relief on the interest payable.

Professional advice should be sought well in advance before setting up this sort of loan.

9.3.4   Other partnership loans

Another situation where it may be appropriate to re-structure existing borrowings is where there is a partnership loan outstanding in the books of the business. The loan might typically have been used to purchase goodwill or the property from which the practice/business is carried on.

In this situation, each partner is required to borrow privately his share of the partnership loan and introduce the monies raised into the partnership. The partner can then claim tax relief on the interest paid personally as a charge on his income on an actual basis.

The partnership collects the monies raised by each partner's loan and uses the funds to redeem the partnership loan. As a result, each partner's share of profits becomes correspondingly higher because no interest is now payable by the partnership. However the situation redresses itself because the higher profits must be used to finance the private borrowing.

In the first year in which this rearrangement takes place, there is in fact a double deduction of interest which results in a one-off dip in the taxable profit.

9.3.5   Example—Borrowing to repay partnership loans

The XYZ partnership prepares accounts to 30 June annually and its balance sheet shows a loan of £180,000 at 30 June 1993 on which interest is payable at ten per cent. The loan has been held for a number of years. On 6 April 1994, each partner borrows £60,000 at ten per cent per annum which is paid into the partnership which in turn uses the monies collected, £180,000, to pay off the partnership loan.

For the 1994–95 tax year, the partnership will be chargeable to tax on the profits for the year ended 30 June 1993, on a preceding year basis and this will include a deduction of £18,000 being interest payable in the twelve months to 30 June 1993.

In addition, each partner will be able to claim a deduction of £6,000 for 1994–95 in his tax return on an actual basis so that effective relief of £36,000 is obtained in 1994–95. This double deduction is also effective for Class 4 NIC purposes.

This kind of rearrangment needs considerable attention to detail and timing to be successful and tax effective, and professional advice should always be sought.

A further advantage of rearranging a partnership loan into individual loans is that the Revenue have issued a consultative paper which proposes to abolish the existing preceding-year basis of assessment in favour of the actual basis. This is likely to happen in the next two or three years but, in the transition from preceding year to actual year, at least twelve months' profits are bound to fall out of assessment. If the partnership loan remains, with the interest being deducted from the partnership profits, tax relief will be lost on twelve months' interest. By rearranging the loan so that relief is claimed on an actual basis, the relief is actually preserved.

9.3.6   Purchase of plant and machinery
(TA 1988, s 359)

Where a partner incurs capital expenditure in the purchase of plant and machinery which is used for the purposes of the partnership's business, and which is eligible for capital allowances, he can claim tax relief on interest paid if the plant or machinery is financed by a loan. The relief is only available in the tax year in which the loan is taken out and the following three tax years. Similar relief is also available for employees who are required to purchase plant or machinery for use in carrying out their duties.

9.3.7   Example—Use of loans to purchase plant and machinery

A partner borrows £10,000 at ten per cent per annum on 6 October 1993 to buy a car which is used for the partnership's business. His private use of the car is agreed at 25 per cent.

Interest relief is available on £375 in 1993–94 and on £750 in 1994–95, 1995–96 and 1996–97.

9.3.8 Property occupied rent-free by partnership

Where a partner takes out a loan to purchase property which is occupied by the partnership for business purposes and the interest is paid by the partnership, no deduction is technically due to the partnership as the interest is not its liability but the partner's. However, Statement of Practice SP4/85 issued in February 1985 regards the interest paid as rent so that it then becomes allowable as a deduction. In the hands of the partner, the rent is taxable but the interest paid will be allowed as a deduction provided the conditions in 9.2.1 are satisfied.

9.3.9 Incorporation of partnership
(Extra-statutory concession A43)

Where a partnership is incorporated into a limited close company, any qualifying loan in existence at the time will continue to attract tax relief provided the conditions for relief in 9.4 below would be met if a new loan was taken out.

9.4 Loans used to invest in close companies
(TA 1988, s 360)

Where interest is paid on a loan used to purchase shares in a close company, or in lending money to such a company which is used for the purposes of the company's business, the interest will be eligible for tax relief, provided that the borrower meets one of two conditions:

(1) The borrower either alone or together with certain associates owns a material interest in the close company (defined broadly as more than five per cent of the ordinary share capital).
(2) The borrower holds less than five per cent of the ordinary share capital, but works for the greater part of his time in the actual management or conduct of the company or an associated company, (a works manager, a production manager or a company secretary would normally satisfy this condition).

The company must exist wholly or mainly for one of the following purposes:

(1) To carry on a trade or trades on a commercial basis.
(2) To make investments in land or property which is let commercially to unconnected parties.

(3)   To hold shares or securities or to make loans to 'qualifying companies' or an intermediate company, all of which are under its control. A qualifying company is one which is under the control of the close company and satisfies the conditions at (1) and (2) above.

(4)   To co-ordinate the administration of two or more qualifying companies.

If the company holds property, the individual must not reside in it unless he has worked for the greater part of his time in the actual management or conduct of the company.

For the definition of a close company see 24.10.1.

9.4.1   Close BES and EIS companies
(*TA 1988, s 360(3A) and FA 1989, s 47*)

Loan interest relief is not available in respect of shares issued after 13 March 1989 if a claim is made to BES relief. Similar rules apply where an individual has used a loan to acquire shares on which relief is due under the Enterprise Investment Scheme (see 11.7).

10 Outgoings paid net of tax

This chapter looks at the various types of outgoings that are paid net of basic rate tax. It covers the following topics:

(1) Deeds of covenant and annuities.
(2) Covenanted payments to charities.
(3) Gift aid.
(4) Vocational training.
(5) Medical insurance.
(6) Trade unions and friendly society subscriptions.
(7) Life assurance premiums.

10.1 Deeds of covenant and annuities
(TA 1988, ss 347A, 663 and 683 and FA 1988, s 36)

A deed of covenant is basically a written promise to pay another person a certain sum of money each year (or each week, month or quarter, etc), either for a fixed number of years or for a period determined by events (for example, until the payer's or the payee's death). A covenant for the payee's life is, of course, a kind of annuity.

At one time, all deeds of covenant operated so as to transfer taxable income from the payer to the payee, so that the payer's taxable income was reduced by the amount of the covenanted payment and the payee's similarly increased. This could save a great deal of money where (as would usually be the case) the payee was subject to a lower rate of tax than the payer. As a result, deeds of covenant were often used to redistribute income around a family.

The Finance Act 1965 provided that a deed of covenant signed after the beginning of the 1965–66 tax year would not transfer income for higher-rate purposes unless the covenanted payment was made:

(1) to a recognised charity; or
(2) to support a divorced or separated spouse; or

(3)   as part of the purchase price of a business; or

(4)   by a partnership to a retired partner, or to the widow or other dependant of a former partner.

A covenant made today which falls within (1), (3) or (4) above will still operate to transfer taxable income from payer to payee, for both basic and higher rate purposes.

Following FA 1965, the position was that most types of covenanted payments counted as the recipient's income for basic rate, but not higher rate, tax purposes and that those payments reduced the payer's income for basic rate, but not higher rate, purposes.

Most such payments were made under deduction of basic rate tax, so that the payer took his relief by reducing the net payment actually made and the payee received his money tax paid. Where the payee had surplus personal allowances, he could claim a repayment from the Inland Revenue.

This situation lasted until 15 March 1988. The position now is that payments under covenants made before 15 March 1988 still operate to transfer taxable income from payer to payee (but for basic rate only) and should still be made under deduction of tax. (This is subject to the overriding rule that a deed cannot transfer taxable income from a parent to his or her own child until that child attains the age of eighteen years.) Payments under covenants made on or after 15 March 1988 (other than for charitable covenants, business purchase annuities and partnership annuities) are simply ignored for tax purposes and should be made gross.

10.1.1   Covenants made between 1965 and 1988

A non-charitable covenant signed between 7 April 1965 and 14 March 1988 (other than a business purchase or partnership annuity) was and is effective for basic rate tax only. Consequently it was, for many years, an effective way of supporting a student child. The parent would covenant to pay, say, £500 a term to the child, but (with basic rate tax then at, say, 30 per cent) would pay a net amount of £350 only. The student could (if he or she had no other taxable income) reclaim tax of £150 from the Inland Revenue and that repayment would represent a net gain to the family. However, even if the parent was a higher-rate taxpayer, no further relief for the payment could be claimed.

Existing pre-15 March 1988 covenants continue to create such tax repayments until they expire. This is subject to the deed's having been produced to the Inland Revenue no later than 30 June 1988 (a 'policing' measure designed to counter the temptation to backdate deeds signed after the 14 March deadline). The payer is required to enter appropriate details on his tax return because, as with charitable covenants, the Revenue may require non-taxpayers to make good the tax they have paid over to the beneficiary.

10.1.2 Covenants signed after 14 March 1988
(FA 1988, s 36)

With the exception of business purchase and partnership annuities, non-charitable covenants signed after 14 March 1988 are ineffective for all tax purposes.

10.1.3 Annuities

For details of the tax treatment of annuities paid to individuals for valuable consideration, for example as consideration for the acquisition of a business or an interest in a partnership, see 6.6.

10.2 Covenanted payments to charities
(TA 1988, s 660 and FA 1989, s 59)

The Government encourages charitable giving through tax relief for deeds of covenant. Under a deed of covenant, the donor agrees to pay a regular weekly, monthly or annual contribution to the charity. Any payment interval may be specified, but there must be at least one payment a year.

To qualify for tax relief, the deed must run for at least three years and a day (though relief will not be lost if payments cease earlier by reason of events outside the control of the donor—for example, the winding-up of the charity or his own death).

10.2.1 Example—Covenanted payments to a charity

B covenants to pay £75 a year for five years to a recognised charity. The donation will be treated as a gift of £100, from which £25 tax has been deducted, and the charity may reclaim that tax from the Inland Revenue.

If B is a basic rate taxpayer, that is the end of the story—the Inland Revenue has simply 'topped up' his £75 donation to £100. If he is a higher-rate taxpayer, B may additionally claim the higher-rate relief of £15. However, if he does not pay tax at all, the Inland Revenue may ask him to make good the £25 it has paid to the charity.

10.2.2   Conditions for relief

There is no requirement that the donor be United Kingdom resident, but the charity must still be administered in the United Kingdom.

Relief is available only for donations in money and, in principle, relief will be lost if the donor, or a member of his family, enjoys any reciprocal benefit. However, it is quite common for those subscribing to charities to receive magazines or newsletters, or to be allowed free admission to places of interest managed by the charity. In determining whether any reciprocal benefit is enjoyed, the Inland Revenue will therefore ignore any right of admission to wildlife sanctuaries or to buildings and land of historic or architectural interest, and any other benefit worth less than one-quarter of the subscription paid.

10.2.3   Practical points

The deed of covenant may specify either the net or the gross sum payable (£75 or £100 in the example above). In practice, almost all deeds specify the net amount because the amount payable under a gross deed will rise or fall if the basic rate of income tax changes, causing administrative problems. (For example, if the donor in the example above covenanted to pay £100 gross and the basic rate of income tax were reduced to 24 per cent, the charity would have to ask him to sign a new banker's order for £76.)

Most established charities will be pleased to supply pre-printed deed of covenant forms. However, if none is available, blank forms are available from the Inland Revenue Claims Branch (see 10.3.4).

The deed must run for at least three years and one day. A deed will typically provide for an annual payment to be made on (say) 1 June 1993, 1994, 1995 and 1996 and such a deed, although running only for the minimum three years and a day, is usually called a four-year deed, because it specifies four payments.

Sometimes a donor, while willing to make regular charitable payments, does not wish to commit himself to supporting a particular charity for four years. Such an individual may covenant to the Charities Aid Foundation, which acts as a clearing house, enabling his donations to be redirected to the charities of his choice. An explanatory leaflet is available from:

> Charities Aid Foundation
> 48 Pembury Road
> Tonbridge
> Kent TN9 2JD

Finally, with covenants, it is essential to put the paperwork in place before handing over the money. This is because a deed of covenant takes effect only from the date it is signed.

10.2.4   Example—Covenant made out of time

On 1 June 1993 A gives £100 to a recognised charity. On 2 June he signs a deed of covenant, promising to make four annual payments, on 1 June 1993, 1994, 1995 and 1996.

The 1993 payment will not be covered by the covenant, because it was made before the deed came into effect, so the charity will not be able to reclaim tax on that payment. Even worse, the total life of the covenant is three years only (2 June 1993 to 1 June 1996) and so the deed is wholly ineffective for tax purposes: therefore no tax may be reclaimed in respect of the 1994, 1995 and 1996 payments also.

10.2.5   Claims by charities

A charity obtains the tax due on deed of covenant payments by submitting a claim to the Revenue. Claim forms and guidance notes are available from Claims Branch (Charity Division) (see 10.3.4).

The original deed of covenant should be retained by the charity. It is no longer necessary to submit deeds with repayment claims, but the Revenue may at its discretion ask for sight of particular deeds.

The donor must provide, on Inland Revenue Form R185 (Covenant) or R185(AP), details of the payment made and of his own address and Tax Office reference. In general such a certificate need only be provided for the first year of a covenant unless Charity Division specifically requires this.

A somewhat unfortunate point is that, although deed of covenant payments must be made in money, experience has taught the Revenue to be suspicious of payments made in cash. (In one case it found that a charity had claimed millions of pounds in respect of payments covenanted but never actually made by supporters.) Where it is claimed that payments have been made in cash, the Revenue will therefore require a proper 'audit trail' establishing receipt of money from the individual covenantors.

Where, for example, members of the congregation of a church have covenanted to donate a pound or two each week, the most practicable method of establishing an audit trail is to provide named envelopes for each contributor's weekly donation.

10.2.6   Deposited covenants

A popular arrangement for an individual wishing to make a single donation of, say, £200 to a charity, was to covenant £50 (net) a year for four years and then to treat the £200 as the first £50 instalment due under the covenant plus a loan of £150. In each following year, there would be an exchange of £50 cheques (the payment of an annual instalment due under the covenant being matched by a partial repayment of the loan). In this way, tax relief was generated for what was in truth a single lump-sum donation.

However, unless the total donation is less than £250, it will nowadays be more convenient to use the gift aid scheme (see 10.3).

10.2.7   Payroll giving scheme
(TA 1988, s 202)

Under a payroll giving scheme an employee asks his employer to deduct an amount from his wage or salary and pay that amount over to a charity (usually a clearing house such as the Charities Aid Foundation—see 10.2.3 above). PAYE is then operated by the employer as if the employee's wage or salary had been the amount remaining after the charitable donation, which has the effect of granting tax relief at the highest rate paid. The maximum donation an individual may make under payroll giving arrangements is £900 a year (£600 up to 6 April 1993).

An employer is not obliged to offer a payroll giving scheme and, if a scheme is offered, employees may decide individually whether they wish to participate. Usually, each employee will specify particular charities to the clearing house but in some cases the money is paid into a fund administered by a workplace committee. However, such funds can cause difficulties, especially where the name of the fund suggests that it was established by the generosity of the employer, rather than the employees themselves.

10.3   Gift aid
(FA 1990, s 25 and F(No2)A 1992, s 26)

'Gift aid', introduced in 1990, is another way in which the Government seeks to encourage taxpayers to support charities. The scheme gives income tax relief (at the higher rate, if paid) for substantial cash donations to charity. However for the purposes of basic rate tax, it operates in a similar way to the schemes for vocational training and medical insurance, ie on a net payment basis. To many people, therefore, gift aid appears to be not so much a tax relief as a mechanism by which the Government tops up their charitable giving.

10.3.1 Example—Gift aid donation

A gives £750 to a recognised charity. Under the gift aid scheme, that will be treated as a donation of £1,000, from which basic rate tax of £250 has been deducted. The charity will be able to claim that tax from the Inland Revenue, so it will receive a total of £1,000.

If A is a basic rate taxpayer, that is the end of the story: he has paid over £750 which the Revenue has 'topped up' to £1,000.

If A is a higher-rate taxpayer, he may claim higher-rate relief on the gift, calculated as follows:

Gross donation made	£1,000
Tax relief at 40 per cent	£400
Less deducted when gift made	£250
Reduction in A's own tax liability	£150

However, whereas tax relief for vocational training and medical insurance is given even to non-taxpayers (see 10.4 and 10.5) the gift aid scheme is less generous. If the donor is not a taxpayer at all, the Revenue will require him to make good the £250 it has paid to the charity.

10.3.2 Qualifying donations

Several conditions have to be satisfied before a donation can qualify under the gift aid scheme:

(1)   The recipient must be a recognised charity established in the United Kingdom (that is to say, the charity must be administered in the United Kingdom: it may carry out its charitable work anywhere in the world). However, many appeal funds and societies established for the public benefit are not technically charities. In case of doubt, intending donors should ask for evidence of charitable status or should consult:

The Charity Commission
57–60 Haymarket
London SW1Y 4QX

By way of exception, four bodies which are not technically charities are deemed to be charities for gift aid purposes: the British Museum, the National History Museum, the National Heritage Memorial Fund and the Historic Buildings and Monuments Commission for England.

(2)   The donor must be resident in the United Kingdom.

(3)   The gift must be of money—it is not possible to claim gift aid relief for donated works of art, or even for goods (such as clothing or

blankets) which will be used to assist distressed people. Also, it is not possible to give money on condition that it be used to buy something from the donor, a member of his family or a company in which he has an interest.

(4)   The gift may be made in cash, by cheque or bank transfer, or by credit card. However, the Revenue does not accept that writing-off an existing loan to the charity is equivalent to a gift of money.

(5)   The donation actually made (that is to say, before adding the Revenue 'top-up') must be at least £250. Until 7 May 1992 the minimum donation was £600 and from 8 May 1992–15 March 1993 the minimum was £400. Currently there is no maximum donation: until 19 March 1991 there was a ceiling of £5 million for donations by a single individual in any year of assessment.

(6)   Any reciprocal benefit received from the charity (by the donor or a member of his family) must not exceed the lesser of 2.5 per cent of the net donation made and £250 for the year of assessment.

10.3.3   Example—Gift aid and reciprocal benefits

In May 1993 A gives £10,000 to a recognised charity and, as a token of appreciation, is sent tickets worth £150 to attend the charity's Summer Festival. The £10,000 qualifies as a gift aid donation, because £150 is less than 2.5 per cent of that donation.

In November 1993, she gives a further £10,000 and is sent tickets, again worth £150, to attend the charity's Christmas Extravaganza. That donation will not qualify under the gift aid scheme, because the total benefits received by A during the year of assessment exceed £250.

10.3.4   Administration

The donor must provide the charity with a certificate (on Inland Revenue Form R190 (SD)), certifying the amount paid and giving his tax office reference and National Insurance number. It is not necessary for this form to be completed at the time the gift is made (so that it is in order, for example, for a charity to write subsequently asking for Form R190 (SD) to be completed).

The charity then submits its claim on Inland Revenue Form R68. As long as the basic rate of income tax remains 25 per cent, the amount it may claim will of course be one-third of the net donation received. If the tax rate changes to produce a more awkward calculation, ready reckoner tables will be provided by the Revenue.

Supplies of forms are available from, and any gift aid queries should be addressed to:

England, Wales and Northern Ireland

Inland Revenue Claims Branch
Charity Division
St John's House
Merton Road
Bootle
Merseyside L69 4EJ

Scotland

Inland Revenue Claims Branch
Charity Division
Trinity Park House
South Trinity Road
Edinburgh EH5 3SD

10.3.5   A word of warning

Gift aid relief is available only for individual donations of £250 or more. Relief is not available where a supporter makes a series of smaller donations which, over a period, total £250, nor where two or more people—even husband and wife—have joined forces to build a single remittance up to £250. However, if a larger remittance is made up of several contributions, each individual who contributed £250 or more may claim gift aid relief in the usual way.

10.4   Vocational training
(FA 1991, ss 32 & 33)

For 1992–93 and subsequent years of assessment, tax relief is available where an individual pays for his or her own vocational training, subject to the following conditions:

(1)   Relief is available for registration, tuition, assessment and examination fees, but not for books, equipment, travel or other incidental expenses.

(2)   Those fees must be paid by the student himself and not, for example, by his employer.

(3)   The student must be resident in the United Kingdom (but not necessarily ordinarily resident).

(4)   The course must lead to, or count towards, a National or Scottish Vocational Qualification (NVQ or SVQ) at levels 1 to 5 inclusive. (Level 5, which covers senior managerial and professional skills, was added with effect from 1 January 1994.)

(5)   The college or other body organising the course must be registered with the Inland Revenue as a 'training provider'.

(6) The student must not be entitled to claim tax relief for his training expenses in any other way. (It is in fact very unlikely that relief would be available in any other way: one possibility is that the student is carrying on business and the course fees count as an expense of that business. However even in the case of a student carrying on a business, fees, will count as a business expense only if the course updates his existing expertise, rather than giving him entirely new skills.)

(7) The student must not be receiving public sector financial support, for example a local authority grant or a subsidised loan under the Career Development Loan Scheme. More detailed information is given in the Inland Revenue leaflet *Tax Relief for Vocational Training* (IR119).

(8) The student must be 16 or over.

(9) The student cannot be in full-time education and qualify for relief unless he is over 18.

On the other hand, there is no requirement that the course must be relevant to the student's current job, or even that the student must be in employment or in business on his own account. Accordingly, tax relief is available on equal terms to unemployed people keen to increase their chances in the job market, to those wishing to embark upon a new career path and to those seeking to update their skills with a view to returning to work after a career break.

Furthermore, provided the study unit could count towards a NVQ or SVQ, tax relief is available even if the student has no intention of pursuing the full qualification.

10.4.1 How relief is given

Basic rate relief is given under MIRAS-type arrangements: that is to say, if the course fee is £200, the college will ask the trainee to pay only £150 and will claim the balance of £50 (25 per cent of £200) from the Government. From the student's point of view, this system offers two advantages. Firstly, relief is obtained immediately and secondly, the reduced fee is payable even if the student is not a taxpayer (for example, is unemployed and so has no taxable income).

The college will ask the student to sign a simple declaration that he fulfils the qualifying conditions. For identification purposes, he will also be required to state his national insurance number. The tax return form asks him to enter the 'name of the training organisation' and the 'net amount paid'—in the example above, the £150 actually paid to the college, rather than the full £200 fee.

If the student is a higher-rate taxpayer, higher rate relief will be given in his tax assessment or PAYE code. (If the student in the example above was a higher-rate taxpayer, the higher rate relief would reduce the tax payable by 15 per cent of £200, or £30.) The tax office may require the student to produce an official college receipt, to verify the fee paid.

Relief is available only where the student pays his own course fees. If, for example, a father wishes to help his son financially, he should give the boy the money, not pay the fees direct. It also follows that the fee paid will not reduce the father's income for higher-rate purposes.

10.4.2 Training providers

A college or other body wishing to register as a training provider should request a copy of the training pack from:

> Inland Revenue (Claims Branch)
> Vocational Training Unit
> St John's House
> Merton Road
> Bootle
> Merseyside L69 9BB

10.5 Medical insurance
(FA 1989, ss 54–57)

Since April 1990, tax relief has been available for premiums paid to provide medical insurance cover for a person aged 60 or more. The arrangements resemble those for vocational training, inasmuch as basic rate relief is given by reducing the premium actually paid (so that the benefit may be enjoyed even by those who are not taxpayers).

The Finance Act 1994 restricts tax relief to 25 per cent. For 1993–94 and earlier years, higher rate relief had been available. Also, up to 1993–94, the grossed up premium constituted an allowable deduction in arriving at an individual's total income for age relief purposes (see 7.6).

It should be noted that relief may be due to a person, even though he is not himself insured, provided the insurance is for a person aged 60 or more.

10.5.1 Example—Premiums paid by a relative

A, aged 35 and a higher-rate taxpayer, pays the premiums to secure medical insurance cover for her mother, B, aged 65, whose sole income is the State pension. If the gross premium is £400, A will pay only £300 and the insurance company will recoup the balance of £100 (25 per cent of £400) from the Government. Prior to 6 April 1994, the company would also (on request) give A a certificate enabling her to claim higher-rate relief, which will reduce her total tax bill by £60 (15 per cent of £400).

10.5.2   Who is eligible?

The person insured must be resident in the United Kingdom and have attained his or her 60th birthday. The only exception is that, where husband and wife are covered by a single policy, tax relief will be given provided either has attained that age. Except in the case of husband and wife, no relief at all will be given where a policy covers two or more people, unless all have attained the age of 60.

The person paying the premiums must be resident in the United Kingdom, but need not be a relative of the person insured. For example, a premium paid to secure cover for a domestic servant will qualify. However, an employer may not claim relief for a premium paid in respect of an employee if that premium is deductible in computing his business profits.

10.5.3   Example—Premiums paid by an employer

A employs B as his butler and C as his farm manager. Both B and C are 62 years old and A provides medical insurance for both.

Only B's policy qualifies for tax relief under the scheme described above. However, the premium paid on C's policy is deductible in computing the taxable profit of A's farming business. Therefore A enjoys effective tax relief for both payments, albeit by different means.

10.5.4   Which policies qualify?

The most important point is that the policy must be limited to reimbursing medical expenses incurred (plus a maximum of £5 per night for out-of-pocket expenses while undergoing treatment in a private hospital bed). Policies that seek to make good the insured's loss of earnings, for example, will not qualify.

No minimum level of cover is required for tax relief to be available. A qualifying policy may cover medical and surgical treatment, including minor operations performed at a doctor's surgery, physiotherapy and consultations with specialists, but it need not cover all of these. A qualifying policy must, however, exclude cosmetic surgery, consultations with general medical practitioners, eye tests and dental treatment (other than specialist treatment carried out by a consultant surgeon).

Tax relief is given (or denied) on an all-or-nothing basis: if the policy offers any non-qualifying benefit, the whole premium is disqualified. Therefore all the well-known medical insurers offer policies tailored to satisfy the Revenue requirements.

The Finance Act 1994 introduced a useful relaxation to the rules. Where a contract covers a married couple, relief can now be given provided that at least one spouse was aged 60 (or over) when the policy was taken out. It was previously the case that where the qualifying spouse died and the surviving spouse was younger than 60, no relief was due on any subsequent premium payments made under that policy. The rules have now been amended so that the surviving spouse will continue to be entitled to relief on premiums paid under the same contract.

10.5.5   Two points to watch

Two points must be emphasised. First, tax relief is available only where the premiums are paid by an individual. No relief, therefore, will be given if premiums are paid direct by the trustees of a family settlement.

Second, the Revenue would regard as fraudulent any kind of arrangement designed to increase the tax relief.

10.5.6   Example—Fraudulent claim for tax relief

A has a private medical insurance policy. On attaining the age of 60, he qualifies for tax relief. However, he is not a higher-rate taxpayer, so he suggests to his son, who is a 40 per cent taxpayer, that the son should in future pay the premiums and claim the higher rate relief. The son will not however be out of pocket, because A will make good his net expenditure.

Both father and son may find themselves in Court, charged with conspiracy to defraud the Inland Revenue—and the same principle applies to any arrangement designed to produce tax relief at a higher rate than that appropriate to the person who has actually borne the cost of the premiums.

10.6   Trade union and friendly society subscriptions
(TA 1988, s 266(6) and (7))

Some trade unions provide pensions and/or death benefits (often called 'funeral benefits') for their members. Each member is entitled to tax relief on half of that part of his subscription which relates to the provision of such benefits. However, this relief is sometimes given by the Revenue making a block payment to the union and the union then charging reduced subscriptions to its members.

The members of some friendly societies also pay a subscription which covers both a death benefit and a sickness benefit. Half of the amount referable to the death benefit qualifies for tax relief.

There is a distinction between relief under the special arrangements for trade union subscriptions and 'mixed' friendly society policies (described above) and the general relief for life assurance premiums (see 10.7). Relief under the special arrangements is available only in the exact circumstances described—and not, for example, for a premium paid under a simple life assurance policy issued by a friendly society. Relief under the special arrangements is, however, available irrespective of the date the insurance came into force, whereas the general relief for life assurance premiums is available only for policies which entered into force before 14 March 1984.

10.7   Life assurance premiums
(TA 1988, s 266)

Most life assurance polices which came into force before 14 March 1984 qualify for a form of tax relief. (The operative date is the day the policyholder's proposal was accepted by the insurance company, not the day the policy was issued.) The Revenue makes a block payment to the insurance company, equal to half the basic rate of tax on the premiums payable on qualifying policies, and the insurance company correspondingly reduces the amount actually paid by the policyholder. For example, if the standard premium was £100, the Revenue would pay £12.50 and the policyholder only £87.50.

That £12.50 is, however, the sum total of the relief available. No additional relief may be claimed if the policyholder is a higher-rate taxpayer.

Furthermore, relief will be lost completely if any material change is made to the policy—for example, if a term policy is converted into an endowment or if the insurance company makes a loan to the policyholder without charging a commercial rate of interest.

No tax relief is available for the premiums on life assurance policies which came into force on or after 14 March 1984. However, an alternative route to tax relief is to arrange your life cover through a personal pension plan as explained in Chapter 12.

11   Tax efficient investment

There is a range of investments where the interest and any gains are exempt from tax. This chapter covers the following:

Investments which provide a tax exempt return

(1)   National Savings investments.
(2)   TESSAs.
(3)   Personal Equity Plans (PEPs).

Investments which qualify for a tax deduction

(4)   Business expansion schemes—general.
(5)   Trading BES companies.
(6)   Assured tenancy schemes.
(7)   Enterprise investment schemes.
(8)   Enterprise zone trusts.
(9)   Venture capital trusts.

11.1   National Savings investments

11.1.1   National Savings certificates
(TA 1988, s 46)

These are certificates which pay an accumulating rate of interest over a five year period. All the returns are tax free. Index linked certificates accumulate at a rate related to the Retail Price Index. If held for the full five years a bonus is payable.

11.1.2   NSB ordinary account interest
(TA 1988, s 325)

The first £70 of interest paid on a National Savings Bank (NSB) ordinary account is exempt from tax (see 5.1.1).

11.2   TESSAs
(TA 1988, ss 326A-326C)

An individual is permitted to have a Tax-Exempt Special Savings Account. This is basically a five year plan under which an individual aged 18 or over can save up to £9,000. The sum must be held on deposit by a bank, building society or other institution authorised under the Banking Act 1987, but the regulations permit an investor to switch from one group to another. The resulting interest is not taxable provided the individual makes no withdrawals during the five year period, or any such withdrawals do not exceed the amount of the interest credited to the account less tax at basic rate.

The following limits apply to the amounts which may be invested in a TESSA:

(1)   Not more than £3,000 may be deposited during the first 12 months.
(2)   Subsequently, not more than £1,800 can be invested in any period of 12 months.
(3)   The total sum invested may not exceed £9,000 in total.

Where a TESSA ceases to qualify, the interest credited to the TESSA becomes taxable income which is deemed to arise at that point in time.

11.3   Personal equity plans (PEPs)
(TA 1988, s 333)

An individual aged 18 or over who is resident in the United Kingdom is permitted to invest up to £6,000 in any tax year in a personal equity plan. In addition, a further £3,000 may be invested in a single company personal equity plan (see below). An individual may not take out more than one of each type of personal equity plan in a tax year.

The investments are held by a PEP manager and once again it is possible for a plan to be transferred to another authorised manager.

Personal equity plans are intended to be a way of encouraging investment in shares. Up to £6,000 may be invested in shares in companies quoted on the Stock Exchange or shares quoted on the unlisted securities market (USM) or in authorised unit trusts or investment trusts who in turn invest at least 50 per cent of their funds in UK equities or shares quoted on EC Stock Exchanges. As an alternative, up to £1,500 may be invested in any other authorised unit trust or investment trust. The balance of any investments over the £1,500 limit must then be invested in qualifying equities or in unit trusts or investment trusts which meet the 50 per cent requirement.

An individual may also invest up to £3,000 a year in a single company PEP where the investment is restricted to shares in one particular company.

All income and capital gains arising within the personal equity plan are exempt from tax. There is one slight *caveat* in the case of personal equity plans which are not invested in shares from the outset. The cash held within the plan will normally be put on deposit and gross interest is obtained. Provided that the PEP is eventually invested in qualifying shares, the interest which has accrued in this way is tax free. However, if the plan were to be cashed in without the money within the PEP ever having been used to purchase qualifying investments, the interest would be taxable income for the owner of the personal equity plan. Such interest is taxable income for the year in which the plan is cashed in.

11.4 Business expansion schemes
(TA 1988, ss 289–312)

11.4.1 Introduction

An individual may claim a deduction for investments under the business expansion scheme (although it should be noted that the business expansion scheme ended on 31 December 1993).

11.4.2 Outline of the relief

BES relief enabled a qualifying taxpayer to deduct the cost of his investment in a qualifying company against his taxable income. The maximum amount of BES relief that could be claimed in respect of any one tax year was £40,000.

BES shares could be issued either at par or at a premium but the minimum subscription to any one company was £500. If, however, the investment was made via an approved investment fund, the £500 limit did not apply.

If BES shares are sold after five years, and relief has not been withdrawn, any capital gain is exempt for capital gains tax purposes. Equally, any capital loss is not allowable.

11.4.3 Claims

No claims are accepted by the Revenue until the company has been trading for four months and, if the company is not trading on the date when the shares are issued, relief will not be given unless the company begins to trade within two years after that date. Even then, relief is only provisional and may be withdrawn in certain circumstances (see 11.4.4).

A taxpayer may elect that the relief be given in part against his previous year's taxation liability in respect of shares issued to him before 6 October. The maximum amount that can be referred back to the previous year is either one half of the investment or £5,000, whichever is the smaller of the two amounts.

11.4.4   Withdrawal of relief

There are various occasions on which BES relief can be withdrawn if certain events occur. The legislation requires the taxpayer to advise the Revenue within 60 days of any event becoming known to him that may lead to the withdrawal of relief. Where relief has already been given, the Revenue may issue an assessment under Schedule D case VI to recover the excessive relief.

Sale of shares
(TA 1988, s 299)

If the shares are disposed of within five years to anyone other than the taxpayer's spouse, the BES relief previously given on those shares will be withdrawn. Relief is withdrawn completely where the sale is not made by way of a bargain at arm's length (and a sale to a connected person— see below—can *never* be a bargain at arm's length for these purposes). Where shares are sold by way of a bargain at arm's length, the withdrawal of BES relief is restricted to the cost of the shares or the disposal proceeds, whichever is the lesser amount.

Linked loans
(FA 1993, s 111)

The receipt of a loan linked to the issue of BES shares may cause BES relief to be withdrawn. Specific legislation was introduced for BES shares issued after 15 March 1993 to combat schemes which involved non-recourse loans.

Receiving value from the company
(TA 1988, s 300)

BES relief may also be withdrawn if the individual receives value from the company. In this case, the amount of BES relief which is withdrawn is equal to the value received.

An individual is deemed to receive value from a company if it does any of the following:

(1) Repays, redeems or repurchases any part of his holding of its share capital or securities, or makes any payment to him for the cancellation of rights.

(2) Repays any debt to him (other than a debt incurred by the company on or after the date on which he subscribed for the shares which are the subject of BES relief).

(3) Pays him for the cancellation of any debt owed to him other than an ordinary trade debt, ie a debt incurred for a supply of goods or services on normal trade credit terms. The legislation specifically provides that normal trade credit does not allow for payment to be left outstanding for a period which exceeds six months.

(4) Releases or waives any liability of his to the company (the liability is deemed to have been waived if the liability is outstanding for more than twelve months) or discharges or undertakes to discharge any liability of his to a third person.

(5) Makes a loan or advance to him if this includes the situation where the individual becomes indebted to the company other than by an ordinary trade debt.

(6) Provides a benefit or facility for him.

(7) Transfers an asset to him for no consideration or for consideration less than market value.

(8) Acquires an asset from him for consideration exceeding market value.

(9) Makes any other payment to him except:
    (a) one which represents payment or reimbursement of allowable expenditure;
    (b) interest at a commercial rate on a loan from the individual;
    (c) dividends representing a normal return on investment;
    (d) payment for supply of goods by the individual to the company (provided that the price does not exceed the goods' market value);
    (e) reasonable and necessary remuneration for services rendered to the company where the individual is chargeable under Schedule D Case I or Case II (the last let-out does not cover remuneration for secretarial or managerial services).

In addition, an individual may receive value from a company if it is wound up and he receives a payment or asset in the course of the liquidation.

11.4.5   Anti-avoidance

In addition to the various provisions that have to be met in order to claim BES relief, there is specific legislation to deny relief unless the shares in question are acquired for *bona fide* commercial reasons and not as part of a scheme to avoid taxation.

A basic feature of the BES is that it is intended to give tax relief to individuals who have no connection with the company other than as investors. It is not designed to enable entrepreneurs to qualify for tax relief in respect of subscription for share capital in their own company.

Even for the outside investor to qualify for tax relief, there are a large number of conditions to be satisfied both by the investor and by the company in its constitution and trading activities. Because there are differences between the rules applying to trading companies and companies offering residential accommodation under assured tenancies, these two types of BES companies are dealt with separately.

11.5   Trading BES companies

11.5.1   The investor
(TA 1988, s 291(1))

The following are the main qualifications for the investor:

(1)   The investor must be resident and ordinarily resident in the United Kingdom on the date on which the shares are issued.
(2)   The investor must not be 'connected' with the company during the 'qualifying period'.

Connected persons
(TA 1988, s 291(2) and (4))

An individual is 'connected' with the company if he, or an 'associate' of his, is one of the following:

(1)   A partner of the company.
(2)   An employee of either the company or of the company's partners.
(3)   A paid director of the company.

An individual is also connected with the company if he controls the company, or he possesses, or he is entitled to acquire, more than 30 per cent of:

(1)   the issued ordinary share capital; or
(2)   the loan capital and ordinary share capital; or
(3)   the voting power of the company; or
(4)   the assets of the company available to shareholders in a liquidation.

'Associate'

An associate in relation to the investor means the investor's partner, or a relative being the investor's:

(1) husband or wife, or
(2) parent or remoter forebear (ie grandparent, great-grandparent etc), or
(3) child or remoter issue (ie grandchild or great-grandchild).

Associate would also cover the trustee of a settlement in which the individual or any relative, as defined above, was the settlor.

Qualifying period

The qualifying period begins on the date the shares are issued and ends five years after that date, except that if the company was incorporated more than two years before the date of the share issue, the qualifying period begins two years before the share issue date and ends seven years later.

11.5.2 Parallel trades
(TA 1988, s 292)

The investor is not entitled to BES relief if, when the trade commences, he is one of a group of individuals who control the company, and he also controls either personally or with others, a second company which deals in the same type of property or services, and serves the same or a similar market.

11.5.3 The company
(TA 1988, s 293)

An investor is not entitled to BES relief unless the company remains a 'qualifying company' at all times during the 'relevant period'. The relevant period is normally three years after the issue of the BES shares. However, where the company was not carrying on a qualifying trade on the date on which the shares were issued, the relevant period extends to three years after the start of the qualifying trade.

Conditions

The principal qualifying conditions for a company are:

(1) The company (which must not be quoted on the Stock Exchange or on the USM) must be incorporated in the United Kingdom and must be solely UK-resident for taxation purposes.
(2) The company must be:
    (a) one that exists substantially for the purposes of carrying on, wholly or mainly in the United Kingdom, one or more qualifying trades; or

    (b)   one whose business consists wholly of:
        (i)   the holding of shares in, or the making of loans to, one or more qualifying subsidiaries; or
        (ii)   both the holding of such shares or the making of such loans, and the carrying on of one or more qualifying trades in the United Kingdom.

(3)   The company's share capital must not include any shares that are not fully paid up.

(4)   A qualifying company will lose that status if a resolution is passed or an order is made for the company to be wound up during the relevant period. This will not apply, however, if the winding up is for *bona fide* commercial reasons (ie not as part of a scheme to avoid tax) and the assets of the company are distributed to the members within three years.

Subsidiaries
(TA 1988, ss 308–309)

Qualifying companies may have subsidiary companies without losing qualifying status provided that:

(1)   The company and each subsidiary exist principally for the purposes of carrying on one or more qualifying trades wholly or mainly in the United Kingdom, or being a property managing or dormant company.

(2)   The subsidiaries are 90 per cent controlled by the company.

(3)   On a winding up, the qualifying company is entitled to 90 per cent of the assets available for distribution in the subsidiaries.

(4)   No arrangement exists for the above to cease to apply.

A subsidiary is a property-managing subsidiary for the purposes of (1) above if it exists mainly to hold and manage property used by a qualifying group company, either for the purposes of carrying on a qualifying trade, or for research and development from which it is intended that a qualifying trade be carried on by a group company.

A subsidiary is a dormant company for the purposes of (1) above if it has no profits for corporation tax purposes and no part of its business consists of the making of investments.

It follows from the above that the existence of one 'non-qualifying' subsidiary, will mean that the parent company is not a qualifying company.

The above conditions must be met until the end of the relevant period, although the sale, winding up or dissolution of a subsidiary for *bona fide* commercial reasons during this period is acceptable. In addition, a subsidiary company may be sold during this period, provided that the sale can be shown to be for commercial reasons and not for the avoidance of tax.

11.5.4 Interests in land
(TA 1988, s 294)

A company is not a qualifying company if at any time in the relevant period the market value of its interests in land and buildings is greater than 50 per cent of the market value of the company's total assets. These provisions, however do not apply to the first £50,000 raised under the BES scheme within the period of one year ending on the date of that particular issue of shares.

11.5.5 Limits on amounts raised
(TA 1988, s 290A)

Trading companies, other than certain ship-chartering companies, were limited as to the amount of share capital they could raise under the BES scheme. The limit was £750,000 in any period beginning six months before the date of issue of shares and ending on that date, or, if longer, the period beginning with the previous 6 April and ending on the date of issue.

11.5.6 The trade
(TA 1988, s 297)

As stated above, a qualifying company must exist for the purposes of carrying on, either on its own account, or via an appropriate subsidiary, a qualifying trade. This trade must be carried out on a commercial basis and with a view to realisation of profits during the relevant period. For this purpose the definition of relevant period is the same as set out in 11.5.3.

The trade must not comprise to any substantial extent of the following:

(1) Dealing in commodities, shares, securities, land or futures.
(2) Dealing in goods otherwise than in the course of an ordinary trade of wholesale or retail distribution. This excludes such trades as dealing in goods that are normally collected or held as investments, dealing in goods with connected parties, 'matching' purchases with future sales or arrangements under which the company does not take physical possession of the goods.
(3) Banking, insurance, money-lending, debt factoring, hire purchase financing or other financial activities.

(4)   Oil extraction activities.
(5)   Providing legal or accountancy services.
(6)   Receiving royalties or licence fees, unless the company is engaged
      in the production of films, or the distribution of films produced by
      itself in the relevant period, and all of the royalties or licence fees
      are in respect of films produced by the company or are in respect
      of sound recordings from those films.
      In addition, the receipt of royalties will not disqualify a company
      if it is engaged in research and development throughout the
      relevant period and all of the royalties received by it in that period
      arise from research and development which it has carried out.
(7)   Leasing, unless the trade consists of the letting of certain ships all
      of which are beneficially owned by the company and are registered
      in the United Kingdom. Individual lettings must not be for a period
      exceeding 12 months and the trade must be conducted on an arm's
      length basis with an unconnected third party. The chartering
      company must be responsible for the general management of the
      ship during the period.

11.6   Assured tenancy companies
(FA 1988, s 50 & Sched 4)

Relief is also available under the business expansion scheme for shares
which were issued by 31 December 1993 for the purposes of raising
money for the provision and maintenance of residential accommodation,
and which the company, or its subsidiary either lets or intends to let on
assured tenancies. This activity must be conducted on a commercial basis
and with a view to the realisation of profits for a period of four years from
the date of issue of the BES shares.

The detailed anti-avoidance rules which need to be borne in mind by
investors are as follows.

11.6.1   The investor

The same conditions apply as for trading BES companies (see 11.5.1).

Connected persons

The same conditions apply as for trading BES companies (see 11.5.1).

An individual is also connected with the company if he, or an associate of
his, occupies a dwellinghouse in which the company holds an interest and,
the interest held by the company is superior to that held by the individual,
(eg. if the company owns the freehold and the individual has a lease, or the
company has a head-lease and the individual has a sub-lease).

The definition of 'associate' is also under 11.5.1.

Qualifying period

This is the same as for trading BES companies (see 11.5.1).

11.6.2   The company

An investor will not qualify for income tax relief for his BES investment unless the company in which he buys shares is a qualifying company throughout the relevant period.

Relevant period

This period commences on the day the shares are issued and ends four years after that date. If, however, the company is not carrying on the 'qualifying activity' (see below) on the date on which the shares are issued, the relevant period extends to four years after the commencement of the qualifying activities.

Status of BES company

The company (which must not be quoted on the Stock Exchange or on the USM), must be incorporated in the United Kingdom and must be solely UK-resident for taxation purposes.

Winding up of company

A qualifying company will lose that status if, during the relevant period, a resolution is passed or an order is made for the company to be wound up. This will not apply however if the winding up is for *bona fide* commercial reasons and not as part of a scheme to avoid tax and, within three years, the assets of the company are distributed to the members.

Shares

The company's share capital must not include shares that are not fully paid-up.

Subsidiaries

Qualifying companies may have subsidiary companies without losing qualifying status provided that:

(1)   each subsidiary is either dormant or exists wholly or substantially for the purposes of carrying on activities which do not include, to any substantial extent, activities that are not qualifying activities; and

(2)   the subsidiaries are 90 per cent controlled by the qualifying company; and

(3)   on a winding up, the qualifying company is entitled to at least 90 per cent of the assets available for distribution; and

(4)   no arrangements exist for the above to cease to apply.

Activities

The company must exist mainly for the purposes of carrying on activities which are either 'qualifying activities' or for the purposes of holding shares in, or making loans to, one or more subsidiary companies which themselves do not carry out to any substantial extent activities which are not qualifying activities.

Qualifying activities are those which consist of the provision and maintenance of dwellinghouses that the company lets or intends to let on 'qualifying tenancies'. The activities must be conducted on a commercial basis and with a view to profits, during the period beginning from the date on which the shares are issued and ending four years later.

11.6.3   Qualifying tenancies

A qualifying tenancy means an assured tenancy, other than an assured shorthold tenancy, as defined by the Housing Act 1988, and is one for which the tenant does not pay a premium, and does not have either personally or through an associate, the option to buy the property.

The following are the principal conditions to be met in order to ensure that the tenancies are qualifying tenancies within the legislation:

(1)   On the date on which the shares are issued, or if later, the date on which the company acquires the dwellinghouse, the market value of each property must not exceed £125,000 if situated in Greater London, or £85,000 if situated elsewhere.

(2)   If the property is divided into flats, the value of each individual flat must not exceed the above limits.

(3)   The property must not be unfit for human habitation and must contain all standard amenities.

(4)   There must not be any arrangements in existence for letting the property at the time it is acquired by the company.

(5)   A qualifying property that is owned by a company entitled to the relief will not qualify again if it is sold to another company.

(6)   A company can either construct property or acquire existing properties for future letting. A company that builds its own properties, however, will have to show that its purpose is to let the properties rather than to build them for onward sale.

(7)   The tenant or joint tenant of the property must be an individual who occupies the property as his only or principal home. The tenant and

the landlord may freely negotiate the terms including rent of the tenancy and the landlord may not normally end the tenancy without the permission of the Court.

(8) Qualifying tenancies do not include company lettings, business tenancies, tenancies of licensed premises or certain types of student or holiday accommodation. They will also exclude properties with a rateable value exceeding £1,500 in Greater London and £750 elsewhere.

11.7 Enterprise investment schemes
(FA 1994 s 137 and Sched 15)

The Chancellor of the Exchequer introduced a new investment incentive scheme in his November 1993 Budget. The scheme is intended to provide a 'targeted incentive' for new equity investment in unquoted trading companies and to encourage outside investors to introduce finance and expertise to a company.

11.7.1 Qualifying investors

A minor departure from the business expansion scheme is that qualifying investors under the EIS do not have to be resident in the United Kingdom. Relief will be available for non residents if they are liable to UK income tax.

Another, perhaps more important change from the BES rules is that an investor can become a paid director without forfeiting EIS relief. However, this is subject to the proviso that the individual was not connected with the company or its trade at any time prior to the EIS shares being issued.

In the same way as under the BES, an individual will be entitled to EIS relief only if his shareholding does not exceed 30 per cent.

11.7.2 Conditions for relief

The relief is available in respect of sums invested by way of subscription for new shares issued by a qualifying unquoted trading company on or after 1 January 1994. A qualifying company is one which carries on a qualifying activity for a minimum of five years following the date that the shares are issued. The rules are slightly more flexible than under the BES in that relief may be available under the EIS for an investment in a foreign company—the requirement is simply that the company must trade in the United Kingdom, it does not have to be incorporated or resident in the UK.

There is a limit of £1m per annum on the amount that a company can raise under the enterprise investment scheme. A higher limit of £5m applies to companies which are engaged in certain shipping activities.

11.7.3   Nature of EIS relief

Provided the various conditions are satisfied, relief is due when an individual subscribes for shares. The relief is given at the 20 per cent lower rate of income tax.

11.7.4   Disposal within five years

The relief is clawed back if the investor disposes of the shares within a period of five years unless the disposal occurs because the company has gone into liquidation.

Where a company does go into liquidation within the five year period, further income tax or capital gains tax relief may be due to the investor. In a case where the investor receives no payment whatsoever under the liquidation, the net amount of his investment may qualify as a capital loss.

11.7.5   Example—EIS tax relief

An individual invests £80,000 under the EIS. He receives tax relief at 20 per cent of £80,000, ie £16,000.

If the entire investment has to be written off, he will be entitled to a capital loss of £64,000.

This loss may be set against an individual's income or relieved against capital gains.

11.7.6   Disposal after five years

Once the shares have been held for five years, there is no claw back of relief on a disposal of shares. Furthermore, the shares are then an exempt asset for capital gains tax purposes so that no capital gains tax will be payable. However, and in contrast to the rules which applied under the business expansion scheme, a loss realised on the disposal of the shares after the five year period may still attract either income tax or capital gains tax relief. Once again, the loss is calculated as the difference between the net of tax cost and the disposal proceeds (see 11.7.4).

11.7.7   Maximum amount which may attract EIS relief

There was a limit of £40,000 for 1993–94 which applied to the aggregate of an individual's investment under the BES and the EIS. For 1994–95 and future years, the maximum amount which may attract EIS relief is £100,000 per annum.

11.7.8 Carry-back

Subject to a maximum of £15,000, up to one half of the amount invested by an individual between 6 April and 5 October in any year can be carried back to the previous tax year (if the individual did not invest the full amount during that year).

11.7.9 Qualifying companies

The company's business must not consist to any substantial extent of any of the following:

(1) dealing in land, in commodities or futures or in shares, securities or other financial instruments;
(2) dealing in goods otherwise than in the course of any ordinary trade of wholesale or retail distribution;
(3) banking, insurance, money-lending, debt-factoring, hire-purchase, financial or other financial activities;
(4) oil extraction activities;
(5) leasing (including letting ships on charter or other assets on hire) or receiving royalties or licence fees;
(6) providing legal or accountancy services;
(7) providing services or facilities for any trade carried on by another person (other than a parent company) which consists to any substantial extent of activities within any of paragraphs (1) to (6) above and in which a controlling interest is held by a person who also has a controlling interest in the trade carried on by the company.

The company must not have more than 50 per cent of its net assets invested in land or buildings.

11.8   Enterprise zone trusts

It is possible to invest in properties in enterprise zones through a syndicate or 'enterprise zone property trust'. An individual who invests in the enterprise zone property trust is treated as if he had incurred a proportion of the trust's expenditure on enterprise zone properties. Similarly, rents (and sometimes interest) received by the trust are apportioned amongst the investors ie the Revenue looks through the trust and treats the individual as if he had acquired an interest in the underlying properties.

Where an individual is treated as having acquired such an interest in an enterprise zone property, the allowances may be set against his other income (see 4.5.4). However, an individual who invests in an enterprise zone property trust is entitled to capital allowances only for the year in which the trust invests in enterprise zone properties. In some cases, there may be a delay in that an individual invests in a trust at the end of one tax year and becomes entitled to allowances only for the following year (because that is the year in which the trust acquires the relevant properties).

11.9   Venture capital trusts

A consultative document was issued in March 1994 setting out proposals for legislation on a new type of investment trust called a venture capital trust. The purpose of the new legislation is to encourage investment in unquoted trading companies by making investors exempt from income tax on any dividend income and from capital gains tax on any disposal of their holdings in the trust.

It is anticipated that legislation will be introduced in the 1995 Finance Bill and, at present, the proposals are still very much at the drawing board stage.

12 Life assurance and pensions

by VINCE JERRARD and STUART REYNOLDS

This chapter covers the tax treatment of life assurance and pensions plans and looks at the treatment of the contributions paid in the funds while they are invested, and the benefits paid out. It covers the following topics:

Life assurance

(1)   Introduction
(2)   Policyholder taxation
(3)   Taxation of life policy proceeds
(4)   Offshore life policies
(5)   Annuities
(6)   Permanent health insurance
(7)   Life policies effected by companies

Pensions

(8)   Approved pension schemes
(9)   Personal pension plans
(10) Retirement annuity contracts (s 226 contracts)
(11) Occupational schemes
(12) Free-standing AVC (FSAVC) schemes
(13) Unapproved schemes
(14) The State pension scheme
(15) Contracting out.

12.1   Introduction—Life assurance

A life assurance policy is simply the evidence of a contract between the individual policyholder and the life assurance company. The general principle is that the company is the collecting house for pooled investments and mortality risks, offering benefits directly to policyholders based on personal contracts.

Life assurance policies can be classified in a number of different ways but the most common, practical classification reflects the nature of the benefits provided under the policy and the periods for which they are provided:

(1) whole of life policies, where the sum assured is payable on the death of the life assured, whenever that occurs;

(2) term policies, where the sum assured is payable on death during the policy term only;

(3) endowment policies, where the sum assured is payable on death during the policy term, or on survival to the end of the term.

Each type of policy has its own characteristics in terms of the blend of life assurance protection and potential investment return. Term policies for a relatively short period are most likely to offer the highest sum assured for each pound of premium while, towards the other end of the spectrum, an endowment policy will have a greater investment element.

An important characteristic of life assurance policies is that they do not produce income, as such, but are essentially medium or long term accumulators. While a policy is held intact, the income and gains arising from the underlying investments held by the life company are taxed in the hands of the life company itself. The policyholder's prospective tax liability generally arises only when he receives payment under the policy.

This chapter deals with the tax consequences on the policyholder paying premiums or receiving benefits under a life assurance policy issued by a UK company or a foreign insurer operating through a branch in the United Kingdom (for 'foreign' life policies see 12.4).

Over the years many changes have been made to this complex and technical area. Unless the contary is clearly the case, this chapter deals with the current life policy tax regime which took effect from its 'appointed day' of 1 April 1976.

12.1.1   The company's tax position
(TA 1988, ss 76, 432 et seq; FA 1989, ss 82–89 & Sched 8; FA 1990 ss 41–48 & Scheds 6–9 and F(No. 2)A 1992, s 65(n))

In respect of their life assurance business, companies are generally taxed on the excess of their investment income and realised capital gains over management expenses (the 'I–E' basis). For proprietary companies there is a formula to determine the proportions of the company's income and gains which should be allocated to policyholders and shareholders, respectively. Tax is charged on the policyholder's share of income and gains at the rate of 25 per cent (20 per cent for the income from directly-held equities), although companies will often make deductions at a rate lower than 25 per cent of policyholder's gains because they are generally able to defer realisations of some types of assets. The company's profits attributable to shareholders are, on the other hand, chargeable to corporation tax at the usual rates.

Registered friendly societies are in a somewhat different position, being exempt from corporation tax in respect of tax-exempt life or endowment business. This is life and endowment business where total premiums under contracts do not exceed £200 per annum and annuities do not exceed £156 per annum. Policies which can be written on the tax-exempt basis are generally qualifying policies provided they satisfy a minimum sum assured test. Such policies can give tax-free proceeds even to higher rate taxpayers but non-qualifying friendly society policies are taxable at basic and higher rates. The remainder of this chapter does not deal specifically with friendly society business.

12.1.2 Review of life assurance taxation

At present, the Inland Revenue is conducting a review of life assurance taxation covering both taxation of life companies and of life policy proceeds.

The current I-E regime collects an aggregated tax in respect of both the company's trading profit and the bulk of the income and gains accruing to the individual's policy but an alternative would be a gross roll-up regime (similar to those found in most EC countries). Under such a regime life companies would be taxed on their profits with the remaining tax charge being levied directly on the individual policyholder when his policy comes to an end.

Although final decisions may be reached during 1994 it is unlikely that any new regime would commence before 1996.

Whatever the outcome of the life company tax review, it seems likely that there will be changes to the life assurance qualifying rules in the next year or so. The Revenue has interpreted the EC 3rd Life Directive as requiring the removal of pre-certification of life policies (see 12.2.1), although the industry does not necessarily agree with that view. What does seem to be agreed, however, is that the current qualifying rules are too complex to be operated with sufficient certainty in the absence of pre-certification by the Revenue.

Accordingly, the loss of pre-certification is likely to be accompanied by simplified 'qualifying policy' rules but the continuance of categories of tax-favoured policies (ie those paying tax-free proceeds even to higher rate taxpayers) is expected.

12.2   Policyholder taxation

For tax purposes, the key classification of policies is between qualifying policies and non-qualifying policies.

The distinction is only relevant to the *individual*. There is no differentiation between qualifying and non-qualifying policies in respect of taxation of the income and gains from the underlying assets, in the life company's hands.

Each of the three types of policy already identified (whole life, endowment and term assurances) is capable of being a qualifying or non-qualifying policy depending on its initial design and the way in which it is dealt with once in force.

12.2.1   Qualifying policies
(TA 1988, s 267 & Sched 15)

These are policies which satisfy the conditions set out in TA 1988 Sched 15, and do not fall foul of the various anti-avoidance provisions.

The main features of the qualifying rules are as follows:

Premiums

(1) must be payable for a period of ten years or more, (though term assurances may be written for shorter periods) and must be payable annually or more frequently, and;

(2) must be fairly evenly spread so that premiums payable in any one period of 12 months are neither more than twice the amount of premiums paid in any other 12 month period, nor more than 1/8th of the total amount of premiums payable over the first ten years (in the case of whole life policies) or over the term of the policy (in the case of an endowment).

The sum assured

(1) for an endowment policy, must not be less than 75 per cent of the total premiums payable during the term of the policy. This percentage is reduced by two per cent for each year by which the life assured's age exceeds 55 years at the issue of the policy;

(2) for a whole of life policy, must not be less than 75 per cent of the total premiums payable if death were to occur at the age of 75 years;

(3) for a term policy, which has no surrender value and ends before the life assured's 75th birthday, need not satisfy any minimum requirement.

Benefits

(1)   may include the right to participate in profits, the right to benefits arising because of disability or the right to a return of premiums on death under a certain specified age (not exceeding 16 years); but

(2)   may not include any other benefits of a capital nature.

The rules for certain special types of policy may vary from those referred to above, eg mortgage protection policies, family income policies and industrial assurances.

Life assurers usually submit standard policy wordings to the Revenue so that they can be certified as satisfying the qualifying rules ('pre-certification'). Policies in those standard forms can then be marketed as qualifying.

Where a policy contains options by which the policyholder may, for example, increase the sum assured, or the premium, or extend the policy term, these options are tested at the outset to ensure that, however any options are exercised, the policy will still satisfy the qualifying rules.

12.2.2   Non-qualifying policies

Non-qualifying policies are all other life policies not satisfying the qualifying rules, and those which, although they may have satisfied the qualifying rules at the outset, have subsequently been changed in some way such that they no longer satisfy those rules.

The most significant category of policies which are non-qualifying are single premium investment contracts (usually referred to as bonds). These are written as whole of life contracts and provide for only a small amount of life cover, being primarily investment vehicles.

12.2.3   Taxation of premiums
(TA 1988, s 266 et seq & Sched 14)

No specific tax relief is available to an individual in respect of premiums paid under a non-qualifying life assurance policy.

Similarly, there is no specific relief for premiums paid under qualifying policies issued in respect of contracts made after 13 March 1984. However, for qualifying policies issued before that date, Life Assurance Premium Relief (LAPR) is still available where the policy was issued on the life of the payer of the premium (or the payer's spouse) and where the payer is resident in the United Kingdom at the time premiums are paid.

Relief is given currently at the rate of 12.5 per cent on premiums up to the greater of £1,500 or one sixth of total income and is usually obtained by deducting the tax relief from the premiums payable to the life company. Relief is lost if the policy becomes non-qualifying or if the benefits secured by the policy are increased, or its term extended, after 13 March 1984.

Where an individual receives the benefit of LAPR but, in effect, recoups himself for his outlay in premiums by withdrawing money from the policy, there is a process by which some or all of the LAPR is 'clawed back' by deduction from the amount withdrawn by him.

12.3   Taxation of life policy proceeds
(TA 1988, ss 539–554)

In view of life policies' position as income accumulators, where liability for gains and income in respect of the underlying assets is dealt with by taxing the life company, the usual income tax principles are inappropriate to life policy taxation. Accordingly, the tax regime which applies to the individual policyholder has been specifically constructed for the purpose. It caters separately for qualifying and non-qualifying policies and for mortality and investment profits realised from policies.

It is first necessary to determine whether any particular action constitutes a chargeable event in respect of the policy. If it does not, no income tax consequence arises from that action, under the life policy regime. If it does, it is then necessary to calculate the 'gain', to determine the rate of tax applicable to the gain, and to determine who is liable to pay the resulting tax.

Despite references to 'chargeable events' and 'gains', this is the income tax regime which applies to life policies (for the capital gains tax position, see 12.3.14).

12.3.1   Chargeable events

Non-qualifying policy
(TA 1988, s 540)

For a non-qualifying policy, the five chargeable events are:

(1)   the death of the life assured;
(2)   the maturity of the policy;
(3)   the total surrender of the policy;
(4)   the assignment of the policy for money or money's worth;
(5)   excesses arising on partial surrenders in any policy year commencing after 13 March 1975 (see 12.3.3).

No chargeable event occurs where an assignment takes place by way of security for a debt (or on the discharge of the security). Similarly, an assignment between spouses living together is not a chargeable event.

Qualifying policy

For a qualifying policy, the chargeable events are the same but subject to the following amendments:

(1)   death or maturity are only chargeable events if the policy has previously been made paid-up (ie premiums have ceased but the policy has remained in force) within the first ten years (or three-quarters of the term of an endowment policy, if shorter);

(2)   surrender, assignment for money or money's worth or an excess will only be a chargeable event if it occurs before the expiry of ten years (or three-quarters of the term of an endowment policy, if shorter) or if the policy was made paid-up within that period.

Three key consequences of the chargeable event rules are that:

(1)   the gift (ie assignment with no consideration) of qualifying or non-qualifying policies is not a chargeable event and so triggers no income tax consequence;

(2)   there is no chargeable event on death of the life assured under, or on the maturity of, a qualifying policy where all due premiums were paid prior to the event in question;

(3)   there is no chargeable event on the assignment for value or surrender (in whole or part) of a qualifying policy where premiums have been paid for the first ten years (or three-quarters of the term), as appropriate.

Where there is no chargeable event in respect of a life policy, there is no charge to income tax under the specific life policy tax regime, irrespective of the tax position of the individual policyholder. In particular, points (2) and (3) above illustrate the key, current advantage of qualifying policies ie their ability to provide tax-free proceeds, even for higher rate taxpayers.

12.3.2   Calculating life policy gains
(TA 1988, s 51)

Broadly speaking, where the chargeable event is a maturity, total surrender or assignment for consideration, the chargeable gain is the investment profit made under the policy. This is calculated by reference to the value of the benefits being received as a result of the chargeable event, plus the amount of any 'relevant capital payments' previously received under the policy (ie any sum or other benefit of a capital nature, other than one paid as a result of an individual's disability), less the amount paid by way of premiums and any taxable gains as a result of previous partial surrenders.

This principle of charging tax only on investment gains also applies where the chargeable event is the death of the life assured. The exclusion of mortality profit from the taxable gain is achieved by using the surrender value of the policy immediately before death instead of the value of the benefits being received under the policy.

12.3.3   Partial surrenders
(TA 1988, s 546)

The fifth of the chargeable events listed in 12.3.1 creates a potential income tax liability on the policyholder surrendering part of his policy (often referred to as making 'withdrawals' from the policy). Partial surrenders include the surrender of a right to a bonus and loans made by (or by arrangement with) the insurance company to the policyholder (unless the policyholder's policy is qualifying and the loan bears a commercial rate of interest or is lent to a full-time employee of the insurer for the purposes of house purchase or improvement).

At the end of each policy year, the policy attracts a 'notional allowance' of five per cent of the total premium then paid under the policy. This allowance is then set against the value of any partial surrenders made up to that date. If the value of those partial surrenders exceeds the current cumulative allowance, a chargeable event occurs; if the cumulative allowance is equal to or exceeds cumulative withdrawals, no chargeable events occurs. Allowances are given up to 100 per cent of the total premiums paid so that, for a single premium investment bond, the allowances are given at the rate of five per cent for 20 years.

Once an 'excess' (ie an occasion on which the cumulative partial surrenders exceed the cumulative allowances) has occurred the cumulative withdrawals and allowances up to that date are considered to have been used and the process of accumulating allowances and withdrawals starts afresh (subject to the '100 per cent of premiums' limit which applies to the allowances).

12.3.4   Example—Cumulation of allowances and withdrawals

A invests £10,000 in a single premium investment bond; £1,200 is withdrawn after four policy years, a further £4,500 after six policy years and £1,000 after eight policy years.

Policy Years	A Cumulative Allowances	B Partial Surrender	C Cumulative surrender between chargeable events	D Taxable Gain (C-A)
	£	£	£	£
1	500 (1 x 500)	0	0	0
2	1,000 (2 x 500)	0	0	0
3	1,500 (3 x 500)	0	0	0
4	2,000 (4 x 500)	1,200	1,200	0
5	2,500 (5 x 500)	0	1,200	0
6	3,000 (6 x 500)	4,500	5,700	2,700
7	500 (1 x 500)	0	0	0
8	1,000 (2 x 500)	1,000	1,000	0
9	1,500 (3 x 500)	0	1,000	0
10	2,000 (4 x 500)	0	1,000	0
etc				

Note: (1) A chargeable event occurs only when C exceeds A.
      (2) The value of the policy is irrelevant to these calculations so that it is possible to have a taxable gain under a policy at a time when the policy itself is worth less than the premiums paid.

When the final chargeable event occurs under the policy (ie death, maturity, final surrender or assignment for value) the total profit on the policy is brought into account. The profit is the final proceeds (excluding any mortality profit where the event is death), plus previous partial surrenders, less premiums paid and any taxable gains from previous partial withdrawals.

12.3.5 Example—Total surrender after partial surrenders

Using the example immediately above, if the policy were totally surrendered at the end of the tenth policy year for £10,400, the taxable gain on that final encashment would be as follows:

£10,400 + £1,200 + £4,500 + £1,000 − (£10,000 + £2,700) = £4,400

Note:
   If, on final termination, the 'gain' calculated in this way is a negative figure, it may be deducted from taxable income, for the purposes of higher rate tax only (see 12.3.6).

12.3.6 Taxing gains on chargeable events
(TA 1988, ss 547 and 550)

In the majority of cases where the policyholder owns the policy for his own absolute benefit, the gain is treated as the top-slice of his income and is taxed appropriately.

However, because the income and gains attributable to the underlying assets of the policy have already been taxed in the hands of the life company, life policy gains are not chargeable to income tax at the basic rate. This applies to both qualifying and non-qualifying policies. Despite the fact that, in effect, the gain is treated as having already suffered basic rate tax, there is no grossing up of the gain for the purposes of higher rate tax.

Accordingly, for an individual paying tax at the higher rate, the maximum rate of tax payable on life policy gains at present will be 15 per cent (40 per cent less 25 per cent). An individual whose income (including the gain) is taxable at the basic rate only will have no further income tax liability on the policy gain. Non-taxpayers or those paying tax at the lower rate of 20 per cent will not be able to make any reclaim in respect of tax notionally paid by the life company.

If the individual realises a loss under the policy, that loss is only available as a deduction from taxable income for the purposes of higher rate tax.

Top-slicing

In view of the fact that the gain will have arisen over a period of years, the legislation recognises that it might be rather harsh to treat the total gain as part of the taxpayer's income in the year of receipt. A measure of relief is afforded by a process known as 'top-slicing'.

Top-slicing first requires calculation of the 'appropriate fraction' of the gain, more usually referred to as the 'slice'. Where the chargeable event in question is death, maturity, total encashment or some of the value, the slice is calculated by dividing the gain by the number of complete policy years for which the policy has been in force. Where the chargeable event is caused by a partial surrender, the gain is divided by the number of complete policy years since the last excess caused by a partial surrender (or by the number of years for which the policy has been in force where the chargeable event is the first excess).

The slice (and not the whole of the gain) is treated as the top part of the policyholder's income and the average rate of tax applicable to the slice (less the basic rate) is calculated. That tax rate will then apply to the whole of the gain to determine the total income tax liability on the gain. The result is that relief is given to individuals whose other income would mean that they pay the tax at no more than the basic rate, but who would be taken into the higher rates of tax if the whole of the gain were added to their income.

12.3.7 Example—No tax on the gain

A invests £20,000 in a single premium investment bond in May 1989 and cashes it in after five years for £27,500. The gain is therefore £7,500 and the 'slice' is £1,500 (£7,500 divided by five).

Taxable income (excluding policy gain)	15,000
'Slice'	1,500
Taxable income	£16,500

The tax rate applicable to the 'slice' is therefore 25 per cent less 25 per cent = 0 per cent.

12.3.8   Example—Slice falling into basic and higher rate bands

B invests £12,000 in a single premium investment bond in May 1989. After five years he cashes it in for £17,000. The gain is £5,000 and the slice is £1,000 (£5,000 divided by five). In that year his other taxable income after reliefs is £23,000.

Tax calculation on gain:		
Taxable income + 'slice'	=	£24,000
Tax Applicable to slice		
On £700 (ie £23,000 to £23,700) at 0% (25%–25%)	=	Nil
On £300 (ie £23,700 to £24,000) at 15% (40%–25%)	=	£45
Total tax on slice	=	£45
Average rate on slice		
$\dfrac{45}{1,000}$ x 100	=	4.5%

The tax payable is £5,000 x 4.5% = £225.

To illustrate the effect of top-slicing, if it had not been available the calculations would have been:

Tax applicable to the gain		
On £700 at 0% (25%–25%)	=	Nil
On £4,300 at 15% (40%–25%)	=	£645
Tax payable	=	£645

Notes:
(1) The whole gain (without top-slicing) is counted as income in determining whether any age allowance should be reduced.
(2) There is no top-slicing where the taxpayer is a company.
(3) Any business expansion scheme relief is left out of account when calculating top-slicing relief.
(4) For top-slicing purposes, total income is computed without reference to amounts chargeable in respect of loss of office or lease premiums chargeable as rent.
(5) The examples given in this chapter assume no reliefs or amounts as mentioned in (3) and (4).

12.3.9   Two policy gains in one tax year
(TA 1988, s 550)

Where an individual has two policies with chargeable gains in a tax year, tax is calculated as if the gains arose under only one policy, with a slice equal to the sum of the individual slices. For example, if two policies are surrendered in the same tax year, one with a gain of £10,000 (having been in force for five years) and one with a gain of £24,000 (having been in force for eight years) tax on the gains is calculated as if one policy had been surrendered yielding a gain of £34,000 and with a slice of £5,000.

This approach can have the effect of increasing the total tax payable (compared to disposing of the policies in separate tax years) depending on the individual's tax position and the performance of the relevant policies.

12.3.10   Persons liable for the charge
(TA 1988, ss 547 and 551)

Where a policy is held by an individual for his own benefit, the tax charge falls on him. The same applies to an individual where the policy is held as security for a debt owed by him.

If the policy is held in trust, the charge falls on the settlor, who can recover the tax paid from the trustees. If a policy is held by a trust created by a settlor who has since died, it is possible that gains realised by trustees in these circumstances may escape tax altogether in view of the impossibility of taxing somebody who has not been alive in the appropriate year of assessment. Although somewhat anomalous, this can be very useful if an individual owns a policy which will not come to an end on his death (eg a joint life policy). By declaring a suitable trust of the policy in his Will, he may be able to put future gains realised under the policy outside the income tax net.

Where the policy is held by a company, or on a trust created by or as security for a debt owed by, a company, the charge falls on the company.

If a policy is assigned by way of gift, chargeable excesses arising during that policy year, but prior to the assignment, are taxed on the assignor. Future gains are taxed on the new beneficial owner.

12.3.11   Timing of the taxation of gains

Where the chargeable event is death, maturity, total surrender or assignment for value, the gain is treated as arising at the time of the appropriate event.

Excesses arising from partial surrenders, on the other hand, are generally only regarded as arising at the end of the policy year in which the excess occurs. Accordingly, if the policy was taken out in June 1990 and an excess occurs as a result of a partial surrender in February 1993, the gain resulting from that partial surrender is treated as arising in June 1993 and so is taxable in the tax year 1993–4.

12.3.12 'Dread disease' policies

A development in the UK life assurance market in recent years has been the ability to include dread disease benefits in a variety of policies. In general, this benefit pays a capital sum if the life assured is diagnosed as suffering from any of the specified 'dread diseases'. The diseases specified will vary from company to company but will usually include heart attack, stroke, cancer, heart by-pass surgery etc.

It is understood that the Revenue accepts that the happening of a dread disease is not a chargeable event so that this benefit is paid free of tax under the life policy tax regime.

12.3.13 Chargeable event certificates
(TA 1988, s 552)

When a chargeable event occurs, the life assurance company is required to provide the Revenue with a chargeable event certificate which gives the name and address of the policyholder, the nature and date of the chargeable event and information required for computing the gain.

12.3.14 Capital gains tax and life policies
(TCGA 1992, s 210)

A policyholder will have no personal liability to capital gains tax on a disposal of the policy if he is its original beneficial owner, or if he is an assignee and acquired the policy other than for money or money's worth.

If a policy is in the hands of an individual who is not the beneficial owner and who did acquire it for money or money's worth, the policy is an asset potentially liable to capital gains tax. However, where the policy is issued in respect of an insurance made after 25 June 1982 the policy also remains subject to the income tax regime which applies to life assurance policies. This may also affect some policies issued before that date. The potential for double taxation (income and capital gains tax) is resolved by TCGA 1992, s 37 which provides, broadly, that money or money's worth charged to income tax will be taken into account and excluded from the capital gains tax calculations.

Where a life policy is subject to the capital gains tax regime, the occasion of the payment of the sum or sums assured and the surrender of the policy are treated as disposals.

12.4   Offshore life policies
(TA 1988, s 553 & Sched 15, paras 23–27)

In general, policies issued in respect of contracts made after 17 November 1983 cannot be qualifying unless they are issued by a UK insurance company or the UK branch of a foreign insurer. Before that date foreign policies could be qualifying, if they satisfied the normal qualifying rules.

Other amendments to the life policy tax regime, as it applies to such foreign policies, are as follows:

(1)   The gain calculated on a chargeable event is reduced by reference to the amount of time, during the life of the policy, the policyholder was resident in the United Kingdom.

(2)   In calculating the 'appropriate fraction' for top-slicing purposes, any complete years during which the policyholder was not resident in the United Kingdom are excluded.

(3)   Taxable gains arising under such policies are charged to basic rate tax as well as higher rate tax, as appropriate.

12.5   Annuities
(TA 1988, ss 656 and 685)

An annuity is an arrangement under which one person agrees to pay another a sum of money for a known period, or a period to be determined by some specified contingency.

Annuities may be immediate (ie the payment will start straightaway) or deferred (where payments will start at some predetermined point in the future). Many annuities are established to continue for the lifetime of the annuitant but temporary annuities will cease at the end of a fixed period or on the annuitant's death, whichever comes earlier. Annuities may be effected on the lives of two or more individuals and, for example, continue until the death of the last survivor. Annuities may be paid monthly, quarterly or annually, may be of a fixed amount or subject to some sort of index-linking. Annuities may also be written with a guaranteed minimum period, so as to reduce the loss which might otherwise be suffered by an individual who dies shortly after purchasing an annuity.

There are four main types of annuity:

(1)   Purchased life annuities, where an individual pays a lump sum to an insurance company in return for the annuity.

(2)   Annuities received as a gift (for example, at one time it was common for testators to direct that annuities be paid out of their estates).

(3) Annuities paid as part of the purchase price of a business or by continuing members of a partnership to a former partner who has retired.

(4) Compulsory purchase annuities, eg those purchased out of pension funds.

Significant changes to the taxation of life companies in respect of general annuity business were made in FA 1991, with effect for accounting periods commencing after 31 December 1991. The changes apply to existing business, subject to transitional relief.

These changes brought the taxation of life company general annuity funds broadly into line with the regime which applies to ordinary life business. Previously, a general annuity fund was not taxed on its income and gains if annuities paid by the company during the tax year equalled or exceeded the investment income and realised gains of the fund.

For the annuitant, a purchased life annuity attracts a special relief in that amounts received by him will be treated in part as a return of the money paid by the annuity (the capital element) and in part as interest on that purchase price. The capital element of each payment is calculated by reference to actuarial tables and is not taxable. This tax exemption applies even where the annuitant lives long enough for the capital element of annuity payments he receives to exceed the original purchase price of the annuity.

Other types of annuity do not receive this favourable treatment in respect of the capital element of annuity payments.

Purchased life annuities are also subject to an income tax regime similar to that previously described as applying to life policies (see 12.3.6).

Chargeable events for life annuities are total surrender, assignment for money or money's worth and 'excesses' (calculated in much the same way as in respect of life policy partial surrenders).

Where a gain arises on a chargeable event, the gain is not charged to basic rate tax where the company offering the annuity has been taxed under the new life company tax regime described above because of the 'credit' which is, in effect, given in respect of tax paid by the life company on the income and gains of its general annuity fund.

For capital gains tax purposes, deferred annuities are also treated in a similar way to life policies, with the effect that no chargeable gain accrues on the disposal of such a contract except where the person making the disposal is not the original beneficial owner and acquired the rights for consideration in money or money's worth.

12.6   Permanent health insurance

12.6.1   Introduction

Permanent health insurance (PHI) policies provide a replacement income for an individual who is unable to work through illness or disability. Contracts are usually available to those aged between 16 and 60 but terminate on the insured reaching his normal retirement date.

Once the disability or illness arises, benefits commence on expiry of a deferred period, typically between one and twelve months, selected by the policyholder. The longer the deferred period, the fewer claims the insurer will expect to pay and so the lower the premium will be per £ of benefit.

PHI contracts can be written as life assurance policies—typically as non-qualifying policies to avoid provision of substantial sums assured payable on death. If structured as a life policy, payment of disability benefits is not treated as a surrender of rights for the purposes of life policy taxation.

12.6.2   Tax consequences

If an individual effects a PHI contract for himself, premiums are not deductible for tax purposes. If an employer effects a policy on an employee in order to enable him to continue to pay the employee's salary during a period of disability or illness, or if the policy covers a revenue loss during such a period, the employer might be able to claim the premiums as a business expense.

Benefits received from an individual's own PHI policy are taxable under Schedule D Case III but receive the benefit of an Inland Revenue extra-statutory concession (A26) which gives him a 'tax holiday'. This means that he will not be taxed on the benefit until it has been paid for a complete tax year: for example, if benefit commences in May 1993 it will not become taxable until the tax year 1995–6. Policies owned by someone other than the insured do not benefit from the tax holiday.

In practice, PHI benefits are paid without deduction of tax by the life company and so must be included in the individual's tax return.

If the contract is effected by an employer in order to maintain the employee's salary during the period of illness or disability, the income will be taxable in the individual's hands, in the same way as salary would have been.

12.6.3   New concession

A Budget press release of 30 November 1993 contained a new concession to replace A26 with effect from 6 April 1994. In summary, the key changes are as follows:

(1) The tax holiday is reduced to a period of 12 months (at present it can be up to 23 months). An individual's tax holiday commences when he becomes entitled to claim appropriate benefits, so that if he has two PHI policies with different deferred periods the tax holiday on the one with the longer deferral will be less than 12 months.

(2) No tax holiday will be available if the benefit does not compensate for loss of income from employment or self-employment.

(3) Insurers will have to deduct basic rate tax from payments to individuals where entitlement to those benefits arises on or after 6 April 1994 (even if the policy was effected before that date).

12.7 Life policies effected by companies
(TA 1988, s 540)

There are a number of circumstances in which a company can effect a life policy. For example, it may do so on the life of a director or other key executive to provide the company with compensation for the death of that individual. Similarly, policies may be effected to provide funds to repay loans.

In general, if a company effects a term assurance for a short period (usually not more than five years), which does not acquire a surrender value and is effected solely to provide protection against the loss of profits resulting from the death of a key man, the premiums will be tax-deductible and the proceeds will be taxable in the hands of the company.

If, on the other hand, the policy is for a longer term, may acquire a surrender value, is effected for a capital purpose, or where the life assured has a material shareholding in the company, the premiums will not be tax-deductible but the proceeds are unlikely to be charged to corporation tax in the company's hands, other than by virtue of the life assurance chargeable event rules.

Prior to FA 1989, policies owned by companies could be qualifying policies (provided they satisfied the qualifying rules) and so could provide tax-free proceeds to the company, in the same way as for individuals. Gains from non-qualifying policies were also tax-free in the hands of the company, except where the company was close.

For policies effected after 13 March 1989 (or those effected before that date but subsequently varied to increase the benefits or the policy term) the rules changed. Such policies cannot be qualifying policies (irrespective of their compliance with the qualifying rules) if, immediately prior to the chargeable event, the policy was owned by a company or was held on trusts created, or as security for a debt owed by, the company. Gains from such policies are treated as the company's income and chargeable under Schedule D Case VI.

There is an exception to this denial of qualifying status where policies are used to secure company debts incurred in purchasing land to be occupied by the company for the purposes of its trade (or in constructing, extending or improving buildings occupied in that way). Broadly speaking, provided that the policy has been used for this purpose since its inception, the chargeable gain will only be the amount by which the policy proceeds exceed the lowest amount of the loan which has been secured by the policy.

12.8   Approved pension schemes

Approved pension schemes offer significant tax reliefs and exemptions. These include tax relief on contributions paid, exemptions from income and capital gains taxes on the investments of the accumulating pension fund and, in the majority of cases, the ability to receive a lump sum free of income tax and capital gains tax. There are also inheritance tax advantages.

These reliefs and exemptions are guarded by a complex set of rules which limit the contributions and benefits which approved schemes can offer. These limits have been tightened over recent years but existing schemes have generally been able to retain the benefits provided by earlier generations of the rules. These changes have been supplemented by significant changes to the State Earnings Related Pension Scheme (SERPS) (see 12.14) and the introduction of personal pensions (see 12.9). The ability to transfer between different types of scheme and between schemes governed by the different generations of rules has made the position even more complicated.

Accordingly, this part of the chapter is an overview and not an exhaustive analysis. For fuller details consult the *Allied Dunbar Pensions Handbook*.

There are three main types of approved pension scheme currently open to new members. These are:

(1)   personal pension plans (PPPs)
(2)   occupational pension schemes, and
(3)   free-standing additional voluntary contribution (FSAVC) schemes.

All three types of scheme offer some or all of the tax reliefs and exemptions previously mentioned but the conditions for membership and the limits on benefits and contributions vary significantly.

12.8.1 Taxation of pension funds

All approved pension funds can provide what is known as a 'gross roll up'. This means that the income and capital gains of the pension fund are totally exempt from UK tax. Where income is taxed at source or is paid with a tax credit (for example, interest on deposits or dividends) the pension scheme can reclaim the tax deducted or the amount of the tax credit.

Pending its abolition, pension funds may be liable to stamp duty on the purchase of investments and, in some cases, usually those involving non-zero rated property transactions, VAT may be payable.

Life assurance companies benefit from identical exemptions on the funds built up in respect of their pensions business.

12.9 Personal pension plans (PPPs)

12.9.1 Types of plan

(1) All PPPs are money purchase schemes where the final benefits are determined by the contributions paid and the rate of investment growth.

(2) PPPs may take the form of life assurance and pension policies provided by life assurance companies. They may also be offered by banks, building societies and authorised unit trust schemes. It is also possible to adopt a self-administered approach with investment in a range of permitted assets.

(3) Where the PPP can invest only in life assurance and pension policies it need not be set up under a trust but a trust is necessary if the other types of PPP investment are used.

12.9.2 Eligibility

(1) A taxpayer will be eligible to make contributions to one of these plans if he is in receipt of 'relevant earnings'. This means either earnings from non-pensionable employments, or from businesses, professions, partnerships, etc. For example, if there is a source of Schedule D Case I or II earnings, the taxpayer normally qualifies for relief from income tax in respect of contributions paid under a PPP approved by the Revenue. This relief is also available in respect of Schedule E earnings (including taxable benefits) from a non-pensionable employment, eg with a firm which does not provide a pension scheme or if the taxpayer is not a member of such a scheme for some other reason.

(2)   If an employer's pension scheme provides only a sum assured payable on death while in the employer's service and/or a pension to a surviving spouse, the earnings from that employment will still be regarded as 'relevant earnings'.

(3)   Where there are two sources of income, one being relevant earnings and the other arising from pensionable employment, it is possible to contribute to a PPP in respect of the non-pensionable earnings, subject to certain limits.

(4)   In two cases it is possible for an individual to have a PPP even though he is not eligible to make contributions to it. The first is that it is possible for an employee who is a member accruing pension benefits under his employer's occupational pension scheme to effect a PPP in order to contract out of SERPS (see 12.14). Such a PPP may not receive any contributions other than protected rights contributions. The second is that a PPP can be established in order to accept a transfer payment from another approved pension scheme or arrangement, even though the individual is not then eligible to make contributions to the PPP.

(5)   Controlling directors of investment companies are not eligible for any form of PPP in respect of earnings from such a company nor are certain other controlling directors who are in receipt of benefits from their employer's occupational scheme.

12.9.3   Tax relief on contributions and limits

(1)   Individuals who have relevant earnings, and pay either single or annual contributions to a PPP within the limits mentioned below, enjoy full income tax relief on those contributions in the relevant years. Employees pay contributions net of basic rate tax, under the Pensions Relief at Source (PRAS) system. Any higher rate relief is claimed either through the PAYE coding or by an adjustment to the assessment at the end of the relevant tax year. The 20 per cent tax band does not affect the rate at which the employee can deduct tax, which remains as the 25 per cent basic rate. The self-employed can set off contributions against their Schedule D income.

(2)   The current annual limits for contributions to PPPs (shown in (3) below) are expressed as a percentage of 'net relevant earnings' (NRE). This means relevant earnings from non-pensionable employment or business, etc. less certain deductions such as expenses, trading losses, capital allowances, etc. Personal charges such as interest or payments under deeds of covenant are not deducted.

(3)   The PPP contribution limits since 1989–90 are as follows (for the limits for previous years see the *Allied Dunbar Pensions Handbook*)

Age at beginning of year of assessment	%
below 36	17.5
36–45	20
46–50	25
51–55	30
56–60	35
61 or more	40

For example, a 48 year old with net relevant earnings of £20,000 can contribute up to £5,000 pa to a PPP. A 58 year old with the same net relevant earnings could contribute £7,000.

(4) There is a limit on the maximum amount of net relevant earnings which can be taken into account in determining the contributions payable to a PPP. The limit was introduced in the 1989–90 tax year and it was originally intended to be increased in subsequent years in line with the Retail Prices Index (RPI), rounded up to the nearest multiple of £600. However, in the March 1993 Budget the Chancellor announced that he intended to keep the limit at its previous level of £75,000 for the 1993–94 tax year. In the November 1993 Budget, the limit was, however, increased to £76,800 for the 1994–95 tax year.

(5) Larger contributions are not possible no matter how far net relevant earnings exceed £76,800. For example, in 1994–95 an individual aged 48 with net relevant earnings of £100,000 can contribute a maximum of £19,200 to a PPP (ie 25 per cent of £76,800).

(6) If an individual has two sources of income, one from pensionable employment, and the other being net relevant earnings, he may contribute up to the maximum limit in respect of his relevant earnings regardless of the level of pensionable earnings. For example, a 58 year old with pensionable earnings as a company executive of £25,000 per annum and net relevant earnings from a part-time consultancy of £8,000 per annum can pay contributions to a PPP of 35 per cent of £8,000 = £2,800.

(7) An amount not exceeding five per cent of net relevant earnings can be used to provide a lump sum payable from the PPP, in the event of death before age 75. Premiums used to provide this life cover must be included as part of the maximum contributions permitted.

(8) If an employer pays contributions to an employee's PPP, these too must be taken as part of the maximum contribution which can be made to the PPP. Employer's contributions are not treated as the employee's income for income tax or national insurance contribution purposes.

(9) Contributions paid to a PPP by the DSS to enable the individual to contract out of SERPS (see 12.14) can be paid in addition to the maximum contribution payable by an individual and/or an employer.

(10) Married couples who both have relevant earnings are entitled to pay separate contributions based on their respective net relevant earnings. It is important that the spouse paying the contributions has sufficient taxable earnings to be able to take full advantage of the relief available. For example, a wife with an income of less than her personal allowances and reliefs will be paying no tax so that, effectively, no relief will be available on the contributions paid by her, unless her salary is increased.

12.9.4   Year for which relief granted and 'carry-back'

(1) Relief for contributions is normally only given against net relevant earnings of the tax year in which contributions are paid. However, it is possible to elect to have any contribution treated for tax purposes as if it had been paid during the preceding tax year; or, if the individual had no relevant earnings for the contribution to be relieved against in that year (eg, because of losses or retirement), then in the tax year before that; ie there is a 'carry-back' period of one or two years.

(2) When electing to obtain relief in this way, it does not matter whether there are any net relevant earnings in the year in which the contribution is paid (or, where carry back is used, for the year in which the contribution is treated as being paid) but if the individual does not have any tax liability in that year he may not be able to utilise the tax relief available. The maximum relief available in any year is the amount of net relevant earnings for that year (or, where carry back is used, for the year in which the contribution is treated as being paid).

12.9.5   Eligibility to pay contributions and 'carry forward'

(1) To the extent that contributions paid in any year fall short of the permitted maximum of net relevant earnings, it is possible to carry forward the shortfall for up to six years and use this (on a first-in first-out basis) to pay a contribution in a subsequent year which exceeds the maximum percentage limit of net relevant earnings for the year in which it is paid. (There are special rules where the tax liability for any year is determined after more than six years have elapsed.)

(2) The earliest year's unused entitlement to pay contributions which may be utilised to permit payment of a contribution paid in 1994–95 is that for 1988–89. The maximum payable by way of contributions in any tax year will be 17.5 per cent (or the

appropriate higher figure for those over 35 years old, based on the age in the appropriate previous year) of the net relevant earnings for that year plus any unused entitlement for the previous six tax years. For example, if an individual is aged 35 or under and pays a contribution of £3,000 in respect of the net relevant earnings of the current year, say £15,000, the first £2,625 (17.5 per cent of £15,000) is permitted because of those relevant earnings, and the remaining £375 only by virtue of any unused entitlement brought forward. The Revenue's interpretation of the legislation is that the maximum contribution payable in any year is the amount of relevant earnings for that year (even where 'carry forward' would have suggested a greater eligibility to pay contributions).

12.9.6 Benefits payable and age at which they may be taken

(1) The PPP scheme established by the pension provider can allow the individual to make more than one 'arrangement' under it. The advantages of this are that, as benefits from an arrangement can, generally, only be taken once if they are to include a cash lump sum, multiple arrangements can give the opportunity to take benefits in stages.

(2) The pension may start being paid at any age between 50 and 75. It is not necessary actually to retire before the annuity may commence. In certain occupations, the Revenue allow an annuity to start earlier than the age of 50 (eg, jockeys, motor racing drivers, cricketers, etc). The pension can also start to be paid before the age of 50 on retirement due to ill health. Under no circumstances may the annuity start later than the age of 75.

(3) The annuity payable can take one of several forms: sterling or unit-linked, guaranteed or non-guaranteed, etc. In most contracts there is a provision that on death before the beginning of the annuity, an annuity is payable to any widow or dependants nominated by the individual or, alternatively, a lump sum could be paid, not exceeding the amount of the contributions plus a reasonable amount of interest or bonuses (this includes capital growth and income attributable to the contributions paid under a unit-linked plan).

(4) The PPP can also incorporate a sum assured, so that on death an additional lump sum would be paid. This can be arranged to be free of inheritance tax by writing it in trust where the PPP scheme itself is not set up under trust.

(5) Any annuity payable to a widow, widower, or dependant would be free of inheritance tax (IHTA 1984, s 152).

(6)   The whole of any annuity payable either to the individual, any spouse or dependants will curently be treated and taxed as income under Schedule D (and not, as is the case with purchased life annuities, partly as income and partly as a return of capital). Basic rate income tax is deducted at source when the pension is paid.

From 6 April 1995 all personal pension annuities, including those already in payment, will be treated and taxed under Schedule E. This will mean that the PAYE system will apply to such payments.

(7)   A lump sum may be taken from the PPP, between the ages of 50 and 75, up to a maximum of 25 per cent of the fund excluding any part of the fund built up from contributions paid by the DSS. For PPPs effected prior to 27 July 1989, the value of the DSS contributions could be taken into account in calculating the cash lump sum available but any fund used to provide benefits for a widow(er) or dependants had to be excluded.

(8)   Instead of taking the annuity from the life company which issued the original pension contract, it is possible to use the fund built up to buy an annuity from any other company, thus obtaining the best terms then available ('open market option'). If the PPP is provided by an organisation which is not a life assurance company, the pension (and life assurance) must be provided by a life company.

12.10   Retirement annuity contracts (s 226 contracts)

Prior to the introduction of PPPs (on 1 July 1988), the self-employed and those in non-pensionable employment were able to contribute to retirement annuity contracts (often called s 226 contracts) which, while broadly similar to PPPs, had several important differences. Although no new s 226 contracts have been allowed since 30 June 1988, those in existence before then can continue much as before with contributions being paid and even increased on a regular basis.

The key differences between s 226 contracts and PPPs include the following:

(1)   employers are not allowed to pay direct contributions into an employee's s 226 contract;

(2)   the Pensions Relief at Source system does not apply to s 226 contracts;

(3)   s 226 contracts cannot be used to contract out of SERPS, and

(4)   the earliest age at which benefits could be taken was age 60 (except for those specific occupations where the Revenue permitted an earlier retirement age or in the case of ill health).

(5)   s 226 contracts will not become subject to the PAYE system when the new rules on the taxation of personal pension annuities are introduced in the 1995–96 tax year.

In addition, there are more favourable rules for determining the maximum lump sum cash which can be taken from an s 226 contract. Instead of being restricted to 25 per cent of the fund, the lump sum can equal three times the annual annuity payable after the cash has been taken (but contracts entered into on or after 17 March 1987 are subject to a maximum cash lump sum of £150,000 per contract).

Section 226 contracts are not subject to the £76,800 cap on the earnings to be taken into account when determining maximum contributions but the maximum percentages of net relevant earnings are different. The current percentages are:

Age at beginning of year of assessment	%
up to 50	17.5
51–55	20
56–60	22.5
61 or more	27.5

Finally, if an individual has an existing s 226 contract he may also pay contributions at the same time to a PPP. However, the contributions to the s 226 contract reduce the amounts that can be paid to the PPP and care is needed to ensure that the interaction between the two sets of rules does not restrict the overall contributions that can be paid.

12.11   Occupational schemes
(TA 1988, s 590 et seq & Sched 23 and FA 1989, Sched 6)

12.11.1   Types of plan

(1)   Occupational pension schemes may be either money purchase schemes or 'final salary schemes', where the benefits are determined as a fraction of the employee's salary at retirement. Final salary schemes are sometimes called 'defined benefit' schemes.

(2)   All occupational pension schemes require the involvement of an employer who will make some contribution to the scheme.

(3)   Occupational pension schemes may be insured, where all benefits are provided in the form of insurance policies either on a group or individual basis, or self-administered with investment in a range of permitted assets. There are special rules for Small Self Administered Schemes (SSAS) with 12 or fewer members.

12.11.2 Eligibility

(1)   All employees, whether part time or full time, are eligible for membership of an occupational pension scheme if their employer participates in such a scheme. There are special rules for employees of overseas employers and for employees who are temporarily seconded outside the United Kingdom.

(2)   Persons assessable under Schedule D (for example, agents and consultants) are not eligible.

(3)   Directors are also eligible for membership of an occupational pension scheme but controlling directors of investment companies are normally not able to benefit from schemes approved under the Revenue's discretionary powers (see 12.11.3).

(4)   It is not possible for an employer to make membership of an occupational scheme (other than one providing death benefits only) compulsory. In general, leaving a good occupational scheme is unlikely to be wise except where its benefits are poor and expert advice should be sought if this is contemplated.

12.11.3 Approval of schemes

(1)   Approval of occupational pension schemes is given by the Pension Schemes Office (PSO) which is a branch of the Inland Revenue. 'Approval' will prevent contributions paid by the employer being taxed in the employees' hands as a benefit in kind.

(2)   In addition, 'exempt approval' will give the additional benefits of the gross roll-up in the fund and tax relief for the employee in respect of regular contributions he makes to the scheme. Exempt approval will also mean that the employer's contributions will be deductible business expenses without relying on the normal rules for deductibility applying to Schedule D income. In order to be exempt approved, the scheme must be set up under irrevocable trusts.

(3)   In most cases approval is given under the PSO's discretionary powers which are extremely wide-ranging. The main conditions for approval include the following:

  (a)   The sole purpose of the scheme must be to provide 'relevant benefits' in respect of service as an employee. Relevant benefits, broadly speaking, include most types of financial benefit given in connection with the termination of an employee's service with a particular employer.

  (b)   The scheme must be recognised by employer and employee and the employee given written particulars of its essential features.

  (c)   The employer must contribute to the scheme although the employee may indirectly provide the necessary funds by agreeing to a reduction in salary, 'a salary sacrifice'.

(d) Pension benefits must be payable on retirement at any age between 50 and 75 and must not exceed a maximum permitted benefit calculated by reference to the employee's final remuneration and the length of service with that employer (see 12.11.5). Benefits may be available in respect of early retirement at any earlier age where retirement is due to ill health. There is also a maximum limit on the permitted pension which can be provided for widows and dependants.

(e) No pension may be surrendered, commuted or assigned, save for commutation on retirement up to a maximum lump sum (see 12.11.5 item (7)).

(f) A scheme may also provide for a lump sum payment of up to four times the employee's final remuneration on death in service and for a return of the employee's contributions in certain cases.

12.11.4 Tax relief on contributions and limits

(1) Contributions by the employer to an exempt approved scheme are deductible business expenses, although relief in respect of non-regular contributions may be deferred by being spread over a maximum of five years.

(2) The employee may make personal contributions of up to 15 per cent of his remuneration subject to the £76,800 salary cap (see 12.11.5 item (6)). Personal contributions attract tax relief at the highest rate paid by the individual.

(3) Unlike PPPs there are no specific limits on the amount of contributions which may be made to an occupational scheme other than those applicable to personal contributions. Instead, the controls operate on a level of benefits which is allowed. If a scheme becomes 'over-funded' (ie, where the scheme has more capital than is necessary to meet its prospective liabilities), payment of further contributions may be restricted or capital may have to be returned to the employer after deduction of tax of 40 per cent.

(4) Where a surplus arises from an employee's voluntary contributions any refund to the employee will have tax deducted at 35 per cent. An employee who is a higher rate taxpayer will be subject to a further charge taking the total to 48 per cent.

12.11.5 Benefits

(1) The maximum pension benefits under an occupational pension scheme are expressed as a fraction of the member's final salary for each year of service with the employer. For example, many

schemes provide a pension of one-sixtieth of final salary for each year of service so that the maximum pension of two-thirds of final salary is reached after 40 years' service.

(2)   The maximum rate at which pension benefits can accrue is one-thirtieth of final salary for each year of service. In order to obtain a maximum pension of two-thirds of final salary it is necessary to complete 20 years' service.

(3)   Final salary or 'final remuneration' must be calculated in a way which is approved by the PSO. The two permitted definitions are:

    (a)   the remuneration in any of the five years preceding retirement, leaving service or death (as applicable) together with the average of any fluctuating emoluments (bonuses, commissions etc) averaged over at least three consecutive years ending with the year in question; or

    (b)   the highest average of the total emoluments from the employer over any period of three consecutive years ending within ten years before retirement, leaving service or death (as applicable).

Company directors who are treated as controlling directors may only calculate final salary using the second permitted definition.

(4)   Final salary excludes any income and gains from shares and options acquired through share option, share incentive and profit sharing schemes. In addition, payments on the termination of employment (eg golden handshakes) cannot be used as part of the calculation of final salary.

(5)   It is possible to increase 'final salary' for previous years in line with the increase in the RPI up to the date when benefits are paid. This increase is known as 'dynamisation'.

(6)   There is a maximum amount of final salary which may be taken into account for pension purposes. For the tax year 1994–95 this amount is £76,800. The 'salary cap' is subject to the same rules relating to annual increases in line with the RPI as the limit on contributions to personal pension schemes (see 12.9.3 item (4)).

(7)   Instead of taking all benefits in pension form, the member may commute part of his pension for a tax-free cash lump sum. The maximum lump sum is three-eightieths of final salary for each year of service up to a maximum of 40 years' service or 2.25 times the pension available before commutation, if greater. The maximum lump sum is, therefore, one and a half times final salary.

(8)   A lump sum of up to four times final salary, together with a refund of the employee's personal contributions, can also be paid on the death of the employee in service. It is also possible to provide a pension for a spouse or dependant up to two-thirds of the maximum pension to which the deceased would have been entitled at his normal retirement date. A pension of a similar amount can also be provided for a spouse or dependant on death after retirement.

(9) Pensions payable are treated as earned income and taxed under Schedule E. The payments will be subject to the deduction of income tax under the PAYE system.

12.11.6 'Grandfathering'

The maximum limits on contributions to and benefits from occupational pension schemes have been restricted over the years. The most notable changes were in 1987 and 1989 when restrictions, including the introduction of the salary cap in 1989, were announced in the Budget. Members who joined schemes prior to the Budget Days in those years may continue to benefit from the old rules which have been preserved or 'grandfathered' for those members eligible. Minor changes have also been made to the Inland Revenue's discretionary practice at other times. Further details can be found in the *Allied Dunbar Pensions Handbook*.

12.12 Free-standing AVC (FSAVC) schemes

12.12.1 Types of plan

(1) FSAVC schemes are money purchase schemes which provide benefits in addition to the benefits provided by an employer's occupational pension scheme.
(2) FSAVC schemes are similar to PPPs in that they may be offered by life assurance companies, banks, building societies and authorised unit trust schemes.
(3) FSAVC schemes are occupational pension schemes for Revenue purposes and must be set up under irrevocable trusts for the sole purpose of providing relevant benefits of the type provided by occupational pension schemes.

12.12.2 Eligibility

(1) An employee will only be eligible to contribute to an FSAVC scheme if he is a member of an occupational pension scheme to which his employer is currently contributing or is a member of a statutory scheme such as the Civil Service scheme.
(2) Contributions may only be paid to one FSAVC scheme in any tax year although if there are earnings from more than one employment separate contributions may be made to an FSAVC scheme in respect of each employment.
(3) Directors who are treated as controlling directors are not eligible for membership of an FSAVC scheme.

12.12.3   Contributions

(1)   The maximum contribution is 15 per cent of the employee's remuneration in any one tax year. In order to calculate the maximum contribution the contribution to the FSAVC scheme must be aggregated with the employee's contributions to his employer's scheme.

(2)   The salary cap of £76,800 will apply if it applies to the benefits provided by the employer's scheme, so that the maximum contribution will be £11,250 in 1993–94 for an employee who is subject to the salary cap.

(3)   Where contributions to the FSAVC scheme exceed £2,400 pa the administrator of the FSAVC scheme must calculate the maximum contribution which is not likely to produce benefits in excess of the Revenue limits. To do this information is provided by the administrators of the employers scheme (or the member himself) about the benefits provided by that scheme. If necessary, contributions to the FSAVC scheme must be restricted.

(4)   Contributions to an FSAVC scheme must be paid net of basic rate tax under the PRAS system. Higher rate tax relief is obtained by either an adjustment to the employee's PAYE coding or to his end of year tax assessment.

12.12.4   Benefits

(1)   The benefits provided by an FSAVC scheme must be aggregated with the benefits provided by the employer's scheme to ensure that the limits on benefits provided by occupational schemes are not exceeded.

(2)   An FSAVC scheme may not provide a tax free cash lump sum on retirement, although the pension provided may be used as part of the '2.25 times pension before commutation' calculation in order to enhance the tax-free lump sum provided by the employer's scheme.

(3)   Where the funds accumulated in the FSAVC scheme are such that the maximum limits on benefits are exceeded, the excess must be returned to the employee after deduction of tax at 35 per cent. An employee who is a higher rate taxpayer will be subject to a further charge taking the total to 48 per cent.

(4)   Pensions payable are treated in the same way as those from occupational schemes and are subject to the PAYE system.

12.13   Unapproved schemes

Unapproved occupational pension schemes were introduced to allow employers the flexibility to provide benefits for those employees who had earnings in excess of the salary cap. However, their use is not restricted to such employees and they may be used to provide benefits in excess of the normal two-thirds maximum pension benefit or to provide greater benefits for those with less than twenty years' service.

12.13.1 Eligibility

(1)   Any person in receipt of income taxed under Schedule E is eligible for an unapproved scheme.
(2)   There is no requirement that the employee is also a member of an approved scheme.

12.13.2 Types of plan

(1)   Such schemes may be funded (ie contributions set aside in order to fund the promised benefits) or unfunded (ie at retirement the benefits will be paid by the company out of a current income or investments).
(2)   There is no requirement that funded schemes are established under trust, but this is commonly the case.

12.13.3 Contributions

(1)   If the scheme is funded, the employer will obtain tax relief on the contributions as a normal business expense. There is no set limit on contributions that may be paid, although excessive contributions may be disqualified from tax relief.
(2)   The employee will be taxed on contributions paid by the employer as if they were emoluments. If no benefits are received by the employee it may be possible to reclaim some of the tax.
(3)   Employee contributions will not be tax deductible and are to be avoided.
(4)   In an unfunded scheme there is no charge to tax on any reserves set up to provide for future benefits. Equally, the employer will not obtain any tax relief until the benefits are actually paid.

12.13.4 Taxation of scheme investments

(1)   Unapproved schemes do not benefit from 'gross roll up' but are not subject to the special rate of income tax of 35 per cent payable by trusts which accumulate their income.
(2)   Unapproved schemes will pay capital gains tax on realised gains at the basic rate of 25 per cent.
(3)   Prior to 30 November 1993, extra tax benefits could be achieved by establishing a funded scheme under an offshore trust, although

care had to be taken to avoid the anti-avoidance legislation which applied to such trusts. The Finance Act 1994 effectively removes the tax advantage of offshore schemes, although existing schemes can continue unchanged.

12.13.5   Benefits

(1)   The scheme must be set up to provide relevant benefits but there are no set limits on the benefits which can be provided.

(2)   Pensions from unapproved schemes, whether funded or unfunded, will be subject to income tax as earned income.

(3)   Lump sums paid from funded schemes may be paid free of tax but those from unfunded schemes are subject to income tax as earned income. Lump sums paid from funded schemes set up after 30 November, or from schemes set up before then which are varied to provide a lump sum, may be taxed if they exceed the amount of the contributions on which the employee was taxed, where the scheme invests in assets which are subject to income or capital gains taxes. This will apply to schemes set up using offshore trusts.

12.14   The State pension scheme

The State scheme currently provides two types of pension; the basic pension and the State Earnings Related Pension Scheme.

The basic pension

This is a contributory scheme which aims to provide a pension of approximately 20 per cent of national average earnings. It is not related to salary but to obtain the maximum pension an individual must have paid (or have been credited with) national insurance contributions for about 90 per cent of his expected working life. The pension (which is taxable as earned income if attributable to an individual's own contributions) is increased each year in line with the RPI.

The State Earnings Related Pension Scheme (SERPS)

SERPS was introduced in 1978 and is based on national insurance contributions made by employers and employees on earnings between the lower and upper earnings limits (for 1993–94 £56 and £420 per week respectively). The earnings between these two figures are often called 'band earnings'. The self-employed neither contribute towards, nor benefit from, SERPS.

SERPS provides a pension at state retirement age expressed as a percentage of band earnings. For those retiring in 2009–10 or later the percentage is currently 20 per cent with those retiring before then receiving a higher percentage up to a maximum of 25 per cent of band earnings. Band earnings are based on average over the whole of your working life, although individuals retiring before 6 April 1999 can use their best 20 years to calculate band earnings.

State pensions do not provide any cash lump sum at retirement or any opportunity of retiring and receiving benefits before state retirement age. Benefits can be postponed for up to five years, in which case the pension will be increased.

The main benefit from the state scheme is a lifelong pension for the individual but SERPS can also, in certain circumstances, provide a widow's pension which will be of a reduced amount unless the widow is aged over 40 and has dependent children (or over 50 with no dependent children).

12.15   Contracting out

It is possible to leave SERPS provided appropriate provision is made to replace the SERPS benefits with a suitable approved alternative. To encourage this, individuals and employers who 'contract out' in this way receive benefits in form of reduced national insurance contributions or a direct payment into individual personal pension plans.

There are currently three ways in which an employee can be contracted out.

These are:

(1)   membership of an appropriate personal pension plan (APPP);
(2)   membership of a contracted-out money purchase pension scheme (COMPS);
(3)   membership of an occupational scheme providing guaranteed minimum pension (GMP).

12.15.1   Appropriate personal pension plans (APPP)

These require no employer involvement at all and are open to all employees who are not contracted-out by another scheme, even those who are also members of an occupational scheme. In order to contract-out the employee and the chosen personal pension plan provider must complete a Joint Notice (Form APP1) which is submitted to the DSS. An individual can use only one APPP to contract out at any time and must contract out for a complete tax year.

Once the Joint Notice is accepted by the DSS payments are made, normally once a year, directly by the DSS to the pension provider. These payments, called protected rights contributions, consist of a National Insurance Rebate, an element of tax relief on the employee's share of the rebate and, for those who are 30 or over at the beginning of the tax year, a payment equal to 1 per cent of the employee's band earnings. Both the employee and employer continue to pay the full rate of national insurance contributions.

The protected rights contributions must be used to provide a pension benefit at State Retirement Age, or a widow(er)'s or dependant's pension or a lump sum on death.

12.15.2   Contracted Out Money Purchase Schemes (COMPS)

These are occupational pension plans where the employer takes the initial decision to contract out, although the employer may allow individuals the choice of whether to contract out or not.

Both the employer and employee pay a reduced rate of national insurance contributions but this saving is balanced by the protected rights contributions which the employer must ensure are paid into the pension scheme on a monthly basis. Payments are not made directly by the DSS and normally both the employer and the employee will contribute their respective shares of the protected rights contributions.

Unlike PPPs, there is no extra payment for employees aged 30 or over and the protected rights contributions do not automatically include an element of tax relief although where the employee is obliged by the employer to pay his share of the protected rights contributions he will effectively receive full tax relief on this part of the contributions. The protected rights contributions must be used to provide benefits in the same way as those provided by an APPP.

12.15.3   Guaranteed minimum pensions

This method of contracting out involves an occupational pension scheme which provides a guaranteed minimum level of pension equivalent to that provided by SERPS. Both the employer and employee benefit from a reduced level of national insurance contribution but the employer has to be prepared to provide the pension scheme with sufficient funds to enable it to meet the guarantee.

Employees who contract out using an APPP or a COMPS must consider whether the money purchase benefits provided by the protected rights contributions will exceed the likely benefits from SERPS. In general contracting out will be of benefit to younger people with older persons likely to benefit more from SERPS. The cut-off ages depend on future investment performance but for those contracting-out using an APPP the ages for 1994–95 are approximately 49 for males and 43 for females. For those contracting out using a COMPS, the ages are approximately 46 for males and 39 for females.

13　Capital gains tax

This chapter deals with the following matters:

(1)　Basic outline of capital gains tax (CGT).
(2)　Who is subject to CGT?
(3)　What assets are chargeable assets?
(4)　Which types of transaction may produce a chargeable gain?
(5)　How gains may be deferred or 'rolled over'.

Unless otherwise stated, the statutory references refer to the Taxation of Chargeable Gains Act (TCGA) 1992.

13.1　Basic outline of capital gains tax

Capital gains are assessed for a tax year. The due date for payment of CGT is 1 December following the tax year concerned, so 1993–94 CGT is due for payment on 1 December 1994. The way in which chargeable gains are computed is quite different from the rules which determine assessable income for tax purposes. A range of exemptions and reliefs may apply and there is a major distinction between CGT and income tax in that allowance is made for inflation in computing capital gains.

The rate of CGT is now governed by whether the individual's income and capital gains are sufficient to put him into the 40 per cent band.

13.1.1　Annual exemption
　　　　　(TCGA 1992, s 3)

You cannot be liable for CGT for 1994–95 unless you have made gains of more than £5,800.

This is because there is an annual exemption. The amount of the exemption for the current year (1994–95) and the past six years is as follows:

	£
1994–95	5,800
1993–94	5,800
1992–93	5,800
1991–92	5,500
1990–91	5,000
1989–90	5,000
1988–89	5,000

13.1.2   No gain/loss on spouse transactions

Provided a couple have not separated on a permanent basis, there can be no chargeable gains on any assets transferred from one spouse to the other, whether by gift or sale. The asset is treated as passing across on a no gain/no loss basis, with the recipient acquiring it at his spouse's cost plus indexation to date (see 14.5 on indexation relief).

13.1.3   Losses

Losses may arise as well as capital gains. The normal rule is that capital losses cannot be off-set against an individual's income but may be carried forward against capital gains of future years. However, losses arising from transactions involving connected persons may only be set against gains arising from transactions with the same person.

Brought forward losses do not need to be set against gains which are covered by the annual exemption. However, current year losses have to be set against capital gains before using the annual exemption.

13.1.4   Rate of tax
(TCGA 1992, s 4)

Once the gains for the year have been computed (net of any losses), the annual exemption is deducted. The balance is then added to the individual's taxable income and the CGT is normally ascertained by working out the additional income tax which would be payable if the capital gains had been taxable income.

13.1.5   Example—Rate of tax

B has 1993–94 taxable income, after personal allowances, of £19,000. Her capital gains for the year are £15,000. After deducting the £5,800 annual exemption, this means adding in an amount of £9,200. The CGT payable would be computed as:

	£
Balance of basic rate band	
£23,700–£19,000 = 4,700 at 25 per cent =	1,175
£4,500 at 40 per cent =	1,800
Total CGT payable	2,975

However, if the individual had no taxable income at all, the calculation is done slightly differently. If the gains were again £15,000, the CGT payable would be:

	£
First £5,800	NIL
£2,500 at 20 per cent	500
£6,700 at 25 per cent	1,675
	2,175

Any unused personal allowances for income tax purposes simply go to waste.

13.1.6 Position where most of the individual's income is made up of dividends

Where an individual has less than £23,700 income, the effective rate of income tax on the dividends is 20 per cent (see 6.3.3). However, where such a person has capital gains, these 'displace' the dividends so that the capital gains use the lower rate band instead.

13.1.7 Example—Tax on gross dividend income

If, in the example at 13.1.5 above, B's other income, after personal allowances, represents gross dividend income the net capital gains of £9,200 for the year will be taxed as follows:

	£
First £2,500 at 20 per cent =	500
Balance of basic rate band	
£23,700 – (£19,000 + £2,500) = 2,200 at 25 per cent =	550
£4,500 at 40 per cent =	1,800
Total CGT payable	£2,850

13.2 Who is subject to capital gains tax?

An individual's residence and domicile status may have a crucial bearing on his liability to CGT.

13.2.1 Significance of residence status
(TCGA 1992, s 2)

An individual will be subject to the CGT legislation only if he is either resident or ordinarily resident for the year in which relevant disposals take place. Residence and ordinary residence are determined in the same way as for income tax (see 21.2).

There is one exception to the above: where a non-resident and non-ordinarily resident person has been carrying on a trade or profession through a branch or agency in the United Kingdom, CGT may be charged on a disposal of assets used in that branch despite the fact that the person would normally be outside the charge on capital gains.

13.2.2 What happens if an individual is non-resident only for part of the tax year?

Technically, an individual is resident or non-resident for the whole of a tax year. The Revenue practice of treating certain individuals as resident for only part of a tax year, is really no more than an extra-statutory concession. Nevertheless, the 'split year' treatment adopted for income tax purposes (see 21.3.1) will normally be followed for CGT—but subject to two exceptions.

Firstly, capital gains may be charged where the individual concerned has returned to the United Kingdom during the year in question *and* he was non-resident for less than 36 months. In such a case, capital gains realised in the tax year in which the individual resumes UK residence may be charged to tax even though the disposals took place prior to the individual's return.

13.2.3 Example—Non-residence for part of tax year

A was classified as non-resident in the United Kingdom from 1 January 1991 when she took up a job in the Middle East. She returned to the United Kingdom on 24 July 1993. For income tax purposes she is regarded as not resident and not ordinarily resident from 1 January 1991–23 July 1993. However, she may be subject to CGT on disposals made during the period 6 April–23 July 1993 as well as on disposals made during the remainder of the tax year 1993–94.

Note, however, that gains realised in 1991–92 and 1992–93 are not subject to CGT as A was neither resident nor ordinarily resident for those tax years. Also, if A had ceased to be resident from (say) 1 June 1990, so that she had been non-resident for 36 months when she returned in July 1993, she would not be subject to CGT on gains realised during the period 6 April–23 July 1993.

The second exception to the split year treatment concerns the year of departure. All the extra-statutory concessions published by the Inland Revenue carry a 'health warning' that they will not be applied in cases where people seek to take advantage of them for tax avoidance. The Revenue's practice is therefore to charge tax on certain gains realised very shortly after an individual moves abroad where they fall in the same tax year.

13.2.4   Having a foreign domicile may make an important difference
(TCGA 1992, s 12)

See 22.1 on Domicile.

An individual who is resident (or ordinarily resident) and domiciled in the United Kingdom will be subject to CGT on gains realised *both* in this country and abroad. By contrast an individual who is not domiciled in the United Kingdom is charged tax on gains from foreign assets only if the proceeds are brought into this country (or, as the legislation puts it, the gains are 'remitted' to the United Kingdom). There are further details on the treatment of foreign domiciled individuals in 22.13. The rest of this chapter deals only with people who are domiciled in the United Kingdom.

13.3   What assets are chargeable assets?

13.3.1   Assets within the scope of capital gains tax
(TCGA 1992, s 21)

Gains on virtually all types of assets are potentially subject to capital gains tax, subject to certain stated exceptions.

TCGA 1992, s 21(1) states:

> All forms of property shall be assets for the purposes of this Act, whether situated in the United Kingdom or not, including:
> (a)   options, debts and incorporeal property generally, and
> (b)   any currency other than sterling, and
> (c)   any form of property created by the person disposing of it, or otherwise coming to be owned without being acquired.

The asset does not have to be transferable or capable of being assigned. The term 'any form of property' is all embracing.

For example, the Courts have held that CGT was due on an employer's right to compensation from an employee who wished to be released from his service agreement. In another case, the right to compensation in respect of property expropriated by the USSR in 1940 was held to be a form of property and therefore an asset for capital gains tax purposes. Similarly, the High Court held in *Zim Properties Ltd v Procter* [1985] STC 90 that the right to bring an action before the Courts constitutes an asset which can be turned to account by the potential litigant negotiating a compromise and receiving a lump sum.

The conclusion therefore is that virtually all forms of property which can yield a capital sum are subject to CGT unless they are specifically exempt.

13.3.2 What assets are specifically exempt?

The following are the main categories of exempt assets:

(1) Chattels which are wasting assets (see 14.8.1) [s 44].
(2) Chattels—where the sale consideration is less than £6,000. There is some alleviation of the charge when more than £6,000 is received (see 14.8.2) [s 262].
(3) Decoration for valour so long as sold by the original recipient [s 268].
(4) Foreign currency acquired for personal expenditure outside the United Kingdom. This includes money spent on the purchase or maintenance of any property situated outside the United Kingdom [s 269].
(5) Winnings from betting—for example the pools, horses, bingo and lotteries [s 51].
(6) Compensation or damages for wrong or injury suffered in a profession or vocation [s 51].
(7) Debts [s 251].
(8) National savings certificates and non-marketable securities, ie those which cannot be transferred or are only transferable with the consent of a Minister of the Crown or National Debt Commissioner [s 121].
(9) Gilt-edged securities and qualifying corporate bonds and any options to acquire or dispose of such investments [s 115]. A qualifying corporate bond is a loan stock which is not convertible and is not a deep discount or a deep gain security (see 5.6 and 5.7).
(10) Shares held in Personal Equity Plans (see 11.3) [s 151].
(11) Shares issued by way of Business Expansion Schemes (see 11.4 [s 222] provided the BES relief has not been withdrawn and the shares are sold etc by the original subscriber or his spouse.
(12) Shares issued under the Enterprise Investment Scheme (see 11.7) provided the EIS relief has not been withdrawn.

(13)   Shares in a Venture Capital Trust (see 11.9).
(14)   Sale of principal private residence (see 14.12) [s 222].
(15)   Motor cars—unless not suitable or commonly used for the carriage of passengers [s 263].
(16)   Woodlands [s 250].
(17)   Gifts to charities, gifts for national purposes to any one mentioned in the Inheritance Tax Act (IHTA) 1984, Sched 3 [s 257].
(18)   Works of art where they are taken by the Inland Revenue in lieu of death duties such as inheritance tax (again see IHTA 1984, Sched 3) [s 258].
(19)   Gifts to housing associations and a claim is made by both transferor and the association [s 259].

Where an asset is exempt no gain is assessable. Unfortunately, it follows that no relief is normally given for losses (losses on a disposal of shares in an enterprise investment scheme are an exception to this general rule).

13.4   Which types of transaction may produce a chargeable gain?
(TCGA 1992, s 28)

13.4.1   Introduction

The most obvious type of disposal is an outright sale with immediate settlement, but there are many other transactions which count as a disposal for CGT purposes, for example:

(1)   Outright sale (possibly with payment by instalments)
(2)   Conditional sale
(3)   Exercise of an option
(4)   Exchange of property
(5)   Compulsory acquisition of asset by local authority, etc
(6)   Sums payable as compensation or proceeds under an insurance policy
(7)   Gifts
(8)   Asset destroyed or becoming of negligible value.

The liability to capital gains tax is determined by the tax year in which the date of disposal falls.

13.4.2   Outright sale
(TCGA 1992, s 28)

The date of disposal is the day on which the unconditional contract is entered into, which may, of course, be different from the date that the vendor receives payment.

Sale with payment by instalments

The date of disposal is fixed by the time that the parties enter into an unconditional contract. It may be possible to pay capital gains tax arising from such transactions by instalments over a period of up to eight years if the Revenue are satisfied that hardship would otherwise result (TCGA 1992, s 280).

The Revenue operate a concession where a purchaser defaults and the vendor takes back the asset in satisfaction of the sums due to him (see extra-statutory concession D18). The disposal is effectively treated as if it has never happened.

13.4.3   Conditional sale
(TCGA 1992, s 28)

A conditional sale is a contract which does not take effect until a stated condition is satisfied.

13.4.4   Example—Conditional sale

A agrees to purchase B's shares in XYZ Ltd provided the local authority grants planning permission over land owned by XYZ Ltd by April 1995. Under this type of agreement, B remains the legal owner of his shares until the condition is satisfied. If the local authority does not in fact grant planning permission, A is under no obligation to buy B's shares.

The date of disposal under such contracts is the day that the condition is satisfied and the contract becomes unconditional, eg in the above example, the date planning permission is granted.

13.4.5   Exercise of an option
(TCGA 1992, s 144)

A 'call' option is a legally binding agreement between the owner of an asset and a third party under which the owner agrees to sell the asset if the other party decides to exercise his option. The purchase price payable upon the exercise of the option is normally fixed at the outset and this constitutes one of the terms of the option.

A 'put' option is one where the other party agrees to buy the asset if the owner decides to exercise an option requiring him to do so.

The grant of either type of option does not constitute a disposal of the asset concerned. This happens only when the option is exercised and the day on which this happens is the date of disposal.

In some cases, payment is made for the option to be granted. This is treated as a disposal of a separate asset unless the option is subsequently exercised.

13.4.6   Exchange of property

An agreement to exchange an asset for another is a disposal of the old asset and an acquisition of the new asset. If there is any cash adjustment, this must also be brought into account. For example, if A exchanges his holding in ICI for B's shareholding in Glaxo, A is treated as if he has disposed of the ICI shares for the market value of the Glaxo shares at the time of the exchange. This type of transaction commonly occurs where an individual transfers portfolio investments to a unit trust in return for units.

There is an important exception to the rule that an exchange constitutes a disposal which may apply where a shareholder takes securities offered to him on a company takeover (see 14.6.7 on such share exchanges). Provided certain conditions are satisfied, the exchange does not count as a disposal and the securities issued by the acquiring company are deemed to have been derived from the original shares, with the shareholder carrying forward his original acquisition value.

13.4.7   Example—Exchange of shares on company takeover

B holds 1,000 shares in XYZ plc which he acquired in 1985 for £9,000. Another company, ABC plc makes a take-over bid and offers all XYZ shareholders a share exchange whereby they receive one ABC share (worth £30 each) for every two XYZ shares that they own. The offer document confirms that agreement has been obtained from the Revenue that TCGA 1992 s 136 applies.

If B accepts, he will receive 500 ABC shares worth £15,000. However, he will be deemed to have acquired them in 1985 for £9,000. No disposal is deemed to have occurred on the share exchange.

13.4.8   Compulsory acquisition of assets
(TCGA 1992, s 22)

The transfer of land to, for example, a local authority exercising its compulsory purchase powers is a disposal for capital gains tax purposes. In some cases, once the compulsory purchase order has been served, contracts are drawn up and the land is transferred under the contract. In such a case, the rules in relation to outright sales and conditional sales apply.

Where the compulsory purchase order is disputed, the date of disposal will normally be the earlier of:

(1) the date on which compensation for the acquisition is agreed or otherwise determined, and
(2) the date on which the local authority enters the land in pursuance of its powers.

13.4.9   Sums payable as compensation or proceeds under an insurance policy
(TCGA 1992, s 22)

In some cases, an asset (for example a building) may be destroyed or damaged and a capital sum is received as compensation for this. In such cases, the asset is deemed to have been disposed of at the date that the capital sum is received. Similarly, where a capital sum is received from an insurance policy following such damage the receipt of the insurance monies is treated as constituting a disposal.

13.4.10   Gifts
(TCGA 1992, s 17)

A gift is treated as a disposal at market value (except where the gift is from one spouse to the other: see 13.1.2). At one time it was possible for assets to be transferred at cost, but this general form of hold-over relief was abolished by Finance Act 1989. In some cases the capital gains may still be held over such as where the gift involves business property or is a chargeable transfer for inheritance tax purposes (see 17.6.1 and 17.10).

A gift will often constitute a transaction between connected persons— see 20.8.

13.4.11   Asset destroyed or becoming of negligible value
(TCGA 1992, s 24)

The total destruction or entire loss of an asset constitutes a disposal. This could be physical destruction (eg by fire) or legal/financial destruction (eg bankruptcy or winding up).

The legislation also permits a person to elect that he should be treated as having disposed of an asset which has become of negligible value. Normally, a capital loss will arise on such an occasion.

'Negligible value' is interpreted by the Revenue as meaning considerably less than small. For example, the Revenue will only agree that shares, loan stock and other securities are of negligible value on being satisfied that the owner is unlikely to recover anything other than a nominal amount on the liquidation of the company. The mere fact that shares have been suspended or de-listed by the Stock Exchange is not regarded as sufficient.

The legislation provides that a disposal is deemed to take place in the year during which the Inspector of Taxes agrees that the asset has become of negligible value. In practice the Revenue permit a claim to take effect up to two tax years prior to the claim provided that the asset was of negligible value in the prior year—see extra-statutory concession D28.

In practice it is not always beneficial for an individual to claim the benefit of ESC D28 or indeed for a claim to be made until such time as there are gains against which the loss can be set (see 13.1.3).

13.5 How gains may be deferred or 'rolled over'
(TCGA 1992, ss164A–164N (inserted by FA 1994)

The Finance Act 1994 has introduced a general form of roll-over relief whereby an individual (or trustee) who has realised a gain on the disposal of an asset of any description may roll over the gain if he re-invests the gain in shares in a qualifying unquoted trading company. Where gains are rolled over, they are not charged to tax, but the gain is deducted from the cost of acquiring the new asset (ie the unquoted shares).

An example of this relief would be if A sold quoted shares and realised a gain of £150,000. Provided he re-invests at least £150,000 in qualifying unquoted shares, and he claims roll-over relief, the gain is not chargeable at all. If he re-invests only £95,000, the chargeable gain would be limited to £55,000.

The relief applies only to gains realised after 29 November 1993. We cover this new relief in detail at 15.4.

14 The calculation of capital gains

The computation of a capital gain (or loss) is more complicated than it looks. Basically, a gain (or loss) is the difference between the disposal value and the original cost after certain expenses, allowances and deductions have been taken into account. However, there are a number of variables.

This chapter deals with the following aspects:

(1) Amount to be brought in as disposal value.
(2) What costs are allowable?
(3) Assets held at 31 March 1982 and 6 April 1965.
(4) Other acquisition values.
(5) Indexation.
(6) How gains are computed on quoted securities.
(7) Foreign currency.
(8) Special rules for chattels.
(9) Land and investment properties.
(10) Unquoted shares.
(11) Foreign property.
(12) Main residence exemption.

14.1 Amount to be brought in as disposal value

14.1.1 Market value
(TGCA 1992, s 18)

The general rule is that market value must be used unless the transaction is at arm's length. In the straightforward situation where a contract is entered into with a third party on a commercial basis, the disposal proceeds will be the actual sale proceeds. An individual is not penalised because he has made a bad bargain and sold an asset for less than it is really worth. On the other hand, if the bargain is not at arm's length and the individual deliberately sells the asset for an amount which is less than its true value, the legislation requires market value to be substituted. If the disposal is to a connected person such as a relative or the trustee of a family settlement or a family company, there is an automatic assumption that the bargain is not at arm's length and market value will always be substituted for the actual sale proceeds if the two amounts are different.

There are two main exceptions to the above:

(1)   Transactions between spouses (see 13.1.2).
(2)   Gifts to charities and similar bodies (see 13.3.2).

14.1.2   Contingent liabilities
(TCGA 1992, s 49)

There may be occasions where the contract may require part of the proceeds to be returned at some time in the future. This is known as a sale with 'contingent liabilities'.

Suppose, for example, that a vendor receives £150,000 for the disposal of a plot of land, but is under an obligation to return £60,000 in certain circumstances. Will the capital gain be charged on sale proceeds of £150,000 or £90,000? In fact, s 49 provides that in these circumstances the capital gain must be computed in the first instance without any deduction for the contingent liability. However, if and when the vendor is required to refund part of the sale proceeds because the contingent liability has become an actual liability, the CGT assessment is adjusted accordingly.

14.1.3   Contingent consideration
(TCGA 1992, s 48)

In a similar way, it is possible that the contract may provide that additional sums may be payable if certain conditions are satisfied in the future. If it is possible to put a value on the further amount of consideration which is 'contingent' (ie which is payable only if certain conditions are satisfied) the full amount which may be received is brought into account at the date of disposal without any discount. If the conditions are not in fact satisfied, so that the further amounts are never received, an adjustment is made later to the CGT assessment.

The position is different where the contingent consideration cannot be ascertained at the date of disposal (this will normally be the situation where the contingent consideration may vary and is not a fixed amount). Basically, the legislation requires that the market value of the right to receive the future consideration should be regarded as the disposal proceeds. The difference between this amount and the amount eventually received forms a *separate* capital gains tax computation for the year in which the final amount of the actual contingent consideration is determined. The treatment of contingent consideration, especially variable contingent consideration, is fairly complex. It normally arises in relation either to land or shares in private companies. This is an area where it is essential to take professional advice.

14.1.4   Deduction for amounts charged as income
(TCGA 1992, s 31)

In some cases the disposal of an asset may give rise to an income tax charge. Where this happens, the amount which is charged as income is deducted from the sale proceeds and only the balance is brought into account for CGT purposes. This commonly arises where a private company buys back its own shares and the transaction is treated as a distribution (see 6.4.7).

14.2   What costs are allowable?

14.2.1   Certain specific types of expenditure

The legislation permits only a limited range of expenses to be deducted in computing capital gains and losses. TCGA 1992, s 38 (1) states:

> . . . the sums allowable as a deduction from the consideration in the computation of the gain accruing to a person on the disposal of an asset shall be restricted to:
>
> (a)   the amount of value of the consideration, in money or money's worth, given by him or on his behalf wholly and exclusively for the acquisition of the asset, together with the incidental costs to him of the acquisition or, if the asset was not acquired by him, any expenditure wholly and exclusively incurred by him in providing the asset,
>
> (b)   the amount of any expenditure wholly and exclusively incurred on the asset by him or on his behalf for the purpose of enhancing the value of the asset, being expenditure reflected in the state or nature of the asset at the time of the disposal, and any expenditure wholly and exclusively incurred by him in establishing, preserving or defending his title to, or to a right over, the asset,
>
> (c)   the incidental costs to him of making the disposal.

14.2.2   The cost of the asset

The market value of the asset at 31 March 1982 or 6 April 1965 may be substituted for actual cost if the asset was held at those dates (see 14.3.1 and 14.3.4).

14.2.3   Incidental costs of acquisition

These are limited to:

(1)   fees, commission or remuneration paid to a surveyor, valuer, auctioneer, accountant, agent or legal adviser;
(2)   transfer/conveyancing charges (including stamp duty); and
(3)   advertising to find a seller.

14.2.4   Enhancement expenditure

The legislation permits a deduction to be claimed in respect of expenditure incurred in order to enhance the value of the asset provided that such expenditure is reflected in the state or nature of the asset at the time of disposal. The latter condition excludes relief for improvements which have worn out by the time that the asset is disposed of. Certain grey areas are worth mentioning:

(1)   Initial expenditure by way of repairs to newly acquired property which is let may be allowable if no relief has been given in computing Schedule A income (see 4.2.1).
(2)   Expenditure means money or money's worth. It does not include the value of personal labour or skill.

14.2.5   Expenditure incurred in establishing, preserving or defending legal title

The case law concerned with the allowable nature of this expenditure hinges on the inter-relationship between the words 'incurred' and 'establishing' etc.

The High Court held in a particular case, that the cost of making an inventory and providing a valuation for a grant of probate was allowable under this head (*IRC v Richard's Executors* (1969) 46 TC 626).

14.2.6   Incidental costs of disposals

The following expenses may be deductible under this head:

(1)   Fees, commission or remuneration for the professional services of a surveyor, valuer, auctioneer, accountant, agent or legal adviser.
(2)   Transfer/conveyancing charges (including stamp duty).
(3)   Advertising to find a buyer.

(4)   Any other costs reasonably incurred in making any valuation or apportionment for CGT purposes, including in particular expenses reasonably incurred in ascertaining market value where this is required. Professional costs incurred in getting a valuation agreed with the Revenue are not allowable.

14.2.7   Part disposals
(TCGA 1992, s 42)

Where a person disposes of part of an asset, the cost is apportioned between the part disposed of and the part retained according to the formula [A ÷ (A+B)] where A is the consideration received or deemed to have been received and B is the market value of the part retained.

14.2.8   Example—Part disposals

B holds 1,000 shares in XYZ Ltd which cost him £10,000. The company is taken over and he receives cash of £5,000 and convertible loan stock issued by the acquiring company worth £15,000 (assume that in this particular case no capital gain arises in respect of the loan stock because it is issued on the occasion of a take over and the necessary Revenue clearances have been obtained (see 13.4.6 and 14.6.7)).

B's acquisition value will be apportioned as follows:

$$\text{£}10,000 \times \frac{5,000}{5,000 + 15,000} = \text{£}2,500$$

ie the proportion of acquisition value which relates to the part sold.

£7,500 is treated as the acquisition value of the part retained, ie it will be taken into account in computing any gain or loss as and when the loan stock is sold.

Special rules may apply where shares are sold out of a shareholding which includes shares held on 31 March 1982 and shares acquired after that date (see 14.6.2).

14.2.9   Small capital receipts
(TCGA 1992, s 122)

There are occasions where the formula [A ÷ (A + B)] does not have to be used, and the amount received is simply deducted from the owner's acquisition value. The most common situation where this arises is where a shareholder sells his entitlement under a rights issue, normally on a nil paid basis. Provided that the amount received is small as compared with the value of the asset, the receipt can be deducted from the owner's acquisition value. 'Small' in this context is interpreted by the Inland Revenue to be an amount not exceeding five per cent of the market value.

14.2.10 Capital sums applied in restoring assets
(TCGA 1992, s 23)

Under normal circumstances, an asset is regarded as having been disposed of for capital gains tax purposes if it is lost or destroyed. However, where a capital sum is received from such an asset (eg the proceeds of an insurance policy), the owner may claim that the asset is not treated as disposed of if at least 95 per cent of the capital sum is spent in restoring the asset.

14.3 Assets held at 31 March 1982 and 6 April 1965
(TCGA 1992, s 35 & Scheds 2–3)

14.3.1 General rebasing
(TCGA 1992, s 35)

The general rule is that where assets were held at 31 March 1982, it is to be assumed that the assets were sold on that date and immediately re-acquired at their market value at that time. This is known as 'rebasing'.

The original cost would still apply in certain circumstances as the rebasing rule is subject to the following qualifications:

(1)   Where the gain since March 1982 is smaller than that measured by reference to original cost (or *vice versa*), the chargeable gain is confined to that figure.

(2)   Where a loss has arisen, the allowable loss is the smaller of the loss measured by reference to original cost and the loss measured by reference to the 31 March 1982 value.

(3)   Where a gain arises when one has regard to original cost, but a loss arises when one takes the 31 March 1982 value (or *vice versa*), the position is regarded as no gain/no loss.

However, even these qualifications are ignored if a universal rebasing election has been made.

14.3.2 Universal rebasing election
(TCGA 1992, s 35(5))

If a person so elects, the rebasing rule is applied to all disposals made by him of assets held on 31 March 1982. In other words, original cost is ignored completely, and regard is had only for the value of the assets held at that date. In some cases, making this election will mean that losses can be claimed which would not otherwise be available (because of the no gain/no loss rule).

A *universal* rebasing election is precisely that. If the election is made the rebasing rule is applied to *all* assets held at 31 March 1982. Furthermore, once made, the election is irrevocable.

There is a time limit for making the election. The legislation requires the election to be made within two years of the end of the year of assessment in which a disposal first takes place of assets which were held both at 6 April 1988 and at 31 March 1982. If no election has been made and assets held at 31 March 1982 have been disposed of during the period 6 April 1988–5 April 1992, it is now too late to make the election.

Married persons

The election may be made by each spouse separately. However, where assets pass from one spouse to another and the spouse who received the asset subsequently disposes of it, the gain or loss on that particular asset will be governed by whether or not the spouse who transferred the asset had made the universal rebasing election.

14.3.3 Time apportionment for assets held at 6 April 1965
(TCGA 1992, Sched 2, para 16)

Special rules apply to the disposal of assets which were held at 6 April 1965 and where a universal rebasing election has *not* been made *and* the assets concerned are not quoted shares or land with development value.

When CGT was first introduced in 1965, it was recognised that it would be unfair to charge tax on capital gains which had accrued before that date. For assets other than shares which were quoted at 6 April 1965 and land which (either at that time or subsequently) had development value, taxpayers were given the general right to compute gains on the basis that the appreciation had occurred at a uniform rate and to exclude the part relating to the period before 6 April 1965. This is known as the 'time apportionment' basis.

The capital gain computed on the time apportionment basis is arrived at by using the following formula:

$$\text{Overall gain} \times \frac{\text{period between 6 April 1965 and date of disposal}}{\text{Total period of ownership}}$$

For example, if an asset had been acquired in April 1953 and sold for an overall gain of £40,000 in March 1993, the time apportionment formula would produce the following result:

$$£40,000 \times \frac{\text{April 1965–March 1993 (28 years)}}{\text{April 1953–March 1993 (40 years)}}$$

ie a chargeable gain of £28,000.

When using this formula, the fraction should be calculated by reference to months of ownership and the divisor cannot reflect a period prior to 6 April 1945.

14.3.4   Market value at 6 April 1965

There may also be circumstances where the market value of an asset at 6 April 1965 can be used or must be used instead of original cost.

Quoted shares

Where an election was made under TCGA 1992, Sched 2, para 4 in respect of securities held on 6 April 1965, either in respect of equity investments or fixed interest investments, all the securities falling into that particular category will be deemed to have been disposed of and reacquired on 6 April 1965 so that the original cost is not relevant. This election would normally have been made some years ago as the deadline was two years after the first relevant disposal which took place after 19 March 1968.

Unquoted shares and other assets

In this situation, capital gains will be calculated on the time apportionment basis unless a specific election is made within two years of the date of disposal, in which case the gain is computed by reference to the market value of the asset at 6 April 1965.

In practice, the desirability of making such an election is fairly remote as it will be beneficial only where the market value of the asset at 6 April 1965 was higher than the value of the asset at 31 March 1982 and time apportionment is not beneficial.

Land with development value
(TCGA 1992 Sched 2, para 9)

Where land has development value at the date of disposal, it is not possible to time apportion the capital gain. One must either use the market value of the land at 6 April 1965 or its value at 31 March 1982.

14.3.5   Assets acquired via a gift made between 1 April 1982 and 5 April 1988
(TCGA 1992, Sched 4)

This section may be relevant where *all* of the following conditions are satisfied:

(1)   The asset was acquired as a gift or transfer from a trust during the period 1 April 1982–5 April 1988.
(2)   The donor held the asset at 31 March 1982.
(3)   The donor claimed hold-over relief so that the recipient was deemed to have acquired the asset at the donor's original cost.

When rebasing was first introduced, it was recognised that it would be unfair not to permit some relief where an asset had been transferred prior to 6 April 1988 and the gain had been held over. The person who received such a gift cannot claim rebasing because he did not own the asset concerned at 31 March 1982. To give rough and ready compensation for this, the legislation included provisions so that when the recipient of such a gift made a disposal after 5 April 1988, half of the held-over gain could be 'forgiven' or left out of account.

14.3.6   Example—Transfer prior to 6 April 1988 with held-over gain

A received a gift of shares in August 1986 from his father B. At the time of the gift, the shares were worth £180,000. B's acquisition value was only £40,000, and indexation (see 14.5) amounted to £10,000. This would normally have meant that B would have had a chargeable gain of £130,000. However, he made a claim under the legislation prevailing at the time which permitted the capital gain to be held over. This meant that B did not suffer a capital gains tax charge, but A was deemed to have acquired the assets with an acquisition value as follows:

	£
Market value at date of gift	180,000
Less held-over gain	(130,000)
Acquisition value	50,000

If A disposes of the asset after 5 April 1988, his acquisition value is increased by 50 per cent of £130,000 so that his acquisition value becomes £115,000.

14.4   Other acquisition values

14.4.1   Assets which have been acquired via an inheritance or from a family trust
(TCGA 1992, ss 62 and 71)

Where a person inherits an asset, he is generally deemed to have acquired the asset for its market value at the date of the testator's death (ie probate value). There is one exception to this. It is possible to claim a form of relief from inheritance tax where quoted securities have gone down in value after the person has died (see 17.11.3). Where such relief has been claimed for inheritance tax, a corresponding adjustment is made so that the person taking the assets concerned is deemed to have acquired them not at probate value, but rather at the value actually brought into account for inheritance tax purposes after taking account of the fall in value.

Where assets have been acquired from a trust, the beneficiary's acquisition value will normally be the market value at the time that the asset is transferred to him. However, the acquisition value may be lower than this where the trustees have claimed hold-over relief either under the general hold-over relief provisions which prevailed up to 5 April 1989 or under the more restrictive provisions which have applied subsequently (see 15.5).

14.4.2   Deemed acquisition value where income tax has been charged
(TCGA 1992, ss 120 and 141)

Where a person is subject to a Schedule E income tax charge when he acquires an asset (for example where he exercises a non-approved share option) he is deemed to have acquired the asset for an amount equal to the value taken into account in computing a Schedule E charge on him.

Similarly, where a person acquires shares by way of a stock dividend (ie, where there is a choice as between a cash dividend or further shares issued by a UK company) the shares are deemed to be acquired for a consideration equal to the amount brought into account for income tax purposes by reason of the stock dividend (for further particulars see 6.3.5).

14.5   Indexation
(TA 1992, s 53–57)

Capital gains tax is charged on real capital gains. A person who makes a capital gain is allowed to deduct not only his actual acquisition value, but also a proportion which represents the increase in the RPI between the month of acquisition and the month of disposal. The formula used is [(RD − RI) ÷ RI] where:

> RD = retail prices index in month of disposal
> RI = retail prices index for March 1982 or month in which expenditure incurred, whichever is the later.

14.5.1 Example—Indexation

A acquired shares in X Plc on 1 June 1990 for £20,000. He sells them in December 1993 for £25,000.

He has a capital gain of £5,000 before indexation, and a gain of £3,020 after taking indexation into account. The indexation relief is computed as follows:-

Cost £20,000 × $\dfrac{\text{RPI for December 1993—RPI for June 1990}}{\text{RPI for June 1990.}}$

That is £20,000 × (141.9 − 126.7) ÷ 126.7 = £20,000 × 0.1199 = £2,398.
The RPI figures are set out in Table 27.2.2 at the back of this book

14.5.2 Restriction to indexation relief
(FA 1994 s 93)

Indexation relief may only reduce or extinguish a gain, it cannot convert a gain into a loss or increase a loss. A different rule applied up to the November 1993 Budget, so that indexation relief may create or increase a loss in relation to transactions prior to 30 November 1993.

14.5.3 Examples of restriction

Acquisition cost £4,000, indexation allowance to date of disposal 1 December 1993, £750.

	£	£	£
Sale Proceeds	5,000	4,500	3,000
Less: Cost	(4,000)	(4,000)	(4,000)
Unindexed Gain/(Loss)	1,000	500	(1,000)
Indexation allowance	(750)	(500)	NIL
Chargeable Gain/(Capital Loss)	250	NIL	(1,000)

There is a modest exception to the rule that indexation allowance may not create an allowable loss. This follows from a last minute alteration which was made to the Finance Bill on 15 April 1994. Individuals and trustees are permitted indexation losses of up to £10,000 (in total) for the period of 30 November 1993 – 5 April 1995. Companies are not entitled to this transitional relief.

Table 14.1—Computing your capital gains

The following can be used as a 'pro-forma' when calculating capital gains (or losses).

Sale Proceeds (consider whether the market value provisions may apply) —see 14.1)	A	
Deduct incidental costs of disposal, see 14.2	B	
Net sale proceeds (A – B)		C
If the asset was acquired after 31 March 1982, enter cost.	D	
Amount of any enhancement expenditure.	E	
If the asset was owned at 31 March 1982 and a universal rebasing election is in force, enter value at 31 March 1982, see 14.3	F	
If the asset was owned at 31 March 1982, but no universal rebasing election is in force, enter cost or value at 31 March 1982, whichever is the higher.[1]	G	
Enter the amount of enhancement expenditure—if 31 March 1982 value is entered at F or G, include only post-31 March 1982 enhancement expenditure.	H	
Enter the total of figures entered in any of D – H		I
Unindexed gain (C – I).		J
Indexation relief on figure in D, F or G, see 14.5	K	
Indexation relief on figure in E or H.[2]	L	
Enter total of K and L.		M
Deduct M from J. The result is the indexed gain.		N

[1] Note that there will not be an allowable loss if there is an overall gain taking the original cost, but a loss taking the 31 March 1982 value.
[2] The figure of indexation relief cannot exceed the figure at J, except in relation to assets disposed of prior to 30 November 1993.

14.6   How gains are computed on quoted securities

The term 'quoted securities' means shares, loan stock, warrants etc. which are dealt in on the London Stock Exchange, the Unlisted Securities Market (USM) and other similar Stock Exchanges recognised by the Revenue as having similar rules and procedures to the London Stock Exchange.

This section deals with the tax treatment of three different types of transactions:

(1) Sale of part of a shareholding.
(2) Pooling.
(3) Bonus issues and rights issues.
(4) Takeovers and mergers.

14.6.1 Sale of part of a shareholding
(TCGA 1992, ss 104–109)

Specific rules apply where a person sells part of his holding in securities of the same class. Securities are treated as being of the same class if they are treated as such under Stock Exchange practice. For example, all ICI ordinary shares are securities of the same class, whereas BP ordinary shares are not and form a different class.

For most quoted securities, (see below for exceptions), the *general* rule on a disposal of part of a shareholding is that the securities sold are identified as follows:

(1) First, with securities of the same class acquired on or after 6 April 1982 which are deemed to form part of a 'new holding' (see 14.6.2).
(2) Second, with securities which are deemed to form part of a 1982 holding, ie securities held at 5 April 1982 other than securities held at 6 April 1965.
(3) Third, with other securities on a LIFO basis (Last In, First Out). This will apply only where a universal rebasing election has *not* been made (see 14.3.2).

There are, however, two exceptions to the general rule:

(1) Disposals on the day of acquisition
(TCGA 1992, s 105)

Securities which are sold on a particular day are matched with purchases on the same day. Where more securities are sold than acquired, the balance will normally be dealt with under the general rule and matched with part of an existing holding. In exceptional cases where this is not possible, the excess of securities over-sold is carried forward and matched with the first subsequent acquisition of those securities.

(2) Acquisitions and disposals within a ten day period
(TCGA 1992, s 107(2))

Securities sold are matched with previous acquisitions during a ten day period (see s 107(3)). The general rule then applies to any sales of securities which cannot be identified on this basis.

Special rules apply for BES shares (see 11.4), securities within the accrued income scheme (see 5.5), deep discount securities (see 5.6), and interests in non-qualifying offshore funds such as roll-up funds (see 5.9).

The decision tree below summarises the position.

Identification of securities sold out of a larger holding

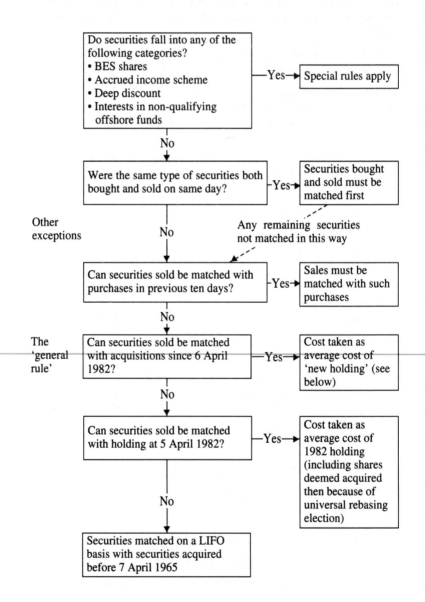

14.6.2 Pooling

Securities acquired on or after 6 April 1982

Any securities of the same class acquired on or after 6 April 1982 and held at 6 April 1985 are 'pooled', ie treated as a single asset which grows or diminishes as acquisitions and disposals are made. The technical term for this asset is a 'new holding' (to distinguish it from holdings at 31 March 1982).

Securities of the same class which are acquired for the first time after 5 April 1985 are pooled as a single asset in the same way.

Technically, the indexed cost of the pool needs to be re-computed every time there is an operative event, ie something which has the effect of either increasing or decreasing the qualifying expenditure.

14.6.3 Example—Securities acquired on or after 6 April 1982

A held 10,000 XYZ plc shares at 6 April 1985. They were all acquired in July 1984 at a cost of £3 per share. On 1 August 1989, A acquired a further 5,000 shares at a cost of £50,000 (£10 per share). A's new holding has an indexed cost computed as follows:

10,000 shares cost July 1984	£30,000
Indexation July 1984–August 1989	£ 8,990
	£38,990
5,000 shares cost August 1989	£50,000
Indexed cost of 15,000 shares at August 1989	£88,990

If A sold 5,000 shares in January 1993, the calculation is:-

Indexed cost of pool at August 1989	£88,990
Indexation August 1989–January 1993	£16,983
Indexed cost of 15,000 shares at January 1993	£105,973

$$\frac{5,000}{15,000} \times £105,973 = \text{Indexed cost of shares sold}$$

$$\frac{10,000}{15,000} \times £105,973 \text{ (i e the balance)} = \text{the indexed cost of the remaining shares.}$$

Thus, the cost of the 5,000 shares sold would be taken as £35,328. A could not take as her cost the actual amount paid for the most recent acquisition of 5,000 shares.

1982 holdings

In much the same way, an individual's shareholding at 6 April 1982 is also treated as a single asset whose cost reduces as and when sales take place.

14.6.4   Example—Assets held in 1982

B had 5,000 shares in XYZ plc at 31 March 1982. He has acquired no shares in XYZ plc since then. The shares cost £1 each in 1979. The value at 31 March 1982 was £2 per share. If B sells 1,000 shares in June 1993, the position is:

5,000 shares 31 March 1982 value	£10,000
Indexation 1 April 1982–30 June 1993 (say)	£7,750
Indexed cost at 30 June 1993	£17,750

Cost of 1,000 shares is taken as

$\dfrac{1,000}{5,000}$ x £17,750 ie £3,550.

The pool cost may increase because of rights issues which take place after 31 March 1982.

14.6.5   Bonus issues and rights issues

A bonus issue or rights issue is related to the shares which produce the entitlement.

14.6.6   Example—Bonus issues and rights issues

C had acquired 4,500 shares in XYZ plc between 1982 and 1993 and also holds 13,500 shares which were acquired before 5 April 1982. The company provides a scrip issue of one new share for every three shares held. C would therefore acquire 6,000 new shares free of charge of which a proportion would be treated as an addition to her new holding with the balance being added to her 1982 holding, ie:

Addition to new holding	1,500 shares
Addition to 1982 holding	4,500 shares

Similarly, if D had a total of 40,000 shares in Y plc which was made up of a new holding of 10,000 shares and a 1982 holding of 30,000 shares, and the company announced a rights issue in March 1993 of one new share at £2 for every existing share held, D might acquire 20,000 new shares at a cost of £40,000. Only the cost of the rights shares which related to his new holding of 10,000 shares could be added to the indexed cost of the new holding. The other rights shares would be treated as forming part of the 1982 holding.

Shareholders sometimes dispose of rights nil paid. Sums received for such disposals will normally be deducted from the indexed pool cost unless (exceptionally) the amount received exceeds five per cent of the market value of the shareholding at the time of disposal (see 14.2.9).

14.6.7 Takeovers and mergers

There is a special relief which may apply where a company issues shares or securities in order to take over another company. The shareholders who accept this offer will not be treated as making a disposal provided they meet one of the following requirements:

(1) together with persons connected with them, they do not hold more than five per cent of the company's share capital; or
(2) the Revenue are satisfied that the share exchange is a *bona fide* commercial transaction which is not entered into with a view to tax avoidance.

So far as quoted securities are concerned, the position is generally straightforward. The offer document forwarded to shareholders will normally state whether clearance has been obtained from the Revenue under TCGA 1992, s 138 confirming that TCGA 1992, s 135 applies. Provided that this is the case, no capital gain will arise on the exchange of shares for securities issued by the company which is making the takeovers.

Of course, matters may not be quite so simple.

What happens if there is a mixture of shares and cash?

Suppose a shareholder in X plc is offered a share in Y plc plus cash of £1 in exchange for every share that he holds in X plc. If he accepts this offer there will be a part disposal.

The value of the new Y plc shares on the first day of trading is taken and the following computation is required:

Amount received via cash element $\boxed{A}$

Take proportion of indexed cost of holding in X Plc

$$\frac{\text{Cash received}}{\text{Cash + value of Y plc shares}} \times \text{indexed cost} \quad \boxed{B}$$

Indexation on amount in B $\boxed{C}$

Total of amounts in B and C $\boxed{D}$

Deduct D from A, the result is the
Capital gain/(loss) on cash element

What happens if there is a mixture of shares and loan stock?

Suppose the shareholder in X plc had instead accepted an offer of one share in Y plc plus £1.25 loan stock. Assume that when the new Y plc shares were first traded they had a price of £2.00 and the loan stock was traded at £80 for every £100 nominal.

The cost of the two types of new securities would be determined like this:

14.6.8 Example—Takeover by mixture of shares and loan stock

Apportioned to Y plc shares:-

$$\frac{\text{Value of Y shares}}{\text{Value of Y shares} + \text{Y loan stock}}$$

ie $\dfrac{£2}{£2 + £1} \times \text{cost of X shares} = \text{Deemed cost of Y shares}$

Apportioned to Y plc loan stock

$$\frac{\text{Value of loan stock}}{\text{Value of loan stock} + \text{shares}}$$

ie $\dfrac{£1}{£1 + £2} \times \text{cost of X shares} = \text{Deemed cost of Y loan stock.}$

This division of the indexed cost of the original holding in X plc will be relevant as and when there is a disposal of either the Y plc shares or loan stock.

14.6.9 Special rules where the share exchange involves qualifying corporate bonds
(TCGA 1992, s 116)

Loan stock will often be a type of qualifying corporate bond, ie an exempt asset for CGT purposes (see 13.3.2). The offer document sent to shareholders on a company takeover will normally draw attention to whether the loan stock falls into this category. If it does, the investor will not be entitled to indexation relief for periods after the take-over. Furthermore, the disposal of the loan stock will create a capital gain calculated according to values at the time of the takeover and *not* the value of the loan stock at the time that it is eventually sold or redeemed.

As a matter of fact, the deferred gain is triggered by any kind of disposal of the qualifying corporate bonds. For example, a gift of the loan stock would cause the deferred gain to become chargeable. Indeed, a chargeable gain could even arise on a deemed disposal such as would apply if the company which had issued the loan stock went into liquidation.

14.6.10   Unit trusts and shares in investment trusts acquired via a monthly savings plan

Many unit trusts and investment trusts operate schemes whereby investors may acquire units or shares via a monthly savings plan. The calculations could become very complicated, but fortunately the Revenue will accept a simplified computation which assumes that the person has made a single annual investment in the seventh month of the trust's accounting year. The cost of the investment will consist of the savings made in that year plus any reinvested income.

For further particulars, see Inland Revenue Statement of Practice SP3/89.

14.7   When may a chargeable gain arise on foreign currency?

There is an exemption for foreign currency provided that it was acquired for an individual's personal expenditure abroad. In all other situations, foreign currency is a chargeable asset and a gain (or loss) will arise when the currency is disposed of. A disposal may take place on the foreign currency being spent, converted into another foreign currency, or converted into sterling. In each of these situations, the sterling equivalent of the foreign currency at the date of acquisition is compared with the sterling equivalent at the date of disposal.

In theory, each separate bank account denominated in foreign currency counts as a separate asset. However, in practice, the Revenue do permit taxpayers to treat all bank accounts containing the particular foreign currency as one account—see Inland Revenue Statement of Practice SP10/84.

14.8   Special rules for disposals of chattels
(TCGA 1992, s 262)

A chattel is defined by the legislation as a tangible, movable asset. Examples include a picture, a silver teapot, a first edition of a famous novel etc.

14.8.1   Chattels which are wasting assets
(TCGA 1992, s 45)

There are special rules which apply for chattels which also fall within the definition of wasting assets. A wasting asset is defined as an asset with a useful life expectancy of less than 50 years. These chattels are exempt regardless of the amount of the sale proceeds. Equally, there is no relief for any losses realised on the disposal of such chattels.

This exemption is not available in respect of assets on which the owner was entitled to capital allowances because the asset had been used in a trade.

14.8.2   Other types of chattel
(TCGA 1992, s 2(2))

A gain arising on the disposal of a chattel which is not covered by the exemption in 14.8.1 is exempt only if the sale proceeds do not exceed £6,000. However, there is a form of marginal relief under which, if the sale proceeds are more than £6,000, the maximum chargeable gain cannot exceed five-thirds of the excess. For example, if a picture costing £900 is sold for £6,900, the chargeable gain cannot exceed 5/3 x £900 ie £1,500.

In some cases, the marginal relief will not help. If the sale proceeds were £6,900, but the picture had cost £5,800, the chargeable gain would be computed on normal principles.

Losses

A capital loss may arise on the disposal of a chattel. However, where the sale proceeds are less than £6,000, the loss has to be calculated on the basis that notional sale proceeds of £6,000 were received. For example, if an uninsured antique table costing £10,000 were destroyed by fire, the proceeds are taken to be £6,000 not nil.

Assets forming a set

Several chattels may be deemed to form a single asset, for example, a set of antique chairs and a table. Where such chattels are sold to the same person, or to persons acting in concert, they may be regarded as the disposal of a single asset. This rule may apply even though the sales take place at different times. As a consequence, gains which would otherwise be exempt because of the £6,000 limit may be brought into charge.

For example, someone may own four antique chairs each worth £6,000. If they were to be sold one at a time to the same person, the total sale would be regarded as the sale of a single asset for £24,000 and the £6,000 exemption would not apply.

14.9 Specific rules which apply to disposals of land and investment properties

14.9.1 Will the gain be subject to income tax?

Speculative or short term transactions in land may well give rise to a claim by the Inspector of Taxes that the individual was dealing in land and therefore subject to tax under Schedule D Case I (see 2.2). Whether a trade is being carried on is a matter of fact. The following 'badges of trade' may be cited by the Inspector of Taxes in support of an assessment under Schedule D Case I:

(1) Evidence that an asset was acquired with a view to its being re-sold in the short term.
(2) A large part of the purchase price being financed by borrowings, especially short term borrowings such as an overdraft.
(3) The taxpayer has a background of similar transactions or has special expertise which assists in achieving a profit on disposal of the asset.

In *Kirkby v Hughes* [1993] STC 76, the Court held that the taxpayer was carrying out a trade and the following were regarded as badges of trade:

(1) The properties were larger than would be expected for sole occupancy.
(2) The periods of occupancy were short.
(3) Another property was purchased while the taxpayer was still resident in the first without any clear intention of selling the first.
(4) There was no proof that the taxpayer had intended to acquire the first house as a personal asset.

Quite separately from the above, TA 1988, s 776 may enable the Inspector of Taxes to assess a gain under Schedule D Case VI. Section 776 may apply where a capital gain is realised and:

(1) UK land was acquired with the sole or main object of realising a gain on its disposal; or
(2) UK land is developed with the sole or main object of realising a gain on the disposal of the land when developed.

There are also circumstances where disposal of shares in a company which owns land may give rise to a Schedule D Case VI assessment (see 20.2.3).

Section 776 can apply whether or not the person is resident in the United Kingdom. Furthermore, the capital gain may be received by a third party and yet still give rise to an assessment under s 776 if an individual has transferred the opportunity of making a gain to the third party. Moreover, s 776 can apply to one or more transactions which form a scheme and any number of transactions may be regarded as constituting a single arrangement or scheme if a common purpose can be discerned in them, or if there is other sufficient evidence of a common purpose. For a fuller account of s 776, see 20.2.

The main disadvantage for UK resident individuals who are assessed to income tax on gains from land, either under Schedule D Case I or Schedule D Case VI, is that they will not be able to deduct either the indexation allowance or the annual exemption. Also, the fact that gains are assessed as income may mean that the individual cannot make use of capital losses which have been brought forward from earlier years or which have arisen during the same year on other transactions. On the other hand, where an individual has *borrowed* to acquire the land, he may be able to deduct the interest in calculating the gain for income tax purposes whereas no deduction will normally be available for capital gains tax purposes.

However, the fact that since 6 April 1988 capital gains tax is normally charged at the same rate as income tax means that it is now less common for Inspectors of Taxes to argue that gains on land transactions should be assessed as income. The main circumstances where the Revenue *is* likely to argue on these lines is where the individual concerned is a builder or developer or estate agent or has entered into a large number of land transactions or the amounts involved in a particular transaction are substantial.

14.9.2 Specific points on the computation of gains on transactions involving land
(TCGA 1992, Sched 8)

Wasting assets

Where a person disposes of a wasting asset, his cost or acquisition value may need to be restricted. This will apply where a person disposes of a leasehold interest in land and the lease has less than 50 years to run at the date of disposal. Table 14.2 below shows how the cost of a lease must be adjusted.

Table 14.2—Depreciation of leases

Years	Percentage	Years	Percentage	Years	Percentage
50 (or more)	100	33	90.280	16	64.116
49	99.657	32	89.354	15	61.617
48	99.289	31	88.371	14	58.971
47	98.902	30	87.330	13	56.167
46	98.490	29	86.226	12	53.191
45	98.059	28	85.053	11	50.038
44	97.595	27	83.816	10	46.695
43	97.107	26	82.496	9	43.154
42	96.593	25	81.100	8	39.399
41	96.041	24	79.622	7	35.414
40	95.457	23	78.055	6	31.195
39	94.842	22	76.399	5	26.722
38	94.189	21	74.635	4	21.983
37	93.497	20	72.770	3	16.959
36	92.761	19	70.791	2	11.629
35	91.981	18	68.697	1	5.983
34	91.156	17	66.470	0	0

The fraction of the cost of the lease which is not allowed is given by the fraction

$$\frac{P(1)-P(3)}{P(1)}$$

where

P(1) = the percentage derived from the table for the duration of the lease at acquisition

P(3) = the percentage derived from the table for the duration of the lease at the time of disposal

14.9.3   Example—Wasting assets

C purchases a 48 year lease in 1980 for £10,000. In 1988 she spends £2,000 on improvements which are affecting the value of the lease. She disposes of it with 36 years left in 1992. Her allowable expenditure is therefore as follows:

Original cost £10,000 x $\frac{(99.289 - 92.761)}{99.289}$ =   £657

Additional £2,000 x $\frac{(95.457 - 92.761)}{95.457}$ =   £58

£715

Total allowable expenditure = £12,000 – £715 = £11,285

Enhancement expenditure

It commonly happens that a person has spent money over the years on improvements. This expenditure can be taken into account provided the improvements are reflected in the state of the property when it is sold.

Where such enhancement expenditure occurred after 31 March 1982, the expenditure is added to the acquisition value and attracts indexation allowance from the time that it is incurred.

Enhancement expenditure prior to 31 March 1982 may be taken into account only if the universal rebasing election (see 14.3.2) has *not* been made and the total of original cost and pre-31 March 1982 enhancement expenditure exceeds the market value at 31 March.

Time apportionment and enhancement expenditure

Where a universal rebasing election has not been made, it may be possible to compute the capital gain on the time apportionment basis (see 14.3.3). This can be difficult where there has also been enhancement expenditure because the overall gain has to be split between the gain on the original cost and the gain relating to the enhancement expenditure. This is an area where professional advice is essential.

14.10 How the Revenue assesses gains on unquoted shares

There are some special features to the way in which gains on unquoted shares are computed. Other aspects follow the principles already covered in this chapter. For example, the identification rules where a person disposes of part of a shareholding of unquoted shares are exactly the same as for quoted securities (see 14.6.1).

There are also practical considerations which do not arise in relation to quoted securities such as the need to negotiate a valuation of the shares at 31 March 1982. Retirement relief will also need to be borne in mind.

14.10.1 Identification of shares sold out of a larger shareholding

The same identification rules apply as they do to quoted securities (see 14.6.1). One aspect which may arise more commonly than in relation to quoted securities is where part of the shareholding was acquired before 7 April 1965. The LIFO (last in, first out) rule applies in these circumstances.

14.10.2 Shares held at 31 March 1982

Where an individual has made a universal rebasing election (see 14.3.2) some of these complications do not arise. The original cost is not relevant as the capital gain is computed only by reference to the value of the shares at 31 March 1982. Even where the election has not been made, it is often fairly clear that the market value at 31 March 1982 will be higher than either original cost or market value at 6 April 1965.

Inevitably, the market value at 31 March 1982 will be the subject of negotiation with the Inland Revenue Shares Valuation Division and professional advice should be taken. The value of the shares will reflect factors such as the nature of the company, its assets and the size of the shareholding.

The general approach adopted by the Shares Valuation Division is to determine the value of the unquoted shares and securities by reference to a completely hypothetical market. It is assumed that any prospective purchaser will have available to him all of the information which a *prudent* prospective purchaser of the asset might reasonably require if he were proposing to purchase it from a *willing* vendor by private treaty and at arms length. Open market value must be assumed and the yardstick is always the requirement of the willing and prudent purchaser and not the wishes etc of the directors of the private company.

The underlying assets of the company are largely irrelevant if a person has only a relatively small minority shareholding, there may be a more important consideration if he has control. Therefore, a quite different valuation might be placed upon shares which form, say, a seven per cent shareholding which allows the owner to retain control. In the former case the valuers will be looking at factors such as the level of dividends paid in the past and the likelihood of such dividends being paid in the future. At the other extreme, a 51 per cent shareholder would place great value on a 7/51sts part of this shareholding as a disposal of such shares will cause him to lose voting control over the company.

For CGT purposes, the value used will normally be the value of the asset taken by the acquirer, not the reduction in value for the person making the disposal. From this point of view, capital gains tax works differently from inheritance tax (see 17.3.3).

14.10.3 Shares held at 6 April 1965

Where a universal rebasing election has *not* been made it may be possible (and beneficial) for the capital gain to be computed on the time apportionment basis.

14.10.4   Example—Shares held at 6 April 1965

B acquired 1,000 shares in a family company on 1 April 1950 and they were then worth £10,000. He sold his shares in April 1993 for £600,000. Assume for illustration purposes that indexation allowance amounts to £160,000. The capital gain on the time apportionment basis is:

$$\frac{\text{Period since 6 April 1965}}{\text{Overall period of ownership}} \times \text{ gain of £430,000 (ie gain after indexation)}$$

The figures work out as follows:-

$$\frac{336 \text{ months}}{516 \text{ months}} \times \text{ £430,000} = \text{£280,000}$$

14.10.5   Situations where time apportionment relief is not available

It is not possible to claim time apportionment relief on the disposal of unquoted shares if there was a capital reorganisation prior to 6 April 1965. A capital reorganisation would include a rights issue or a merger between two companies.

Furthermore, time apportionment relief may be severely restricted where an individual has, since 6 April 1965, transferred or sold a property to a company in which he holds shares. Once again, this is a situation where you should seek professional advice.

14.10.6   Retirement relief

This relief is covered in more detail at 15.8 It is frequently relevant to disposals of shares in family *trading* companies. It is not covered here since there are numerous other conditions which need to be fulfilled and there are therefore many situations where a sale of unquoted shares does not attract the relief (for example, where the company concerned is an investment company).

14.11   Disposal of foreign property

14.11.1   Gains must be computed in sterling

Just as a chargeable gain may arise on the disposal of foreign currency, there may similarly be a currency gain on the disposal of certain foreign assets, such as a house or flat in a foreign country. Where overseas assets are disposed of, it is not correct to calculate the gain or loss in terms of the foreign currency and then convert that gain or loss into sterling at the time of the disposal. Instead, the following formula should be used:

Market value of foreign currency received at sale
(converted at exchange rate applying at that time).   *v*

Deduct sterling equivalent of cost of asset on acquisition
(converted at exchange rate applying at the time of
acquisition).   *w*

_____

x

Deduct indexation relief   *y*

_____

Chargeable gain   *z*

=======

14.11.2   Example—Disposal of foreign property

A acquired a property in West Germany in 1983 for DM 1m (exchange rate DM4
x £1) and sells it in 1994 for DM 900,000 (exchange rate DM2 = £1), the gain
would be computed as follows:

	£
Sale proceeds	450,000
Less cost	250,000
	200,000
Less indexation on £250,000 — say	150,000
Chargeable gain	50,000

This can produce some unexpected consequences. Suppose that A had borrowed
the purchase price in deutschmarks. When she repaid the mortgage on selling the
property, she might well be left with no cash in hand. In fact, the profit on the
sale of the property in sterling terms was matched by the increase in the sterling
value of her mortgage debt. However, there is no CGT relief for this increase and
the gain of £50,000 would still be chargeable.

14.11.3   Relief for foreign tax
(TCGA 1992, ss 277–278)

Many overseas countries reserve the right to charge capital gains tax on
the disposal of real estate situated in that country, whether or not the
owner is resident in that country. Where a UK resident has had to pay
foreign tax in these circumstances, he may claim double tax relief. In
effect, the overseas country's tax is available as a credit against the UK
tax.

14.11.4   Example—Relief for foreign tax

B has a property in Italy which cost 160m lire (at the time of purchase this was the equivalent of £90,000). The property is sold for 220m lire and there is a chargeable gain for UK tax purposes of £50,000 (assume that Italian CGT of £7,000 is payable).

If B's £50,000 gain was chargeable to tax at 40 per cent, the position would be:

UK capital gains tax	20,000
Less double tax relief	7,000
UK CGT actually payable	13,000

However, there is no relief for any excess. Thus, if B had unrelieved losses brought forward such that his UK tax had been only £6,500, there would be no relief for the balance.

Sometimes there will be a liability for foreign tax, but no capital gains for UK tax purposes.

14.11.5   Example—Foreign CGT only

C disposes of a property in Sierra Leone at a £40,000 loss in sterling terms. However, there was a gain in terms of local currency and the tax bill in Sierra Leone is £10,000. C can claim a deduction for this amount as if it were a deduction from his sale proceeds, and this would mean that his loss for UK CGT purposes would be increased from £40,000 to £50,000.

14.11.6   Foreign gains which cannot be remitted
    (TCGA 1992, s 279)

Where a person realises a gain on the disposal of assets situated abroad, but is genuinely unable to transfer that gain to the United Kingdom because of restrictions imposed abroad or because the foreign currency is not convertible, the amount of the gain may be omitted from assessment for the year in which it arose. Instead, the gain will be assessed to capital gains tax only when it becomes remittable. Claims to this relief have to be made within six years of the year in which the gain was realised.

14.12   Main residence exemption

Despite the stagnation in house prices over recent years, the largest gain that most people realise is on the sale of their main (or only) residence. This is not surprising as, for the majority of the population, their home is their single largest investment. In the majority of circumstances, this gain will be exempt from capital gains tax provided certain conditions are satisfied.

14.12.1   Basic conditions which must be satisfied
(TCGA 1992, s 222)

There is a total exemption from CGT where a gain is realised by an individual on the disposal of a property which has been his sole or main residence *throughout* his period of ownership.

The legislation also provides exemption for land which forms part of the property (the garden or grounds) up to the 'permitted area'. The permitted area will always be at least 0.5 of a hectare (approximately one acre), but may be more where the land is required for the reasonable enjoyment of the property. (see 14.12.3).

A married couple who are living together can have the exemption in respect of only one property for a particular period.

14.12.2   Occupation test
(TCGA 1992, s 223(3))
(Statement of Practice D4)

A delay of up to 12 months between a property being acquired and the owner taking up residence does not prejudice the exemption; the property is still treated as if it were his main residence. The 12 month period can be extended if it can be shown that there were good reasons for the owner not taking up residence, such as the need to carry out alterations or building work or there was an unavoidable delay in the owner being able to dispose of his previous residence.

The last three years of ownership are treated as qualifying for the exemption, whether the owner lives in the property or not, *provided* the property has previously been his main residence.

14.12.3   The permitted area

The legislation also provides exemption for a larger area of gardens or grounds than 0.5 hectare if it can be shown that the larger area was 'required for the reasonable enjoyment' of the property as a residence. If the taxpayer and the Inspector of Taxes cannot agree on this, the matter can be determined by the Commissioners.

Relevant factors here include considerations such as the extent to which other similar properties have gardens or grounds larger than 0.5 hectare, the need for an area of land to provide privacy or to provide a buffer between the property and (for example) a motorway and the need to have room for other facilities and amenities which are appropriate to the property.

The last-mentioned factor is often the most difficult to argue with the Revenue which relies on a judgment by Du Parcq J in a 1937 compulsory purchase case, the so-called *Newhill* case [1938] 2 All ER 163. Du Parcq J stated:

> 'Required'. ... does not mean merely that the occupiers of the house would like to have it, or that they would miss it if they lost it, or that anyone proposing to buy the house would think less of the house without it. ... 'Required' means, I suppose, that without it there will be such a substantial deprivation of amenities or convenience that a real injury will be done to the property owner ...

The Revenue's interpretation is not free from doubt, as the CGT legislation is worded differently from the compulsory purchase legislation, and the question has not yet been considered by the Courts. This is an area where it is essential to take professional advice.

14.12.4   What is the residence?

There have been several cases which concerned a property where part of the premises were occupied by servants.

In one case (*Batey v Wakefield* [1981] STC 521) the property consisted of the main house and a caretaker's lodge. The lodge was occupied (rent free) by the caretaker/gardener and his wife who was the owner's housekeeper. The main house and the lodge were separated only by the width of a tennis court. The Court of Appeal upheld the taxpayer's claim that his residence consisted of the main house and all related buildings which were part and parcel of the property and were occupied for the purposes of the owner's residence.

At the other extreme, the Court of Appeal decided against a taxpayer who claimed the exemption should cover a gardener's cottage which was located some 170 metres away and which was not within the same curtilage as the taxpayer's house. This case *(Lewis v Rook* [1992]STC 171) may go on to the House of Lords; the Revenue has said that it may argue that the exemption cannot apply to a separate building at all, regardless of how close it is to the house occupied by the owner.

This is another area where specialist advice should be taken if substantial sums are involved.

14.13 Possible restrictions on the exemption

14.13.1 Part of the property used for business purposes
(TCGA 1992, s 224(1))

If part of the property has been used *exclusively* for the purposes of a trade or business or a profession or vocation, the exemption does not cover the part of the gain attributable to that part.

This restriction does not apply where the relevant rooms are used partly for business and partly for personal reasons. For example, if a journalist's living room doubles up as a work room from which he carries on business as a journalist, there will be no restriction under this provision.

14.13.2 Part of the property let out
(TCGA 1992, s 223(4))

Where the owner has let out part of his home, there may be a similar restriction. Thus, if the owner had let approximately one-third of her home, the exemption would normally be confined to two-thirds of the gain on disposal. However, the normal rule may be overridden if the lettings are as *residential* accommodation.

The gain on the part of the property let out in this way may still be exempt up to the lesser of:

(1)   the exemption on the part of the property occupied by the owner; and
(2)   £40,000.

Where a husband and wife own a property jointly each of them can claim an exemption of up to £40,000 against their share of the gain.

14.13.3 Expenditure incurred with a view to gain
(TCGA 1992, s 224(3))

The exemption is not available if a gain arises from the purchase of property which was made wholly or partly for the purpose of realising a gain.

14.13.4 Example—Expenditure with a view to gain

C is a partner and has lived in a flat owned by his firm. He is offered the opportunity to buy it for £75,000 and he accepts because he knows that he will be able fairly quickly to find a buyer at £120,000. He realises a gain of £45,000. The Inland Revenue are likely to argue that the gain is a chargeable gain because of s 224(3).

Similarly, a person who holds a leasehold interest and who acquires the freehold because it will enable a better price to be obtained may suffer a restriction under s 224(3) if the Revenue can show that this was the *only* purpose of buying the freehold.

14.13.5   Sale of part of gardens

Special care is needed if it is decided to sell surplus land for development. In a 1976 case *(Varty v Lynes* [1976] STC 508) the taxpayer had owned and occupied a house and the garden was less than one acre (the permitted area at that time). He sold the house and part of the garden in June 1971. Slightly less than 12 months later, he sold the rest of the garden to a builder and realised a substantial gain because he had secured planning permission in the meantime. He was assessed on the gain on the land sold to the builder and the High Court decided that the main residence exemption did not apply. Brightman J held that the exemption for the garden or grounds could apply only in relation to garden or grounds occupied as such by the owner at the date of sale.

The Revenue has subsequently stated that it will invoke this only where land is sold with development value.

The following principles should be borne in mind:

(1)   A sale of land out of a parcel of land greater than 0.5 hectare may be vulnerable even where the owner remains in occupation. The fact that the owner continues to live in the property suggests that the surplus land was not required for the reasonable enjoyment of the property.

(2)   A sale of land with development value at the same time as the owner ceases to live in the property is not open to attack in the same way as in *Varty v Lynes.*

(3)   A sale of land with development value after the owner has moved out is likely to result in a tax charge.

14.13.6   What happens where there are two homes?

An individual may live in more than one property without necessarily owning both properties. The Revenue view is that a person has two *residences* if, for example, he owns a large house in Gloucestershire and rents a modest flat in Central London where he lives during the week.

If necessary, the Commissioners decide which of an individual's two or more residences is his main residence. The test is not necessarily where the individual lives most of the time, and it is often not clear in a particular case what view the Commissioners might take.

14.13.7 Taxpayer's right of election
(TCGA 1992, s 222(5))

Fortunately, the owner is able to settle the matter by formally electing that one property be treated as his main residence. The election may be varied from time to time, but only in relation to the last two years prior to the variation.

There is a time limit for a notice under s 222(5) of two years. The Revenue view has been that the time limit refers to the point in time that the individual starts to have a second residence.

This interpretation has recently been upheld by the High Court, in *Griffin v Craig Harvey* [1994] STC 54, although this case may go to the appeal on the basis that the notice under s 222(5) can be given at any time, although only with effect from two years prior to the election.

There is one circumstance where the Revenue will accept an election outside the two year time limit. Inland Revenue extra-statutory concession D21 provides that:

> Where for any period an individual has more than one residence, but his interest in each of them, or in each of them except one, is such as to have no more than a negligible capital value on the open market (for example a weekly rented flat or accommodation provided by an employer) the two-year time limit will be extended where the individual was unaware that such a nomination could be made. In such cases the nomination may be made within a reasonable time of the individual becoming aware of the possibility of so doing, and it will be regarded as effective from the date on which the individual first had more than one residence.

14.14 Living in job-related accommodation

14.14.1 Meaning of job-related accommodation

Job-related accommodation is defined as accommodation provided for an individual or his spouse by reason of his employment:

(1) where it is necessary for the proper performance of his duties that he should live there; or

(2) where it is provided for the better performance of his duties and the employment is one where employers customarily provide accommodation; or

(3) where the accommodation is provided as part of the special security arrangements for the employee's safety.

14.14.2   Right to nominate a property
(TCGA 1992, s 228(8))

Where an individual is required to live in job-related accommodation, a house owned by him and intended to be occupied as his residence in due course is treated as if it were his residence. Such a house may therefore qualify for exemption even if the owner had let it and never actually occupied it himself before disposing of it, provided that he nominates it as his only or main residence.

14.14.3   Similar provisions for self-employed individuals

A self-employed individual who is required to live at or near his place of work (for example, a publican) can nominate a property under s 222(8) for eventual use as his main residence. This also applies if the individual's spouse is required to occupy such premises. Only periods after 5 April 1982 can qualify under this heading.

14.15   Treatment where the property has not been occupied throughout

14.15.1   Proportion of gain may be exempt

The exemption under s 222 is not necessarily an 'all or nothing' test. The legislation makes provision for a proportion of the capital gain to be exempt where the necessary conditions are satisfied for part of the period of ownership. The exempt proportion of the gain will normally be:

$$\frac{\text{Period of qualifying use}}{\text{Total period of ownership}} \times \text{indexed gain}$$

14.15.2   Periods prior to 31 March 1982 ignored

A period of non-qualifying use is ignored if it is prior to 31 March 1982.

14.15.3   Example—Incomplete period of occupation

A property was acquired in March 1970 and let as an investment until March 1983. Thereafter it is the owner's sole residence. It is sold in March 1994 for a gain of £240,000.

The exempt proportion of the gain would be:

$$\frac{11}{12} \times £240,000 = \qquad £220,000$$

14.15.4 Last 36 months of ownership
(TCGA 1992, s 223(2))

Provided that the property has at some time qualified as the owner's main residence, the last three years of ownership will also qualify for exemption. This still applies if the property is let or another property is nominated as his main residence for all or part of that period. It also applies even where the period when the property was occupied as the individual's main residence was before 31 March 1982.

The period was 24 months for disposals prior to 19 March 1991. The three year period may be cut back in the future if the housing market improves.

14.15.5 Periods spent working abroad
(TCGA 1992, s 223(3)(b))

If, during a period when the owner's property was used as his main residence, the owner has to work abroad, the property will continue to be regarded as the owner's main residence (and therefore exempt from CGT), if the owner was employed abroad under a contract of employment and all the duties of the employment were performed overseas.

The condition requiring the property to be the owner's only or main residence after working abroad is treated as satisfied if the individual is unable to resume residence because the terms of his new employment require him to work elsewhere (extra-statutory concession D4).

14.15.6 Periods spent working elsewhere in the UK

A period of up to four years during which the owner's employment necessitated his living elsewhere in the United Kingdom is also a qualifying period. A period (or periods) which in total exceed four years is covered to the extent of four years.

Again, it is normally necessary that the period be followed by a period of occupation, but extra-statutory concession D4 applies if the individual cannot resume occupation because his current employment prevents this.

14.15.7 Other periods which can qualify

A further period of absence of up to three years can be treated as qualifying for exemption, provided the period is both preceded and succeeded by a period of actual occupation.

14.15.8 Summary

The flow-chart below (Table 14.3) may help in computing the position in a particular case.

The exempt gain is (X) + (Y).

Table 14.3—Computation of exempt gain on a main residence

Number of complete months since 31 March 1982 when the property was actually occupied as the owner's main residence. See 14.12.2	(A)
The lesser of 36 months or such part of the last 36 months which does not already fall within A. (24 months for disposals prior to 19 March 1991). See 14.12.2	(B)
Months spent working abroad when the property was not occupied as the individual's main residence provided that the individual resumed residence after his overseas employment ceased or would have done so if he had not been required to take up employment elsewhere in the UK. Note exclude any period which already falls to be included in B above. See 14.15.5	(C)
Number of months spent living elsewhere because the individual's employment required him to live in another part of the UK (subject to a maximum of 48 months). Again, exclude any period already included in B. Note, an entry is appropriate here only if the individual resumed occupation of the property at the end of the period. See 14.15.6	(D)
Any further period of absence which was both preceded and succeeded by the individual occupying the property as his main residence. (Subject to a maximum of 36 months). Again exclude any period already included in B. See 14.15.7	(E)
Apply the following fraction to the overall gain which arose on the disposal of the property: $$\frac{A + B + C + D + E}{\text{months of ownership since 31 March 1982.}}$$	(X)
A further exemption may also be due where the property has been let. The additional exemption is the lessor of X or £40,000. See 14.13.2	(Y)

14.15.9 Dependent relatives
(TCGA 1992, s 226)

In addition to the main residence exemption, an individual may qualify for exemption in respect of a property occupied by a dependent relative as his or her main residence *provided* the property was so occupied before 6 April 1988.

To qualify for this exemption, the property must have been occupied by the dependent relative rent free, and without any other consideration.

A widowed mother (or mother in law) is automatically regarded as a dependent relative. In other situations, the relative is regarded as dependent only if prevented by old age or infirmity from maintaining himself or herself. The exemption is not available for a property acquired after 5 April 1988, even if the property is a replacement for another property previously occupied by a dependent relative.

In some cases, it may be appropriate to form a settlement with the trustees owning the property occupied by the dependent relative as the trustees may still qualify for exemption in respect of a property occupied by a beneficiary as his or her main residence (see 18.4.11).

15 Capital gains tax and business transactions

This chapter focuses on the CGT aspects of various business transactions. It deals with the following matters:

(1) Loans to private businesses.
(2) Losses on investment in unquoted shares.
(3) Relief for replacement of business assets.
(4) Roll-over relief for reinvestment in unquoted shares.
(5) Hold-over relief for gifts of business property.
(6) Partnerships and capital gains.
(7) Transfer of a business to a company.
(8) Retirement relief—general provisions.
(9) Retirement relief and unincorporated traders.
(10) Retirement relief and full-time directors or employees.

15.1 Loans to private businesses

A very common type of transaction is a loan to a sole trader or partnership (an 'unincorporated business') or to a private company. Almost as common are situations where a person gives a guarantee to a bank etc which makes a loan to a business. This section deals with the CGT position if a loan becomes written off or a person is required to make a payment under a bank guarantee that he has given.

15.1.1 Loans to unincorporated businesses
(TCGA 1992, s 253)

A CGT loss may be deemed to arise if the Revenue is satisfied that a loan has become irrecoverable.

There are various conditions which need to be fulfilled:

(1) The borrower must not be the lender's spouse.

(2) The borrower must be resident in the United Kingdom.
(3) The borrower must have used the loan wholly for the purposes of a trade carried on by him. The trade must not have been a trade which consists of (or includes) lending money.

When a claim is submitted, the Inspector of Taxes must satisfy himself that any outstanding amount of the loan is irrecoverable and that the lender has not assigned his right to recover the loan.

Strictly speaking, relief is due only when a claim is made and admitted but, in practice, the Revenue permits claims to be made within two years of a year of assessment provided the other conditions were satisfied at the end of that year of assessment (extra-statutory concession D36).

The allowable loss is restricted to the amount of the loan which is irrecoverable; there is no indexation relief in these circumstances (and this has always been the case, even where the disposal took place before 30 November 1993).

15.1.2 Loans to companies
(TCGA 1992, s 253)

Similar provisions apply where a person has made a loan to a company which proves to be irrecoverable.

The principal conditions which need to be satisfied are:

(1) The company must be UK resident.
(2) It must be a trading company.
(3) The lender must not be a company which is a member of the same group of companies.

In all other respects, the relief normally applies exactly as described in 15.1.1.

Disposals before 30 November 1993

There is an additional complication which may apply to a disposal of a 'debt on a security' before 30 November 1993. A debt on a security is a special type of loan. In broad terms, such loans are usually evidenced by a debenture deed and are transferable, a typical example being a loan stock.

If a loan falls into this category, it is then necessary to ascertain whether it also falls into another sub-class, ie whether it is a qualifying corporate bond (see 13.3.2 item (9)). If it is a qualifying corporate bond then relief is once again due as set out in 15.1.1 (see TCGA 1992, s 254). However, additional relief may be due if the loan is a debt on a security but is not a qualifying corporate bond, since this type of loan is an asset which qualifies for indexation relief. The most common situation where this will apply is if the loan stock is convertible into shares.

15.1.3   Payments under loan guarantees
(TCGA 1992, s 253(4))

Instead of lending money to a relative or friend or his private company, a person may have given a guarantee to a bank etc. Similarly, a director of a company may have had to give personal guarantees in respect of bank loans to his company.

Where the borrower cannot repay the loan, the bank will call on the guarantor to pay the amount due. In these circumstances, the guarantor may be able to claim a CGT loss as if he had made a loan which was irrecoverable.

The following conditions need to be satisfied in order for relief to be claimed in this way:

(1) Payment has been made under a guarantee.
(2) The payment should arise from a formal calling in of the guarantee. A voluntary payment attracts no relief.
(3) The original loan met the requirements listed in 15.1.1.
(4) The amount paid under the guarantee cannot be recovered either from the borrower or from a co-guarantor.

15.2   Losses on unquoted shares
(TA 1988, s 574)

From time to time, an individual may invest in a private company, either as a working director/shareholder or perhaps as a 'passive' investor with a minority shareholding. Investments may also be made in companies which, whilst they are technically public companies as defined by the Companies Act, are not quoted companies.

15.2.1   Special relief for subscribers

A loss may arise on a disposal of shares in such a company. If the investor acquired existing shares by purchasing them, the loss is a normal CGT loss and the only way in which it can be relieved is as set out in 13.1.3. However, if the individual acquired his shares by *subscribing* for new shares, it may be possible to obtain income tax relief for the loss. Subject to certain conditions, the capital loss may be off-set against the individual's income for the year in which the loss is realised.

The following conditions need to be satisfied:

(1) Firstly, the loss must arise from one of the following:

(a) a sale made at arm's length for full consideration (this rules out a sale to a connected person); or

(b) a disposal which takes place when the company is wound up; or

(c) a deemed disposal where the shares have become of negligible value.

(2) Secondly, there are conditions which attach to the company itself, in particular:

(a) The company must have been resident in the United Kingdom throughout the period from its incorporation until the date of the individual's disposal.

(b) The company must not have been a quoted company at any time during the individual's period of ownership. The fact that any class of shares has had a Stock Exchange quote rules out relief under s 574 even though the loss may have arisen on a class of share which did not have a quote.

(c) The company must be a trading company, or the holding company of a trading group, at the date of disposal or it must have ceased to have been a trading company not more than three years prior to the date of disposal and it must not have been an investment company since that date.

(d) The company's trade must not have consisted wholly or mainly of dealing in shares, securities, land, trades or commodity futures.

(e) The company's trade must have been carried on on a commercial basis.

15.2.2 Relief also available for the spouse of the subscriber

The spouse of a person who subscribed for shares may also claim relief under s 574 where he has acquired the shares in question through an *inter vivos* transfer from his spouse. However, shares which are acquired on the death of a spouse do not entitle the widower/widow to s 574 relief on a subsequent disposal.

15.2.3 Nature of relief

The loss is calculated according to normal capital gains tax principles.

If the loss is eligible for relief under s 574, the individual may elect within two years for the loss to be set against his taxable income. The loss may be set either against the individual's taxable income for the year of the loss, or (up to 1993–94) his taxable income for the following year (different rules will apply for losses realised after 5 April 1994: the loss will be available for offset against income of the year of loss or the *preceding* year). Either claim may be made independently of the other. Where an individual has losses which are available for relief under s 574 and he is also entitled to relief for trading losses, he can choose which losses should be relieved in priority to the other.

Any part of the capital loss which cannot be relieved under s 574 can be carried forward for off-set against capital gains in the normal way.

15.3   Relief for replacement of business assets
(TCGA 1992, s 152–160)

Relief may be available where a person sells an asset which is used by him in a trade (or in certain circumstances, an asset which is used by his family company) and re-invests in replacement assets used for business purposes. This relief is termed 'roll-over' relief.

15.3.1   Nature of roll-over relief

A gain is said to be rolled over in that it is not charged to tax, but is deducted from the person's acquisition cost of the new assets.

15.3.2   Example—Roll-over relief

A sells a farm for £450,000. His capital gain is £200,000. He starts up a new business and invests £500,000 in a warehouse.

By claiming roll-over relief, A avoids having to pay tax on the gain of £200,000. The acquisition cost of his warehouse is reduced as follows:

Annual cost	£500,000
Less rolled-over gain	£200,000
Deemed acquisition cost	£300,000

The relief is really a form of deferment since a larger gain will arise on a subsequent disposal of the replacement asset.

15.3.3   Conditions which need to be satisfied

The asset that has been disposed of must have been used in a business and must have fallen into one of the following categories:

(1)   land and buildings;
(2)   fixed plant and machinery;

(3)   ships;
(4)   goodwill;
(5)   milk and potato quotas;
(6)   aircraft;
(7)   hovercraft, satellites and spacecraft.

The replacement assets must also fall into one of these categories.

It is not possible to claim roll-over relief on the disposal of shares in a family company, nor is it possible to claim s152 relief for expenditure on such shares on the basis that this is replacement expenditure (but see 15.4 regarding a different type of roll-over relief introduced by FA 1994).

The replacement assets must normally be acquired within a period starting one year before the date of the disposal of the original asset and ending three years after the date of disposal. The time limit can be extended (at the Revenue's discretion) if the acquisition of replacement assets within three years was not possible because of circumstances outside the person's control.

15.3.4   Example—Full relief available only where all the sale proceeds are reinvested
(TCGA 1192, s 152(3)–(11))

Using the same figures as in 15.3.2, A sells his farm for £450,000, making the same capital gain of £200,000. He starts up a new business but invests only £400,000 in the new warehouse. The part of the £450,000 disposal consideration for the farm which is not applied in acquiring the warehouse is £50,000. This is less than the gain which arose on the disposal of the farm and the balance of the gain may be rolled-over. The acquisition value of the warehouse is reduced by £150,000.

15.3.5   Old assets not used for business throughout ownership

If the old asset was not used for business throughout the period of ownership, s 152 applies as if a part of the asset used for the purposes of the trade was a separate asset to that which had not been wholly used for the purposes of the trade.

15.3.6   Example—Old assets

In April 1992, B sells his ship for a gain, after indexation has been calculated, of £50,000. It had originally been bought in April 1984 but had been used in his trade only since April 1986. The amount of gain which can be rolled over into the purchase of a new asset is calculated as follows:

Chargeable gain £50,000 x $\dfrac{\text{period of trading use of old asset}}{\text{period of ownership}}$

This equals £50,000 x 6/8 ie £37,500

The balance of £12,500 (£50,000 – £37,500) is a chargeable gain.

15.3.7 Treatment where replacement assets are wasting assets
TCGA 1992, s 154)

The roll-over relief is modified where the replacement expenditure consists of the purchase of a wasting asset (an asset with an expected useful life of less than 50 years) or an asset which will become a wasting asset within ten years. Plant and machinery is always considered to have a useful life of less than 50 years. Furthermore, the acquisition of a lease with less than 60 years to run will also constitute the acquisition of a wasting asset. Rather paradoxically, the goodwill of a business is not regarded as a wasting asset.

The capital gain in these circumstances is not deferred indefinitely, but becomes chargeable on the first of the following occasions:

(1)   the disposal of the replacement asset; or
(2)   the asset ceasing to be used in the business; or
(3)   the expiry of ten years.

15.3.8 Examples—Roll-over relief on wasting assets

(1) B sells a factory and re-invests in a 59 year lease of a warehouse which he uses in his business. In the sixth year the warehouse is let as an investment property.

The rolled-over gain would become chargeable in year six.

(2) C also rolls over into a 59 year lease. He is still using the property after ten years, but because it has become a wasting asset within that period, the rolled-over gain becomes chargeable in year ten.

15.3.9 Reinvestment in non-wasting assets

On the other hand, if the person acquires new non-wasting replacement assets during the ten years, the capital gain which was originally rolled over into the purchase of the wasting assets can be transferred to the new replacement assets. Assume in example (1) above that B had bought the goodwill of a business in year five. He could transfer his roll-over relief claim to the new asset. No gain would then become chargeable in year six when he lets the warehouse.

15.3.10 Furnished holiday lettings

A property acquired for letting as furnished holiday accommodation (see 4.9) may qualify for roll-over relief and gains from the disposal of such properties may be rolled over.

15.3.11 Assets used by a partnership
(Inland Revenue Statement of Practice D11)

Roll-over relief can be secured where the replacement assets are used by a partnership in which the owner is a partner.

15.3.12 Assets used by a family company
(TCGA 1992, s 157)

Relief can also be obtained where an individual disposes of a property etc which is used by his 'personal trading company', but only if the replacement asset is acquired by him and is used by the same company. A company is an individual's personal trading company if he personally owns at least five per cent of the voting shares. Prior to 16 March 1993 relief was due only if he held 25 per cent of the voting shares or his family owned more than 50 per cent.

The individual need not be a director of the company, indeed he need not even be employed by it. Also, roll-over relief is not lost because he has charged the company rent.

15.3.13 Assets owned by an employee or office-holder

An employee or office-holder may claim roll-over relief where he disposes of an asset used in the employment. This condition may apply to a person such as a sub-postmaster who has an 'office' for tax purposes, but who generally owns the sub-post office premises. For further details, see Statement of Practice SP5/86.

There are circumstances where these provisions mean that a director of a family company who has sold an asset used by one company and bought new assets used by another family company is entitled to roll-over relief. However, this is a difficult area where professional advice is essential.

15.3.14   Roll-over relief for entrepreneurs
(FA 1993, s 87 & Sched 7)

The Finance Act 1993 introduced a new relief to assist people wishing to sell their private company and either start a new business or invest in other growing businesses.

The relief permits deferment of CGT on the sale of shares in the individual's own company provided the sale proceeds are reinvested in other qualifying trading companies. The gains are deferred until a disposal of the replacement shares takes place or the individual emigrates.

To obtain the relief the individual must reinvest some or all of the proceeds from the sale of shares in the business in a qualifying unquoted trading company. He must:

(1)   dispose of shares in an unquoted trading company; and
(2)   have been a full-time working officer (eg a director) or employee engaged in a managerial or technical capacity with that company; and
(3)   have owned at least five per cent of the shares in that company for at least one year; and
(4)   reinvest in a qualifying unquoted trading company by acquiring or adding to a holding of at least five per cent within a period beginning one year before and ending three years after the sale of the original shares.

Qualifying unquoted trading companies do not include those with more than fifty per cent of their assets in land, or companies carrying on financial, leasing or land dealing activities. Companies letting residential property under assured tenancies and investors not exposed to any real risk will also not qualify for this relief.

Relief is withdrawn if the company ceases to be a qualifying company within a period of three years.

This relief applies to disposals made on or after 16 March 1993. The relief was broadened by Finance Act 1994 in that the relief is now available to cover gains realised on the disposal of all types of asset. We cover the expanded relief in more detail at 15.4, the original FA 1993 provisions are now relevant only to gains realised during the period 16 March–29 November 1993.

15.4   Roll-over relief for reinvestment in unquoted shares
(FA 1994 s 91)

The Finance Act 1994 has made it possible for individuals and trustees to secure reinvestment relief on any capital gain made on or after 30

November 1993 where the gain is reinvested in shares in a qualifying unquoted trading company. It should be noted that the previous requirement that the individual/trustee should acquire at least a five per cent holding in the new company no longer applies. Reinvestment relief is therefore available for any investment in a qualifying unquoted trading company.

Reinvestment must take place within a period beginning one year before and ending three years after the disposal which has given rise to the capital gain. It should be noted that it is possible to claim reinvestment relief where investment has been made in qualifying unquoted companies prior to 30 November 1993, but within 12 months of a capital gain being realised after that date.

As under the previous provisions (see 15.3.14), a company is a qualifying company only if it carries on a trade other than farming, dealing in land, or various financial activities. Moreover, a company is not a qualifying company if more than half of its chargeable assets consists of land or an interest in land. The full list of prohibited activities is set out in Table 15.1.

Table 15.1—Prohibited activities of a company for re-investment relief

(1) dealing in land, in commodities or futures or in shares, securities or other financial instruments;

(2) dealing in goods otherwise than in the course of any ordinary trade of wholesale or retail distribution;

(3) banking, insurance, money-lending, debt factoring, hire-purchase, financial or other financial activities;

(4) oil extraction activities;

(5) leasing (including letting ships on charter or other assets on hire) or receiving royalties or licence fees;

(6) providing legal or accountancy services;

(7) providing services or facilities for any trade carried on by another person (other than a parent company) which consists to any substantial extent of activities within any of paragraphs (1) to (6) above and in which a controlling interest is held by a person who also has a controlling interest in the trade carried on by the company;

(8) property development;

(9) farming.

The relief is clawed back where a company ceases to meet the qualifying conditions within three years of the reinvestment. The gain is treated as arising at the point in time when the conditions are breached.

A clawback may also arise where the individual who has qualified for reinvestment relief ceases to be resident in the United Kingdom within the three year period.

Most trustees are eligible for the new relief. The main exclusion is where the beneficiaries of the trust are not individuals.

15.5   Hold-over relief for gifts of business property
(TCGA 1992, s 163)

15.5.1   Background and nature of hold-over relief

Under the legislation which applied up to 5 April 1989, a UK resident individual could transfer an asset to another UK resident person on a no gain/no loss basis by claiming hold-over relief.

15.5.2   Example—Hold-over relief

B transferred shares in X plc to her brother C in 1988. They were both resident in the United Kingdom.

B's shares were worth £29,000 and her capital gain would normally have been £13,000.

By claiming hold-over relief, B could avoid having a chargeable gain of £13,000. C's acquisition value was then taken as:

Market value at acquisition	29,000
Less held-over capital gain	13,000
	16,000

In 1989, the Chancellor abolished the hold-over relief for gifts in general. However, the same type of hold-over relief can still be claimed on gifts of business property.

15.5.3   Definition of business property

Business property is defined for these purposes as:

(1)   an asset used by the transferor in a trade, profession or vocation;
(2)   an asset used by the transferor's family company in a trade;
(3)   an asset used for a trade by a subsidiary of the transferor's family company;
(4)   unquoted shares in a trading company;
(5)   quoted shares if the company concerned is the transferor's family company (it will be very unusual for this condition to be satisfied);
(6)   agricultural land which qualifies for the inheritance tax (IHT) agricultural property relief.

15.6   Partnerships and capital gains

The way in which CGT affects partnership transactions can at times be complex. If you are a partner you should familiarise yourself with Inland Revenue Statement of Practice D12—and take regular professional advice. The following section describes some key aspects.

15.6.1   Partnership's acquisition value

Although individual partners' entitlement to profits may vary over the years, the partnership's acquisition value for the firm's chargeable assets is not affected unless there are cash payments from one partner to another to acquire a greater interest in the firm or unless assets are revalued as part of the arrangements for changes in profit-sharing.

15.6.2   Assets held by the firm at 31 March 1982

The partnership may make a universal rebasing election for the values at 31 March 1982 to be used instead of cost (see 14.3.2). This is quite separate from the individual partners' position in relation to their personal assets when a disposal of an asset takes place. There may be partners who were not in the partnership at 31 March 1982, but this does not affect the computation of the gain.

15.6.3   Partnership gains divisible amongst the partners

Where a partnership asset is sold at a capital gain (or loss), the gain is divided amongst the partners in accordance with their profit-sharing ratios. Each partner is personally assessable on his share of the gain.

The partner's actual capital gains tax liability will depend upon his own situation, ie whether he has other gains for the year, has available losses, can claim roll-over relief or is entitled to retirement relief (see 15.8).

15.6.4   Revaluations and retirement and introduction of new partners

Problems may arise where a partnership has substantial assets which are chargeable assets for CGT purposes and which are worth more than their book value (ie the value at which they are shown in the firm's accounts).

A revaluation to bring the book value of the assets into line with their market value can produce a liability for individual partners if there is a reduction in their profit-sharing ratios.

This commonly happens when existing partners retire or new partners are introduced.

15.6.5   Example—Retirement of partner

A is a partner in a five partner firm and is entitled to 20 per cent of the profits. He retires and his colleagues then share profits on the basis of 25 per cent each.

As part of the arrangements for his retirement, the book value of the firm's office block is increased from £150,000 to its current value of £750,000. The surplus is credited to each partner's account so that A is credited with £120,000.

A is treated as if he had realised a gain on the disposal of a one-fifth share of the building. This would be based on the £120,000.

The remaining four partners are not treated as having made a disposal. Indeed, they each have made an acquisition of a five per cent interest in the building for an outlay of £30,000.

15.6.6   Example—Introduction of new partner

B and C are partners. Their premises are included in their firm's balance sheet at £200,000 (original cost), but are actually worth £500,000. B and C agree to admit D as an equal partner in return for his paying in new capital into the firm of £700,000. They revalue the premises before admitting D as a partner, and the surplus of £300,000 is credited to their accounts. In this case, B and C will each be regarded as having made a disposal of a one-sixth interest in the premises. This is because D's new capital will go into the firm as a whole. After coming in, he effectively owns one-third of all the assets (and is responsible for one-third of the liabilities).

The former partners' ownership of the premises has been reduced from 50 per cent to a one-third interest.

15.6.7   Retirement and introduction of partners with no revaluation of assets

There is no such problem where partners leave or come in and there is no revaluation of assets. In such a case, the remaining or incoming partners normally take over the outgoing partners' acquisition values for the firm's asset.

15.6.8   Example—Change of partners with no revaluation of assets

A and B are in partnership. They own premises which have a book value of £94,000 (equal to cost in 1980). A retires and is replaced by C. The premises are not revalued.

Later the premises are sold for £244,000. B and C are assessed on their share of the gain.

The gain will be computed by reference to the original cost (£94,000) or the premises' market value at 31 March 1982, *not* their value at the time that C became a partner.

This does *not* apply where the partners are connected persons (perhaps because they are relatives), or where cash payments are made to acquire an interest in the firm. In either of these categories you should seek specialist advice.

15.7 Transfer of a business to a company
(TCGA 1992, s 162)

Where a person transfers a business to a company (ie he 'incorporates the business'), there is a disposal of the assets which are transferred to the company. Not all the assets will necessarily be chargeable assets for capital gains tax purposes, but a gain may arise on assets such as land, buildings and goodwill.

Fortunately, there is a relief which may cover such situations.

15.7.1 Nature of relief

The main relief applies only where a business is transferred to a company in return for an issue of shares to the former proprietors of the business. Where the necessary conditions are satisfied so that s 162 relief is available, the gains which would otherwise arise on the transfer of chargeable assets are rolled-over into the cost of the shares issued.

15.7.2 Example—Transfer of a business to a company

A transfers a business to X Ltd in return for shares which are worth £75,000.

There are capital gains of £48,000 on the assets transferred to the company.

If s 162 relief applies, A will not have any assessable capital gain, but her shares in X Ltd will be deemed to have an acquisition cost of £27,000 computed as follows:

	£
Market value	75,000
Less rolled-over gain	48,000
	27,000

15.7.3 Conditions which must be satisfied

In order for s 162 relief to be available, *all* the assets of the business other than cash must be transferred to the company. It is not acceptable to the Inland Revenue for certain assets of the unincorporated business such as trade debts to be excluded, even though this might otherwise be advisable in order to save stamp duty.

Relief is available only in so far as shares are issued by the company instead of other forms of payment such as loan stock. The market value of the shares issued in return for the transfer of the business must be at least equal to the capital gains arising on the transfer of assets.

15.7.4 Example—Limitations of s 162 relief

A transfers a business with a net value of £400,000 to Y Ltd, a new company specially formed for the purpose. Shares in X Ltd are issued to him, and these have a value of £400,000. However, closer examination reveals that the business's value is depressed by heavy bank borrowings. Furthermore, capital gains of a total of £490,000 arise on chargeable assets transferred as part of the business.

Section 162 relief would be limited to £400,000. The balance of £90,000 would be taxable in the normal way.

15.7.5 Conditions which are not required

(1) Relief is not confined to a transfer of a business to a company by a sole trader; the same relief is available where a partnership transfers its business to a company.

(2) The shares which are issued need not be ordinary shares.

(3) Relief does not seem to be confined to a business which is classified as a trade which falls under Schedule D Case I or Case II. It is arguable that the relevant business might, for example, consist of letting a group of properties.

(4) There is no requirement that the company should be incorporated or resident in the United Kingdom. It can be both of these things, but relief is not prejudiced just because a foreign company is involved.

15.7.6 Relief may be due on a proportion of the capital gains

Some relief will still be available if the business is transferred to the company in return for a mixture of shares and loan stock, or shares and cash. The formula to be used is:

$$\text{Chargeable gain} \times \frac{\text{value of shares received}}{\text{value of whole consideration received}}.$$

15.7.7   Alternative incorporation relief

It may sometimes be possible to transfer a business to a company and avoid any capital gains tax liability by relying on the hold-over provisions (see 15.5). Professional advice is essential when implementing such arrangements.

15.8   Retirement relief—general provisions
(TCGA 1992, s 163–164)

This is an important relief which may be available on the sale of a business, or an interest in a partnership, the disposal of assets used in a partnership, sale of shares in a family company, the liquidation of such a company, or sales of assets used by such a company. The relief is available only if the individual is aged at least 55 or is having to retire early because of ill health.

15.8.1   Nature of the relief

The maximum relief is £250,000 plus a further amount of 50 per cent of gains in excess of £250,000 (up to an overall ceiling of £1m). The £250,000 and £1m limits came into force on 30 November 1993; prior to that date the limits were £150,000 and £600,000.

The maximum relief is based on all of the requirements being met for a period of ten years. The relief is tapered using the 'appropriate percentage' which starts off at ten per cent for one year and rises to 100 per cent for the full ten years.

15.8.2   Example—Retirement relief

A who is 57 years old and fulfils all of the criteria, disposes in May 1994 of his business in which he has been a full-time working director for 15 years. He realises gains qualifying for relief of £400,000. The relief is as follows:

Appropriate percentage—100 per cent—of first limit =	£250,000
Excess of gains over this limit =	£150,000
Relief on excess at 50 per cent =	£75,000
Therefore total relief =	£325,000
Taxable gain	£75,000

The relief can be split between gains on disposals of two or more different businesses, but the aggregate relief will be restricted to the £250,000 and £1m limits. In some cases, the gains may arise in different tax years.

15.8.3 Retirement through ill health

The legislation provides that retirement relief should be available to an individual who is being required to dispose of his business because ill health makes it impossible for him to carry on.

In practice, the Revenue requires claimants to provide a medical certificate, signed by a qualified medical practitioner (whether or not the claimant's own general practitioner). The Board will themselves take advice from the Regional Medical Service of the Department of Health, and in some cases a further medical examination by the Regional Medical Officer will be required.

The Revenue have made it clear that retirement relief will *not* be given to someone aged below 55 where he has ceased work because of the ill health of someone else, for example his spouse.

15.8.4 Conditions needing to be satisfied for ten years if full relief is to be available

The full relief is given only if the individual has satisfied various requirements for a period of ten years. During that period he must have been in business as a sole trader or partner or have been a full-time officer (eg a director) or employee of a personal trading company (see 15.3.12).

15.8.5 Example—Limited relief

In example 15.7.2, if A had owned the business for six years, the relief would be as follows:

Appropriate percentage of £250,000	£150,000
Excess of gain over £150,000	£250,000
50 per cent thereof	£125,000
Total relief	£275,000
Taxable gain	£125,000

Separate periods during which an individual satisfied one of these requirements can be aggregated in certain circumstances.

15.8.6 Specific conditions for unincorporated traders and full-time directors and employees

There are a number of very specific requirements in relation to disposals by sole traders, partners and full-time directors and employees of personal trading companies. These are dealt with separately at 15.9 and 15.10 respectively.

15.8.7 Retirement relief for trustees

There are certain circumstances where the sale by trustees of family settlements of business property or shares can attract retirement relief. This is an area where professional advice should be taken.

15.9 Retirement relief and unincorporated traders

The sale of a business may be broken down for tax purposes into the disposal of distinct assets (goodwill and buildings, plant and equipment, stock debtors and cash). The CGT position needs to be looked at separately in relation to each asset.

15.9.1 Retirement relief for sole traders

The legislation requires that a capital gain should arise on the disposal of a business or part of a business.

There have been several cases concerning farmers where the individual concerned has disposed of part of his land. In each of these cases, the Courts have held that retirement relief was not due since the asset disposed of was an asset used in the business rather than part of the business itself. A similar point would arise if a sole trader sold a warehouse or office block, but continued in business.

In practice, the Revenue resists relief for farmers unless the disposal concerns at least 50 per cent or more of the total area being farmed.

15.9.2 Retirement relief for partners

A gain may attract retirement relief where it arises on a disposal which takes place on the introduction of a new partner or on some other change in profit sharing ratios combined with a revaluation of partnership assets (see 15.6.4).

In some cases, a partner may own an asset which is used by his firm. Retirement relief is available to cover a gain arising from the disposal of such an asset provided the following conditions are satisfied:

(1) The disposal of the asset must take place as part of the withdrawal of the individual from participation in the business carried on by the partnership.
(2) Immediately before the disposal (or the cessation of the business) the asset must have been used for the purposes of the partnership business.

(3)   During the whole or part of the period in which the asset has been in the ownership of the individual, the asset must have been used:.

  (a)   for the purposes of the business; or

  (b)   for the purposes of another business carried on by the individual or by a partnership of which the individual concerned was a member; or

  (c)   for the purposes of another business carried on by the individual's family trading company (in this instance, the individual must have been a full-time working director at the time).

The amount of retirement relief on the disposal of an asset of this nature may be restricted where the partner has charged his firm a commercial rent for use of the property.

15.10   Retirement relief and full-time directors and employees
(TCGA 1992, ss 163–164 as amended by FA 1993, s 87)

This section focuses on the way in which the capital gain on the sale of shares in a personal trading company and assets owned privately by the shareholder may qualify for retirement relief.

15.10.1   Full-time working directors

It was necessary up to 15 March 1993 that the individual should have been a full-time working director if he were to qualify for retirement relief. For disposals after that date, it is sufficient for the individual to work for the company on a full-time basis in a managerial or technical capacity.

There is no statutory definition of what full-time means in this context. In practice, it is understood that the Revenue accepts that a director whose normal working week is 30 hours qualifies for relief (the 30 hours would exclude meal breaks). A person is required to devote more or less the whole of his time if that is what his job and service contract involve. Absence through illness does not prejudice entitlement to the relief.

In some cases, the individual will be working full-time for a group of related companies. Relief is available where a person is required to devote more or less the whole of his time to the service of a commercial association of companies which carry on businesses and which are of a nature that the business of a company and the associated companies taken together may be reasonably considered to make up a single composite undertaking.

This is clearly an area where professional advice may be required in the light of the circumstances of the particular case.

A director who has retired from full-time employment, but who continues to spend an average of at least ten hours per week in the conduct and management of the company's business may qualify for relief. However, his entitlement is based on the period of full-time service which he had up to the date of his retirement.

It is also a condition for an individual to qualify for retirement relief that he has a shareholding in the company of at least five per cent. Prior to 16 March 1993 it was necessary that he should hold twenty five per cent or he and his family should have held more than fifty per cent.

15.10.2   Possible restriction of retirement relief

Where a company has investments as well as business interests, the gain which may attract retirement relief is restricted to the proportion of the gain determined by the following fraction:

$$\frac{\text{Chargeable assets used for business purposes}}{\text{Total chargeable assets}}$$

Where a company has disposed of business assets within six months of a disposal of shares, the individual may elect for the restriction to be computed by reference to the position if the company had not sold the assets concerned.

15.10.3   Sale of premises etc used by company

An individual who has been a full-time director or employee may own property or some other assets which are used by his personal trading company. Retirement relief may be claimed in respect of a disposal of such assets provided the following conditions are satisfied:

(1)   The disposal of the asset must take place as part of the withdrawal of the individual concerned from participation in the business carried on by the company; and

(2)   the asset must be in use for the purposes of the company's business at the time of the disposal or it must have been so used at the time that the company's business ceased; and

(3)   the asset must have been used in the whole or part of the period in which the individual has owned it:
    (a)   for the purposes of the business carried on by the company; or

    (b)   for the purposes of another business carried on by the individual or by a partnership of which the individual was a member;

    (c)   for the purposes of another business carried on by a personal trading company.

16 Some ways of reducing capital gains tax

Where a capital gain arises, the transaction tends to be an exceptional or 'one-off' event and the capital growth on an invesment which may have been held for many years falls entirely into the tax year in which the disposal takes place instead of being spread evenly over the whole period of ownership. This can often mean that a large amount of tax is involved. There are a number of possible ways of mitigating tax and it is usually a good idea to take professional advice. The following suggestions should be borne in mind, but they are only suggestions rather than definitive advice.

(1) Make use of both spouses' annual exemptions.
(2) Realise gains to avoid wasting the annual exemption.
(3) Make sure you get relief for capital losses.
(4) Bed and breakfast transactions.
(5) Try to make gains taxable at 25 per cent rather than 40 per cent.
(6) Saving tax by making gifts to relatives.
(7) Roll-over relief and furnished holiday accommodation.
(8) Sale of a family company.

16.1 Make use of both spouses' £5,800 annual exemption

16.1.1 Inter-spouse transfer can be a way of saving tax

All individuals are allowed to realise capital gains of £5,800 in 1994–95 before they become liable for CGT. This applies to husband and wife, but there are no provisions under which any unused amount may be transferred to a spouse.

16.1.2   Example—Inter-spouse transfers

If A has gains of £3,000 and his wife B has gains of £7,000, the position is as follows:

A	B	
No CGT	Gains	£7,000
liability	Less exempt	£5,800
	Taxable	£1,200

There will often be a way of avoiding this type of mismatch. If B had transferred assets to A before he sold them, she could effectively transfer her gain to him. A transfer between spouses does not count as a disposal for tax purposes and A would take over B's base cost. So, with a little forethought, the position could have been:

A		B	
Gains	£5,000	Gains	£5,000
Exemption	£5,800	Exemption	£5,800
	NIL		NIL

16.2   Realise gains to avoid wasting the annual exemption

Any unused annual exemption cannot be carried forward for use in a future tax year. Dealing costs may be a disincentive but, provided you expect to sell shares etc, at some time or other in the future, it can make sense to 'top up' any net gains to make full use of the £5,800 exemption.

It could be appropriate to realise gains by entering into 'bed and breakfast' transactions if you are not ready to sell the shareholding concerned. A bed and breakfast deal involves a sale near close of business on one day and a repurchase first thing on the following day.

16.2.1   Example—Bed and breakfast deals

A has made no chargeable disposals during the current year. For a long time, she has had a large holding in one particular company which shows a 'paper' gain of £40,000. The market is expected to rise further but, even so, it will make sense to bed and breakfast part of the holding to use up her £5,800 exemption. If A does this for three years running and then sells her holding, the total saving could be between £4,350 and £6,960 depending on whether A is subject to tax at 25 per cent or 40 per cent.

16.3   Make sure you get relief for capital losses

It may be possible to save tax in a different way by a transfer of an asset between spouses before it is sold to an outsider. Capital losses for previous years attach to each spouse separately and can now be set only against that spouse's gain.

16.3.1   Example—Relief for capital losses

If A's wife B has losses of £35,000 and A has an asset which has appreciated by £50,000, it will make sense for him to transfer it to B before it is sold. Instead of the position being like this:

	£
A's gains	50,000
Less exemption	5,800
Taxable	44,200

the position will be:

	£
B's gains	50,000
Less capital losses	35,000
	15,000
Less exemption	5,800
Taxable	9,200

Of course, the ideal position would be achieved by A transferring part of the asset to B, so that they eventually make a joint disposal, use B's losses and take advantage of both of their £5,800 annual exemptions.

16.3.2   Negligible value claims

You may have made an investment in the past which has gone badly. Indeed, you may have written it off in your own mind but, if you have not sold it, the loss is normally only a paper loss which is not allowable for CGT purposes. However, there is an exception to the normal rule whereby you may be able to establish an allowable loss even though there has been no disposal. If the Revenue can be persuaded that the asset has become of 'negligible value' (ie, virtually worthless) you can claim a loss (see 13.4.11). In practice, the Revenue issues lists of quoted shares which have been suspended and which are recognised to be of negligible value, so you should ask your Inspector of Taxes whether your defunct investments are on the Revenue's list. It may also be possible to establish losses on unquoted shares and other investments.

16.4   Bed and breakfast transactions

There may be yet another way of saving tax by carrying out any bed and breakfast deals towards the end of the tax year. Once again, you may need to rearrange the way you and your spouse hold assets.

16.4.1   Example—Bed and breakfast deals

A has made a capital gain of £75,000 in June 1994 on selling a property in Yorkshire. Her husband B is sitting on a paper loss of £40,000 on an ill advised gamble in penny shares. How can he set his loss against A's gain? The answer is for B to transfer the penny shares to A and for her to carry out the bed and breakfast before 5 April 1995. She will take over B's base cost of, say, £48,000 and when she sells the shares, she, and not B, will have realised the loss.

16.5   Try to make gains taxable at 25 per cent rather than 40 per cent

The rate of tax depends upon the level of your income, rather than the amount of gain you make. If you have taxable income of more than £23,700 after deducting your personal allowances etc, the gains will be taxed at 40 per cent. If you have little or no income, the first £23,700 of any capital gains will normally attract tax at a maximum rate of 25 per cent. It can therefore make sense for you to transfer an asset to your spouse to sell and realise a gain if the gain will be taxed at a lower rate.

16.5.1   Example—Transfers to reduce the rate of CGT

If A's wife has no income, A could transfer shares with a paper gain of £25,000 to her. If A sold them he would be taxed at 40 per cent, but his wife's disposal will attract tax only as follows:

	£
Gain	25,000.00
Less exemption	5,800.00
Taxable	19,200.00
Tax at 20% on £3,000	600.00
Tax at 25% on £16,200	4,050.00
	4,650.00

16.6 Saving tax by making gifts to relatives

If you are planning to sell unquoted shares it may be possible to save tax.

16.6.1 Example—Sale of unquoted shares

A holds all the shares in a private trading company. He has reached broad agreement with a potential purchaser to sell his shares for £1,000 each which will produce a gain of £400 per share. The resultant capital gain will attract tax at 40 per cent because of the level of A's other income and gains.

If A so wishes, he could transfer some shares to his son B, to enable him to use his annual exemption, ie, A would give B 14 shares in the company and claim hold-over relief. No capital gain need arise for A on his gift to B who would then dispose of the shares to the ultimate purchaser.
B's capital gain would then be as follows:

Capital gain: 14 x £400 =	£5,600
Less annual exemption	£5,800
Taxable	NIL

The overall effect is that A's family saves tax of £2,240 (ie 40 per cent of £5,600).

16.7 Roll-over relief and furnished holiday accommodation

There will be many situations where a person has realised a capital gain on the disposal of a business and does not wish to embark on further trading activities. Under such circumstances, roll-over relief may still be available. One particular type of property investment qualifies in this way because where a property is acquired for letting as furnished holiday accommodation, the owner is deemed to have acquired an asset for a trade and roll-over relief may be available. Two points are of particular interest:

(1)   The property need not be located at the seaside. A property in (for example) Central London could qualify provided that it is let for at least part of the year on a short term basis (see 4.9 and 15.3.10).

(2)   Roll-over relief may be obtained provided the property is let as furnished holiday accommodation for a period. If the property is subsequently let on a longer term basis or used for some other purpose (for example used as a second home) the roll-over relief is not normally withdrawn. The one exception to this would be if

the owner has acquired a leasehold interest on the property concerned and the lease has less than 60 years to run at the time that it is acquired. Taking such a property out of use as furnished holiday accommodation would mean that the deferred gain would become chargeable (see 15.3.8).

16.8 Sale of a family company

16.8.1 Pre-sale dividend

There may be situations where it makes better sense for the owners of a private company to take a dividend which is taxable as income, before disposing of their shares. Clearly, the purchaser will pay less, but the difference in the tax treatment of dividends and capital gains may mean that the vendors are better off.

16.8.2 Example—Sale of a family company

A owns all the shares in X Ltd. He is planning to sell the shares for a total of £1.2m. The capital gain which would result is £800,000. However, his accountant advises him that no additional tax would be payable by X Ltd if a dividend were taken of £800,000. The timing of the company's tax payments might be advanced by anything between nine and 18 months if it pays such a dividend, but assume that this is acceptable to the purchaser (provided the price for the shares is reduced to £400,000). If A receives a dividend he will be liable only for higher rate tax ie,

	£
Dividend	800,000
Tax credit	200,000
	1,000,000
40 per cent income tax	400,000
Less tax credit	200,000
	200,000

Because the sale price is reduced to £400,000 A has no capital gains tax liability.

If A had not taken the dividend his capital gain would have been £800,000 on which tax would be payable of £320,000. So by taking the dividend he has cut his tax bill by £120,000.

There is sometimes a constraint in that the payment of a really sizable dividend may result in the company paying additional tax which is not recoverable in the immediate future. This will depend upon the facts, but will constitute a problem if the advance corporation tax payable by the company (24.5.4) cannot be offset against mainstream tax for the year in which the dividend is paid or one of the six preceding years. Even here there may be ways around the difficulty and you should take professional advice.

16.8.3 Maximising retirement relief

This is a complex area, but consideration should be given to matters such as:

(1) careful planning in relation to disposals of assets which are owned by full-time working directors or senior employees and used in the company's business;

(2) transfer of shares between spouses if this will increase gains which are eligible for retirement relief;

(3) possible purchase by the individual shareholders from the company of all or some of its investments if this will avoid or reduce the restriction imposed by the principle that only the following proportion of a gain on the sale of shares may qualify for retirement relief:

$$\frac{\text{Company's chargeable business assets}}{\text{Company's total chargeable assets}}$$

(see 15.10.2)

17 Inheritance tax and individuals

Inheritance tax (IHT) is a combined gift tax and death duty. It applies to gifts and deemed gifts made during a person's lifetime and to his estate on death. The first £150,000 of chargeable transfers (the nil rate band) is free of IHT. Cumulative transfers in excess of this which take place either at death or within seven years of death are taxed at 40 per cent (though the overall impact may be reduced on transfers that take place more than three years before death). On all other occasions when IHT is payable, the rate is 20 per cent.

This chapter covers the following topics:

(1) Who is subject to IHT?
(2) When may a charge arise?
(3) Transfers of value.
(4) Certain gifts are not transfers of value.
(5) Exempt transfers.
(6) Potentially exempt transfers.
(7) Reservation of benefit.
(8) Business property.
(9) Agricultural property and woodlands.
(10) Computation of tax payable on lifetime transfers.
(11) Tax payable on death.
(12) Life assurance and pension policies.

17.1 Who is subject to IHT?

An individual who is domiciled in the United Kingdom is subject to IHT on all property owned by him, whether it is located in the United Kingdom or overseas. By contrast, a person who has a foreign domicile is subject to IHT only on property which is situated in the United Kingdom. Domicile is a concept of general law and is distinct from a person being resident or ordinarily resident (for a fuller description of domicile, residence etc see Chapters 21 and 22).

Section 267 of the Inheritance Tax Act (IHTA) 1984 contains a special rule which applies for IHT purposes whereby an individual may be deemed to be domiciled in the United Kingdom for a tax year if he has been resident in the United Kingdom for 17 out of the 20 tax years which end with the current year.

17.2   When may a charge arise?

Inheritance tax can apply in the following circumstances:

(1)   On a gift made by an individual during his lifetime.
(2)   On a lifetime transfer of value which is regarded as a 'chargeable transfer'.
(3)   On the death of an individual.

A person who has an interest in possession under a trust or settlement is normally regarded as if he were entitled to the capital. When the beneficiary dies the full value of the trust property is treated as part of his estate for IHT purposes (see 18.4.15).

Table 17.1 below indicates the circumstances under which a gift may be a chargeable transfer for IHT purposes.

17.3   Transfers of value

17.3.1   Not all transfers are gifts
(IHTA 1984, s 3)

The legislation refers mainly to *transfers* rather than gifts. The reason for this is that all gifts are transfers of value but not all transfers of value are gifts. For example, where a person deliberately sells an asset at less than market value, he may not be making a gift but he is certainly making a transfer of value. Similarly, deliberately omitting to exercise a right can also be a transfer of value but this is not a gift in the normal sense of the word. To give a third example, a transfer can even involve property which is not owned by the person since the IHT legislation deems a person to make a gift if his interest in possession under a trust comes to an end.

17.3.2   There must be gratuitous intent
(IHTA 1984, s 10)

IHT will not normally apply to a gift unless there is an element of 'bounty', ie there is a deliberate intention to make a gift. An unintentional loss of value (for example, a loss made on a bad business deal), is not subject to IHT because there was no intention to pass value to another person.

Table 17.1—Is a gift a chargeable transfer?

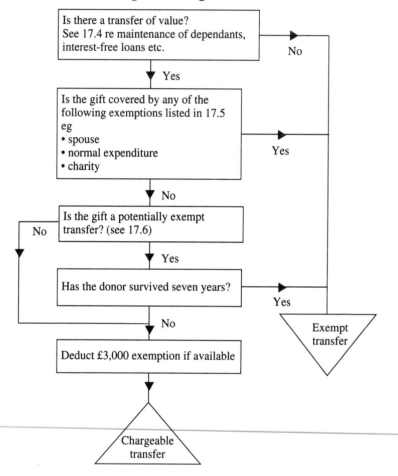

17.3.3   How a transfer is measured
(IHTA 1984, s 3)

The amount of any transfer of value is determined by the reduction in the donor's wealth. This is not necessarily the same as the increase in the recipient's wealth.

This can be shown by considering the situation where a person owns 51 out of 100 shares in a company. He has control because he has the majority of the shares. If he were to give two shares to his son, he would relinquish control of the company and his remaining 49 shares might be worth considerably less because of this. The two shares given to his son might not be worth very much in isolation, and the son may not have acquired a very valuable asset, but the father's estate would have gone down in value by the difference between the value of a 51 per cent shareholding and the value of a 49 per cent shareholding.

17.4 Certain gifts are not transfers of value

Certain gifts and other transactions are not regarded as transfers of value so the issue of whether they are chargeable transfers simply does not arise. These include:

- Maintenance of dependants
- Waivers of dividends
- Waivers of remuneration
- Interest free loans
- Disclaimers of legacies
- Deeds of variation.

17.4.1 Maintenance of dependants, family etc
(IHTA 1984, s 11)

The legislation specifically provides that the following lifetime payments are not transfers of value:

(1) Payments for the maintenance of a spouse or former spouse
(2) Payments for the maintenance, education or training of a child or stepchild under the age of 18
(3) Payments made to maintain a child over 18 who is in full time education or training
(4) Reasonable provision for the care or maintenance of a dependent relative, ie someone who is incapacitated by old age or infirmity from maintaining himself, or a widow or a separated or divorced mother or mother-in-law.

17.4.2 Waivers of dividends
(IHTA 1984, s 15)

A waiver of a dividend is not regarded as a transfer of value provided certain conditions are satisfied:

(1) The dividend must be waived by deed.

(2)   The deed must not be executed more than 12 months before the right to the dividend has accrued.
(3)   The deed waiving the dividend must be executed before any legal entitlement to the dividend arises.

The position is slightly different for interim and final dividends as the point in time at which entitlement may arise can be different.

Interim dividends

A shareholder has no enforceable right to payment prior to the date on which a board resolution has declared that a dividend shall be payable. Therefore, a deed waiving a dividend should be executed before any board resolution is passed.

Final dividends

A company might declare a dividend without stipulating any date for payment. In such circumstances, the declaration of the dividend creates an immediate debt and it is therefore too late to execute a waiver.

In other cases where a final dividend is declared as being payable at a later date, a shareholder *may* waive his entitlement provided that he does so before the due date for payment.

In practice, a final dividend will require the shareholders' approval and an individual shareholder may therefore waive a dividend provided that the deed is executed before the company's annual general meeting.

17.4.3   Waivers of remuneration
(IHTA 1984, s 14)

There is a specific provision whereby a waiver of remuneration does not constitute a transfer of value. The terms of this exemption are based upon the income tax treatment. In practice, the Inland Revenue accept that remuneration is not subject to income tax under Schedule E if it is waived and the Schedule E assessment has not become final and conclusive, and:

(1)   the remuneration is formally waived (usually by deed), or, if it has already been paid, it is repaid to the employer, and
(2)   the employer's assessable profits are adjusted accordingly.

17.4.4   Interest-free loans
(IHTA 1984, s 29)

The IHT legislation specifically provides that an interest-free loan is not to be treated as a transfer of value provided that the loan is *repayable upon demand.*

This exemption would not cover a situation where a loan was made for a specific period, with the lender having no legal right to call for repayment before that time. The grant of such a loan could be a transfer of value, with the Revenue assessing the transfer as the difference between the amount of the loan and the present market value of the loan if it were to be assigned.

17.4.5   Disclaimer of legacies
(IHTA 1984 s 142)

If a person becomes entitled to property under a Will or an intestacy or under a trust (for example, on the death of a life tenant), he may disclaim his entitlement. Such a disclaimer is normally effective for IHT purposes and is not treated as a transfer of value provided that:

(1)   no payment or other consideration is given for the disclaimer, and
(2)   the person has not already accepted his entitlement, either expressly or by implication.

17.4.6   Deeds of variation
(IHTA 1984, s 142)

A deed of variation may be entered into where a person has died leaving property to a beneficiary, the effect being to redirect property. Where the necessary conditions are fulfilled, the revised disposition is treated as having taken place on the deceased person's death. Once again, a person who gives up an entitlement is not treated as making a transfer of value.

The following conditions need to be satisfied:

(1)   The deed of variation must be executed within two years of a death and an election must be filed within six months of the deed being executed.
(2)   The deed must be in writing and must specifically refer to the provisions of the Will etc which are to be varied.
(3)   It must be signed by the person who would otherwise have benefited, and anyone else who might have benefited.
(4)   Only one deed of variation in respect of a particular piece of property can be effective for IHT purposes.
(5)   No payment or other consideration may pass between beneficiaries to induce them to enter into the deed of variation (except that a variation is permitted which consists of an exchange of inheritances and a cash adjustment).

17.5   Exempt transfers

Even if a transfer takes place, it will not attract IHT if it is an exempt transfer.

The full list of exempt transfers is as follows:

(1)   Gifts to spouse
(2)   Normal expenditure out of income
(3)   £250 small gifts exemption
(4)   Annual £3,000 exemption
(5)   Exemption for marriage gifts
(6)   Gifts to charities
(7)   Gifts for national purposes
(8)   Gifts for public benefit
(9)   Gifts to political parties
(10) Certain transfers to employee trusts.

17.5.1   Gifts to spouse
(IHTA 1984, s 18)

There is normally an unlimited exemption for transfers between husband and wife. For this purpose, a couple are regarded as husband and wife until a decree absolute has been obtained. The exemption covers outright gifts, legacies and a transfer of property to a trust under which the spouse has an interest in possession. (The transfer may either be a lifetime transfer or a transfer which takes place on death.)

The exemption is restricted in the case where a UK-domiciled spouse makes transfers to a foreign domiciled spouse. In this situation, the exemption is limited to £55,000. However, the deemed domicile rule which treats individuals as domiciled where they have been resident in the United Kingdom for 17 out of 20 years applies for *all* purposes of the inheritance tax legislation except where expressly excluded. Consequently, a gift by a UK-domiciled individual to a spouse who has a foreign domicile but who is treated as UK domiciled for inheritance tax purposes under the 17 year rule, qualifies for the unlimited exemption.

17.5.2   Normal expenditure out of income
(IHTA 1984, s 21)

A lifetime gift is exempt if it is shown that the gift was made as part of the normal expenditure of the donor and comes out of income. The legislation requires that the gift should be normal ie the donor had a habit of making such gifts. The legislation also requires that by taking one year with another, the pattern of such gifts must have left the donor with sufficient income to maintain his normal standard of living.

Gifts which take the form of payments under deed of covenant or the payment of premiums on life assurance policies written in trust frequently qualify as exempt because of this rule.

17.5.3 £250 small gifts exemption
(IHTA 1984, s 20)

Any number of individual gifts of up to £250 in any one tax year are exempt. However, where gifts to an individual exceed £250, the exemption is lost completely.

17.5.4 Annual £3,000 exemption
(IHTA 1984, s 19)

This exemption is available to cover part of a larger gift. The exemption is £3,000 for each tax year. Furthermore, both husband and wife have separate annual exemptions.

If the full £3,000 is not used in a given year, the balance can be carried forward for one year only and is then allowable only if the exemption for the second year is fully utilised.

17.5.5 Example—Annual £3,000 exemption

Situation 1

Gifts made in year one		£1,000
Balance of exemption carried to year two		£2,000
Gifts made in year two		£4,000
Annual exemption for year two	£3,000	
Part of unused exemption for year one	£1,000	£4,000
Chargeable gifts		Nil

The balance of exemption from year one of £1,000 may not be carried forward to year three.

Situation 2

Year one as in situation 1—unused exemption		£2,000
Exemption for year two	£3,000	
Gifts in year two	£2,000	
Balance of year two exemption to be carried forward to year three	£1,000	

The balance of the year one exemption of £2,000 may not be carried forward to year three.

17.5.6   Gifts in consideration of marriage
(IHTA 1984, s 22)

Gifts made to the bride or groom in consideration of their marriage are exempt up to the following amounts:

Gifts made by	Maximum exemption
Each parent	£5,000
Grandparents	£2,500
Bride or groom	£2,500
Any other person	£1,000

Parents may make gifts to either party to the marriage—their exemption is not restricted to gifts made to their own child. This means that, for example, in relation to the groom each of the bride's parents may give up to £5,000.

The gifts should be made so that they are conditional upon the marriage taking place.

17.5.7   Gifts to charities
(IHTA 1984, s 23)

Gifts to charities which are established in the United Kingdom are exempt regardless of the amount. A charity may be established or registered here even though it carries out its work overseas and the exemption covers gifts to such charities. However, donations made to a foreign charity which is established abroad do not normally qualify.

17.5.8   Gifts for national purposes
(IHTA 1984, s 25)

Gifts to certain national bodies are totally exempt. These bodies include colleges and universities, the National Trust, the National Gallery, the

British Museum and other galleries and museums run by local authorities or universities.

17.5.9   Gifts for public benefit
(IHTA 1984, s 26)

It is necessary to clear the position in advance with HM Treasury if this exemption is to be available. It covers gifts of eligible property such as historic buildings, land of outstanding scenic, historic or scientific interest, works of art and collections of national, scientific, historic or artistic interest.

17.5.10   Gifts to political parties
(IHTA 1984, s 24)

Gifts to 'qualifying political parties' are exempt only if certain conditions are satisfied. A political party qualifies if it had at least two members of parliament returned at the last general election, or if it had at least one member and more than 150,000 votes were cast for its candidates.

17.5.11   Certain transfers to employee trusts
(IHTA 1984, s 28)

Transfers by an individual to an employee trust of shares in a company can be exempt provided the following conditions are satisfied:

(1)   The beneficiaries of the trust include all or most of the persons employed by or holding office with the company.
(2)   Within one year of the transfer:
    (a)   the trustees must hold more than 50 per cent of the ordinary share capital of the company and have voting control on all questions which affect the company as a whole; and
    (b)   the trustees' control is not fettered by some other provision or agreement between the shareholders.
(3)   the trust deed must not permit any of the trust property to be applied at any time for the benefit of:
    (a)   a participator in the company (ie a person who holds a five per cent or greater interest);
    (b)   any person who has been a participator at any time during the ten years prior to the transfer;
    (c)   any person connected with a participator or former participator.

A further restriction may apply where a company makes a transfer to an employee trust.

17.6   Potentially exempt transfers
(IHTA 1984, s 3A)

17.6.1   Definition of a potentially exempt transfer

Irrevocable gifts made during an individual's lifetime may, provided certain conditions are satisfied, be 'potentially exempt transfers' (PETs).

These gifts become actually exempt only if the donor survives seven years. If the individual dies during that period, the potentially exempt transfer becomes a chargeable transfer. The tax payable depends upon the rates of inheritance tax in force at the date of death. The donee is liable to pay the tax.

The main conditions that need to be satisfied for a gift to be a PET are that:

(1)   the gift is made to an individual; or
(2)   the gift is made to a trust for the disabled (see 18.7 below); or
(3)   the gift is made to an accumulation and maintenance trust (see 18.6).

A gift which is subject to a reservation of benefit (see 17.7) cannot be a PET. Furthermore, a gift to a discretionary trust is a chargeable transfer.

17.6.2   Taper relief
(IHTA 1984, s 7)

Where an individual makes a potentially exempt transfer and dies within the seven year period, taper relief may reduce the amount of tax payable.

The tax payable on the transfer which has become a chargeable transfer is subject to the following reduction:

Years between gift and death	*Percentage of the full charge*
Three to four	80
Four to five	60
Five to six	40
Six to seven	20

17.7   Reservation of benefit
(FA 186, s 102 & Sched 20)

17.7.1   Introduction

Property which has been gifted may still be deemed to form part of a deceased person's estate unless:

(1)   possession and enjoyment of the property was *bona fide* assumed by the donee; and

(2)   the property was enjoyed virtually to the entire exclusion of the donor and of any benefit to him by contract or otherwise.

The reference to the property being enjoyed virtually to the entire exclusion of the donor means that for all practical purposes this is an 'all or nothing' test. The Revenue's view is that the exception is intended to cover trivial benefits such as might arise where, for example, the donor of a picture enjoyed the chance to view it when making occasional visits to the donee's home.

Is there reservation of benefit?

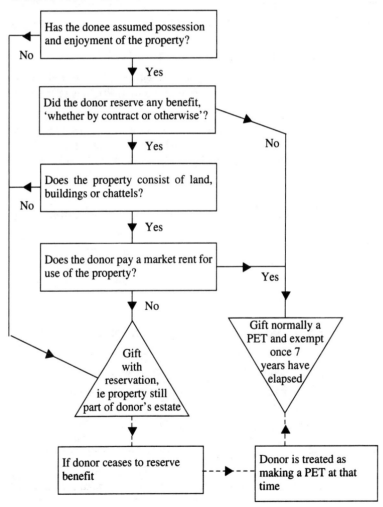

The Act refers to a benefit reserved 'by contract or otherwise' and this is meant to refer to arrangements which are not legally binding but which amount to an honourable understanding. This might arise where a person gifts away a house but remains in occupation. A reservation of benefit would arise even if there is no legal tenancy and the donee could, in law, require the donor to vacate the property at any time.

Starting date

The reservation of benefit rules apply to gifts made on or after 18 March 1986. Where a gift or transfer was made before that date, and the donor has reserved a benefit, the gift is effective for IHT purposes and the capital does not form part of that person's estate.

17.7.2   Two specific exemptions

The legislation specifically states that occupation of property or use of chattels does not count as a benefit provided a market rent is paid by the donor.

The legislation also provides that a benefit enjoyed by a donor occupying property can be ignored in a case where the donor's financial circumstances have changed drastically for the worse after the gift has been made.

17.7.3   Position where reservation of benefit ceases

Where a person makes a gift and initially reserves a benefit, but then relinquishes that reservation, the donor is treated as making a potentially exempt transfer at the time that he gives up the reserved benefit. The amount of the PET is governed by the market value of the property at that time.

17.7.4   Example—Giving up reservation of benefit

A gives property worth £150,000 in July 1989 but reserves a benefit.

The benefit is relinquished in July 1994 when the property is worth £220,000. A dies in October 1996.

If no benefit had been reserved, the gift would have been completely exempt by August 1996 (ie seven years after the gift) but because a benefit was retained until July 1994, the seven year period starts only from that date.

The full £220,000 (ie the value at July 1994 when the reservation of benefit came to an end) would form part of A's estate for inheritance tax purposes.

17.7.5   Settlements and trusts

The position is less clear cut where a person has sought to reserve the *possibility* of a benefit, for example where an individual has created a settlement and he is a potential beneficiary. It is the opinion of the Revenue that a benefit is reserved where the settlor creates a discretionary trust and is a member of a class of potential beneficiaries. This would also apply where the settlor may be added to a class of potential beneficiaries.

In contrast to this, the Revenue has confirmed that no reservation of benefit arises where a person creates a settlement and is a contingent or default beneficiary. This might apply, for example, where property is put into trust for the settlor's children but the property would revert to the settlor in the event of the children dying or becoming bankrupt.

The legislation does not require that the donor's spouse should be excluded from benefit and where a discretionary settlement is created it would be possible to include the donor's spouse, any future spouse or widow/widower as a potential beneficiary. However, if property were to be distributed to the donor's spouse from the trust and that property were then to be applied for the benefit of the *settlor,* the Revenue might well take the view that, looked at as a whole, there had been a reservation of benefit.

The Revenue has confirmed that a settlor may be a trustee of a settlement created by him without this constituting a reservation of benefit. Also, where the settled property includes shares in a family company, the settlor/trustee may also be a director of the company and may be permitted under the trust deed to retain his remuneration provided the remuneration is reasonable in relation to the services rendered.

17.8   Business property
(IHTA 1984, ss 103–114)

17.8.1   Basic requirements

A special deduction is given against the value of business property where the following conditions are satisfied:

(1)   The property must have been owned during the previous two years or it must have been inherited from a spouse and, when the spouse's period of ownership is taken into account, the combined period of ownership exceeds two years.

(2)   Property must not be subject to a binding contract for sale.

17.8.2   Rates of business property relief

Unincorporated businesses

The sole proprietor's interest in his business qualifies for a 100 per cent deduction. A partner's interest in his firm also qualifies for 100 per cent relief.

A 50 per cent deduction is available in respect of an asset owned by a partner but used by his firm.

Shares and debentures

Business relief is available on shares only where the company concerned is a trading company or the holding company of a trading group.

The 100 per cent relief is available on shares and debentures in a company where the transferor had voting control before the transfer. Relief is available in these circumstances even where the company concerned is a quoted company.

The 100 per cent relief is also available for a transfer of shares in an unquoted trading company provided that the transferor had control of more than 25 per cent of the voting rights before the transfer. A 50 per cent deduction is given for other shareholdings in unquoted trading companies.

Shares dealt in on the unlisted securities market (USM) are not regarded as quoted shares. A similar treatment applies to US shares which are dealt in on the Nasdaq Exchange.

Where a controlling shareholder transfers an asset which is used by his company, or where such an asset passes on his death, 50 per cent relief is available.

17.8.3   Businesses which do not qualify

Business relief is not normally available where the business carried on consists wholly or mainly of dealing in securities, stocks or shares, land or buildings or in making investments.

Where a transfer involves shares, business relief may be restricted if the company owns investments. The legislation refers to such investments as 'excepted assets', which are defined as assets which are neither:

(1)   assets used wholly or mainly for the purposes of the business, nor
(2)   assets required for the future use of the business.

Where a company has subsidiaries, it is necessary to look at the group situation (ie shares in subsidiaries may have to be treated as excepted assets if the subsidiaries are investment companies).

17.9   Agricultural property and woodlands
(IHTA 1984, ss 115–124B)

Agricultural relief is available on the agricultural value of farmland in the United Kingdom, Channel Islands or Isle of Man.

17.9.1   Land occupied by the transferor

Relief is available where the individual has occupied the farmland for the two years prior to the date of the transfer. Where a farm has been sold and another farm has been acquired, the replacement farm normally qualifies for agricultural property relief provided that the owner has occupied the two farms for a combined period of at least two years in the last five years. Agricultural property relief is also available in respect of land owned by an individual but occupied by a firm of which he is a partner or by a company of which he is the controlling shareholder for the two years preceding the date of the transfer.

17.9.2   Relief for other land

Relief is also available on land which is not occupied by the owner provided that he has (or had) the legal right to regain vacant possession within a period not exceeding twelve months. In order to qualify under this head, the individual must normally have owned the land for at least seven years.

17.9.3   Relief for tenanted farmland

A 50 per cent deduction is available for farmland which is let and where the owner cannot obtain vacant possession within twelve months. This would generally be the case where the land is let under an agricultural tenancy. Once again, the land must normally have been owned for seven years.

17.9.4   Woodlands
(IHTA 1984, ss 125–130)

The tax treatment of woodlands is largely beneficial.

(1)   Business relief is normally available after two years of ownership.
(2)   The charge can be postponed until the timber is eventually sold provided that it has been owned for five years.
(3)   If the charge on standing timber is postponed and the new owner dies before it is sold, the potential charge is eliminated.

Five year ownership requirement

The person who has died must have been the owner of the land for five years or he must have acquired it by way of inheritance or gift. A person who is a life tenant of a trust which owns the land is treated as meeting these requirements.

Election for postponement

A formal election needs to be submitted within two years of a person's death. The election has the consequence that IHT is not charged on the *standing timber* (the land itself is still chargeable). When the timber is sold (or otherwise disposed of) the net disposal proceeds on market value must be brought into charge. The rate of tax is governed by the rate which applied on the rest of the person's estate ie not necessarily the rate at the date of death. Business relief is available if it would have been due had deferment not been claimed.

The net disposal proceeds are the proceeds of the sale of timber less the costs of replanting unless they are allowed for income tax purposes (they will not normally be allowable).

17.10   Computation of tax payable on lifetime transfers

In practice, IHT is likely only to be paid during a person's lifetime in respect of chargeable transfers made by him to a discretionary trust.

The tax payable is calculated as follows:

Initial calculation

Chargeable transfers made during the preceding seven years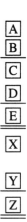

Add   Amount of chargeable transfer

Deduct   Nil rate band

IHT thereon at 20 per cent

Deduct   IHT on a notional transfer of ⌊A⌋ minus ⌊D⌋ as if it took place at the same time.

IHT payable in respect of the chargeable transfer

Position if the donor dies within three years

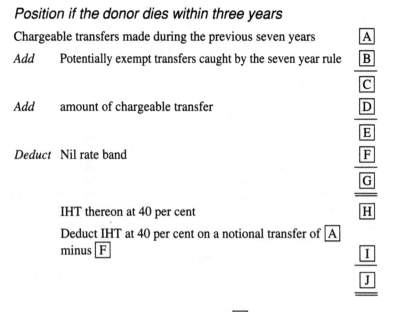

Chargeable transfers made during the previous seven years [A]

Add   Potentially exempt transfers caught by the seven year rule [B]

[C]

Add   amount of chargeable transfer [D]

[E]

Deduct Nil rate band [F]

[G]

IHT thereon at 40 per cent [H]

Deduct IHT at 40 per cent on a notional transfer of [A] minus [F]

[I]

[J]

The donee is liable to pay additional IHT of [J] minus the amount already paid under [Z] above.

Position if the donor dies during years four to seven

The above will be liable for additional IHT computed as [J] above, but subject to the IHT on PETs caught by the seven year rule being reduced by taper relief, see 17.6.2.

17.11   Tax payable on death

17.11.1   Normal basis of computation

The charge on death is normally computed as shown in the flowchart overleaf:

The IHT will be the tax on the figure in box 6 minus the tax payable on a normal transfer equal to the amount in box 4 as if the notional transfer took place immediately prior to the death. Some taper relief may be due on the PETs caught by the seven year rule, see 17.6.2.

However, there are a number of special reliefs which may be available.

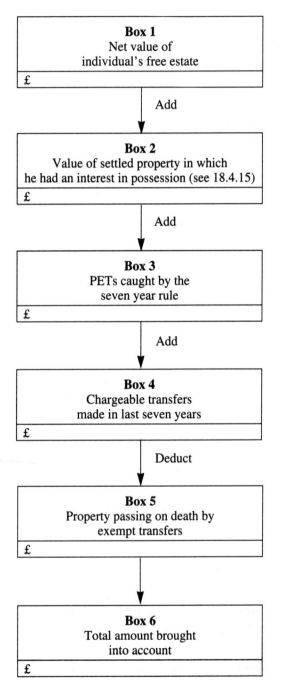

17.11.2 Death on active service
(IHTA 1984, s 154)

Ever since the Second World War the death duty legislation has contained an exemption for a person who dies from wounds suffered whilst on active service.

The exemption applies to the estates of those killed in the Falklands conflict, the Gulf War and to estates of members of the RUC killed by terrorists in Northern Ireland.

The exemption may well apply more often than people think. Death does not have to be immediate, nor need the wound be the only cause of death. The High Court held in 1978 that the exemption was owed to the estate of the fourth Duke of Westminster because serious wounds that he had suffered in 1944 contributed to his death in 1967.

17.11.3 Sales of quoted securities at a loss
(IHTA 1984, ss 178–189 as extended by FA 1993, s 198)

Relief is given where quoted securities or unit trusts are sold at a loss within 12 months of death. Where shares are suspended, FA 1993, s 198 permits similar relief to be claimed by reference to the value of the shares when they return from suspension. It is not possible to pick and choose — the relief is confined to the amount of any overall loss. Executors must, in effect, elect that the total proceeds of any sales should be substituted for the value at date of death.

17.11.4 Example—Sale of quoted securities at a loss

A died on 1 October 1993. His estate included a portfolio worth £70,000. The executors had to sell some of the securities and realised an overall loss of £25,000. The estate can be reduced by this amount so that, in effect, only £45,000 is taken into account.

The overall loss of £25,000 may have been made up of a gain of £5,000 and losses of £30,000. Relief is, however, limited to the net figure.

17.11.5 Relief restricted where executors purchase quoted securities

Furthermore, the relief is restricted where the executors repurchase quoted securities within two months of the last sale.

17.11.6   Example—Restriction of relief on quoted securities

A's executors sold the securities on 14 November 1993. On 10 January 1994, they reinvested £10,000 in new securities. The £25,000 loss cannot be claimed in full, it has to be reduced by

$$\frac{10,000}{45,000} \times £25,000, \text{ ie } £5,556$$

17.11.7   Sales of land at a loss
(IHTA 1984, ss 190–198 as amended by FA 1993, s 199)

Relief is due where land and buildings are sold at a loss within four years of death, provided the loss is at least £1,000 or five per cent of probate value (whichever is less). The net proceeds are substituted for the value at the date of death and the IHT is re-computed. However, this relief applies only where the property is sold to an arm's-length purchaser rather than to a connected person.

The four year period was three years in relation to deaths before 16 March 1990.

17.11.8   Debts which may be disallowed
(FA 1986, s 103)

The Finance Act 1986 introduced a general rule that debts are not deductible where the deceased has made a capital transfer to the person who subsequently made a loan back to the deceased. This rule applies only to loans made after 18 March 1986 but there is no such time limit on the capital transfers. A debt may be disallowed because the deceased had made a capital transfer to the lender even though that capital transfer took place before 18 March 1986. It is also of no help that the loan was made on normal commercial terms and a market rate of interest was payable.

17.11.9   Legitim: special rules for Scotland
(IHTA 1984, s 147)

Where the deceased was Scottish, the 'legitim' rules need to be considered. Scottish Law provides that a person must leave a set part of his estate to his children: their entitlement is called 'legitim'. If a person makes a Will which does not take account of this, the children can have it set aside. In practice children often decide to renounce their right to legitim, especially where a person's Will bequeaths all his property to his widow. The legislation provides that children who renounce their entitlement are not treated as making a chargeable transfer and the property is treated as passing to the widow in accordance with the Will.

Practical problems arise where children who are minors are involved since a child under the age of 18 does not have the legal capacity to renounce his entitlement. In such cases the executors have a difficult choice. They can either account for IHT on the basis that the child takes his entitlement or on the assumption that the child will renounce his rights when he reaches 18.

Position where executors assume legitim rights are taken

Inheritance tax will have to be paid to the extent that the property which passes to the children exceeds the nil rate band. When each child attains 18, he may elect to renounce his rights so that the widow benefits. The spouse exemption will then mean that no tax should have been paid. The Revenue will then repay the IHT paid and pay interest.

Position where executors assume that legitim will be renounced

No IHT will be paid in the first instance. However, if it turns out that one of the children decides not to renounce his entitlement, IHT on the death is re-computed and the tax payable attracts interest from the date that it should have been paid.

17.11.10 Quick succession relief
(IHTA 1984, s 141)

Suppose a person has recently inherited property from someone else. If he were to die and the full rate of IHT applied, the same property would have been subject to IHT twice within a relatively short period of time.

Quick succession relief is intended to alleviate this. The relief works by giving credit for a proportion of the tax charged on the first occasion against the tax payable on the second death. The proportion is set out below:

Both deaths occur	Proportion
within one year	100%
within two years	80%
within three years	60%
within four years	40%
within five years	20%

17.11.11   Example—Quick succession relief

A person inherited property worth £150,000 in June 1990. Inheritance tax was paid on that estate at an average rate of 25 per cent, so the grossed up amount was £200,000 (£150,000 x $\frac{100}{75}$) and the tax suffered was £50,000.

The recipient dies in August 1993. The maximum amount on which quick succession relief can be claimed is:

$$\frac{150,000}{200,000} \times £50,000 \text{ ie } £37,500$$

This has to be reduced to 40 per cent of £37,500 as three complete years have elapsed.

The relief is *not* affected by the fact that property has been sold or given away before the second death takes place.

17.11.12   Treatment of gifts which are caught by the seven year rule
(IHTA 1984, s 113A)

Tax on a PET which becomes a chargeable transfer because of the transferor's death is payable by the recipient of the gift.

Business relief is available on a PET that becomes a chargeable transfer only if the conditions in 17.8 are satisfied both at the time of the gift and at the time of death.

17.11.13   Examples—Business relief on PETs

(1)   A owns all the shares in a family company. He gives his son a 24 per cent shareholding. Three years later, the company is sold and the son receives cash for his shares. One year after that A dies.
Business relief will not normally be available as the necessary conditions are not satisfied by the donee at the time of A's death. If the son had reinvested the proceeds in another private company, business relief might have been available after all.

(2)   In this case the basic position is as in (1) ie A has made a gift to his son of a 24 per cent shareholding. However, this time, the son retains his shares, but by the time that A dies, the shares are quoted. No relief is due as the son does not control the company and his shares are quoted shares.

(3)   The basic position is as in (1) but, in this case, the son retains the shares and they are still unquoted at the time of A's death. The shares attract the 100 per cent relief and this is not lost even if the son disposes of the shares shortly after A's death.

17.11.14   Replacement property

Where a donee has disposed of business property but acquires replacement property, the PET may yet attract business relief. Until 30 November 1993, the rule was that the replacement property had to be acquired within one year.

Section 247 FA 1994 has now extended this period to three years.

17.12   Life assurance and pension policies

17.12.1   Life assurance

Life assurance is one of the best ways of providing for inheritance tax, but the tax treatment of policies needs to be watched carefully. The following is only a summary of a complex area.

17.12.2   Death of policyholder

A life assurance policy beneficially owned by the deceased is property that is subject to IHT in the same way as any other property owned by him.

17.12.3   Gifts of policies

Gifts of policies may generally be made in two ways:

(1)   Writing the policy in trust or making a subsequent declaration of trust.
(2)   Assignment of the policy.

In either case subsequent premiums may be paid: (a) by the donor direct; (b) by the beneficiary out of cash gifts from the donor; (c) by the beneficiary out of his resources; (d) by a combination of the above.

In general, if the gift is to an individual, an accumulation and maintenance trust, a trust for the disabled or (with effect from 17 March 1987) a trust in which there is an interest in possession, it will constitute a potentially exempt transfer and will only be taxable if the donor dies within seven years of making the gift. Gifts to other trusts such as discretionary trusts may attract lifetime IHT.

If any of the usual inheritance tax exemptions apply (see 17.5) neither the gift of the policy nor any gifts of premiums that have been made will be taxable, eg:

(1)   The gift of the premium or policy falls within the annual

exemption—currently £3,000 (note that if the policy is a qualifying policy and premiums are payable net of life assurance relief then it is the net premium that constitutes the gift; if the premiums are paid gross, it is the gross premium that constitutes the gift).

(2)   The premiums come within the donor's normal expenditure out of income exemption (note that this applies to payment of premiums not to the gift of an existing policy).

(3)   The gifts fall within the marriage settlement exemption.

(4)   The gifts fall within the small gifts exemption—outright gifts of not more than £250 per donee (for example a premium on a policy written in trust for the absolute benefit of a child).

(5)   Policies written by husband or wife in trust for the other.

If none of the exemptions applies, IHT may be payable in respect of the gift of the policy or the payment of subsequent premiums (unless they fall within the first £150,000 of non-exempt gifts in respect of which a nil rate is payable).

If IHT is payable, the chargeable transfers are the premiums paid by the donor; or, if a gift of an existing policy is made by assignment or declaration of trust, the chargeable transfer is generally the greater of the total gross premiums paid or the market value of the policy (usually the surrender value).

If cash gifts have been made to enable the premiums to be paid by the beneficiary, the amount of the cash gifts will usually be PETs. The proceeds of the policy on death, maturity or surrender will not be subject to IHT in the hands of the recipient of the assignment or a beneficiary having an interest in possession in the trusts.

17.12.4   Life of another policies

On the death of the life assured the proceeds are totally free of IHT. Clearly they do not form part of the life assured's estate, as the policy is not owned by him. The surrender value will, however, be potentially chargeable in the policyholder's estate if he dies before the life assured.

If the policyholder is enabled to pay the premiums by virtue of cash gifts from the donor, the cash gifts will be taxable for the donor, unless the exemptions mentioned above apply, but the proceeds will be free of IHT in the policyholder's hands.

17.12.5   Use of policies

Life assurance policies can be used in two main ways in IHT planning:

(1)   as a vehicle for making gifts to beneficiaries; and

(2)   to create a fund for the eventual payment of the tax.

Thus they may help both to minimise the amount of tax payable and offer a means of paying any unavoidable liability whenever it arises.

17.12.6   Inheritance tax and pension plans

Although the legislation does not permit a policyholder to alienate his right to a retirement pension, it is possible to assign any death benefits provided under retirement annuity or personal pension plans, whether provided as a sum assured or as a return of the retirement fund. The IHT rules are broadly similar to those applicable to life policy assignments except that:

(1)   discretionary trusts of these assignable benefits will not be subject to the usual IHT charging regime of ten-yearly and exit charges, (see 18.5.12) provided the benefits are distributed within two years of the individual's death;

(2)   the right to a pension is not treated as giving rise to an interest in possession in the pension fund;

(3)   the gift of a 'return of fund' death benefit will usually be regarded as having no value, provided the individual is in good health. Similarly, subsequent contributions to the pension will be treated as being attributable to the provision of the pension benefits and not the death benefit, providing the individual is in good health at the time the contribution is made.

Occupational schemes are usually written under discretionary trusts and also achieve the same inheritance tax exemptions on payment of contributions and distribution of benefits.

18   The taxation of trusts

by MARK FRANCIS

This chapter covers the taxation of trusts under the following headings:

(1)   When are trustees liable to pay UK income tax?
(2)   When are trustees liable for UK capital gains tax?
(3)   Bare trusts.
(4)   Fixed interest trusts.
(5)   Discretionary trusts.
(6)   Accumulation and maintenance trusts.
(7)   Trusts for the disabled.
(8)   Protective trusts.
(9)   Charitable trusts.
(10) Executors and personal representatives.

18.1   When are trustees liable to pay UK income tax?
(FA 1989, s 110)

A liability to pay UK income tax arises for all trusts which have at least one UK resident trustee (even though there may be a majority of non-resident trustees) unless the trust was created by a person of foreign domicile, in which case the UK trustee is liable only in respect of UK income.

In the main, trustees are liable for tax at the basic rate but trustees of discretionary and accumulation trusts are subject to tax at 35 per cent.

A non-resident trust will be subject to tax on UK income such as interest taxed at source and dividends. Where the non-resident trust receives untaxed interest, there is in theory a tax liability, but in practice the trustees may escape tax because of extra-statutory concession B13 (see 21.4.2).

Trustees are not entitled to personal allowances (see Chapter 7).

18.2 When are trustees liable for UK capital gains tax?
(TCGA 1992, ss 2 and 69)

Trustees are subject to capital gains tax only if the trust is resident in the United Kingdom. A trust is regarded as resident unless:

(1) the majority of the trustees are not resident in the United Kingdom; *and*

(2) the ordinary administration of the trust is carried on outside the United Kingdom.

This rule is therefore slightly different from that used for income tax purposes.

There is an exception to the above general rule in the case of property settled by a person of foreign domicile who was neither resident nor ordinarily resident in the United Kingdom at the time that the trust was created. Provided the UK trustees are professional trustees whose business consists of or includes the management of trusts, the facts that the majority of the trustees are UK resident and the management of the trust is carried on within the United Kingdom do not make the trust resident in the United Kingdom.

UK resident trusts

In general trustees are responsible for reporting gains and paying tax, but this rule does not apply where either the settlor or his spouse can receive benefit.

Capital gains made by trustees of such a trust are generally taxed as if they were personal gains of the settlor (see 18.10).

18.2.1 Annual exemption
(TCGA 1992, Sched 1)

For a number of years the annual capital gains tax exemption available to trustees has been half the individual exemption, eg for 1994–95 £2,900 (half of £5,800).

Where a settlor has created a number of settlements since 6 June 1978, the annual exemption is shared equally. The minimum annual exemption for each settlement is £580 ie 1/10th of the annual individual exemption. An unused part of the exemption for one settlement cannot be utilised by another settlement.

Consequently, if a person created three trusts in 1975 and four trusts in 1989, the exemption for the 1975 trusts would be £2,900 each, and the four trusts created after 6 June 1978 would each have an exemption of £725. If all seven trusts had been created after 6 June 1978, each would have an annual exemption of £580.

18.3   Bare trusts

A bare trust is one where trustees hold property on behalf of someone who is absolutely entitled to that property, or would be absolutely entitled if he were not a minor.

Income and capital gains received by trustees of a bare trust belong to the person who is absolutely entitled to the property concerned. The trustees have no liability to tax.

18.4   Fixed interest trusts

A fixed interest trust is one where a beneficiary is entitled to receive income as it arises, either during his lifetime or for a specific period. A simple type of fixed interest trust would be a trust under which the beneficiary is entitled to receive all the income during his lifetime with the trust coming to an end on his death, perhaps with the capital then passing to the beneficiary's children. A beneficiary who is entitled to receive trust income in this way during his lifetime is called a 'life tenant'.

There may also be a situation where a life tenant is entitled to receive a proportion of the trust income, say 50 per cent, with the other 50 per cent being held upon different types of trust. It is also possible to have an entitlement to income (an 'interest in possession') for a specific period, so that a trust under which someone had a right to all of the income for a fixed period of ten years would be a fixed interest trust until the end of that period.

18.4.1   Income tax

Where property is held upon fixed interest trusts, income tax is charged on the trustees at the basic rate. There is no deduction for personal allowances (only individuals are entitled to personal allowances), but if a trust owns investment properties on which an entitlement to capital allowances arises, such capital allowances may be set against the trustees' income in the same way as for individuals. Similarly, if the trustees carry on a trade, any losses may be relieved against other income. Subject to this, the trustees will either suffer basic rate tax at source or be assessed to basic rate tax on all income arising to them, with the assessments being made under the different Schedules.

18.4.2 Ascertaining the beneficiary's income

It will not generally be possible for the trustees to pay over to a beneficiary the full amount of the income left to him after tax. Inevitably, there will be some expenses such as bank charges, interest, professional fees and so on, which are properly charged to income, and there may also be the trustees' own fees. Such expenses are not deducted in arriving at the *trustees'* taxable income, but they need to be taken into account in determining the amount of the *beneficiary's* income.

In broad terms, the proper procedure is to ascertain the trustees' taxable income for a year (some income may, of course, be charged to tax under the preceding year basis—for example, untaxed interest). The tax paid by the trustees for the year concerned should then be deducted, and a further deduction should be made for expenses which are properly charged against income. The net amount must then be 'grossed up' and this is the amount that the beneficiary will need to declare on his tax return.

18.4.3 Example—Tax treatment of income from a fixed interest trust

The trustees of a fixed interest trust have a taxable income of £20,000. They pay tax of £5,000. There are expenses of £1,500 which are properly chargeable against the income. The balance belongs to the life tenant.

The life tenant's gross income will be ascertained as follows:

	£
Trustees' taxable income	20,000
Less basic rate tax	5,000
	15,000
Less expenses	1,500
	13,500
£13,500 grossed up at basic rate =	£18,000

This income forms part of the life tenant's income for the year *whether or not it is actually paid out to him*. If the life tenant is subject to higher rate tax, he must pay the difference between the 40 per cent rate and basic rate tax.

18.4.4 UK dividend income
(FA 1993 s 79 & Sched 6)

For 1993–94 onwards, it is necessary to distinguish UK dividend income included in the amount due to the life tenant, as this part of his trust income carries a tax credit of only 20 per cent. Trustees' expenses are deemed to be set first against UK dividend income, so as to minimise the restriction of the tax deemed to be withheld from the trust income.

18.4.5   Tax returns

Where the trust is wholly fixed interest the tax returns which are usually completed are Forms 1 and R59. A tax deduction certificate (Form R185E) should also be completed by the trustees or their professional advisers showing the appropriate gross, tax and net figures in respect of the beneficiary's income. For 1993–94 and subsequent years, the amount represented by UK dividends will need to be shown separately on the certificate.

18.4.6   Income mandated to a beneficiary

Trustees sometimes take the view that it is simpler to mandate dividends and other income to the beneficiary so that such income does not pass through the trustees' hands. This does not alter the fact that the trustees are still the legal owners of the assets which produce the income.

Although this income can be entered directly in the beneficiary's personal tax return, care should be taken to ensure that it is entered in the correct section for *trust* income so as to avoid any confusion with the beneficiary's *personal* income.

Where this happens, the Revenue will assess the beneficiary rather than the trustees. However, if the trustees incur expenses, these may not be deducted as in 18.4.2 above. This even applies where the beneficiary reimburses the trustees for such expenses later on.

18.4.7   Beneficiary's exempt income

It is sometimes possible for UK-resident trustees to take advantage of a beneficiary's tax exemption to avoid paying tax which the beneficiary would then have to claim back. For example, where a beneficiary is entitled to all the income of the trust and he is resident outside the United Kingdom, the trustees can agree with the Revenue that the income which arises outside the United Kingdom (and any other income which is exempt for a non-resident eg interest from exempt gilts—see 21.4.3) should not be taxed in the trustees' hands.

This treatment is not normally available where a non-resident beneficiary is entitled only to a proportion of the trustees' income.

18.4.8   Taxable income which is not income for trust purposes

Difficulties can arise where the trustees receive something which constitutes income for *tax* purposes, but is not income for *trust* purposes.

For example, if trustees of a fixed interest trust receive a lump sum premium which is taxable income for Schedule A purposes (see 4.4) this is not income which belongs to the life tenant. Similarly, a distribution such as may arise on a company buying back its own shares may be *income* for income tax purposes (see 6.4.7) but is *capital* for trust purposes. In both these situations, the trustees must pay tax on such deemed income, but the amounts must be excluded when calculating the life tenant's income for tax purposes.

Another situation where taxable income, but not trust income, may arise is where trustees have acquired an Enterprise Zone Building (or indeed any type of industrial building) and a balancing charge arises on a disposal. Such a balancing charge will be taxed at basic rate only. Because it is a capital receipt, it will not normally be possible for the trustees to pay it to a life tenant and it will therefore not constitute part of his income for tax purposes.

There are certain situations where the legislation makes special provision. Where trustees dispose of a loan stock cum-interest, the trustees will generally be subject to assessment under the accrued income scheme (see 5.5) in respect of the interest which has arisen on the loan stock during their period of ownership. However, this is not income which the trustees will be able to pay out to a beneficiary since a life tenant will be entitled only to *actual* income, not *deemed* income. In this specific case, the legislation provides that trustees should be taxed at 35 per cent on income assessed under Schedule D Case VI in respect of the accrued income scheme.

A similar rule applies where trustees realise gains on the disposal of shares in an offshore roll-up fund (see 5.9).

18.4.9   Exempt receipts which are income for trust purposes

The converse may happen. For example, a trustee may receive income in the form of a repayment supplement which is exempt (see 19.11). This will still constitute income for trust law purposes and the life tenant will generally be entitled to receive the full amount, but it is not taxable income for him.

The treatment of dividends arising from demergers (see 6.3.10) also gave rise to concern, but a test case involving the ICI demerger has established that such receipts by trustees are capital rather than income from the point of view of trust law so in this particular case the treatment for trust law and taxation will normally be the same.

18.4.10   Capital gains tax

The basic rule is that trustees of fixed interest trusts are subject to tax at 25 per cent on any capital gains. No further CGT liability (or income tax liability) will normally arise on the trustees' distributing cash to a beneficiary after they have realised a capital gain by selling an asset.

18.4.11   Exemption for property occupied by a beneficiary
(TCGA 1992, s 225)

There is an exemption for trustees in respect of a property which is owned by them, but which is occupied by a beneficiary as his main residence (provided he is entitled to do so under the terms of the trust deed). The beneficiary may not also claim exemption for a property owned by him. Where an individual has more than one residence, and it is desired to elect that a property owned by trustees be treated as the individual's main residence, a joint notice needs to be given by the trustees and the individual concerned.

18.4.12   Liability may arise on deemed disposals as well as actual disposals

A capital gain may arise on a deemed disposal such as where the trustees distribute assets to a beneficiary, or where a beneficiary becomes absolutely entitled to capital under the terms of a trust. Hold-over relief is available only if the disposal involves business property (see 15.5).

18.4.13   Transfer of capital losses to a trust beneficiary

Where capital is distributed to a beneficiary, or when he becomes absolutely entitled to the capital, capital losses which are attributable to the property to which he becomes entitled pass across to the beneficiary and are available to cover future capital gains realised by him.

18.4.14   Death of the life tenant
(TCGA 1992, s 73)

There is one type of deemed disposal which does not give rise to a CGT charge. Where an interest in possession ceases on a death, the assets are treated as having been disposed of and reacquired at their value at that date, but there is no chargeable gain for the trustees. This does *not* apply where the trustees hold assets which were subject to a hold-over claim by the settlor at the time that he transferred the assets to the trustees.

18.4.15 Inheritance tax
(IHTA 1984, s 49)

Where a beneficiary has an interest in possession, he is treated for IHT purposes as if he owned the capital of the trust. On death, the value of the trust capital is brought into account as part of the individual's estate and IHT is charged accordingly. However, the trustees are responsible for paying the IHT on the proportion of the tax attributable to the trust property.

18.4.16 Example—IHT liability on a fixed interest trust

A dies owning property in his personal capacity worth £200,000 (this is called his 'free estate') and he is also the life tenant of a trust which has a capital value of £350,000.

The total inheritance tax payable is:

	£
Free estate	200,000
Trust	350,000
	550,000
Less nil rate band	150,000
	400,000
IHT thereon at 40 per cent	160,000

The inheritance tax is payable as follows:

Executors

$$\frac{£200,000}{550,000} \times 160,000 \qquad = £58,182$$

Trustees

$$\frac{£350,000}{550,000} \times 160,000 \qquad = £101,818$$

18.4.17 Exempt pre-13 November 1974 Will Trusts
(IHTA 1984, Sched 6, para 2)

These are trusts created by the Will of a person who died before 13 November 1974 and left property in trust on the following terms:

(1) his surviving spouse was entitled to an interest in possession;
(2) the surviving spouse was not entitled to demand that the capital should be paid out to her.

These trusts are exempt from the normal charge that arises when the surviving spouse's interest in possession comes to an end. The reason for this is that prior to 13 November 1974, estate duty was levied on the death of an individual even if he left property in trust for his spouse. However, the estate duty legislation then provided an exemption on the death of the surviving spouse and this has been carried over to IHT.

Will Trusts which came into being after 12 November 1974 are treated differently because of the exemption which applies for IHT purposes where property passes to a surviving spouse. Property held in a post 12 November 1974 Will Trust is subject to IHT on the death of the life tenant.

18.4.18 No charge where a life tenant becomes absolutely entitled to the trust property
(IHTA 1984, s 53(2))

There are no IHT implications where a life tenant (or any other beneficiary entitled to an interest in possession) becomes absolutely entitled to the trust property. The reason for this is that the beneficiary was already regarded for IHT purposes as if he owned the capital concerned. All that has happened is that the beneficiary's interest has been enlarged and, whilst this may have CGT consequences, it does not give rise to an IHT charge.

18.4.19 Consequences of an interest in possession terminating during a person's lifetime
(IHTA 1984, ss 3A, 23 and 52)

Where a beneficiary's interest in possession comes to an end during his lifetime and he does not personally become entitled to the trust property, he is treated as making a transfer of value. The transfer will normally be either a potentially exempt transfer (PET—see 17.6) or a chargeable transfer, according to what happens as a result of the interest in possession coming to an end.

Potentially exempt transfer

If the effect of the beneficiary's interest coming to an end is that:

(1)   another individual becomes entitled to an interest in possession; or
(2)   another person becomes absolutely entitled to the trust property; or,
(3)   the trust becomes an accumulation and maintenance trust;

the person whose interest in possession has terminated is treated as having made a PET.

Where a person is treated as making a PET, IHT is charged *if and only if* the person dies within the following seven years. If this should happen, the trustees will be liable to pay the IHT unless the settled property passed to a beneficiary through his becoming absolutely entitled on the termination of the interest in possession. In such a situation the person who became absolutely entitled is liable to pay any such IHT.

Exempt transfer

Occasionally, the effect of a person's interest in possession coming to an end is that the spouse becomes entitled to an interest in possession. Where this happens, the person whose interest in possession has come to an end is treated as having made an exempt transfer. This treatment also applies if a trust becomes a charitable trust as a result of a beneficiary's interest in possession coming to an end.

Chargeable transfer

Where a person's interest in possession comes to an end, and the trust thereby becomes a discretionary trust, the person is treated as having made a chargeable transfer. If the person's cumulative chargeable transfers bring him over the nil rate band, IHT is payable right away at the lifetime rate of 20 per cent. If the person should then die within three years, the rate increases to 40 per cent (see 17.10).

18.4.20 How the transfer of value is computed on a lifetime transfer

The legislation contains an anomaly. Where an individual makes a gift in his personal capacity, the transfer of value is deemed to be the amount by which his estate is reduced in value (see 17.3.3). This rule does not apply where a person's interest in possession comes to an end as, in this case, the amount of the transfer of value is taken as the value of the property in which the interest in possession has terminated.

18.4.21 Example—Calculation of value of lifetime transfer

A owns 90 per cent of a company in his personal capacity and is the life tenant of a trust which owns the remaining 10 per cent.

The value of a 100 per cent shareholding in the company is worth £500,000. The value of a 90 per cent shareholding is £450,000. However, a 10 per cent shareholding valued in isolation is worth only £20,000.

If A had made a gift of 10 per cent out of his personal shareholding, his transfer of value would be taken to be:

Value of a 100 per cent shareholding	£500,000
Less value of remaining 90 per cent shareholding (taking his own shares and the trust together)	£450,000
Reduction in value of his estate	£50,000

However, if A surrenders his life interest in the trust so that his interest in possession comes to an end, the value transferred is taken as £20,000.

18.5 Discretionary trusts

In contrast to a fixed interest trust, a discretionary trust is one where the trustees can control the way in which the income is used. In some cases, the trustees have power to accumulate income, in which case it may be retained by them either with a view to its being paid out in later years or as an addition to the trust capital.

In other cases, the trustees will have no legal right to accumulate income, but the trust is regarded as discretionary because no beneficiary has a fixed entitlement (ie the trustees must distribute the income, but they can choose how the income is distributed and which particular beneficiary should receive income).

18.5.1 Income tax
(TA 1988, s 686)

There is a difference between 1993–94 and previous years. Trustees of discretionary trusts are liable for tax at 35 per cent for 1993–94, ie 'the rate of tax applicable to trusts'. Where part of the trust income is subject to a fixed interest trust and the balance is held on discretionary trusts, the 35 per cent rate is charged only on the income held on discretionary trusts.

In respect of most income, the trustees suffer basic rate tax at source and then pay an additional 10 per cent. However, a liability arises at 15 per cent on dividend income since this will have suffered only 20 per cent tax at source.

For 1992–93 and earlier years, trustees of discretionary trusts were subject to tax on all income at the basic rate (25 per cent) and at the additional rate (10 per cent).

Notional income which is left out of account

Certain types of income are not taken into account for additional rate purposes, ie sums which are capital profits under trust law such as:

(1) Premiums treated as rent (see 4.4)
(2) Profits on sale of certificates of deposit (see 5.8)
(3) Deemed distributions such as may arise where a company buys back its own shares (see 6.4.7).

This income is subject to tax at only 25 per cent. Income which is taxed under the accrued income scheme is charged at 35 per cent. This comes to the same thing, but such deemed income is not technically subject to the additional rate.

18.5.2 Computing the trustees' liability to the rate applicable to trusts

The trustees' liability for basic rate tax is calculated in exactly the same way as for trustees of fixed interest trusts. A separate computation is then required for the purposes of the 35 per cent rate.

Expenses paid out of net income are 'grossed up' and the resulting amount is then deducted from the income which is subject to the 35 per cent rate. Examples of such expenses are:

(1) Bank charges
(2) Interest which does not qualify for tax relief
(3) The costs of administering the trust
(4) Charges made by professional trustees
(5) Deficits on properties where the deficiency cannot be relieved against other Schedule A income.

Costs such as premiums on an insurance policy (excluding fire insurance), or property expenses such as the cost of maintenance or insurance of a property or charges made for the collection of rents, cannot be included directly as a deduction in computing liability for additional rate tax.

18.5.3 Example—Calculating the 35 per cent tax on discretionary trusts

A discretionary trust received net dividends of £12,000 during 1993–94. Expenses which are not allowable in computing income for basic rate tax purposes, but which are properly chargeable to income, amount to £960.

The trustees' liability for tax at the 35 per cent rate is computed as follows:

Net dividends—grossed up	
£12,000 x $\frac{100}{80}$	£15,000
Less expenses—grossed up	
£960 x $\frac{100}{80}$	£1,200
	£13,800
Tax at 15 per cent	£2,070

If the trustees had also received interest or some other income which was not dividend income, this would normally be taxed at 10 per cent, ie 35 per cent less basic rate tax withheld at source. Administrative expenses are set off against dividends first. Any balance is then grossed up at the rate of $\frac{100}{75}$ and then set against non-dividend income for the purposes of calculating the 35 per cent rate.

18.5.4   Income distributions in excess of the trustees' taxable income
(TA 1988, s 687)

There may be situations where trustees make distributions in excess of their taxable income. Such distributions also give rise to a liability for the trustees to account for tax at 35 per cent.

There are several situations in which such a liability can arise:

(1)   A trust may have income on which income tax does not have to be paid. If such income is paid out to a beneficiary as an income distribution, the trustees must account for tax at 35 per cent.

(2)   Similarly, trustees may make payments of an income nature which are subject to tax as *income* in the hands of the beneficiary even though they come out of the trust *capital*. In practice, the Revenue would not normally assess such distributions unless they were made regularly.

If the income is fully distributed each year and foreign securities are held, there will be an *additional* liability to tax when the foreign income is distributed to beneficiaries. The liability is equal to the credit allowed against basic rate tax for double taxation relief.

18.5.5   Tax returns

The tax returns which are usually completed are Forms 31 and 32. Form 32 calculates the liability to additional rate tax and also the pool of tax suffered by trustees to match against the tax stated as having been deducted when making a distribution to a beneficiary. If insufficient tax is available in the pool the trustees will have to pay the excess.

A tax deduction certificate form R185 should be completed by the trustees or their professional advisers showing the appropriate gross, tax and net figures.

18.5.6 The beneficiary's position

A beneficiary needs to include on his tax return the grossed up amount of any income distributed to him by the trustees during the tax year. Because the trustees are subject to the additional rate, the beneficiary's income is treated as net of 35 per cent tax.

18.5.7 Accumulated income subsequently distributed as capital

A distribution of capital which represents income which has been accumulated is not normally taxable income for the beneficiary. Such a distribution is treated as a capital distribution though, of course, this presupposes that the trustees have power to accumulate income. In cases where they have no power to accumulate income, any distributions will remain as income.

18.5.8 Capital gains tax
(TCGA 1992, s 5)

All the capital gains of a discretionary trust are taxed at 35 per cent. It is not possible, (as it is for income tax purposes—see 18.5.1) to separate two parts of a trust so that gains arising within a part of a trust which is subject to a fixed interest are taxed only at 25 per cent. Furthermore, the 35 per cent tax rate applies where a trust (or part of a trust) is discretionary at any time during the tax year. This means that if a small part of the trust is held on discretionary trusts until 6 April 1994, but thereafter the whole trust is a fixed interest trust, the trustees' gains for 1994–95 are all taxed at 35 per cent.

As with a fixed interest trust, no further CGT (or income tax) liability will normally arise on the trustees' distributing cash to a beneficiary after they have realised a capital gain by selling an asset.

18.5.9 Exemption for property occupied by a beneficiary
(TCGA 1992, s 225)

The Courts have held that trustees of a discretionary trust are entitled to this exemption where they permit a beneficiary to occupy a property as his main residence, even though the trust deed did not confer a right for the beneficiary to require the trustees to provide such a property.

18.5.10 Deemed disposals/hold-over relief
(TCGA 1992, s 71)

A capital gain may arise on a deemed disposal such as where the trustees distribute assets to a beneficiary, or where a beneficiary becomes absolutely entitled to capital under the terms of a trust. Hold-over relief will normally be available where a disposal of the property arises on a capital distribution to a beneficiary.

18.5.11 Transfer of capital losses to a trust beneficiary

Where capital is distributed to a beneficiary, or when he becomes absolutely entitled to the capital, capital losses which are attributable to the property to which he becomes entitled pass across to the beneficiary and are available to cover future capital gains realised by him.

18.5.12 Inheritance tax
(IHTA 1984, ss 64–65)

By definition, no beneficiary has an interest in possession in a discretionary trust and it follows that the trust capital is not treated as forming part of his estate. There is therefore no IHT charge on the death of a beneficiary of a discretionary trust.

To make up for the absence of such a charge, the legislation imposes a lower charge every ten years (the 'periodic charge'). The theory is that a generation is approximately 30 years and the tax charged on three separate occasions by reason of the periodic charge will approximate to the tax payable on property passing down to the next generation.

There is also an 'exit charge' which applies where property leaves a discretionary trust.

There are different rules for discretionary trusts created before and after 26 March 1974.

18.5.13 Trusts created after 26 March 1974

Periodic charge
(IHTA 1984, s 66)

The periodic charge arises on the tenth anniversary of the creation of the trust and on every subsequent tenth anniversary. The maximum rate is at present six per cent, computed as follows:

Tax payable at lifetime rate (20 per cent) x 30 per cent.

Actually, the computation is more complex and involves the following process:

Amount of chargeable transfers made by the settlor in the ten years prior to the creation of the trust	A
Value of the trust property at the tenth anniversary	B
Add A and B	C
Deduct nil rate band	D
	E

The next step is to compute the inheritance tax payable on E and on A – D. The tax payable by the trustees on the periodic charge is 30 per cent of the difference.

18.5.14 Example—Periodic charge

A created a discretionary trust in 1983. He had previously made chargeable transfers of £190,000. In 1993, the trust is worth £160,000. The periodic charge is therefore computed as follows:

		£
Amount of previous chargeable transfers	(A)	190,000
Value of trust property in 1993	(B)	160,000
	(C)	350,000
Deduct nil rate band	(D)	150,000
	(E)	200,000
Inheritance tax on E	=	40,000
Inheritance tax at lifetime rates on A – D	=	8,000
		32,000

Periodic charge is 30 per cent of £32,000 ie £9,600.

18.5.15 Trusts created prior to 26 March 1974

This type of trust is simpler in that there cannot have been any chargeable transfers made by the settlor prior to the creation of the trust. The computation is therefore:

Value of the trust property at the tenth anniversary	X
Deduct nil rate band	Y
	Z

Inheritance tax at lifetime rates on Z

Periodic charge is 30 per cent of this amount.

18.5.16 Position where the trustees have made capital distributions during the preceding ten years

Where the trustees have made a capital distribution within the previous ten years or property has otherwise ceased to be held upon discretionary trusts (eg by reason of a beneficiary being entitled to an interest in possession) the value of the capital distribution must also be brought into account in arriving at the periodic charge. The computation is as follows:

Amount of chargeable transfers made by the settlor in the ten years prior to the creation of the trust *and* capital distributions since the last periodic charge	A
Value of the trust property at the tenth anniversary	B
Add A and B	C
Deduct nil rate band	D
	E

The next step is to compute the IHT payable on E and on A – D. The tax payable by the trustees on the period charge is 30 per cent of the difference.

18.5.17 Treatment of undistributed income

The Revenue accepts that undistributed income which has not been accumulated should be excluded in arriving at the value of the trust capital at the tenth anniversary. The reason for this is that such income remains income held for the benefit of beneficiaries and is not capital.

Where income has been formally accumulated, it must be brought into account for the purposes of the periodic charge. However, such accumulated income is treated as if it were additional capital added to the trust at the date that the trustees resolved to accumulate it.

18.5.18 Exit charge (also known as the proportionate charge)

The way in which the exit charge is computed varies according to whether capital leaves a discretionary trust within the first ten years or only after there has been a periodic charge.

18.5.19 Exit charge during the first ten years
(IHTA 1984, s 68)

The position here is that a notional rate of charge should be computed which is the average rate of inheritance tax which would have been payable if the settlor had made a chargeable transfer at the time that he created the trust equal to the value of the trust property at that time.

18.5.20 Example—Exit charge during first ten years

A created a trust in February 1990 and the original trust property was worth £300,000. The entry charge would have been computed as follows:

	£
Value of the trust property in February 1990	300,000
Less nil rate band at that time	128,000
	172,000

£172,000 at 20 per cent = £34,400

Effective rate $= \dfrac{34,400}{300,000} \times 100$

The entry charge would therefore have been 11.47 per cent and the tax payable if property leaves a discretionary trust within the first ten years is levied as a proportion of this rate. The exact proportion is determined by the number of complete periods of three months (or quarters) during which the trust has been in existence. Thus, if the exit charge occurred after the trust had been in being for three years seven months, the charge would be at the rate of:

$\dfrac{14}{40} \times 30$ per cent of 11.47 per cent.

18.5.21 Exit charge after a periodic charge
(IHTA 1984, s 69)

The position here is that the rate of tax charged under an exit charge is fixed by the effective rate charged on the previous periodic charge. However, the charge applies only to the proportion of the property which leaves the discretionary trust, with the proportion being determined by the following formula:

$$\frac{\text{Number of complete quarters since the periodic charge}}{40}$$

A distribution during the first quarter following the ten year charge *is entirely free of inheritance tax.*

18.6 Accumulation and maintenance trusts
(IHTA 1984, s 71)

An accumulation and maintenance trust is a special form of discretionary trust which has been set up for a stated class of beneficiaries.

The following conditions must normally be satisfied:

(1)   One or more beneficiaries will become entitled to an interest in possession in the trust property on attaining a specified age which must not exceed age 25.

(2)   Until one of the beneficiaries becomes beneficially entitled, the income of the trust must be held on a discretionary basis with income being applied only for the maintenance, education or benefit of the beneficiaries or accumulated for the benefit of such persons.

(3)   The trust must have a life of not more than 25 years or it must be a trust for the benefit of grandchildren of a common grandparent.

Where an accumulation and maintenance trust was in existence at 15 April 1976, the 25 year period runs from that date, ie, to 14 April 2001, and not from the date that the trust was created.

18.6.1   Taxation

The same rules apply, and the same returns and certificates need to be completed, for income tax and CGT as for discretionary trusts. There are, however, different rules for CGT hold-over relief and IHT.

18.6.2   Hold-over relief for trustees
(TCGA 1992, s 260)

Where trustees dispose of assets to a beneficiary, hold-over relief may be available if the property concerned is business property (see 15.5).

As regards other assets, hold-over relief will normally be available if the disposal takes place when a beneficiary becomes absolutely entitled to capital and income at the same date.

There is a problem area for trustees of accumulation and maintenance trusts in that many trusts provide that a beneficiary should become entitled to income when he reaches age 18, but capital vests only at age 25. If the beneficiary became entitled to the capital at age 18, there would be no problem but, because there is a gap in time between the accumulation period coming to an end and the beneficiary becoming absolutely entitled to the capital, it is not possible for trustees to claim hold-over relief (unless, of course, the trust property consists of business assets).

18.6.3   IHT privileges for an accumulation and maintenance trust

An accumulation and maintenance trust is not subject to the periodic charge described above. Furthermore, there is no exit charge on a beneficiary becoming entitled to an interest in possession under the trust or becoming absolutely entitled to trust property.

18.7 Trusts for the disabled
(TCGA 1992, Sched 1 and IHTA 1984, ss 74 and 89)

A trust for a disabled person is a type of discretionary trust which enjoys certain tax privileges. The trustees are entitled to the full CGT exemption of £5,800 and there is no liability for the IHT periodic and exit charges.

The terms of the trust must be such that not less than half of the settled property and income must be applied for the benefit of a disabled person who is treated as if he had an interest in possession.

A disabled person is one who, at the time that the trust was created, was:

(1)   incapable by reason of mental disorder within the meaning of The Mental Health Act 1983 of administering his property or managing his affairs; or
(2)   in receipt of an attendance allowance under The Social Security Contributions and Benefits Act 1992, s 64; or
(3)   in receipt of a disability living allowance under Social Security Contributions and Benefits Act 1992, s 71.

The two conditions which need to be satisfied are as follows:

(1)   Not less than half of the property within the trust should be applied for the benefit of the beneficiary concerned; and
(2)   The person should be entitled to not less than 50 per cent of the income arising from the property (this condition is regarded as satisfied where the trust provides that no income may be applied for the benefit of any other person).

Income is deemed to be applied for the benefit of a person where it is held by the trustees for that person on protective trusts.

18.8 Protective trusts

This is a term under the Trustee Act 1925, s 33. The protective trust is one under which a person (known as the principal beneficiary) is entitled to an interest in possession in the trust unless he forfeits his interest, eg by assigning his interest or by becoming bankrupt. Protective trusts are normally worded so that if a principal beneficiary forfeits his interest, the trust property is held on discretionary trusts for a class of beneficiaries which includes the principal beneficiary.

18.8.1   The position where the principal beneficiary dies

The periodic charge does not apply whilst property is held on protective trusts because the principal beneficiary has forfeited his interest. However, an IHT charge arises on his death.

The charge varies according to whether the principal beneficiary forfeited his interest before or after 12 April 1978.

Where the principal beneficiary forfeited his interest before 12 April 1978, the tax charged on his eventual death is calculated at a fixed rate on the value of the trust property according to the following formula:

	Cumulative Total
0.25 per cent for each of the first 40 quarters	10 per cent
0.20 per cent for each of the next 40 quarters	8 per cent
0.15 per cent for each of the next 40 quarters	6 per cent
0.10 per cent for each of the next 40 quarters	4 per cent
0.05 per cent for each of the next 40 quarters	2 per cent
Maximum rate chargeable after 50 years	30 per cent

The nil rate band is *not* available.

18.8.2   The position where the principal beneficiary forfeited his interest after 11 April 1978

In this situation, the trustees are subject to a charge on the death of the principal beneficiary as if he had an interest in possession at the date of his death.

18.9   Charitable trusts

Provided that property is held for charitable purposes only, income and capital gains received by the trustees are normally exempt from tax.

Exemption from income tax
(TA 1988, s 505)

There is total exemption from income tax for all income other than trading profits. The exemption is, however, dependent upon income being applied for charitable purposes.

Exemption from CGT
(TCGA 1992, s 256)

There is also total exemption from CGT provided that the charitable trust applies the capital gains for charitable purposes.

18.9.1   Application for charitable purposes
(TA 1988, s 505)

A charity's exemption from tax may be restricted where income is not applied for charitable purposes. In particular, where a charity has income and capital gains which exceed £10,000 in a tax year, exemption is restricted where the following two conditions are satisfied:

(1)   The charity's relevant income and gains exceed the amount of its qualifying expenditure.
(2)   The trust incurs or is treated as incurring non-qualifying expenditure.

'Qualifying expenditure' for these purposes means expenditure actually made during the year for charitable purposes and commitments for such expenditure entered into during the year.

Where payments are made to bodies outside the United Kingdom, these will count as qualifying expenditure only to the extent that the charity can show that it has taken such steps that are reasonable in the circumstances in order to ensure that the payments will be applied for charitable purposes.

Expenditure for charitable purposes also includes reasonable administrative and fund raising expenses.

Non-qualifying expenditure includes things such as political activities, trading expenses, excessive administration costs. Furthermore, the legislation specifically mentions certain types of investments or loans which are to be regarded as not being qualifying expenditure. This is intended to catch investments in a company controlled by a connected person (for example the settlor) or loans to such a company. Indirect arrangements may also be caught such as where a charity makes loans or investments which are used as security for borrowings by a connected person.

Where a charitable trust makes a payment to another connected charitable trust, this does not count as application of the income for charitable purposes unless the trust that receives the payment actually applies it for charitable purposes.

18.9.2   Inheritance tax position

Property held upon charitable trusts is exempt from the periodic and exit charges. If the property is held upon temporary charitable trusts, a charge will arise on those charitable trusts coming to an end with tax being charged according to the same formula in 18.8.1.

18.10   Executors and personal representatives

18.10.1   Meaning

When a person dies, his assets vest in his executors/personal representatives. If he does not leave a Will, it is normally necessary for letters of administration to be obtained and the person who acts in this way is treated for tax purposes as if he were an executor. The term 'personal representative' covers both executors in the case of a Will and administrators in the case of an intestacy.

The fact that at least one personal representative is resident in the United Kingdom would normally mean that the estate is subject to UK tax. However, there is an exception to this where the deceased was not resident, ordinarily resident, or domiciled in the United Kingdom at the time of his death. In such a situation, provided that at least one of the personal representatives is not resident in the United Kingdom, the estate is not regarded as resident in the United Kingdom.

Personal representatives of a deceased person are treated as a single body of persons so that there is no tax implication if an executor retires or dies. The estate is treated as a single entity for tax purposes.

18.10.2   Income tax
(TMA 1970, s 40)

Personal representatives of a deceased person are liable to pay tax on income received by the deceased person up to the date of his death. The Revenue must issue the relevant assessments within three years following the tax year in which the person died. The tax is assessed in exactly the same way as if the individual were still alive, ie all the normal allowances and reliefs are due. The only difference is that the personal representatives are responsible for settling the tax (they are also entitled to any repayments).

Quite separately, personal representatives are also charged to tax on income received by them following the death. No personal allowances are given. During the administration period, the income is charged at the basic rate; there is no higher rate liability for the personal representatives.

Although there are cases where income has to be apportioned pre- and post-death for *legal* purposes, for *tax* purposes any income received after a person's death is treated as income of the estate.

Where, under the terms of the Will, a trust evolves, the executors become trustees upon the completion of the administration period. Depending upon the type of trust, the trustees may become chargeable to additional rate income tax first on the balance of accumulated income at that date and second upon receipt of subsequent income. There is no date fixed by law to determine the completion of the administration period, but it is generally agreed that it is the date on which the residue is ascertained.

18.10.3   Beneficiary's position
(TA 1988, s 695–696)

A beneficiary of a Will may receive an annuity. This income is taxable for the year in which it is payable unless, as a matter of fact, the annuity is paid out of capital in which case the annuity is income for the year in which it is paid.

Beneficiaries of specific legacies are normally entitled from the date of death to the income which arises on the property that they have inherited.

Other beneficiaries will be entitled to the residue, either through a limited interest (eg a life tenant entitled to income arising from the residuary estate) or by an absolute entitlement.

During the administration period, sums paid to a beneficiary who has a limited interest are initially treated as income for the year of payment. In the case of beneficiaries with an absolute entitlement to the residue, the payments made to them are initially treated as income for the year to which they relate. However, once the administration has been completed, the position is re-computed. In the case of beneficiaries with a limited interest, the income is deemed to have accrued evenly during the administration period and is apportioned between the tax years concerned. In the case of a beneficiary with an absolute entitlement, the income which is assessable for tax purposes is the actual income which arose in each tax year (or the appropriate proportion of such income if there is more than one residuary legatee).

Where income which has accrued to the date of death is treated as capital of the estate for IHT purposes and as residuary income, there is higher rate tax relief available to beneficiaries. Form 922 is used to calculate this relief.

18.10.4   Capital gains tax
(TCGA 1992, ss 3 and 62)

Personal representatives are also subject to CGT (once again at 25 per cent) on any capital gains realised by them. For this purpose, assets which were held by the deceased person at the date of his death are deemed to be acquired by the personal representatives at their market value at that date (the probate value). However, the probate value may need to be adjusted where securities are sold at a loss within 12 months of the death and relief from IHT has been claimed.

If a claim has been made to substitute the sale proceeds of property or land within four years of the date of death, the original probate value and not sale proceeds continues to be the acquisition value for CGT purposes.

Assets which are transferred to beneficiaries, either during the course of the administration period of an estate or on the completion of the administration period, do not give rise to a chargeable gain since the beneficiary is regarded as having himself acquired the asset at the date of the person's death and at the probate value.

Personal representatives of an estate in the course of administration are entitled to the full individual annual exemption for CGT purposes for the year of death and the following two tax years, but are not entitled to any exemption thereafter. Again, if a Will Trust evolves upon completion of the administration period, the trustees will then become entitled to their own exemption.

Losses made by personal representatives during the administration period, and not utilised, are not available to be transferred to residuary beneficiaries with absolute interests, but are available to the ongoing trustees where a Will Trust evolves.

18.10.5   Property owned by the estate, but used by a beneficiary as his main residence

The Revenue treat the exemption for a property occupied by a beneficiary of a trust as his main residence as applying where personal representatives dispose of a property which has been used by a beneficiary of the estate as his only or main residence both before and after the deceased's death (see extra-statutory concession D5).

18.10.6   Deeds of variation

Where the terms of a Will have been varied by a deed of variation (also known as a deed of family arrangement), there are important consequences so far as IHT is concerned (see 17.4.6). Similarly, the Court of Appeal held in *Marshall v Kerr* [1993] STC 360 that where the variation takes place within two years of the relevant person's death and an election is made under TCGA 1988, s 62 (7), the terms of the deed of variation are read back into the original Will for CGT purposes so that the parties entering into the deed of variation are not deemed to have made a disposal for CGT purposes. (The Inland Revenue has appealed against this decision in the House of Lords.)

Unfortunately, the income tax treatment is less favourable. Even where the deed specifically provides that all income is to be paid to a beneficiary named in the deed, this has no effect for income tax purposes in relation to income which arose prior to the deed's execution. The original beneficiary or beneficiaries named in the Will remain liable for any higher rate tax on such income which arose at a time when they were entitled to it. Furthermore, a person who gives up an entitlement under a Will by executing such a deed is treated as a settlor for income tax purposes.

19 Dealing with the Revenue

This chapter deals with the following aspects:

(1)   How the Inland Revenue is organised
(2)   Assessments and right of appeal
(3)   Postponement of tax
(4)   Interest on delayed payment of tax
(5)   Set-offs
(6)   Certificates of tax deposit
(7)   Default interest under s 88
(8)   Back duty and Revenue investigations
(9)   The Revenue's powers to impose penalties
(10) Remission of tax by the Revenue
(11) Repayment supplement
(12) Error or mistake relief
(13) Liability to make other deductions.

19.1   How the Inland Revenue is organised

In your dealings with Inland Revenue officials, you should bear in mind that there are three main divisions of responsibilities:

(1)   Collectors of Taxes
(2)   Inspectors of Taxes
(3)   Certain specialist offices such as the Capital Taxes Office (CTO) which deals with inheritance tax and the Stamp Duty Office.

The collection of tax is dealt with by Collectors of Taxes, who are also responsible for collecting national insurance contributions from employers. There are various collection offices around the country. Staff at the Collector's office do not get involved at all in *assessing* the tax payable, this is the job of the Inspector of Taxes.

There are 666 tax offices within the United Kingdom at which Inspectors of Taxes are located. These offices have responsibility for issuing tax returns and reviewing the completed returns when they come in. In the light of this information, the Inspector of Taxes issues assessments and will negotiate with the taxpayer (or his adviser) if an appeal is made.

Once tax is found to be payable, the Inspector will pass over the responsibility for collection to the Collector of Taxes.

Each individual taxpayer dealt with by the Revenue has a main tax district (the Revenue term is GCD—General Claims District). In the case of an individual who has one job, the tax district will be determined by the address of his employer. Where a taxpayer is self-employed, the main tax district will be decided by the address from which the business is carried on. Individuals who have only investment income are normally dealt with by the tax district which deals with the area in which they live.

In some cases, a second or third tax district may be involved. For example, if an individual is employed in London he will be dealt with by a tax district dealing with that area. If he also has a farm in Canterbury or Yorkshire, the accounts for that business will be dealt with by a district which deals with the area concerned. The district which deals with the farm (or any other business) will issue assessments on profits arising from that business.

The Revenue also has a number of specialist offices which deal with matters such as inheritance tax and stamp duty and, from time to time, the Inspector of Taxes may need to liaise with a section of such a specialist office. An Inspector of Taxes is concerned to agree *principles* and ensure that tax is properly *assessed*. He is not responsible for agreeing valuations. Where land or property needs to be valued, he will liaise with the District Valuer; where unquoted shares are concerned, he will deal with the Shares Valuation Division, a division within the CTO.

19.2 Assessments and right of appeal

It is most unusual for the Revenue to issue an assessment which is correct and agreed for payment first time. The reason for this is that most assessments issued by the Revenue are made in the absence of a completed return. All that the Inspector of Taxes can do is to issue an estimated assessment on the basis of information available to him (normally the main determinant is the assessable income for the previous tax year).

When an estimated assessment is received, the taxpayer may appeal. He may also ask for all or part of the tax which has been assessed to be held in abeyance, or 'postponed' (see 19.3). The appeal is normally settled (or 'determined') by agreement as and when the Inspector is supplied with full particulars of the actual income or gains concerned.

However, there may be differences of opinion, either on matters of principle or concerning the actual income received. It is normal for taxpayers to correspond with the Revenue in order to try to narrow such differences of opinion but, in the last resort, the matter may need to be settled by an independent arbiter. This is the role of the Commissioners.

There are two types of Commissioners, Special Commissioners (who are full-time officials with a legal expertise) and General Commissioners (who are lay people who have agreed to act as Commissioners for a particular area). When a taxpayer appeals against an assessment, he should specify which type of Commissioners he wishes to hear his appeal if the matter cannot be resolved by agreement with the Inspector of Taxes.

The main role of the Commissioners is to act as a tribunal of fact. Findings of fact reached by the Commissioners are not normally set aside by the Courts unless the finding of fact is totally at odds with the information provided to the Commissioners.

The Commissioners will also make decisions on law. However, from time to time they may not be properly advised. Decisions by the Commissioners on matters of law are open to appeal and the Courts may (and regularly do) overrule the Commissioners on such matters.

It may be necessary for the Commissioners to hear evidence in order to arrive at a decision. The Revenue are normally represented before the Commissioners by the District Inspector, whereas a taxpayer may argue his case in person or may be represented by an accountant or lawyer. Each side bears its own costs.

If the decision goes against the Revenue, it is necessary for the Inspector to express dissatisfaction in order to keep the matter open. After consulting with his head office, an appeal may be taken to the High Court. From this point onwards, costs become a major consideration since the party that loses before the Court must bear the other side's costs.

Once the High Court has made a decision, it is possible for either side to appeal to the Court of Appeal. Subsequently, an appeal may be made to the House of Lords. At each stage, costs arise and the higher courts may (and usually do) award costs to the victor so that the other side must bear both parties' legal costs.

In Scotland, a slightly different procedure arises in that an appeal from the Commissioner's decision will be heard by the Court of Session and an appeal against such a decision then goes to the House of Lords (in other words, there is no equivalent in Scotland to the High Court stage of proceedings).

19.3   Postponement of tax
(TA 1988, s 5)

The fact that an appeal is made against an assessment does not of itself affect the liability to make payment. However, it is normal for an application to be made to postpone (ie defer) payment of tax whilst an assessment is under appeal. The postponement application may be made on a separate part of the standard appeal form which is issued by the Inspector of Taxes when he sends out the assessment concerned.

Tax due under assessments where no postponement application has been made falls due for payment on the later of two dates, the 'due date' or 30 days after the date the assessment was issued.

The due dates are as follows:

(1)   *Income tax under Schedule A*—1 January during the year of assessment.
(2)   *Schedule D Cases I and II*—first instalment 1 January during the year of assessment. Second instalment 1 July following the end of the year.
(3)   *Schedule D Case III*—1 January during the year of assessment.
(4)   *Schedule D Cases IV and V*—1 January during the year of assessment.
(5)   *Schedule D Case VI*—1 January during the year of assessment.
(6)   *Schedule E*—14 days after the Collector applies for payment (SI 1973 No 334, reg 52(2)).
(7)   *Higher rate tax on investment income*—1 December following the year of assessment.
(8)   *Capital gains tax*—1 December following the year of assessment.

Where a postponement application is made, the tax not in dispute becomes payable 30 days after the Inspector issues a notice agreeing the postponement application.

19.4   Interest on delayed payment of tax
(TMA 1970 ss 86 and 88)

Interest may be charged in one of two different situations.

(1)   If a taxpayer simply delays paying tax for which an assessment notice has been issued, he will be charged 'interest on overdue tax' under s 86.
(2)   If too much tax has been postponed, and the final liability exceeds the amount paid on account, interest may be charged under s 86.

Technically, if the taxpayer fails to submit his return on time and then also fails to pay the assessment, he will be liable to interest under s 88 for the whole period down to the eventual date of payment. However, interest is charged at the same rate under both s 86 and s 88, so in practice the section under which interest is charged will not affect the amount payable.

19.4.1 Interest on delayed payment of tax (s 86)

The rules for determining the date from which s 86 interest runs are complex. Also, different rules apply for wages and salaries taxed under Schedule E than for all other types of income and for capital gains.

Interest on a Schedule E assessment runs from fourteen days after the Collector first applies for payment of the relevant tax. Clearly, he cannot apply for payment until an assessment notice has been issued by the Inspector and, in practice, no such application is usually made until the thirty days allowed for an appeal have expired or, if an appeal is entered, until that appeal is settled.

Interest on a Schedule A, Schedule D or capital gains tax assessment usually runs from the date shown in 19.3 above.

However, interest will not run until thirty days after the issue of the relevant assessment notice, if that would produce a later date. In practice this will mostly apply where an assessment is issued late because of a mistake or delay in the Inspector's office. If an assessment is issued late because of mistake or delay on the part of the taxpayer, interest will usually be chargeable under s 88, as explained below.

19.4.2 Interest charges where too much tax has been postponed

Where an appeal is entered against an assessment, and a postponement application has been made, the tax must be split into two parts: that which the taxpayer and the Inspector agree is payable in any case, and that which will only become payable if the taxpayer loses his appeal. Interest on the first part is calculated as if the tax were charged by an assessment made the day the Inspector agreed the amount payable; interest on the second begins to run only when the appeal has been settled and the Inspector has sent the taxpayer a statement of the tax outstanding.

However, interest on either or both parts will run from the date shown below, if that produces an *earlier* base date for the interest charge:

Interest calculation dates (the 'reckonable date') following an appeal

Type of income or gain	*Interest runs from*
Higher rate (for individuals) and additional rate (for trustees) on income received net of basic rate tax	1 June fourteen months following the end of the year of assessment
All other income charged under Schedule A or Schedule D	1 July following the year of assessment
Capital gains	1 June fourteen months following the end of the year of assessment

The overall effect of the rules set out above is that an appeal cannot defer by more than six months the date from which interest starts to run.

19.4.3 Example—Interest on tax paid late

A carries on a business taxable under Case 1 of Schedule D. His 1993–94 tax would therefore normally be payable in two equal instalments, on 1 January and 1 July 1994.

In November 1993 the Inspector of Taxes issues an estimated assessment for 1993–94, showing tax payable of £10,000.

A appeals against that assessment, stating that he expects his tax bill for the year to be only £6,000. On 25 January 1994 the Inspector agrees to allow the balance of £4,000 to be postponed.

On 26 February A pays £3,000, being his estimate of the first instalment of the Schedule D tax. On 12 July he pays a further £3,000, being his estimate of the second instalment.

The appeal is finally settled on 6 September, when it becomes apparent that a further £2,000 is payable. A pays this £2,000 on 20 September.

The interest position is as follows:

(1) The agreed payment on account was £6,000, divided equally between the first and second instalments. Interest on the first instalment (of £3,000) runs from 30 days after the Inspector agreed the payment on account down to the date of payment. The payment on account was agreed on 25 January, so the thirty days expired on 24 February. Interest is therefore payable for one day, 25 February.

(2) The agreed payment on account of the second instalment (also £3,000) should have been made on 1 July. Interest will therefore run on that £3,000 for the period 1 July to 11 July.

(3)   Interest on the balance of £2,000 also runs from 1 July (see 19.4.1). This is of course both *after* the normal date for payment of the first instalment (and half the £2,000 will be attributable to the first instalment) and *before* the date the appeal was settled.

19.4.4   Tax outstanding at a person's death

There is an extra-statutory concession which applies where a person dies after receiving an assessment, but before paying the tax. Extra-statutory concession A17 provides that s 86 interest is charged only from the date that probate or letters of administration are obtained.

19.4.5   Rate of interest charged

The rate of interest charged varies according to the general level of interest rates. The rates for the last five years have been:

6 August 1988 to 5 October 1988	9.75%
6 October 1988 to 5 January 1989	10.75%
6 January 1989 to 5 July 1989	11.5%
6 July 1989 to 5 November 1989	12.25%
6 November 1989 to 5 November 1990	13%
6 November 1990 to 5 March 1991	12.25%
6 March 1991 to 5 May 1991	11.5%
6 May 1991 to 5 July 1991	10.75%
6 July 1991 to 5 October 1991	10%
6 October 1991 to 5 November 1992	9.25%
6 November 1992 to 5 December 1992	7.75%
6 December 1992 to 5 March 1993	7%
6 March 1993 to 5 January 1994	6.25%
6 January 1994 onwards	5.5%

Each new rate is applied to all outstanding liabilities. Thus if tax which should have been paid on 1 January 1993 is not paid until 31 March, interest for the period 1 January to 5 March will be charged at 7 per cent per annum and for the period 6 to 31 March at 6.25 per cent.

Interest is *not* compounded.

A ready reckoner, entitled *Interest Factor Tables*, is available, free of charge, from:

Inland Revenue Public Enquiry Room
Somerset House
Strand
London WC2R 1LB

A final point is that interest charged on tax paid late is *never* deductible in computing taxable income. For example, a trader who is charged interest on tax paid late may *not* deduct that interest in calculating his taxable profits.

19.4.6   Escaping interest on tax paid late

Where tax is paid late, a demand for the relevant amount of interest will automatically be generated by the Revenue's computer and sent to the taxpayer. Until recently, it was the practice to waive interest if the total charge did not exceed £30, but that rule does not apply where:

(1)   Schedule E tax was first demanded on or after 19 April 1993; or
(2)   An assessment for Schedule A or Schedule D tax, or for capital gains tax, was issued on or after 19 April 1993.

Because the demand is generated automatically, no-one in the Revenue will have considered whether any circumstances exist making it unfair or unreasonable to charge that interest. It is therefore up to the taxpayer to raise the point.

The Revenue has stated that, where a tax office takes more than seven months to answer a taxpayer's letter or deal with his enquiry, any interest which accrued on tax which remained unpaid because the taxpayer was awaiting an answer will be waived.

Experience suggests, however, that interest will be waived wherever the taxpayer can make out a reasonable case for saying that the Revenue were in some way at fault—for example, that they failed to issue a demand note for the July instalment of Schedule D tax. Typically, a letter giving the taxpayer's reasons for believing that interest should not be charged will never be answered, but at the same time no further action to collect the interest charged will be taken. If there is *any* arguable case for blaming the delay on the Revenue, it is worth a letter. Interest itself paid late does not attract further interest, so there is nothing to lose.

19.5   Set-offs

It is possible for an individual to seek postponement (see 19.3) on the grounds that he has overpaid tax elsewhere, or is due a repayment. However, some care is required.

First, the Inland Revenue's view is that s 86 interest may run on an assessment until such time as the individual formally claims that an overpayment should be set against the tax assessment concerned. This may result in a degree of inequity where the overpayment does not qualify for repayment supplement because of the twelve month rule.

Second, the Revenue may allocate reliefs and allowances differently from the way that the individual or his adviser expect and this may mean that an overpayment does not in fact arise after all. This problem is particularly likely to arise where an individual has a number of different sources of income, possibly with different districts being involved.

An overpayment by one spouse cannot be off-set against tax payable by the other, except in relation to 1989–90 and earlier years. Even then, the offset may be restricted to tax on investment income where an election was made for separate taxation of the wife's earnings.

Situations may arise where tax has been assessed, payment has been made late, s 86 interest has been charged and paid and the individual then reduces or eliminates the tax liability by claiming relief for losses etc. In a case such as this, it is necessary to claim repayment of the s 86 interest as an adjustment is not made automatically.

19.6   Certificates of tax deposit

A taxpayer may make deposits with Collectors of Taxes to cover tax liabilities. A certificate is issued and the deposit is held for the general benefit of the individual until such time as he surrenders all or part of the certificate to cover tax liabilities.

Where a deposit is used to cover a tax liability, s 86 interest cannot run from the date that the deposit was made. They are therefore commonly used to cover a tax liability which cannot easily be quantified, eg a capital gain on a sale of unquoted shares where a value at 31 March 1982 needs to be negotiated with the Shares Valuation Division.

Interest is credited from the date the deposit is made to the due date (see 19.3). The rate of interest is fixed by reference to money market rates and is taxable. Interest is paid at a lower rate where deposits are encashed rather than used to settle tax liabilities.

There is an extra-statutory concession whereby the Revenue will give a person the benefit of interest at the lower rate for encashment up to the reckonable date and this will often be beneficial in a situation where an assessment has been issued between the due date and the reckonable date.

Deposits are not transferable except to personal representatives of a deceased person. They cannot even be transferred to a spouse, although the Collector of Taxes will accept a certificate on the basis that it is treated as encashed with the resultant proceeds being applied to cover a spouse's tax liability. The problem with this procedure is that it does not protect the spouse from a liability to interest under s 86 if the assessment concerned has been outstanding for some time.

19.7 Default interest under s 88

Where the Revenue has been unable to issue an assessment at the proper time, because the taxpayer either failed to submit his return or submitted an incorrect or incomplete return, interest may be charged from the usual due date (as set out in 19.3 above) to the date of payment. For s 88 purposes, the due date for tax charged under Schedule E is taken as 1 January in the year of assessment.

For this purpose, an individual or trust tax return counts as 'late' if it is not in the Inspector's hands by 4 pm on the last business day of October following the year of assessment. For example, the absolute deadline for a return for the year to 5 April 1994 was 4 pm on Friday, 29 October 1993. Fortunately, 31 October 1994 is a Monday so taxpayers have three extra days in 1994 to comply with their responsibility to make returns.

19.7.1 Example—Default interest under s 88

In the 1993–94 tax year A and B each realised capital gains of £1 million from exercising unapproved share options which gave rise to a Schedule E income tax charge. A delivers his return by hand to the Inspector's office at 3 pm on Monday 31 October 1993. At exactly the same time, B posts his return, which accordingly arrives at the Inspector's office on Tuesday, 1 November.

The Inspector issues assessment notices to both A and B on Thursday, 15 December 1994. Because A submitted his return before the deadline, he will not be charged interest under s 88 and has thirty days (until 15 January 1995) to pay his tax before becoming liable to a s 86 interest charge. However, because B missed the deadline, he will be liable to a s 88 charge and interest could run from 1 January 1994 to the day he pays the tax.

This shows the importance of submitting returns on time.

19.7.2 Escaping default interest

Interest under s 88 will not be charged, even where a taxpayer has not submitted his full return, if he has provided (by the end-of-October deadline) sufficient information for the Inspector at least to make a reasonable estimate of his liability. For example, if a large capital gain was made in 1993–94, it should at least be possible to advise the gross proceeds by the end of October, even if the exact taxable gain cannot be calculated, perhaps because 31 March 1982 valuations are required.

Interest will not be charged if the taxpayer was unable, through no fault of his own, to submit his return by the deadline. Most commonly, this will apply where the taxpayer has been incapacitated by illness or by a family crisis, such as bereavement. Of course, interest will still be charged if the return is not prepared within a reasonable time of those difficulties abating.

19.8   Back duty and Revenue investigations

'Back duty' is the term given by the Revenue to tax which should have been paid for earlier years, but which has not been paid because of a failure by the taxpayer properly to disclose his income. A back duty case may arise from a failure to disclose income altogether (for example a bank deposit account) or because profits from a business have been understated (perhaps because cash takings have not been included in sales).

Where the Inspector of Taxes believes that back duty may be payable, he will commence an enquiry. In some cases, a specialist arm of the Inland Revenue, the Enquiry Branch, will become involved. If back duty is found to be payable, interest and penalties will also be payable.

19.9   The Revenue's powers to impose penalties
(TMA 1970 ss 7, 11A, 93 and 95)

19.9.1   Deliberate deception

Anyone who has deliberately understated his taxable income or chargeable gains may be prosecuted for fraud, false accounting, theft or the beautifully old-fashioned, but still rather serious, offence of 'cheating our Sovereign Lady the Queen'. If you have understated your business profits, failed to declare all your investments or claimed allowances to which you are not entitled, you are in serious trouble and at risk of imprisonment.

If you find yourself in this position, you should seek the advice of a solicitor or accountant experienced in settling 'back duty' cases *immediately*—even if the Revenue has not yet shown signs of suspecting you. The point is that it is very difficult for the Revenue to amass enough evidence to mount a successful criminal prosecution, but an unrepresented taxpayer may find himself out of his depth at a Revenue enquiry.

19.9.2 Failure to submit a return

More usually, however, the problem will be that the taxpayer has simply failed to submit his return in time, or has made mistakes in preparing the figures.

For failing to complete and submit a return form issued by the Inspector, the General Commissioners may impose an initial penalty of up to £300. If the return is not then submitted, a further penalty of up to £60 per day (counting from the day the initial penalty was imposed) may be levied.

If the return is not made by the end of the tax year following that in which it was issued, an additional penalty equal to the tax on the undeclared income becomes due—in other words, there is a double assessment.

19.9.3 No tax return form issued by Inspector

The end-of-October deadline mentioned at 19.7 does *not* apply where the Inspector has not sent the taxpayer a return form to complete. The obligation on such a taxpayer is to notify the Inspector of any unassessed liabilities no later than the first anniversary of the end of the year of assessment (so by 5 April 1995 for 1993–94 liabilities). Only if he fails to meet that extended deadline will he become liable to default interest.

Tax returns are sent annually to all those known to be self-employed, in receipt of income from property, or having investments which may produce capital gains. The 5 April deadline is likely, therefore, in practice to apply only to someone who has recently commenced self-employment or acquired substantial investments.

19.9.4 Failure to notify Revenue of taxable income or gains

A taxpayer who has not received a return form is still obliged to inform the Inspector of any taxable income or gains (other than income taxed under the PAYE scheme, income taxed by deduction at source and income and gains already assessed) within twelve months of the end of the year of assessment (by 5 April 1995 for income and gains arising in 1993–94). If he fails to do so, he becomes liable to a penalty equal to the tax chargeable on the undeclared income—in other words, a double assessment.

19.9.5   Submission of an incorrect return

If a taxpayer submits an incorrect return, he is liable to a penalty equal to the difference between the tax charged on the income or gain returned and the true income or gain. Strictly, such a penalty is only chargeable if the taxpayer has been fraudulent or negligent, but the Revenue's approach has always been that the mere fact that the return is wrong proves that the taxpayer must have been guilty at least of negligence. Moreover, the taxpayer is not allowed to blame a third party (for example, his accountant) for the error, although he may be able to insist that the accountant reimburses any penalty suffered.

19.9.6   Mitigation of penalties for incorrect return

The penalty for an error in a return (including, of course, a set of business accounts submitted with a return) is, therefore, a potential doubling of the tax chargeable on the income or gains under-declared. This will be levied in addition to any interest charge due under ss 86 or 88.

However, the Revenue's practice is to reduce or mitigate the potential penalty by reference to three factors.

Taking the maximum penalty as a surcharge of 100 per cent, the possible reductions are as follows:

(1)   For disclosure, a maximum of 30 per cent if the taxpayer goes to the Inspector admitting that a mistake has been made and a maximum of 20 per cent if the taxpayer makes a complete disclosure as soon as he is challenged by the Inspector.

(2)   For co-operation, a maximum of 40 per cent. 'Co-operation' means, for example, answering the Inspector's questions and providing any back-up documentation within a reasonable timespan.

(3)   For reduced culpability, a maximum of 40 per cent. For example, nothing will be allowed under this head if it is clear, even though the Inspector cannot prove it, that the taxpayer set out deliberately to cheat the Revenue. A reduction of perhaps 15 per cent to 25 per cent will be allowed if the taxpayer has been guilty of gross carelessness and between 30 per cent and 40 per cent where he has simply misunderstood information supplied by a third party (for example, where he has entered the net instead of the gross interest received on a building society account).

The usual procedure is for the Inspector to suggest an overall settlement figure to include underpaid tax, interest and any penalty. However, he will also provide a computation showing how the overall figure was calculated and it is open to the taxpayer to argue for a bigger reduction of the penalty element. If the Inspector does not agree, he must submit the case to his Head Office, which is often willing to accept a lower settlement than originally proposed by the Inspector.

Payment by instalments is possible where the taxpayer does not have readily realisable capital, but this will of course increase the interest (though not the penalty) payable.

19.9.7 Two common questions

Two common questions are: 'Am I obliged to point out to the Inspector that he has made a mistake in my favour?' and 'How should I deal with 'grey areas', such as outgoings which may or may not be allowable as trading expenses?'.

Not infrequently, because of some error by the Inspector, a taxpayer may receive an assessment which is clearly inadequate or even a repayment which the taxpayer knows is not due. It is *always* best in such circumstances to point out the Inspector's error. Cashing a repayment warrant which you know has been issued in error is certainly a criminal offence and, depending on the exact circumstances, keeping quiet about an error in an assessment may be a criminal offence as well.

Similarly, do not attempt to deflect attention from 'grey areas'. The distinction between presenting your case in the best light and actively misleading the Inspector can be a fine one, but often one that is easier to discern with the wisdom of hindsight. The rule of thumb is: do not hide anything you would be embarrassed for the Inspector to discover.

19.10   Remission of tax by the Revenue

The Revenue's policy is to remit tax where arrears have arisen because of failure by the Revenue to make proper and timely use of information supplied. Remission of tax in this way is available where the taxpayer could have reasonably believed that his affairs were in order. In practice, the Revenue's policy is to remit tax only where the Revenue fails to issue assessments by the end of the tax year following that in which the liability arose.

The extent to which tax is remitted depends upon the individual's total income for the year. Normally, the Revenue has regard to the individual's income for the preceding tax year, but where an individual's income is reduced, it will work on the basis of estimated income for the current year.

The practice currently adopted with regard to remitting tax is as follows:

Gross Income £	Remission
15,500 or less	All
15,501–18,000	3/4
18,001–22,000	1/2
22,001–26,000	1/4
26,001–40,000	1/10
40,001 or more	None

19.11   Repayment supplement
(TA 1988, s 824)

The Revenue is required to pay interest or 'repayment supplement' on overpayments of tax. However, the Revenue is not required to give repayment supplement until one complete year has elapsed following the end of the year of assessment concerned. Furthermore, where an assessment is issued more than 12 months after a year of assessment, repayment supplement runs only from the end of the year of assessment in which the tax was paid.

It will be noted that the period during which s 86 interest may accrue and the period in which entitlement to repayment supplement may arise do not match up. There may be a period of nine months during which an overpayment does not qualify for repayment supplement even though interest may be accruing under s 86 on an assessment for the same tax year raised under a different schedule.

Special rules apply where tax has been overpaid under Schedule E. Where Schedule E assessments for different years are raised at the same time, the net tax overpaid at the end of a year is normally carried forward to the next year's assessment. For the purposes of attributing a repayment, the Revenue's practice is to treat an overpayment as arising in the earliest year possible.

19.11.1   Example—Repayment supplement on Schedule E

An individual's Schedule E assessments show the following net position at the end of each year.

	£
1988–89	1,000
1989–90	1,100
1990–91	1,300

The tax repayment is treated as arising as follows:

	£
1988–89	1,000
1989–90	100
1990–91	200

If the 1989–90 assessment had shown a net overpayment at 5 April 1990 of only £700, the treatment would be:

	£
1988–89	700
1989–90	NIL
1990–91	600

Difficulties may arise where there are overpayments for earlier years which are extinguished by an underpayment for a subsequent year. Consequently, if the above individual's assessment for 1991–92 included a large amount of untaxed income (eg a share option) so that the assessment for 1991–92 showed an overpayment brought forward of £1,300, but an underpayment at the end of the year of £1,000, there would be no repayment of tax and therefore no repayment supplement.

19.12   Error or mistake relief

Some errors are made the other way round—against the taxpayer. Relief may be claimed within the six year time limit against any over assessment to income tax or CGT due to an error or mistake in, or an omission from, any return or statement. However, relief is not due where the information was not used to form the basis of an assessment, or where the assessment was made in accordance with practice generally prevailing at the time of issue.

It should be noted that s 33 relief may be claimed in respect of an assessment made in the past six years, even where the assessment related to an earlier year.

19.13   Liability to make other deductions

19.13.1   Payments to employees

Employers are required to withhold tax under PAYE.

An employer who fails to operate PAYE takes a substantial risk. The primary liability to account for the tax rests with the employer and the scope of PAYE does not extend simply to deducting tax from the gross pay of an employee and remitting it to the Inland Revenue. Instead, an employer must remember that PAYE can also apply to all forms of casual labour, which may or may not be paid through the payroll, and additionally to individuals who may be considered to be self-employed (see 2.2).

Another area frequently overlooked is that of expenses (see 3.4.1) which constitute part of the emoluments of an employee and accordingly fall within the scope of PAYE. Whilst genuine business expenses incurred *wholly, exclusively and necessarily* in the course of an employee's duties are allowed tax-free, there remain several areas where employers are required to operate PAYE. These include the payment of *all* round sum allowances which have not been approved by the Inspector of Taxes in the form of a dispensation, and the payment of unauthorised or unvouched expenses. Even the payment of travel expenses may not be permitted tax-free in circumstances where the employee's workplace is deemed to be his normal place of work. As an example, a site-based employee living in London and working on a site in Aberdeen will be taxed on all his expenses for travel between London and Aberdeen, showing that special attention needs to be paid to such payments and the circumstances surrounding them.

Whilst the Collector of Taxes will invariably seek to recover any unpaid tax from the employer in the first instance, the relevant Regulations (SI 1973/334) do permit the Collector to direct that unpaid tax shall be recovered from the employee, but there is no legal requirement that the Collector should give such a direction. The Regulations make it clear that the Collector will make such a direction only if he is satisfied that the employer took reasonable care to comply with the PAYE regulations and the underdeduction of tax was due to an error made in good faith. Errors arising simply from confusion or ignorance of the rules are not, however, considered to be a reasonable excuse. In such situations, the Collector will not only seek recovery of all duties underpaid but is likely to add interest (from April 1993) and penalties as well.

SI 1973/334, reg 26B(3) provides that the Collector may pursue the employee if he has received his remuneration knowing that the employer has wilfully failed to deduct PAYE tax, but the Revenue will normally pursue this course of action only after they have endeavoured to collect from the employer.

All lump sum payments generally should be treated with caution in times when termination payments are increasingly common. Basically, if there is any contractual obligation or expectation, on the part of the employee, to receive a sum then the employer is likely to be considered liable to make a deduction of tax.

A more comprehensive list of the type of payments from which tax should be withheld under PAYE is contained at 3.2.1.

19.13.2   Payments to agency workers

Where the services of an individual are provided to a trader through an agency, and the manner in which the individual performs his work is controlled and supervised as if he were an employee, TA 1988, s 134 requires the trader to operate PAYE.

There are situations where the Revenue regard payments to a 'one man' company as caught by this provision so that the person paying the money to the company should deduct PAYE as if he had made payments to the individual worker concerned. This is increasingly relevant as many employers use service contracts to reduce their overheads and maximise the benefits available to the worker. The Revenue, however, are likely to apply the same criteria to payments made in such circumstances as those they apply to the self-employed, as covered in detail in paragraph 2.2.2.

19.13.3   Payments to sub-contractors in the construction industry

Where a person is carrying on a business which includes construction work, the payments to a sub-contractor in respect of 'construction operations' may be subject to a deduction of tax.

A contractor includes any person carrying on a business which includes construction industry operations even where these are not the main trading activity. If construction work is regularly commissioned on their own trading or investment properties, that person will be considered to be a contractor for the purposes of deducting tax if their expenditure exceeds £250,000 on average over a three year period.

Construction operations

The Regulations define construction so as to include the installation of heating, lighting or drainage, the internal cleaning of buildings in the course of their construction, alterations or repair work, internal or external painting, as well as the construction, alteration, repair or demolition of buildings.

All payments made to sub-contractors who are unable to produce valid and up-to-date tax exemption certificates (Form 714) are liable to a 25 per cent deduction of tax. This includes any travel or expense payment unless the amount can be authenticated as being for genuine building materials required in the course of the work. Where a tax exemption certificate is produced, full details of the certificate must be recorded and, whilst payments can be made gross, a 715 voucher must be obtained from the sub-contractor as a receipt for every payment made. These vouchers must be sent to the Inland Revenue periodically.

19.13.4   Interest and penalties for late payment of PAYE

Over recent years, the Revenue has progressively tightened its policing of employers operating PAYE schemes. The current position is as follows:

(1)   Interest will be charged on PAYE tax and employer's and employees' national insurance contributions not remitted to the Collector of Taxes by fourteen days after the end of the tax year (that is to say, by 19 April 1995 for 1994–95).

(2)   Penalties may be imposed on employers who do not submit their end-of-year returns (Forms P14 and P35) by 19 May following the end of the tax year. The penalty is likely to be £100 per month per unit of 50 employees (rounded up, so that 51 employees count as two units).

(3)   A penalty of £300 may be imposed for each Form P11D (return of expenses payments and benefits provided) not submitted by 6 June following the end of the tax year, with a daily penalty of £60 per return if the forms are not submitted once the initial penalty has been imposed. The penalty for submitting a single incorrect P11D is £3,000.

These very substantial financial penalties mean that all employers must devote adequate resources to the preparation of PAYE returns.

20 Anti-avoidance legislation

There are numerous anti-avoidance provisions which must be borne in mind, especially when a tax planning exercise is being carried out. These provisions are generally intended to ensure that a person cannot reduce his tax liability by carrying out a given transaction in a roundabout way.

This chapter covers:

Income tax

(1) Interest income
(2) Transactions in land
(3) Transactions in securities
(4) Transfer of assets overseas
(5) Trust income taxed on the settlor
(6) Transactions involving loans or credit

Capital gains tax

(7) Disposals by a series of transactions
(8) Transfers to a connected person
(9) Value shifting
(10) UK-resident settlements where the settlor has retained an interest
(11) Offshore companies
(12) Non-resident trusts.

20.1 Interest income

20.1.1 Background

The Taxes Acts contain extensive legislation which is designed to prevent the conversion of taxable income into capital.

20.1.2　Sale of loan stock with right to purchase
(TA 1988, s 729)

At one time it was possible to enjoy the benefit of income in a capital form which was not subject to tax. This was achieved by selling loan stock or other interest bearing securities and retaining a right to repurchase them. For example, a person holding £1 m 3½% War Loan might sell the stock to a charity for £400,000 cum-interest whilst retaining the right to repurchase the War Loan once it had gone ex-interest for (say) £385,000, an overall profit of £15,000. He would have to forgo the income of £17,500 but that would be taxable and worth less than £15,000. The charity, however, would get the income tax free and so the transaction made sense to it.

There is now specific legislation designed to catch such arrangements. Where s 729 applies, the interest is treated as remaining taxable income of the person who sold the loan stock with a right to repurchase. Thus, in the above example, the interest payments actually received by the charity would be treated as income of the individual who had sold the War Loan stock with the right to repurchase it.

20.1.3　Sale of right to income
(TA 1988, s 730)

A variation on the above scheme worked for a number of years. It was common for individuals to sell to a charity or other exempt body the right to receive interest payments for a specified period of time, whilst retaining legal ownership of the securities themselves. This is now caught by TA 1988, s 730. If the loan stock is a UK security, the income which arises is assessed on the vendor. If it is a foreign loan stock, the proceeds of the sale are assessable as if they were income.

20.2　Transactions in land
(TA 1988, s 776)

20.2.1　Introduction

Section 776 was intended to prevent tax avoidance by persons concerned with land or development of land. Section 776 may apply where a capital gain is realised and one of the following conditions applies:

(1)　The gain arises from UK land (or some other asset deriving its value from land) and the land was acquired with the sole or main object of realising a gain.

(2)   The gain arises from the disposal of UK land which is held as trading stock.

(3)   The gain arises from a disposal of UK land which has been developed with the sole or main object of realising a gain on the disposal of the land.

Where s 776 applies, all or part of the capital gain is charged as income under Schedule D Case VI.

The definition of land includes buildings, and also assets deriving their value from land such as options. Consequently, s 776 could apply if a person received a lump sum for assigning the benefit of an option.

20.2.2   Exemption

There is an exemption for gains which arise on the disposal of an individual's principal private residence. This exemption continues to be available even where the capital gains tax exemption is not due because the property was acquired with a view to realising a gain (see 14.13.3).

20.2.3   Sales of shares

Section 776 may apply where a person disposes of shares in a land-owning company. If a non resident individual were to dispose of (say) a controlling shareholding in a company which itself owned a valuable UK property, the individual might be subject to tax under Schedule D Case VI on the whole of his capital gain.

There is a let-out in the case of a land-owning company which holds land as trading stock (ie a company which is a builder or developer or which deals in land as a trade). No liability arises under s 776 on a sale of shares in such a company, provided that the land held by the company is disposed of in the normal course of its trade and a full commercial profit from that land is received by the company.

Despite this let-out, s 776 may still be a problem on a sale of a land-owning company since the company may be an investment company (in which case it will not hold the land as trading stock).

20.2.4   Clearance procedure

It is possible for a person to apply for advance clearance from the Revenue that s 776 will not apply in relation to a particular disposal. This clearance may be sought either in relation to a sale of land or a sale of shares in a land-owning company. The legislation requires that the person should supply full written particulars to the Inspector of Taxes who must then make his decision within 30 days. Once clearance has been given, the Revenue cannot subsequently charge tax under s 776 unless the clearance application was invalid because it did not accurately set out all the facts.

20.3   Transactions in securities
(TA 1988, s 703)

20.3.1   Introduction

Legislation was originally introduced in 1960 to enable the Revenue to counteract tax advantages obtained by transactions in securities. The legislation is often applied by the Revenue to prevent tax savings being achieved because a right to income has been converted into a capital gain. An example of the type of transaction which might be caught in this way is where a person sells shares with a right to repurchase them for a lower amount after a dividend has been received by the purchaser (this is not caught by s 729 which has been mentioned at 20.1.2 above because that legislation applies only to loan stock and other fixed interest securities). However, the legislation also applies to other more devious types of transactions where the tax advantage is less obvious at first sight.

20.3.2   Conditions which must be satisfied before the legislation can apply

For s 703 to apply, the following three conditions must be satisfied.

(1)   There must be one or more transactions in securities; and
(2)   A person must have obtained, or be in a position to obtain, a tax advantage; and
(3)   One of the prescribed circumstances set out in s 704 must have occurred.

If s 703 does apply, an income tax assessment may be made under Schedule D Case VI to counteract the tax advantage.

20.3.3   Transactions in securities

This term is widely defined so as to include transactions of whatever description relating to securities. It includes in particular:

(1)   the purchase, sale or exchange of securities;
(2)   the issuing of new securities;
(3)   alteration of rights attaching to securities.

The term 'securities' is, in turn, defined as including shares and loan stock.

20.3.4 Tax advantage

In general, a tax advantage is deemed to arise if there is any increased relief, or repayment of tax, arising from transactions in securities, or if the transactions result in a reduction in the amount of tax which would otherwise be assessed.

The Courts have taken the view that a tax advantage may arise wherever the Revenue can show that an amount received in a non-taxable form could have been received in a way which would have given rise to an income tax liability. Going back to the example given in 20.3.1 the Revenue would say that a tax advantage arises when a person sells shares and has a right to buy back at a lower price after a dividend has been paid because he could simply have retained the shares and received the dividend.

20.3.5 Prescribed circumstances

Section 704 lists five circumstances and at least one of them must apply before the Revenue can invoke s 703.

Section 704A

This requires:

(1) the receipt of an abnormal dividend;
(2) a dividend should be received by someone entitled to an exemption or relief.

One example of this would be where shares are sold to a charity, the company then pays a dividend and the charity is able to reclaim tax because it is exempt from income tax. Another less obvious example of the circumstances caught under s 704A is where an abnormally large dividend is paid to an individual who is able to set losses against the dividend.

Section 704B

This section applies in specific circumstances which are outside the scope of this book.

Section 704C

This applies where a person receives consideration without paying income tax on it as a result of a transaction whereby another person subsequently receives an abnormal amount by way of dividend.

The consideration received must represent:

(1)   the value of assets which are available for distribution by way of dividends; or

(2)   future receipts of the company; or

(3)   the value of trading stock of the company.

Section 704D

This sub-section applies where a person receives consideration which is not subject to tax and which represents:

(1)   the value of assets which are available for distribution by way of dividend; or

(2)   future receipts of the company; or

(3)   the value of the trading stock of the company.

This sub-section is obviously similar to s 704C but s 704D can apply even though there has been no abnormal dividend.

Section 704D can apply only to transactions involving specified companies, ie:

(1)   companies which are under the control of not more than five persons; or

(2)   transactions involving any other unquoted company.

Section 704E

Again, this section applies to special situations which are outside the scope of this book.

20.3.6   Exemption for *bona fide* commercial transactions

If there is a transaction in securities and the prescribed circumstances apply, a taxpayer may still avoid assessment if he can show that transactions were carried out for *bona fide* commercial reasons or in the ordinary course of making or managing investments, and that none of them had as their main object the obtaining of a tax advantage.

20.3.7   Clearances

Section 707 provides a procedure whereby a person can give details of the proposed transactions to the Revenue and request clearance that the Board will not apply s 703.

Once a written application has been made under s 707, the Revenue has 30 days in which to request further particulars; such further information must then be provided within 30 days.

The Revenue must give a decision either within 30 days of receiving the original application or within 30 days of receiving the further information.

Where the Revenue has notified someone that it is satisfied that s 703 should not apply, the Revenue may not subsequently change its mind. However, where information given in the application is incomplete or inaccurate, any clearance given by the Revenue may be void.

20.3.8   Situations where clearance should be sought

It is standard practice for vendors, or their advisers, to seek clearance under s 707 where a private company is being sold for a substantial amount. Quite apart from anything else, the vendor would otherwise be at the mercy of the purchaser who might extract an abnormal dividend and thus bring s 707 into consideration.

It is also advisable to seek clearance under s 707 where a company is liquidated, the reserves are extracted in a capital form and it is intended that the company's business should be carried on by a new company owned by the current shareholders.

20.4   Transfer of assets overseas

Legislation was originally introduced in 1936 to prevent tax savings for resident and ordinarily resident individuals arising from their transferring assets overseas.

The legislation refers to avoidance of income tax. Capital tax avoidance is not subject to counteraction by s 739 or s 740, although separate anti-avoidance legislation also exists for capital gains tax (see 20.12).

20.4.1   Where the individual or his spouse can benefit

Section 739 applies where a person has made a transfer and either he or his spouse may benefit as a result of the transfer of assets. A person is deemed to meet this test if he has 'power to enjoy' income which arises overseas. Power to enjoy income exists in the following circumstances:

(1)   The income accrues for the benefit of the individual.
(2)   The receipt of the income increases the value to the individual of any assets held by him or for his benefit.
(3)   The individual may become entitled to enjoy the income at some future point in time.

(4)   The individual is able in any way whatsoever, and whether directly or indirectly, to control the way in which the income is used.

Where s 739 applies, the transferor or spouse are assessed on the income as it arises, even if it is not actually paid out to them.

20.4.2   Exemption for *bona fide* transactions

Section 741 provides a clearance procedure. The individual must show to the satisfaction of the Revenue that:

(1)   the purpose of avoiding tax was not one of the purposes for which the transfer of assets was carried out; or
(2)   the transfer of assets, and any associated operations, were *bona fide* commercial transactions and not designed for tax avoidance.

20.4.3   Assessment of income caught by s 739

Income which is caught by s 739 will normally be assessed under Schedule D Case VI. However, where the income is UK dividend income, or other income which has borne tax at source, relief is given for such tax and the assessment will be for higher rate tax purposes only.

20.4.4   Liability of non transferors
(TA 1988, s 740)

A person may not be assessed under s 739 unless he or his spouse has made a transfer of assets. However, a UK-ordinarily resident individual may be assessed if he receives a benefit from a transfer made by another person. This particularly applies to beneficiaries of non-resident settlements created by someone other than the individual and his spouse.

In contrast to s 739, a liability may arise under s 740 only when the individual concerned receives a benefit.

The term 'benefit' is not specifically defined although the legislation states that a benefit includes a payment of any kind. It is understood that an interest free loan or the provision of accommodation are also regarded by the Revenue as constituting a benefit.

20.4.5   Matching income with benefits

The legislation provides for benefits to be matched with income received in either earlier or later years.

20.4.6 Example—Matching benefits with income

An overseas trust receives income of £10,000 in 1993–94. In 1995–96 a capital payment of £100,000 is made to a UK-resident and ordinarily resident individual. In the year 1998–99, the trustees receive further income of £120,000.

If s 740 applies, the individual will be taxed as follows:

	£
1995–96	10,000
1998–99	90,000

20.4.7 Assessment under s 740

Where income is taxed under s 740, there is no credit for any UK tax suffered at source. This can give rise to double taxation. Thus, going back to the previous example, if the trustees' income represented dividends from UK companies, the total tax suffered would really be as follows:

$$\text{Tax at source on dividends: } £100,000 \times \frac{20}{80} = \quad £25,000$$

$$\text{Tax charged on beneficiary under s 740} = \quad \underline{40,000}$$

$$\underline{\underline{65,000}}$$

20.4.8 Clearances

Once again, it is possible to obtain clearance from the Inland Revenue that s 740 should not apply because the transfer of assets concerned was not carried out for the purposes of tax avoidance.

20.5 Trust income taxed on the settlor

20.5.1 Introduction

There are a number of separate provisions under which income on property which belongs to trustees may be taxed as if it were income which belonged to the settlor.

20.5.2 Trust where the settlor may benefit
(TA 1988, s673–674)

Legislation may catch income which arises to a trust under which the settlor or his spouse may benefit. The legislation provides that the settlor/spouse should be treated as capable of benefiting where they *may* benefit in any circumstances whatsoever except in one of the following exceptional cases:

(1)   The bankruptcy of a person who is beneficially entitled under the settlement.
(2)   The death under the age of 25 of a person who would be beneficially entitled to the trust property on attaining that age.
(3)   In the case of a marriage settlement, the death of both parties to the marriage and of all or any of the children of the marriage.

The Revenue interpret this legislation rather literally. For example, if a person creates a trust for the benefit of his son, and the trust deed states that the property should revert to the settlor if the son dies before age 35, the Revenue takes the view that s 673 applies because the let-out applies only where property reverts on the death of someone before he attains age 25.

Sometimes the trust deed is silent on a matter. For example, a person creates a trust for the benefit of his three children and the trust deed makes no reference to the capital coming back to the settlor. In such circumstances, the Revenue is apt to say that the property *could* revert to the settlor if all his children died and they left no children of their own. To avoid this kind of argument, it is normal for a trust to contain a clause which provides that the capital shall in no circumstances whatsoever come back to the settlor but shall be held for the benefit of (say) a charity in the event that all the named beneficiaries die before the capital is distributed.

The Revenue do not take the view that a person has reserved the benefit simply because his spouse may benefit after his death as his widow. On the other hand, cases have actually arisen where the settlor and his wife were excluded but the Revenue said that s 673 *should* apply because the settlor's current marriage might come to an end and he might marry someone who could benefit. Once again, it is best to make sure that the trust deed excludes such an interpretation by expressly providing that any future spouse of the settlor should be excluded from all benefit.

Where a settlor's spouse can benefit, the settlor is assessed on the trust income. This means that the benefits of independent taxation cannot be secured by putting capital into trust for a spouse.

20.5.3   Settlements on minor children
(TA 1988, s 664)

Where a person gives capital to his minor children, the resulting income may be taxed as if it belonged to the parent. This treatment applies where the following three conditions are satisfied:

(1)   The child is a minor.
(2)   The child is unmarried.

(3)   The income exceeds £100 per tax year for each child.

Similarly when a person makes a settlement under which his minor children may benefit, income which is distributed to the children before they are 18 is treated as the settlor's income (subject to the £100 *de minimis* exemption). This applies even where the individual is separated or divorced and the children live with his former wife.

For purposes of s 664, a child includes an adopted child and illegitimate child. Once again, the Revenue interpret this legislation strictly and they have been known to tax a grandparent who set up a trust for his daughter's (illegitimate) child whom he subsequently adopted and brought up as his own child.

There are two circumstances where s 664 does not apply:

(1)   Where the child has married.
(2)   Where the settlor is not resident in the United Kingdom.

The legislation does not stop here. Any capital payments made to the children are also caught so far as the capital payments may be matched with accumulated income within the trust. This is less serious than in the past since trustees will normally pay 35 per cent tax on accumulated income (see 18.5.1) so even if the income is then deemed to be the settlor's income because a capital sum has been paid out to the child, the additional tax payable cannot exceed five per cent (i.e the difference between the 40 per cent top rate and 35 per cent paid by the trustees).

Somewhat surprisingly, s 664 does not apply where a parent gives capital to bare trustees who hold it for the absolute benefit of the child but do not pay out the income before the child attains age 18.

20.5.4   Capital payments to the settlor
(TA 1988, s 677)

There is even a section which may apply to enable the Revenue to charge tax on income received by the trustees of the settlement under which the settlor and spouse are both totally excluded from benefit.

Section 677 may apply where the trustees of the settlement have accumulated income and they have made a capital payment to the settlor. The capital payment is treated as if it were income for the year in which the payment is made provided there is sufficient undistributed income.

If only part of the capital payment can be 'matched', the balance is matched with income for subsequent years, and amounts matched in this way are then taxable for those years.

20.5.5   Example—Matching of capital payments

In 1993–94 A received a capital payment of £18,000 from a trust set up by him in 1985. The trust has net undistributed income of £30,000.

A will be assessed under s 677 as if he had received gross income which after tax at the rate applicable to trusts (35 per cent) would have left £18,000, ie £27,692.

In 1994–95 A receives a capital payment of £50,000. The trustees have undistributed income for that year of £20,000. The trustees make no further capital repayments but in 1995–96 and 1996–97 they have undistributed income of £10,000 and £9,000.

The following amounts are taxable under s 677:

		£
1994–95 £32,000[1] grossed up	=	49,230
1995–96 £10,000 grossed up	=	15,385
1996–97 £8,000 grossed up	=	12,308

[1] ie balance of the undistributed income available at the end of the year 1994–95.

20.5.6   Income may be matched with capital payments made in the previous twelve years

Undistributed income can be identified with past capital payments for up to 12 years. The only way to get round this is for the whole of the capital sum to be repaid by the settlor, but even doing this does not affect the position for past years and the year in which the capital sum is repaid.

20.5.7   Loans may also be caught

A loan from the trustees to the settlor may be treated under s 677 as if it were a capital payment. Furthermore, the *repayment* of a loan by the settlor to the trust can also be treated as a capital payment.

20.5.8   Example—Treatment of loans

In 1993–94 A makes a £150,000 loan to a trust created by him. The trustees repay the loan in full during 1996–97. At that time, the trustees have undistributed income of £45,000.

A would be taxed under s 677 on £45,000 grossed up at 35 per cent ie £69,231.

If the trustees had undistributed income of £30,000 for 1998–99 and £85,000 for 2001–2002, the position would be that assessments could be made on £30,000 grossed up for 1998–99 and £75,000 grossed up for the year 2001–2002.

20.5.9 Payments by companies connected with the trustees

A liability may also arise under s 677 if a company which is connected with the trustees makes a capital payment to the settlor. There have to be three conditions here:

(1) The trustees must have undistributed income.
(2) There must be 'associated payments' by the trustees to the company. An associated payment may include a capital payment (for example a subscription for shares) or the transfer of assets at an undervalue by the trustees to the company.
(3) The company must make a capital payment to the settlor, or make a loan to him or repay a loan made by the settlor to the company. This event must occur within five years of the associated payment having taken place.

20.6 Transactions involving loans or credit
(TA 1988, s 786)

Specific legislation exists to prevent any tax avoidance which could otherwise arise if a person who was liable to pay non-allowable interest found a way of converting his liability to pay interest into some other payment which is tax deductible. Section 786 may apply where a transaction is effected with reference to the lending of money. It can apply whether the transaction is between the lender and borrower or involves other persons connected with them.

(1) Section 786 (3) states that if the transaction provides for payment of any annuity or other annual payment it shall be treated as interest for all purposes of the Taxes Act.
(2) Section 786 (4) states that if the borrower agrees to sell or transfer to the lender any securities or other property carrying a right to income then the borrower may be chargeable under Schedule VI on an amount equal to the income which arises from the property before he repays the loan.
(3) Section 786 (5) refers to income being assigned, surrendered, waived or forgone and states that the person who has assigned, surrendered etc, may be charged to tax under Schedule D Case VI on the amount of income assigned, surrendered, waived or forgone.

In theory, s 786 could apply to interest free loans. The Revenue have given some degree of comfort in that they have said that in the straightforward situation where one person lends money to another and then waives the interest, and there is no further transaction linked in any way to the arrangements, s 786 will not be invoked. There has been some concern, in the past, that s 786 could apply where, for example, a client deposited a large lump sum with his accountant on the basis that the accountant would not pay interest but would reduce his accountancy fees by the amount of the interest that would have been paid at commercial rates on the client's deposit. It is possible to read s 786 (5) as permitting the Revenue to make an assessment in this way even though the type of transactions described are somewhat different from those envisaged when the legislation was originally enacted.

20.7   Disposals by a series of transactions

20.7.1   Basic principle behind the legislation
(TCGA 1992, s 19)

There are certain assets which are worth more in total than the sum of their various parts. For example, a 55 per cent shareholding in a private company will almost always be worth a great deal more than five times the value of an 11 per cent shareholding since a 55 per cent shareholder has control of the company. It follows from this that if there were not specific anti-avoidance legislation, a person could reduce his exposure to CGT on a gift to a relative etc by transferring the asset in stages.

In fact, in certain circumstances, the Revenue may look at the value transferred by a series of transactions and assess the value transferred by each separate transaction according to an appropriate part of the total value transferred.

20.7.2   Legislation may have a wide application

The legislation can also apply in unexpected ways. For example, if an individual with a 75 per cent shareholding in an investment company decided to give 25 per cent to each of his brother's three children and even arranged to make the gifts over a period of two (or more) years, the Revenue could still apply s 19 so as to catch the total value transferred.

20.7.3   Circumstances which will cause s 19 to apply

The following circumstances may result in the Revenue applying s 19:

(1)   A person disposes of assets to another person (or persons) who fall within the definition of connected persons.
(2)   There are 'linked transactions' which fall within a period of six years.
(3)   The disposals have all taken place since 19 March 1985.

(4)   The aggregate value transferred by the series of linked transactions is greater than the total of the values transferred by the individual transactions.

A transaction may be caught by s 19 even if it is a *sale* rather than a gift.

20.7.4   Section 19 can result in retrospective adjustments

If the Revenue invokes s 19, it may result in assessments for previous years being re-opened. For example, C may have made a gift to her father in 1989–90 of a ten per cent shareholding in X Ltd and the value of the shares may have been agreed with the Revenue as, say, £20,000. If C makes a further gift to her brother in 1993–94 of a 70 per cent shareholding, the position may have to be re-opened. If the Revenue establish that a 80 per cent shareholding is worth £800,000 at the time of the gift to C's brother, the effect of applying s 19 will be:

Deemed disposal proceeds on the 1989–90 gift	– £100,000
Deemed disposal proceeds on the 1993–94 gift	– £700,000

20.7.5   Hold-over relief may cover the position

In some circumstances, the donor may not have to pay extra tax because he and the donee may have agreed that the hold-over provisions should apply (see 15.5). However, hold-over relief will not always be available since the asset will not always fall within the definition of business property or the donee may not be resident in the United Kingdom.

Professional advice is clearly essential where a person is contemplating making a series of gifts to connected persons.

20.8   Transfers to a connected person

Another potential pitfall arises from special rules which govern the way in which market value is to be determined when assessing a gain on a transaction between connected persons (whether the transaction is a gift or a sale).

20.8.1   Some restrictions may be taken into account
(TCGA 1992, s 18)

A gift or sale to a connected person may involve an asset over which the acquirer already has certain rights. Thus, A may own the freehold of a building and his daughter may have valuable rights as a tenant. Suppose that the freehold is worth £230,000 with vacant possession, but is worth only £180,000 if his daughter's lease is taken into account. When A sells the freehold to his daughter will the market value be taken as £230,000 or £180,000?

The legislation states that the market value shall be taken to be the market value of the asset less the lower of:

(1) the value of the interest held by the connected person who acquires the asset; or
(2) the amount by which the transferor's asset would increase in value if the connected person's rights did not exist.

Consequently, A would be deemed to make a disposal of an asset worth £180,000.

20.8.2 Some restrictions are ignored
(TCGA 1992, s 18(7))

Certain valuable rights may have to be left out of account. One example of this is an option. Suppose the facts set out in 20.8.1 had been slightly different so that A had vacant possession of a property worth £230,000, but his daughter had an option under which she could acquire it for £180,000. If A sells the property to his daughter or if she exercises her option he will receive only £180,000, but he may be assessed as if he had received £230,000.

This is because the legislation requires options to be ignored or left out of account when computing the market value of an asset. Similarly, legal rights which, if exercised, would effectively destroy or impair the asset also have to be ignored. Market value is determined as if such rights did not exist.

20.9 Value shifting
(TCGA 1992, s 29)

The legislation contains provisions which are intended to ensure that disguised gifts are assessed as a disposal at market value.

20.9.1 Type of transaction which may be caught

A controlling shareholder might exercise his control over a company to transfer value in an indirect way.

20.9.2   Example—Value shifting

B owns all the shares in Y Ltd. The company has 1,000 £1 ordinary shares in issue. Assume that the value of these shares is £300,000.

If B allowed his son C to be issued with 2,000 £1 shares at par, he would not have made a disposal of his own shares. However, C would have acquired a valuable asset in that his 2,000 shares will probably be worth in excess of £200,000 compared with the £2,000 that he had paid to acquire them. Furthermore, B's 1,000 shares will have gone down in value since he will have become a minority shareholder.

Where the Revenue can apply s 29, the person who has transferred value (in this example B) is treated as if he had disposed of an asset.

20.9.3   An omission to exercise a right

There can be circumstances where s 29 is relevant because a person has failed to exercise a right. For example, if A and his grandson D were 50:50 shareholders in Y Ltd and the company announced a rights issue of three new shares for every one share already held and the amount payable for each share was £1 (par), s 29 would come into operation if A chose not to exercise his entitlement to the rights issue, as this omission would mean that after the rights issue the shares in Y Ltd would be owned as to:

A   20 per cent
D   80 per cent

Control would have thereby passed to D.

20.10   UK resident settlements where the settlor has retained an interest

20.10.1   Introduction
(TCGA 1992, s 77)

Capital gains realised by trustees of a UK resident settlement may be taxed as if they were the settlor's own gains if he is deemed to have retained an interest in the trust. The gains are simply added to his personal gains and he is responsible for paying the CGT. He can, however, re-claim the tax from the trustees.

This does not apply unless the settlor is resident or ordinarily resident in the United Kingdom for the tax year concerned. These provisions can apply to a settlement which was created some years before the introduction of this legislation in 1988.

20.10.2   Circumstances in which the settlor is deemed to have retained an interest

A settlor is regarded as having retained an interest if there are any circumstances whatsoever under which the property within the settlement or income arising to the trustees may become payable to him or his spouse. Furthermore, he may be deemed to have retained an interest if he or his spouse enjoys a benefit derived directly or indirectly from the settled property.

There are some circumstances in which a settlor is not deemed to have retained a benefit even though he might receive a benefit. These exceptions relate to the possibility of the settlor or spouse benefiting in the event that a beneficiary becomes bankrupt or dies under the age of 25 years or, in the case of a marriage settlement, the death of the married couple and their children.

20.10.3   Considerable care needed

There is no 'proportionality' here so the retention of even a very small interest could result in the settlor being taxed on considerable gains which he did not (and perhaps never could) enjoy.

There are two areas of special concern: loans by a settlor and remarriage.

Loans by a settlor

If the settlor lends money to the trustees there is a risk that he might be said to have an interest in the settled property and this situation should therefore be avoided.

Remarriage

The possibility of the settlor's current marriage coming to an end and his remarrying may be remote, but will be considered by the Revenue to bring s 77 into operation if such a future spouse is not specifically excluded from benefiting under the settlement.

20.10.4   Death of the settlor

Once the settlor has died, s 77 ceases to apply. His widow cannot then be charged on the trustees' gains.

20.11   Offshore companies
(TCGA 1992, s 13)

A person who is resident and ordinarily resident in the United Kingdom (see 21.2) may be liable for a proportion of capital gains realised by a non-resident company in which he has a shareholding.

20.11.1 Example—Offshore companies

A owns all the shares in Z Ltd, a company incorporated and resident in Bermuda. The company realises a capital gain by disposing of a US property that it owns.

The legislation enables the Revenue to assess A as if he made the capital gain himself. However, certain conditions need to be satisfied before the Revenue can assess a capital gain in this way (see 20.11.2).

20.11.2 Conditions which need to be satisfied

The following conditions need to be satisfied:

(1) The company must be controlled by five or fewer shareholders or shareholder directors must between them own more than 50 per cent of the company's shares.
(2) The individual concerned must be resident (or ordinarily resident) *and* domiciled in the United Kingdom (see 22.1 and 22.14).
(3) The individual must have a shareholding of at least five per cent and be entitled to at least one-twentieth of the company's assets on a liquidation.

20.11.3 Certain gains not assessable under s 13

The legislation is really intended to catch gains on investment assets etc held through an offshore company. There is therefore an exemption under s 13(5) for:

(1) Gains arising on the disposal of foreign currency where the currency represents money in use for a trade carried on by the company outside the United Kingdom.
(2) Gains arising from the disposal of 'tangible property' used for the purposes of a trade carried on by the company wholly outside the United Kingdom.
(3) Gains arising from disposals of assets used by a UK branch of the company.

20.11.4 Distribution test
(TCGA 1992, s 13(5)(d))

Where an offshore company has realised gains which are not exempt under 20.11.3, the individual may still escape assessment if he can show that the offshore company has distributed the gains within two years, either as a dividend or on the company being wound up.

However, if the individual is resident in the United Kingdom at the time that he receives such a distribution, he will be assessed on it (either for income tax or, in the case of a liquidation, for capital gains tax).

20.12   Non-resident trusts
(TCGA 1992, s 86 & Sched 5)

20.12.1   Introduction

Trustees of a trust may be resident outside the United Kingdom and the administration of the trust may be carried out overseas. Provided *both* these conditions are satisfied, the trust is not resident and there will not normally be any liability for the trustees so far as UK capital gains tax is concerned. However, there may be a liability for either the settlor (ie the person who set up the trust) or the beneficiaries (who may include the settlor).

20.12.2   Post 18 March 1991 offshore trusts
(TCGA 1992, s 86 & Sched 5)

The legislation refers to these type of trusts as 'qualifying settlements'. In fact, they qualify for an adverse CGT treatment in that the trustees' gains are deemed to be the settlor's personal capital gains.

The conditions under which the trust's capital gains will be treated in this way are as follows:

(1)   The settlor must be UK resident or ordinarily resident for the year concerned.
(2)   He must not have died during the course of the year.
(3)   The people who benefit from the trust include one of the following:

    (a)   the settlor;
    (b)   the settlor's spouse;
    (c)   the settlor's children (and spouses);
    (d)   a company connected with the settlor.

20.12.3   Pre 19 March 1991 offshore trusts
(TCGA 1992, s 97(1))

Provided that the trust does not become a qualifying settlement, there will be no capital gains tax liability for beneficiaries until such time as 'capital payments' are received.

UK resident and domiciled beneficiaries may be assessed for capital gains tax purposes on a proportion of the trustees' capital gains which can be 'matched' with capital payments received.

20.12.4   Example—Pre 19 March 1991 offshore trusts

Trustees of an offshore trust make capital gains in 1989–90 of £200,000. In 1989–90–1991–92 the trustees distribute income, but their doing this does not have any CGT consequences. In 1993–94 they make a capital payment of £50,000 to A who is UK resident.

A would be assessed as if he had personally made capital gains of £50,000 for 1993–94. The tax actually payable will depend upon whether he has made other capital gains, whether he has capital losses available for off-set and his rate of tax.

A supplementary charge may be made of 10 per cent of the tax for each complete year between 1 December following the year in which the trustees realised the gain and the time that the trustees make the capital distribution. The supplementary charge cannot exceed 60 per cent.

The receipt of a benefit may count as a deemed capital payment.

A pre-19 March 1991 offshore trust may become a qualifying settlement if:

(1)   property is added after 18 March 1991;
(2)   the trust is varied so that a person becomes a beneficiary who previously could not have been expected to benefit.

The preservation of the beneficial tax treatment of pre-19 March 1991 offshore trusts is an area where a specialist tax adviser should be consulted.

21   Residence status

This chapter covers the following:

(1)   Consequences of residence in the United Kingdom
(2)   Various criteria for determining residence status
(3)   Ceasing to be resident in the United Kingdom
(4)   UK income and capital gains received by non-residents
(5)   Non-resident investment companies
(6)   When tax should be withheld from payments to non-residents.

21.1   Consequences of residence in the United Kingdom

The basic principle of UK taxation is that an individual may be charged tax on his world-wide income if he is resident in the United Kingdom. If the individual is not resident in the United Kingdom he will still be liable for tax on income that arises in the United Kingdom but not for tax on income which arises overseas.

There is an exception to this in that an individual who is resident in the United Kingdom but not domiciled here may have to pay tax only on UK income. The concept of domicile is different from residence—for further details see 22.1.

The rest of this chapter proceeds on the basis that an individual has a UK domicile.

21.2   Various criteria for determining residence status

21.2.1   Introduction

For the purposes of UK taxation, the 'United Kingdom' means England,

Scotland, Wales and Northern Ireland. It does not include the Republic of Ireland, the Channel Islands or the Isle of Man. A person may be resident in more than one country so the fact that an individual is treated as resident in, for example, the USA or South Africa does not necessarily mean that he is not resident in the United Kingdom.

A person is resident or not resident for a tax year. A person may also be ordinarily resident if he is habitually resident in the UK as opposed to simply being resident for one year in isolation.

Somewhat surprisingly the word 'resident' is not defined in the Taxes Acts. There is, however, considerable case law and the position is summarised below.

21.2.2 Two basic tests

An individual will always be treated as resident in the United Kingdom for a tax year if he is caught under either of the following tests:

(a) *The six-month rule*, ie the individual is present in the United Kingdom for 183 days or more during the tax year.
(b) *The three-month average rule*, where the individual is present in the United Kingdom for an average of 90 days or more *per annum* measured over a period of four tax years.

Days of arrival and departure are normally left out of account for these tests.

Until recently, it was also possible for an individual to be regarded as resident in the United Kingdom if he had accommodation available for his use in the United Kingdom and he visited this country during the tax year. This rule (which did not normally apply to individuals who worked abroad on a full-time basis), was abolished with effect from 6 April 1993.

21.2.3 Existing UK residents

So far as a person who has been resident in the United Kingdom for a number of years is concerned, he is likely to continue to be regarded as UK resident despite temporary periods of absence from this country unless the following conditions are satisfied:

(a) he works full-time abroad, and the period spent overseas includes a complete tax year, or
(b) he has no accommodation in the United Kingdom and he lives abroad for at least one full tax year.

The treatment of UK residents who move overseas is covered at 21.3.

21.2.4   Foreign nationals coming to the United Kingdom

The residence status of individuals who come to the United Kingdom is now governed by the six-month and the three-month rules set out in 21.2.2.

Individuals who regularly visit the United Kingdom, and are therefore caught by the three-month rule, are normally treated as ordinarily resident only from the fourth year. However, an individual may once again be regarded as ordinarily resident from year one if it is clear that he intended to spend an average of three months per annum in this country.

21.2.5   Visits for education

A person who comes to the United Kingdom for a period of study or education which is expected to last more than four years will be regarded as resident and ordinarily resident from the date of his arrival. If the period is not expected to exceed four years, he may be treated as not ordinarily resident, but this will depend on whether:

(1)   he has accommodation available here, or
(2)   he intends to remain in the United Kingdom when his education is complete, or
(3)   he proposes to visit the United Kingdom in future years for average periods of three months or more per tax year.

If, despite his originally intending not to do so, the individual remains in the United Kingdom for more than four years, he will be treated in any event as ordinarily resident from the beginning of the fifth year of his stay. This applies both to a person who comes to the United Kingdom for his own education or a parent or guardian of a child who comes in connection with the child's education.

21.2.6   Double taxation agreements

The United Kingdom has entered into a large number of double taxation agreements (also known as double tax treaties) with other countries. Provisions of such an agreement may override UK tax law. Specifically, the agreement may provide exemption for certain income received by a person who is resident overseas even though the income arises in the United Kingdom. For example, most double taxation agreements provide that a resident of the foreign country concerned may claim exemption from UK tax in connection with interest income arising in the United Kingdom.

Most double taxation agreements also make provision for the situation that an individual may be resident in both the foreign country concerned and the United Kingdom. The agreements usually contain a clause along the following lines:

(1) If the individual has a permanent home in only one country, he is deemed to be resident in that country.

(2) If the position has not been resolved by (1), then the individual is treated as resident where he has the centre of his personal and economic interests.

(3) If the above tests do not resolve the position, the individual is treated as resident in the country where he has an 'habitual abode'.

(4) If the individual has an habitual abode in both countries he is deemed to be a resident of the country of which he is a national.

(5) If he is a national of both countries, or if he is not a national of either country, the Revenue authorities of the United Kingdom and the foreign country may settle the matter by mutual agreement.

These provisions apply only for the purposes of determining residence under the agreement. They are deeming provisions and, under UK law, an individual might still be regarded as resident in the United Kingdom even though he may be treated as resident in the foreign country for the purposes of the double taxation agreement. However, the terms of a double taxation agreement override UK tax law and, if an individual is deemed to be resident in a foreign country under the agreement, his liability to UK tax will then be computed in accordance with other provisions of the double taxation agreement.

21.3 Ceasing to be resident in the United Kingdom

21.3.1 Working abroad

Up to 1992–93 there was an important distinction between individuals who worked full-time abroad and other people who lived overseas in that the legislation specifically provided that, where an individual worked full-time abroad, the fact that he had accommodation available for his use was not regarded as a relevant factor in determining his residence status. As from 6 April 1993, this distinction became less important as the legislation now provides that an individual shall not be regarded as resident just because he has available accommodation in the United Kingdom. Nevertheless, it is still easier to establish non-resident status if you are working overseas.

A key Revenue publication (IR20) states that if a person goes abroad for full-time service under a contract of employment and:

(1)   all the duties of his employment are performed abroad or any duties he performs here are incidental to his duties abroad; and

(2)   his absence from the United Kingdom and the employment itself both extend over a period covering a complete tax year; and

(3)   any interim visits to the United Kingdom during the period do not amount to:

    (a)   six months or more in any one tax year; or

    (b)   an average of three months or more per tax year

he is normally regarded as not resident and not ordinarily resident in the United Kingdom on the day following the date of his departure until the day preceding the date of his return. On his return, he is regarded as a new permanent resident.

The treatment whereby a person is treated as not resident for part of a tax year is called the 'split year' concession.

IR20 specifically refers to individuals working abroad under a contract of employment. Self-employed people can also qualify for non-resident status, but the split year concession does not normally apply to a self-employed person.

21.3.2   Example—Treatment of self-employed person working overseas

A is self-employed and normally lives in the United Kingdom. He works full-time abroad from 1 May 1992–31 August 1995. He is likely to be regarded as resident and ordinarily resident up to 1992–93 and for the year of return (1995–96), but he should be treated as not resident for the years in between. Note that if A had been an employee he would be treated as not resident and not ordinarily resident from 1 May 1992–31 August 1995.

21.3.3   Involuntary residence
(Statement of Practice SP2/91)

The Revenue operates a concession which covers individuals who are forced to spend time in the United Kingdom because of exceptional circumstances outside their control, eg someone who was working abroad in a Gulf state, but who had to return to the UK prematurely at the outbreak of the Gulf War, may be allowed some leeway when the Revenue apply the three-month average test. Similarly, where an individual spends days in the United Kingdom because of illness, these may be left out of account in certain circumstances.

These concessions do *not* apply where an individual returns to the United Kingdom because his employer has prematurely terminated his contract of employment. Also, and more fundamentally, the Revenue's concession does not affect the rule that an individual is treated as resident in the United Kingdom if he spends 183 days or more in the United Kingdom during a particular tax year.

21.3.4 Other individuals who live abroad

Different rules apply where a person does not work full-time abroad (eg where an individual moves to a foreign country on retirement), or where he works overseas but continues to perform duties in the United Kingdom which are not incidental to the work carried out abroad. A person who falls into this category will continue to be treated as resident where he spends an average of three months per annum in the United Kingdom over a four-year period.

21.4 UK income and capital gains received by non-residents

A person who is not resident in the United Kingdom for a tax year may still be subject to tax on UK source income, but is not liable to tax for income which arises abroad. The following types of income are deemed to arise within the United Kingdom and are therefore subject to tax even where the individual is not resident here:

(1) Employment income which relates to duties performed in the United Kingdom.
(2) Trading profits from a branch or permanent establishment in the United Kingdom.
(3) Rents from UK properties.
(4) Dividends from UK companies.
(5) Interest paid by a person who is resident in the United Kingdom.
(6) 'Annual payments' made by a UK resident person.

21.4.1 Earned income

Where an individual is non-resident, profits from a trade carried on outside the United Kingdom are not subject to UK tax. Where such a person has a branch or permanent establishment in this country, a liability to UK tax may arise from profits earned by that branch. Provisions of a double taxation agreement may govern what type of presence in the United Kingdom is deemed to constitute a branch or permanent establishment.

Earnings from an employment may attract UK tax where the duties are performed in the United Kingdom (see 21.4.5 on double taxation agreements).

Where an individual works full-time abroad under a contract of employment, the resulting income will not be subject to UK tax even though the employer may be a UK company. However, a Crown employee or a member of the Armed Forces is regarded as performing the duties of his employment in the United Kingdom and he may therefore be subject to UK tax even though he performs all his duties overseas and is not resident in the United Kingdom.

Problems have arisen in recent years where an individual was granted a non-approved share option at a time when he was resident in the United Kingdom and subject to tax under Schedule E Case I, with the option subsequently exercised after the individual has ceased to be resident in the United Kingdom. The Revenue's view is that a liability may arise in these circumstances even if the individual is no longer employed by the company concerned.

Pensions paid by UK-resident persons are subject to tax unless the recipient can claim the benefit of a double taxation agreement (see 21.4.5).

21.4.2   Concession for bank and building society interest

In practice, certain income which arises from a UK source is not subject to UK tax. In particular, bank deposit interest is not subject to deduction of UK tax at source provided the non-resident person certifies that he is not ordinarily resident in the United Kingdom (TA 1988, s 481(5)(*k*)). The Revenue will not assess such income unless the account is managed or controlled by a UK resident agent. However, the Revenue may take this income into account when repaying tax which has been withheld at source from other sources of UK income, see extra-statutory concession B13. The concession also applies to interest or dividends paid gross by a building society, discount (eg discount on deep discount bonds), gains on deep gains securities, and interest on certificates of tax deposit.

21.4.3   Exempt gilts

Interest paid on certain British Government securities is not subject to UK tax where the person who owns the security is not ordinarily resident in the United Kingdom (unless the interest forms part of the profits of a trade carried on in the United Kingdom). The exempt securities are the following:

9% Conversion Stock 2000

9% Conversion Stock 2011

13$^{1}/_{4}$% Exchequer Loan 1996

6% Funding Loan 1993

2$^{1}/_{2}$% Treasury Index-linked 2024

4$^{1}/_{8}$% Treasury Index-linked 2030

4$^{3}/_{8}$% Treasury Index-linked 2004

4$^{5}/_{8}$% Treasury Index-linked 1998

5$^{1}/_{2}$% Treasury 2008/12

6$^{3}/_{4}$% Treasury 1995/98

7$^{3}/_{4}$% Treasury 2012/15

8% Treasury 2002/06

8$^{1}/_{2}$% Treasury 2000

8$^{1}/_{2}$% Treasury 2007

8$^{3}/_{4}$% Treasury 1997

9% Treasury 1994

7$^{1}/_{4}$% Treasury 1998

7$^{3}/_{4}$% Treasury 2006

8% Treasury 2003

8% Treasury 2013

8$^{3}/_{4}$% Treasury 2017

9% Treasury 1992/96

9% Treasury 2008

9% Treasury 2012

9$^{1}/_{2}$% Treasury 1999

10% Treasury 1994

12$^{3}/_{4}$% Treasury 1995

13$^{1}/_{4}$% Treasury 1997

13$^{3}/_{4}$% Treasury 1993

14$^{1}/_{2}$% Treasury 1994

15$^{1}/_{4}$% Treasury 1996

15$^{1}/_{2}$% Treasury 1998

3$^{1}/_{2}$% War Loan 1952 or after

21.4.4   Income from property

Rental income received by an individual from a UK property is subject to UK tax even if the individual is not resident in the United Kingdom. A tenant who pays rent direct to a non-resident landlord should withhold basic rate tax at source. In other cases, where rent is paid to a UK agent, the tenant should pay the rent without deduction, but the agent may be assessed on behalf of the owner of the property under TMA 1970, s 78.

21.4.5   Double taxation agreements

Where an individual is not resident in the United Kingdom but is resident in a foreign country which has a double taxation agreement, it may be possible for certain income which would normally suffer UK tax at source to be exempt from UK tax, or subject only to a lower rate.

Remuneration for work performed in the United Kingdom

Most double taxation agreements provide an exemption from UK tax for employment income, provided the following conditions are satisfied:

(1)   the recipient of the remuneration is present in the United Kingdom for a period not exceeding 183 days in aggregate in the tax year concerned; and

(2)   the remuneration is paid by, or on behalf of, an employer who is not resident in the United Kingdom; and

(3)   the remuneration is not borne by a permanent establishment or a fixed base which the employer has in the United Kingdom.

Pensions

Double taxation agreements generally provide for exemption from UK tax in respect of a pension paid by a UK company or pension scheme, although such a pension will then be subject to tax in the foreign country concerned.

Interest

In general, most double taxation agreements provide for a person resident in the foreign country concerned to be exempt from UK tax on interest. The company etc which pays the interest can be given authorisation to pay the interest gross. In cases where tax has been withheld at source the individual may be entitled to a repayment.

Dividends

The double taxation agreement may provide that the person who receives a dividend from a UK company should be entitled to the benefit of the tax credit and should be repaid part of the tax credit (so that the UK tax withheld at source represents an effective rate of 15 per cent).

Royalties

Most double taxation agreements provide that where a royalty is received by a person resident in the foreign country concerned, the royalties shall be free from UK tax.

21.4.6   Allowances and reliefs

A British subject is entitled to a full personal allowance for a tax year, even if he is not a UK resident. Prior to 1990–91, a different rule applied in that British subjects who were resident abroad were entitled only to a proportion of the personal reliefs due to a UK resident person. A person who is resident abroad because of his employment, and who expects to return within four years, may continue to have MIRAS relief in respect of mortgage interest.

A non-resident person is not generally entitled to repayment supplement (see 19.11) so it is normally important that tax should not be overpaid where this can be avoided. However, EC nationals may be entitled to supplement even though they are not UK resident.

21.4.7   Capital gains

A non-UK resident is not normally subject to CGT except where capital gains arise from the disposal of assets used by a branch or permanent establishment of a business carried on by the non-resident in the United Kingdom.

21.5   Non-resident investment companies

A non-UK resident who has significant investment income arising within the United Kingdom may take certain steps to minimise his UK tax liability. Where he cannot claim the benefit of a double taxation agreement, it may be advisable for UK income-producing assets to be held through a non-UK resident company. This will mean that any tax liability will be confined to basic rate tax and there will be no question of any higher rate liability.

In such a case, it would still be sensible for some investments to be retained in the individual's own name if he is a British subject or is otherwise entitled to claim a personal allowance. Sufficient personal income should arise to use such an allowance as this will be wasted if all income arises within an offshore company.

It is generally advisable for a non-resident landlord to appoint a UK agent since, where tax is withheld at the basic rate from rental income, the tax deducted at source is likely to exceed the actual liability for the year (because the landlord will have expenses which may be set against the rental income). This is particularly likely to be the situation where the individual has raised a qualifying loan to purchase the property (it should be borne in mind that the £30,000 ceiling for MIRAS does not apply to loans which have been used to purchase an investment property).

In some cases, a non-resident landlord should form an offshore company to acquire UK properties. The offshore company may raise a qualifying loan to purchase the properties from the individual concerned and interest payable on the loan may then be offset against the non-resident company's rental income. This is a way in which an individual who already owns a property which is not subject to a mortgage may create a situation where interest is payable on a qualifying loan which is deductible in computing Schedule A income.

21.6   When tax should be withheld from payments to non-residents

21.6.1   Payments to non-resident sportsmen and entertainers

Basic rate tax must be withheld from most payments made to non-UK resident sportsmen and entertainers in respect of work performed in the United Kingdom. In addition, where benefits in kind are provided to a non-resident sportsman or entertainer, the cost must be 'grossed up' for tax of 25 per cent and accounted for. A tax voucher must be provided in respect of each payment and the person making the payments needs to account for tax on a quarterly basis.

21.6.2   Payments caught by this scheme

Payments or benefits subject to these regulations include:

(1)   Prize money.
(2)   Appearance or performance fees.
(3)   Endorsement fees where the individual has appeared in the United Kingdom (whether or not his appearance is to promote the goods that he is endorsing).
(4)   Payments which finance any of the above (such as commercial sponsorship).

Certain payments are specifically excluded from the scheme:

(1)   Payments subject to deduction of tax.
(2)   Payments subject to PAYE.
(3)   Payments solely for the use of copyright in words or music.
(4)   Payments made to the Performing Rights Society.
(5)   Payments which are made to UK residents and which are ancillary to a performance (this will include the cost of hiring a venue and payments for the services of UK-resident performers appearing with a non-resident).
(6)   Payments as royalties on the sale of records and tapes.
(7)   Payments amounting to less than £1,000 in a tax year. This *de minimis* limit applies in respect of all payments made in a tax year in connection with the same event. Furthermore, payments made by the same or connected persons have to be aggregated and the £1,000 exemption applies only if the total is less than £1,000.

21.6.3   Special arrangements

It is possible for a payer to secure the Revenue's agreement to a lower rate of withholding tax provided an application is made at least 30 days in advance. Such authorisation may be given on the basis that:

(1)   the organiser can arrange that he is responsible for accounting for the tax; or

(2)   the sponsor can apply for clearance on the grounds that the tax will be collected from someone else; or

(3)   the payer can see authority to withhold tax at a lower rate, possibly to reflect the fact that the non-resident will have certain allowable expenses or perhaps because only some members of a group are non-resident.

21.6.4   Indirect payments also caught

The regulations provide that the withholding system should apply to payments made to:

(1)   any person who is under the control of the non-resident sportsman or entertainer;

(2)   any person who is:
      (a)   not resident in the United Kingdom; and
      (b)   not liable to tax in a territory outside the United Kingdom where the rate of tax charged on profits exceeds 25 per cent;

(3)   any person in receipt of a connected payment or value transferred by a connected transfer;

(4)   any person who receives any connected payment or connected transfer where there is a contract or arrangement under which it is reasonable to suppose that the entertainer (or other person who is connected with him) is, will, or may become, entitled to receive amounts not substantially less than the amount paid.

21.6.5   Interest paid to a non-resident lender

Basic rate tax must normally be deducted where the interest is chargeable under Schedule D Case III and the lender is not resident in the United Kingdom. However, it may be possible for the lender to make a claim under a double taxation agreement. Where such a claim has been made, the Revenue may authorise payment of interest without deduction of tax.

21.6.6   Copyright royalties

Copyright royalties paid to a non-resident person are normally subject to deduction of tax. Where the payment is made via a commission agent, basic rate tax has to be withheld for the net amount which is paid on to the non-resident. A statement made in the House of Commons in 1969 indicates that this obligation to withhold tax does not apply where copyright payments are made to professional authors who are resident abroad.

21.6.7   Purchase of British patent rights

There is an obligation for basic rate tax to be withheld where a person sells all or part of his patent rights and the vendor is not resident in the United Kingdom. Once again, the provisions of a double tax agreement may override this, but a person making payment for such rights must deduct tax unless he is authorised not to do so by the Inspector of Foreign Dividends.

21.6.8   Rent payable to a non-resident landlord

A person who pays rent to a non-resident landlord is required to withhold tax at the basic rate and to account for this to the Revenue. This obligation arises whether the payment is made within the United Kingdom or by payment out of a bank account held overseas.

The obligation to withhold tax does not arise where the tenant pays rent to an agent in the United Kingdom since the agent may be assessed under TMA 1970, s 78. The Revenue would not normally pursue a tenant who had failed to deduct tax where the tenant could not have known that the landlord was non-resident and nothing had happened to put him on notice.

Where a UK-resident person pays a premium to a non-resident landlord, the same requirement to withhold tax arises.

21.6.9   Payments in respect of UK land

There are no provisions for tax to be withheld at source from capital payments made to a non-resident person in respect of UK land. However, where the Revenue serve a notice on a person who is liable to make such a payment, he is required to treat the sums paid by him as an annual payment.

Where a tenant has failed to withhold tax, he may be required to account for it to the Revenue. In such circumstances, there is no legal right for the tenant to withhold sums from subsequent payments of rent to cover the amounts paid over to the Revenue.

22 The income and capital gains of foreign domiciliaries

This chapter deals with the tax treatment of individuals who are resident but not domiciled in the United Kingdom.

(1)   Meaning of domicile

Earned income

(2)   Foreign emoluments
(3)   Travelling expenses
(4)   'Corresponding payments'
(5)   Overseas pension funds
(6)   Self employment
(7)   Partnerships controlled outside the United Kingdom
(8)   Pensions benefits

Investment income

(9)   The remittance basis for investment income
(10) What constitutes a remittance?
(11) Position if foreign domiciliary acquires a UK domicile
(12) Managing the remittance basis

Capital gains tax

(13) Remittance basis for capital gains on foreign assets
(14) Use of offshore companies and trusts

Inheritance tax

(15) UK and foreign situs property.

22.1   Meaning of domicile

Domicile is a fundamentally different concept from residence and ordinary residence. It is not the same as nationality, although an individual's nationality may be one factor which is relevant in determining his domicile. The basic concept is that a person is domiciled in the country which he regards as his real home. The fact that an individual may be prevented from living in that country or may need to live elsewhere because of temporary reasons (such as business and/or employment) does not mean that the individual is domiciled in the country in which he resides. Under English law, an individual normally acquires his father's domicile at birth and he retains this domicile unless his father changes his own domicile before the individual attains age 16. The mother's domicile may apply instead where a child is illegitimate or the parents divorce. The domicile acquired in this way is called the individual's 'domicile of origin'.

An individual may change his domicile to a 'domicile of choice'. Normally this would happen by his leaving his country of origin and taking up permanent residence abroad with the intention of never returning to live in the country of origin on a permanent basis. An individual's domicile of origin will revive if his intentions alter and he decides not to make his permanent home in the new country after all.

Married women

Where a woman married before 1 January 1974, she generally acquired her husband's domicile (this was referred to as a 'domicile of dependency'). This domicile continued after divorce or the death of the husband, although the woman could discard her domicile of dependency in which case she would regain her domicile of origin. A domicile of dependency in the United Kingdom may be discarded by the woman establishing that she no longer intends to remain permanently in this country and by her ceasing to be resident here. The mere intention is not itself sufficient. For example, an Australian woman who had acquired a domicile of dependency in England was held to be domiciled here, despite her intention to return to Australia, because she had not ceased to be resident.

Where a couple have married after 31 December 1973, the law is somewhat different. The Domicile and Matrimonial Proceedings Act 1973 allows a woman to retain an independent domicile on her marriage.

Changes on the way?

Following the publication of a report on the law of domicile by the Law

Commission, the UK Government announced that it intends to introduce new legislation on the law of domicile 'when a suitable opportunity arises'.

The draft Domicile Bill broadly contains the following provisions:

(1)   A child will be domiciled in the country with which he is, for the time being, most closely connected.

(2)   On becoming an adult, a person retains the domicile he had immediately before becoming an adult.

(3)   An adult will acquire a domicile in another country if he is both present there and intends to settle there for an indefinite period.

(4)   The burden of proof to demonstrate a change of domicile will not be so great as it is under the present rules.

However, on 26 May 1993, a reply given by the Prime Minister to a written parliamentary question, stated that the Government 'has no immediate plans to introduce legislation on this subject'. The Lord Chancellor's office indicated at the time that the reference to 'immediate' meant that legislation would not be introduced during the current parliamentary session, but no formal statement has ever been issued.

22.2   Foreign emoluments

22.2.1   Introduction

A foreign-domiciled individual who is employed by a UK-resident employer is basically treated no differently from a UK-domiciled individual in a similar position. The earnings from such an employment are taxed under Case I or Case II of Schedule E according to whether the individual is ordinarily resident in the United Kingdom as well as resident here (for the taxation of such earnings, see Chapter 3).

However, where a person domiciled outside the United Kingdom is employed by a non UK-resident employer, the tax treatment is fundamentally different. Earnings from such an employments are called 'foreign emoluments'. Their tax treatment is as set out Table 22.1 below.

22.2.2   The employer need not be resident in the country in which the individual is domiciled

It is not necessary that the employer should be resident in the same country as that in which the individual is domiciled (although this will, of course, often be the situation). An individual who is domiciled in (for example) Switzerland and who is employed by a company which is resident in the United States has foreign emoluments.

Table 22.1—Tax treatment under Schedule E of earnings by a foreign domiciled individual from a non UK resident employer ('foreign emoluments')

	Duties of employment performed wholly or partly in the UK		Duties of employment performed wholly outside the UK
	In the UK	Outside the UK	
Employee resident and ordinarily resident in the UK	Liable to UK tax (Case I)	Liable to UK tax (Case I)	Liable if remitted to the UK (Case III)
Resident but not ordinarily resident	Liable to UK tax (Case II)	Liable if remitted to the UK (Case III)	Liable if remitted to the UK (Case III)
Not resident	Liable to UK tax (Case II)	Not liable	Not liable

22.2.3   Earnings from an employer who is resident in the Republic of Ireland
(TA 1988, s 192)

There is one exception to the general rule that foreign emoluments arise from an employment by a person not domiciled in the United Kingdom from an office or employment with a non UK-resident employer. Where the employer is resident in the Republic of Ireland, the earnings are not regarded as foreign emoluments.

22.2.4   Earnings of a person who is not ordinarily resident in the United Kingdom

Where an individual has foreign emoluments and he is resident in the United Kingdom, but not ordinarily resident (see 21.2.1 for meaning of ordinary residence), it is necessary to divide the emoluments between those which relate to duties performed in the United Kingdom and those which are performed overseas. The remuneration which is referable to the UK duties is taxed on an arising basis under Schedule E Case II but the remuneration for the duties performed overseas is taxed on the remittance basis under Schedule E Case III.

22.2.5 Split contract needed for a person who is resident and ordinarily resident in the United Kingdom

A different rule applies where an individual is both resident and ordinarily resident in the United Kingdom. The earnings from an employment with a foreign employer are subject to tax in the United Kingdom on an arising basis where all *or any part* of the duties are performed in the United Kingdom. There are no provisions whereby remuneration can be split between earnings relating to work done in the United Kingdom and work performed overseas. However, if an individual has a contract of employment where *all* the duties are performed outside the United Kingdom, the earnings are taxed on the remittance basis under Schedule E Case III. In practice, it is possible to take full advantage of this treatment by an individual having two separate contracts of employment, one covering duties performed in the United Kingdom and the other covering duties performed overseas.

22.3 Travelling expenses
(TA 1988, s 195)

There are special provisions which apply for individuals of foreign domicile. Certain travel expenses which are paid or reimbursed by an employer are not assessable income where all the following conditions are satisfied:

(1)   The expenses must be paid during the five year period which begins from the date of arrival in the United Kingdom.

(2)   The expenses must relate to a journey between the individual's usual place of abode and the place in the United Kingdom where he works.

(3)   The expenses must relate to journeys made by the employee, unless he is in the United Kingdom for a continuous period of 60 days or more for the purposes of performing duties. In this event, the expenses of a visit by his spouse or minor child will also be allowable, although there is a limit of two visits by any such person in a tax year.

In order to secure this exemption it is also necessary that the individual must not have been resident in the United Kingdom in either of the two tax years which precede the year in which he took up his UK employment.

22.4   'Corresponding payments'
(TA 1988, s 192(3))

Certain payments made by an individual out of foreign emoluments qualify for tax relief where they are made 'in circumstances corresponding to those in which the payments would have reduced his liability to income tax' had they been paid in the United Kingdom. Payments which can be relieved under this heading include contributions to an overseas pension fund (see 22.5 below) and mortgage interest. Alimony and maintenance payable under pre-15 March 1988 foreign Court Orders may also be deducted from foreign emoluments.

22.5   Overseas pension funds

An overseas pension fund will not normally be an approved retirement benefit scheme for the purposes of UK tax. However, where the benefits provided by an overseas pension fund are broadly similar to those which arise from UK-approved retirement benefit schemes, the Revenue may regard the employer's contributions as not constituting remuneration for the purposes of Schedule E and any contributions made by the employee may be deducted as corresponding payments (see 22.4). In some situations, the Revenue will accord this treatment only where the individual's rights under his overseas pension scheme are adapted or restricted. For example, a US National who has an individual retirement plan may be required to give notice to the US administrators so as to waive his ability to take a lump sum in circumstances where this would not be permitted under the rules which govern UK-approved retirement benefit schemes.

22.6   Self-employment

Where an individual is resident in the United Kingdom, any earnings from a business carried on as a sole trader are taxed under Schedule D Case I on the arising basis. This even applies in a situation where all the work is actually performed overseas. The basis for this interpretation by the Courts is that a business is deemed to be carried on from where it is controlled and, in the case of a sole trader, control is located where the proprietor is resident.

A foreign domiciled individual who carries on self-employment and who performs a substantial amount of work overseas should consider forming a company. In particular, if an overseas company were to be formed and the company employed the individual and supplied his services outside the United Kingdom to customers, the earnings from that employment would constitute foreign emoluments. Provided that no work is performed in the United Kingdom under the contract of employment, interposing an offshore company in this way would mean that the individual could take full advantage of the remittance basis for earnings which are taxable under Schedule E Case III.

22.7 Partnerships controlled outside the United Kingdom

Where a UK-resident individual is a partner in a firm which is controlled outside the United Kingdom, his earnings from that firm will be taxed as follows:

(1) Profits from a UK branch—Under Schedule D Case I on the arising basis.
(2) Overseas profits—Under Schedule D Case V under the remittance basis.

22.8 Pension benefits

22.8.1 Lump sums paid under overseas pension schemes
(Extra-statutory concession A10)

Income tax is not charged on lump sum benefits received by an employee (or by his personal representatives or any dependant) from an overseas retirement benefit scheme or an overseas provident fund where the employee's overseas service comprises:

(1) not less than 75 per cent of his total service in the employment concerned; or
(2) the whole of the last ten years of his service in that employment (subject to the total service exceeding ten years); or
(3) not less than 50 per cent of his total service in that employment, including any ten of the last 20 years, provided the total service exceeds 20 years.

If the employee's overseas service does not meet these requirements, relief from income tax is given by reducing the amount of the lump sum which would otherwise be chargeable by the same proportion as the overseas service bears to the employee's total service in that employment.

22.8.2 Pensions

An individual who receives a pension paid by a person who is not resident in the United Kingdom is subject to tax under Schedule D Case V on the remittance basis. However, there is no such reduction as exists for UK-domiciled individuals who are taxed on only 90 per cent of such pensions. If the whole of the pension is remitted, tax arises under Schedule D Case V on the full amount.

22.9 The remittance basis for investment income

22.9.1 Remittance basis

Chapters 5 and 6 cover the overseas investment income of an individual who is ordinarily resident and domiciled in the United Kingdom; such individuals are taxed under Schedule D Cases IV and V in respect of income as it arises. A completely different rule applies for individuals who are not ordinarily resident or not domiciled in the United Kingdom; their assessable income is fixed by reference to the amount of income remitted to the United Kingdom.

22.9.2 Exception for income arising within the Republic of Ireland
(TA 1988, s 68)

Where a foreign-domiciled individual has income which arises within the Republic of Ireland, the income is taxed as it arises and not on the remittance basis. The income is taxed on the current year basis.

22.9.3 Assessment under the preceding year basis
(TA 1988, s 65)

Where an individual is taxed under the remittance basis, the assessable amount will generally be the amount of income remitted to the United Kingdom during the preceding tax year. However, the current year basis applies in relation to the first two tax years and also the final tax year in which an individual owns a particular source of overseas income. The Revenue also has the option to assess the penultimate year on the actual basis.

22.9.4 Treatment of individuals who become UK resident

The opening years provisions do *not* come into force on an individual's taking up residence in the United Kingdom. Where an individual has had a particular source of overseas income for a number of years before becoming resident in the United Kingdom, the preceding year basis of assessment may apply from the outset. Where he has actually made remittances of income to the United Kingdom in the tax year prior to the year in which he takes up residence, the remittances will normally form the basis of the assessable income for the year of arrival. In fact, the preceding year basis will apply from the outset unless he made no remittances to the United Kingdom whatsoever during the two years prior to the year of arrival in the United Kingdom.

Where an individual ceases to have a source of overseas income during the period between his arrival in the United Kingdom and the end of that tax year, the assessable income is restricted to the amount of the income which arises during that period. Where an individual ceases to have a source of income in the tax year following the tax year in which he becomes resident in the United Kingdom, the assessable income for the year of arrival is restricted to a proportion of the amount of income which is strictly assessable on the preceding year basis, with the proportion being determined as follows:

$$\frac{\text{Period from date of arrival} - 5 \text{ April}}{365}$$

22.9.5 Each source of overseas income to be dealt with separately
(TA 1988, ss 67 and 73)

The Inland Revenue will generally issue an assessment under Schedule D Case IV or Case V which includes all the individual's income which falls to be taxed under that schedule. However, the opening year and closing year provisions apply separately in relation to each source of overseas income.

22.9.6 No assessment can be made if the individual ceases to have the source of income

A Schedule D Case IV or Case V assessment can only be made for a tax year if the individual had the source of income during that year. Care needs to be taken as to what constitutes a source of income. It is not thought to be prudent to rely upon this principle by closing a bank account and opening a new deposit account with the same bank. It is arguable that the source of income is represented by the debt due by that *particular* bank and so the individual continues to have the source of income in question.

22.9.7   Income previously subject to deduction at source
(TA 1988, s 66)

If income from overseas securities etc has previously been subject to UK tax at source, and the income ceases to be subject to tax deduction in this way, it is treated as a new source of income for Schedule D Case IV and Case V purposes.

22.9.8   Income which becomes subject to deduction of tax at source
(TA 1988, s 66)

If income from an overseas source becomes subject to deduction of UK tax at source, the individual is treated as having disposed of that particular source. The Schedule D Case IV or Case V assessment for the final year prior to tax being withheld at source will be adjusted to the actual income remitted.

22.9.9   Deemed cessation
(TA 1988, s 67)

If an individual makes no remittances of overseas income for six consecutive years, he can claim that the source of income should be deemed to have ceased in the tax year when remittances were last made. Similarly, where an individual actually ceases to have a source of income, he may elect for a source to be treated as having ceased at the time when he last remitted income. Such a claim cannot be made more than eight years after the year in which income was last received.

22.9.10   Relief for foreign tax
(TA 1988, s 793)

Where overseas income has borne foreign tax, credit may be claimed for this against the UK tax assessed on the same income.

22.10 What constitutes a remittance?

22.10.1 General principles

A remittance arises where an individual brings money into the United Kingdom, either in cash or by transferring money to a UK bank account. However, no remittance occurs if money is spent abroad or if liabilities which fall due for payment overseas are settled directly from a foreign bank account.

22.10.2 Constructive remittances
(TA 1988, s 65)

The legislation deals with constructive remittances and states that a remittance is deemed to have occurred if an individual applies overseas income towards the satisfaction of:

(1) a debt (or interest thereon) for money lent to the individual in the United Kingdom;
(2) a debt for money lent to him abroad and brought to the United Kingdom;
(3) a loan incurred in order to satisfy such debts.

Case law also indicates that a constructive remittance is deemed to have occurred if an individual borrows from a UK bank but has his borrowings formally secured against money held in an overseas bank account.

The Courts have held that a complex arrangement whereby money was transmitted between two South African companies, with the individual receiving a loan from one of them, constituted a constructive remittance of income. Since the Courts are increasingly having regard for the overall consequences of a series of transactions, it would be unwise to rely upon an artificial scheme which enabled an individual to enjoy sums in the United Kingdom which could be matched with overseas income.

22.10.3 Unauthorised remittances

In one case, a bank remitted untaxed overseas income by mistake. Because the bank acted contrary to its customer's instructions, it was held that there was no liability under the remittance basis.

22.10.4 Gifts of unremitted income

The safest course of action is for a gift to take the form of a cheque to be drawn on a foreign bank account, with the recipient paying the sum into a foreign bank account. If matters are handled in this particular way, there can be no question of the gift constituting a remittance.

Where an individual makes a gift of foreign income, he is not affected by what happens subsequently. The money loses its income quality once it has been given away and the recipient can bring the money into the United Kingdom without any liability under the remittance basis. In principle, this rule ought also to apply to gifts between spouses, although one should expect the Revenue to carefully scrutinise such arrangements so as to ensure that there are no hidden arrangements which govern the way in which the recipient must use the money given.

22.11   Position if foreign domiciliary acquires a UK domicile

Where an individual is assessable under the remittance basis, but then acquires a UK domicile of choice, the remittance basis ceases to apply and the individual's overseas income is taxable under the arising basis. No tax liability arises if he then remits money which would formerly have given rise to a liability under the remittance basis.

22.12   Managing the remittance basis

22.12.1   Maintaining separate bank accounts

Where a foreign-domiciled individual has substantial overseas income, it is normal for arrangements to be put in place so that remittances to the United Kingdom may be identified, as far as possible, with capital.

The way that this is normally dealt with is by arranging for the individual to have three separate bank accounts, as follows:

(1)   The first account is capital, ie the cash actually held by the individual at the time that he took up residence in the United Kingdom. It is normal for further sums to be paid into this bank account where the cash relates to the sale proceeds of assets sold at a loss for CGT purposes or the proceeds arise from the sale of exempt assets. The bank should be instructed so that any interest on this bank account is not credited to the account, but paid to the income account (see below).

(2)   The second account should contain the proceeds of sales of assets which give rise to capital gains.

(3)   The third account should be kept for income, including interest on the capital account and the capital gains account.

Clearly, in practice, an individual may minimise his liability under the remittance basis by taking remittances from the capital account in (1).

In some situations, it may be sensible to go one stage further and to keep two income accounts with one account containing income which has not borne tax at source (for example, overseas bank deposit interest) and the other account containing income which has borne foreign tax. By organising matters in this way, remittances of income can come out of the account which contains income which has suffered foreign tax, and this will further minimise any UK tax liability.

There may be CGT savings from having different types of capital gains account (see 22.13.5).

22.12.2 Use overseas income accounts to fund expenditure outside the United Kingdom

A foreign-domiciled individual should also organise matters so that all possible expenditure outside the United Kingdom is funded out of the income account and, where relevant, out of the income account which represents income which has not borne any foreign tax at source.

22.12.3 Closing a bank account so that a source ceases to exist

Where an individual has a separate source of income (eg a bank deposit account) it may be possible to take full advantage of the rule that no assessment may be made for a tax year after the individual ceases to have the source of income concerned. This could be achieved by the individual's closing the bank deposit account, and transferring the cash to a new account with another bank (see 22.9.6). Remittances from that new account may then be made in the following tax year and no liability should arise under the remittance basis since such remittances will represent capital (even though the capital was built up out of income which arose whilst the individual possessed the particular source of overseas income concerned).

22.12.4 Trustees may use unremitted income to buy investments from the settlor

A further possibility whereby a foreign-domiciled individual may minimise the income he requires in the United Kingdom is for him to transfer unremitted income to foreign trustees who then use that income to make capital investments by buying property from the settlor.

22.12.5   Example—Trustee's use of unremitted income

A has accumulated overseas income of £45,000 which will become taxable if it is remitted to the United Kingdom.

If A transfers the £45,000 to an offshore trust and then sells his main residence to the trustees, he should not be chargeable to tax under Schedule D Case IV or V as if he had remitted the income, even though the £45,000 is brought into the United Kingdom after the sale of the property.

If A remains in occupation as a beneficiary of the trust, this will not of itself constitute a remittance or a deemed remittance.

22.13   Remittance basis for capital gains on foreign assets

22.13.1   Introduction
(TCGA 1992, s 12 and s 275)

A person of foreign domicile may be subject to CGT if he is either resident or ordinarily resident in the United Kingdom. Gains on UK assets are charged in the same way as gains realised by UK-domiciled individuals. However, gains realised on assets which are situated overseas are subject to UK CGT *only* if the proceeds are remitted to the United Kingdom.

The following rules determine whether an asset is deemed to be situated in the United Kingdom or abroad:

(1)   Real estate and rights over such property are situated in the country where the real estate is located.

(2)   Tangible movable property and rights over such property are situated in the country where the property is located.

(3)   Debts are normally situated in the country where the creditor is resident.

(4)   Stocks, shares and securities are generally situated in the country where the company maintains its principal register.

(5)   Goodwill is treated as situated where the trade or business is carried on.

(6)   Patents, trade-marks and designs are situated in the country where they are registered.

22.13.2   Definition of remittance

Capital gains are remitted if they are brought into the United Kingdom or enjoyed here. For example, payment of the disposal proceeds into a UK bank account counts as a remittance, as does a payment into a UK bank account from an overseas bank account containing such proceeds. Less obviously, the gains will be enjoyed in the United Kingdom if an individual has a large deposit account outside the United Kingdom and he formally secures a UK bank loan against this deposit account. However, if the money is spent outside the United Kingdom, it is not deemed to have been remitted. Payment of disposal proceeds into a bank account in the Channel Islands or Isle of Man does *not* constitute a remittance to the United Kingdom. An outright gift which takes place outside the United Kingdom will not normally be a remittance provided a cheque etc is paid into an overseas bank account for the recipient.

22.13.3   Losses not allowable
(TCGA 1992, s 16(4))

Where a loss arises on an overseas asset, a person of foreign domicile cannot claim a capital loss. In some situations this could give rise to hardship.

22.13.4   Example—Losses not allowable

A has gains of £90,000 on UK assets and capital losses of £60,000 on foreign assets. Unfortunately, there is no relief for the £60,000 losses so he would be taxed on gains of £90,000.

22.13.5   How to take full advantage of the remittance basis

In some cases it may be that there is no likelihood of the individual needing to bring the proceeds of a sale of foreign assets into the United Kingdom. In such a situation the payment of CGT is something that the individual may or may not choose to do since he can control the amount of his chargeable gains. Where it is going to be necessary to bring money into the United Kingdom at some stage in the future, it is advisable for the individual to keep separate bank accounts.

One account should receive the proceeds of assets which have been sold at a loss when measured for UK CGT purposes. This account may be used to fund remittances to the United Kingdom which are not going to give rise to a CGT liability. A second account should contain the proceeds of sales of assets which are subject to foreign CGT. Remittances out of this account will give rise to a CGT assessment, but double tax relief will be due in respect of the foreign CGT which has been paid. Other sales of assets which have produced a gain should be kept in a third account, and should be remitted only as a last resort.

22.13.6 Position where foreign domiciliary acquires UK domicile

The law is not clear here. A Special Commissioners' decision indicates that a liability may arise for a UK-domiciled individual if he remits sums which would have been subject to capital gains tax if they had been remitted before he acquired a UK domicile of choice. Caution is advisable.

22.14 Use of offshore companies and trusts

The formidable range of anti-avoidance provisions covered in Chapter 20 do not have the same impact where a foreign domiciled individual is concerned.

22.14.1 Offshore companies

The anti-avoidance legislation contained in TCGA 1992, s 13 (see 20.11) does not apply to foreign-domiciled individuals and there are no other ways in which a person may be charged to tax on capital gains realised by an offshore company, even though the UK-resident individual may own all the share capital of such a company. Consequently, gains on UK assets may be taken outside the ambit of CGT if a foreign-domiciled individual makes his investments indirectly by setting up an offshore company which then makes the relevant investments. However, care needs to be taken to ensure that a company which is incorporated overseas is not resident in the United Kingdom because central management and control are exercised here (see Statement of Practice SP1/90).

22.14.2 Offshore trusts

Offshore or non-resident trusts can be extremely tax-efficient where foreign-domiciled individuals are concerned. A settlement established by a foreign-domiciled individual after 18 March 1991 cannot be a 'qualifying settlement' which means that there are no provisions for charging a settlor to tax on gains realised by the trustees of his non-resident settlement.

The provisions of TCGA 1992, s 86 which charge beneficiaries when they receive capital payments have no application where the settlor was not domiciled in the United Kingdom and is not domiciled in the United Kingdom at the time that gains are realised. Even if these exemptions do not apply, s 86 still does not come into force if a beneficiary who receives a capital payment is not domiciled in the United Kingdom. There are no other provisions which may allow the Revenue to tax a beneficiary on gains realised by offshore trustees and so the creation of an offshore trust may enable a foreign-domiciled individual to escape from any CGT charge, whether on foreign or UK assets.

Professional advice should be taken to avoid potential pitfalls arising from income tax and other legislation.

22.15   UK and foreign situs property

Inheritance tax may be charged on the death of an individual who is not deemed to be domiciled in the United Kingdom but only to the extent that his estate consists of property situated in the United Kingdom. No charge arises on foreign situs property as this is classified as 'excluded property'. The table below indicates which types of property are regarded as situated in the United Kingdom.

There is a special rule for IHT whereby an individual may be deemed to be domiciled in the United Kingdom if he has been resident for 17 of the 20 tax years ending with the current year.

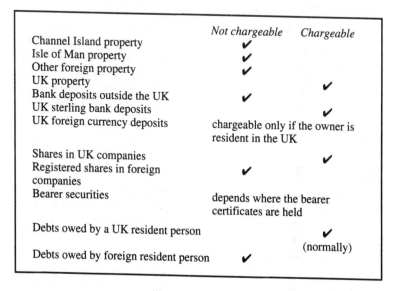

	Not chargeable	*Chargeable*
Channel Island property	✔	
Isle of Man property	✔	
Other foreign property	✔	
UK property		✔
Bank deposits outside the UK	✔	
UK sterling bank deposits		✔
UK foreign currency deposits	chargeable only if the owner is resident in the UK	
Shares in UK companies		✔
Registered shares in foreign companies	✔	
Bearer securities	depends where the bearer certificates are held	
Debts owed by a UK resident person		✔ (normally)
Debts owed by foreign resident person	✔	

23 National insurance contributions and social security benefits

This chapter covers the following topics:

(1) Class 1 contributions
(2) Class 2 contributions
(3) Class 3 contributions
(4) Class 4 contributions
(5) Social security benefits

Where rates are quoted, they are the 1994–95 figures.

23.1 Class 1 contributions

23.1.1 Introduction

Individuals who are employed are liable for Class 1 national insurance contributions (NICs). No contribution is payable unless the employee earns at least £57 a week. If he earns £57 or more, contributions are charged at two per cent on the first £57 plus ten per cent of earnings between £57 and £430 a week. No contribution is payable on earnings in excess of £430 (the 'upper limit'). Lower contributions apply if the individual is contracted out of SERPS.

Women who married before 7 April 1977 and who have chosen to pay a reduced rate are subject to pay NICs of only 3.85 per cent. This right is lost if the woman is divorced but is not lost if she is widowed.

Contributions are normally assessed by reference to weekly earnings but if the employee is paid less frequently, contributions are calculated on the corresponding figures for a monthly basis or whatever other period is covered by the payment of salary to the individual.

Where an individual has a period of unemployment during a year this will not affect his liability when he resumes employment. Each 'earnings period' is looked at in isolation and there is no principle which corresponds to that used for income tax whereby a tax year is looked at as a whole (there is a slight exception to this for company directors (see 22.1.3) but this is basically an anti-avoidance provision).

23.1.2 Deferment

Where an individual has more than one job, and his total earnings are likely to exceed the upper limit, he may apply for deferment so that the DSS may authorise individual employers not to withhold contributions from his remuneration. The deferment application is made on Form CF379. Ideally this form should be submitted before the start of a tax year for which deferment is sought. In any event, deferment will not be granted for 1994–95 unless the DSS receives the application by 14 February 1995. The DSS are also reluctant to grant deferment for a year in which the individual will reach pensionable age. Where a deferment application is made, the individual cannot choose which earnings should be subject to deduction for NICs. In practice, the DSS will always defer contributions at the non-contracted out rate.

After the end of a tax year, the position is reviewed. It may be that the individual has not had the anticipated level of earnings from a particular employment and this may mean that the liability for the year has not been satisfied. In such a case, the DSS will apply for payment of the balance and this falls due for payment within 28 days of the DSS making such a demand. Where an individual does not apply for deferment, he is still entitled to repayment of contributions withheld from his remuneration in so far as they exceed the maximum for the year.

23.1.3 Company directors

Remuneration paid to a company director is normally assessed for NICs as if it arose on a yearly basis. This means that a payment of fees or a bonus in a lump sum may attract the maximum contributions for a year rather than the maximum contributions for one week or one month.

23.1.4 Example—Assesment on lump sum payments

A company director receives remuneration of £22,500 paid in a single sum. The liability for contributions is the liability for the year, ie

52 x (£430 – £57) x 10 per cent ie	£1,939.60
plus 52 x £57 x 2 per cent ie	£59.28
	£1,998.88

It is not just the maximum for one week's earnings, ie two per cent of £57 and ten per cent of £373.

23.1.5   Definition of earnings

Earnings for national insurance purposes include all cash remuneration. Contributions are also payable on sick pay, holiday pay etc. The definition of earnings is quite different from that used for income tax purposes. For example, NICs are assessed on individual's pay before superannuation contributions and before any charitable donations made under a payroll deduction scheme. Profit-related pay is another type of earnings which may be exempt for income tax purposes, but gives rise to a liability for NICs.

Where an employer settles his employee's pecuniary liabilities, the sum paid is treated as earnings for national insurance purposes even though it is not pay for PAYE purposes. In general, no contributions are payable in respect of benefits in kind. However, there is an exception to this in respect of certain types of benefits in kind which can easily be converted into cash. For example, the DSS takes the view that premium bonds and national savings certificates are earnings for national insurance purposes because they may be encashed by the holder surrendering them.

For some years, financial instruments such as gilts, unit trusts, quoted shares etc, have been treated as earnings for national insurance purposes, as have derivative instruments such as warrants and options. Gold bullion and other commodities and vouchers exchangeable for gold or commodities were also brought into charge for NIC purposes from 30 November 1993. Where an employer acquires an insurance policy such as an investment bond and transfers it to an employee, the value of the policy is regarded as earnings for national insurance purposes.

Vouchers are not normally regarded as earnings provided the vouchers are exchangeable only for goods and may not be surrendered for cash. However, the DSS is looking very closely at arrangements in which a wide variety of vouchers (which are accepted by retailers and suppliers), are offered.

23.1.6   Problem areas

One major problem area concerns directors' drawings. The DSS takes the view that where a director arranges for a personal liability to be settled by his company and charged to his drawings account, the payment constitutes earnings for national insurance purposes unless the drawings account is in credit.

23.1.7 Example—Directors' drawings

A has a drawings account with his company which is £60 in credit. The company pays a personal bill for A of £100 and debits his drawings account with £100, thus turning the credit balance into an overdrawn balance of £40.

The DSS takes the view that £60 of the payment of the £100 bill is a repayment of a loan and attracts no national insurance liability, but the balance of £40 is a payment of earnings and the grossed up amount is subject to NICs.

23.1.8 Loans from the employer

Curiously, the DSS takes the view that if an individual arranges for a loan from his employer and the loan is used to settle a personal liability, there is no liability for NICs unless (and until) the loan is written off by the employer.

There is clearly a need to take considerable care in dealing with any documentation and structuring the arrangements properly with a view to minimising liability for national insurance contributions on payments of this nature.

23.1.9 Employer's national insurance contributions

In addition to the contributions paid by the employee (these are called 'primary contributions') employers are also required to pay contributions ('secondary contributions'). There is no ceiling on the amount of an employee's earnings which attract secondary contributions. Furthermore, employers are liable for Class 1A contributions where the employee has a car which is available for private use. The amount of the scale benefit as used for income tax purposes is treated as if it were additional earnings subject to secondary contributions. A further charge may arise if the employee is provided with fuel for private mileage, with the Class 1A charge again being based on the scale benefit used for income tax purposes.

No liability for secondary contributions can arise unless there is a liability for primary contributions. Some directors of private companies have relied on this in order to avoid their company being liable for Class 1A contributions. Such individuals have arranged matters so that their company car is provided by a subsidiary or other group company which pays them no remuneration. The provision of a company car in these circumstances gives rise to a Schedule E income tax charge on the scale benefit, but Class 1A contributions are not due.

There is no ceiling on the amount of an employee's earnings which attract secondary contributions.

23.2   Class 2 contributions

23.2.1   Introduction

A self-employed individual is liable to Class 2 NICs of £5.65 per week unless his earnings are less than £3,200 per annum and he has applied for a Certificate of Exemption.

23.2.2   Earnings from employment and self-employment

Where an individual has income from both employment and self-employment, both Class 1 and Class 2 NICs will be payable unless he applies for deferment. However, the maximum that an individual may pay for any year is an amount equal to the maximum Class 1 primary contributions on 53 weeks earnings. Consequently, for 1994–95 the maximum is £2,037.32. A repayment may be claimed if an individual has paid a mixture of Class 1 and Class 2 NICs in excess of this amount.

23.2.3   Small earnings exception

A person may avoid paying Class 2 NICs by applying in advance for the small earnings exception. The amount of the limit for small earnings exemption for 1994–95 is £3,200.

Earnings for this purpose are measured by reference to actual earnings for the tax year. For example, if a trader makes up accounts to 30 September, the small earnings exception will be available only if his earnings for 1994–95 are less than £3,200 when computed as follows:

> 6/12 x profits for the year ended 30 September 1994
> 6/12 x profits for the year ended 30 September 1995

Where a person has paid Class 2 NICs, he may apply for repayment. The repayment claim must normally be made between 6 April and 31 December following the end of the tax year and thus the deadline for making a repayment claim for 1993–94 will be 31 December 1994.

A false economy?

In general, choosing not to pay Class 2 NICs could prove a false economy as entitlement to benefits such as pensions and sick pay may be affected.

23.3   Class 3 contributions

These are a type of voluntary contribution. A person who is neither employed nor self-employed may pay voluntary Class 3 NICs in order to secure the State retirement pension. The weekly rate is set just below that of Class 2 NICs and is currently £5.55.

23.4   Class 4 contributions

These are payable by self-employed individuals according to the level of their profits as determined for income tax purposes. At present, Class 4 NICs are levied at the rate of 7.3 per cent of Schedule D profits between £6,490 and £22,360.

Where an individual pays interest on a business loan or has suffered trading losses, such amounts may be set against his earnings for the purposes of assessing liability for Class 4 NICs. This situation applies even where the losses have been relieved for income tax purposes by way of offset against his other income.

23.5   Social security benefits
(TA 1988, s 617)

The following types of benefit are taxed as earned income under Schedule E:

> Industrial death benefit (if paid as pension)
> Invalid care allowance
> Invalidity allowance when paid with retirement pension
> Job release allowance
> Old person's pension
> Retirement pension
> Statutory maternity pay
> Statutory sick pay
> Income support when paid to unemployed and strikers (see below)
> Unemployment benefit
> Widowed mother's allowance
> Widow's pension.

The following benefits are not taxable:

> Maternity allowance
> Sickness benefit
> Attendance allowance

Child benefit
Child dependency additions paid with widow's allowance,
   widowed mother's allowance, retirement pension, invalid care
   allowance, unemployment benefit or supplementary benefits
Child's special allowance
Christmas bonus for pensioners
Disability living allowance
Disability working allowance
Employment rehabilitation allowance
Fares to school
Guardian's allowance
Home improvement, repair and insulation grants
Invalidity allowance when paid with invalidity pension
Invalidity pension
Job search allowances
Mobility allowance
One parent benefit
Severe disablement allowance
Employment training allowance
War orphan's pension
War widow's pension
Widow's payment
Youth training scheme allowance.

Means-tested benefits

Educational maintenance allowance
Family credit
Hospital patients' travelling expenses
Housing benefit
Income support
Social fund payments
Student grants
Uniform and clothing grants.

War disablement benefits

Disablement pension, including:

Age allowance
Allowance for lowered standard of occupation
Clothing allowance
Comforts allowance
Constant attendance allowance
Dependant allowance
Education allowance

Exceptionally severe disablement allowance
Invalidity allowance
Medical treatment allowance
Severe disablement occupational allowance
Unemployability allowance.

Industrial injury benefits

Industrial death benefit child allowance
Disablement benefit, including:

Constant attendance allowance
Exceptionally severe disablement allowance
Reduced earnings allowance
Retirement allowance
Unemployability supplement.

Adoption allowances
(Extra-statutory concession A40)

Sums paid under schemes approved under the Children Act 1975, s 32 are exempt from income tax.

24 Tax and companies
by PETER SWASH

This chapter looks at the taxation of companies under the following headings:

(1)   How 'profits' are defined.
(2)   Accounting periods, rates and payment of tax.
(3)   Companies' capital gains.
(4)   Interest and other charges.
(5)   Dividends and advance corporation tax.
(6)   Losses.
(7)   'Pay and file'.
(8)   Double taxation relief on foreign income.
(9)   Groups of companies.
(10) Close and investment companies.
(11) Claims and elections.
(12) Should you operate via a company?

24.1 How 'profits' are defined

24.1.1 Computation of profits
(TA 1988, s 6)

The income and chargeable gains of a company, collectively termed 'chargeable profits', are chargeable to corporation tax. The computation of chargeable profits can be a very complex process bearing in mind the detailed tax legislation and extensive case law. There are also myriad Inland Revenue Statements of Practice, press releases and extra-statutory concessions which may need to be borne in mind when calculating chargeable profits upon which corporation tax is payable.

Although the general principles of profit adjustment closely follow the rules for income tax, the assessment of income under the various schedules is computed on an actual or arising basis, as opposed to the preceding year basis for income tax purposes.

24.1.2 Capital allowances
(CAA 1990, s 144)

Although depreciation is not regarded as an allowable expense for tax purposes, tax relief is given for expenditure on qualifying capital assets by means of capital allowances. The principles follow very closely those which apply in the case of individuals (see 2.5) and therefore the main provisions are not covered in detail here. Capital allowances in respect of a trade carried on by a company are regarded as trading expenses for the accounting period in which they arise. They are therefore taken into account in arriving at the chargeable profits or overall tax loss for the accounting period.

Capital allowances in respect of non-trading activities are primarily deductible from the income arising from that source. Any surplus allowances may be carried forward against similar source income arising in later accounting periods or deducted from overall chargeable profits for the accounting period in which they arise.

24.1.3 Interest and other annual payments
(TA 1988, s 338)

Unlike individuals, a company is liable to account to the Revenue for income tax on annual interest and certain other annual payments which it makes. Such annual payments (termed 'charges on income'), are deductible from a company's profits in arriving at the amount assessable to corporation tax. The basic principle is that these charges on income are offset against the total profits of the payer, not merely against a particular source of income with which the payment is connected.

A payment will count as a charge on income only if the following conditions are met:

(1) It has been made out of the company's profits brought into charge to corporation tax.
(2) It is made under a liability incurred for a 'valuable and sufficient consideration' (or the payment is a covenanted donation to charity).
(3) The payment must not be one charged to capital or one not ultimately borne by the company.
(4) Where the payment is interest it must be wholly and exclusively laid out for the purposes of the company's trade.
(5) It must not be in the nature of a dividend or distribution made by the company.

Payment must actually be made in the accounting period for it to count as a charge for that period.

Where there is a requirement to deduct and account for income tax on the payment, no deduction will be allowed until this requirement is satisfied.

Where the total profits for an accounting period are insufficient to absorb charges on income, excess charges in respect of payments made wholly and exclusively for the purposes of the company's trade may be carried forward and utilised against future trading income of the company. Non-trade charges may not be carried forward in this manner and no further relief is available.

24.1.4   Who pays corporation tax?
(TA 1988, ss 11–12 and FA 1988, s 66)

Corporation tax is levied on the chargeable profits of companies which are resident in the United Kingdom for tax purposes. A company is generally defined as meaning any body corporate or unincorporated association, but does not include a partnership, a local authority or a local authority association. The definition also extends to authorised unit trusts, the detailed provisions for which are set out in TA 1988, s 468.

Corporation tax also extends to non-resident companies carrying on a trade in the United Kingdom through a branch or agency. Such companies are chargeable to tax on any income attributable to the branch or agency and on any capital gains arising on the disposal of assets used in the United Kingdom for the purposes of the branch or agency trade. Any income of a non-resident company from sources within the United Kingdom which is not charged to corporation tax will be liable to income tax.

A company which was incorporated in the United Kingdom is regarded as resident here regardless of where the directors exercise their management and control. However, some of the double taxation conventions negotiated with other countries override this in practice and treat a dual resident company as if it were not resident in the United Kingdom.

A company which was incorporated overseas may still be regarded as resident in the United Kingdom on the basis that its central management and control is exercised in this country. Questions relating to the residence status of a foreign incorporated company are usually determined by reference to the guidelines set out in Inland Revenue Statement of Practice SP1/90 dated 9 January 1990.

24.2 Accounting periods, rates and payment of tax

24.2.1 Accounting periods for tax purposes
(TA 1988, s 12)

Companies pay corporation tax by reference to their accounting periods and the income included is assessed on an actual or accruals basis rather than the preceding year basis which applies for income tax purposes. Accounting periods may straddle two financial years (which for corporation tax purposes run from 1 April to 31 March). If this is the case, the chargeable profits are apportioned on a time basis for the purposes of determining the rate of tax to apply to the overall profit.

An accounting period begins for corporation tax purposes:

(1) when the company comes within the charge to corporation tax either by becoming resident in the United Kingdom or acquiring a source of income; or

(2) when the previous accounting period of the company ends without the company ceasing to be within the charge to corporation tax.

An accounting period runs on for a maximum of twelve months from its commencement. It will end earlier if the company's own accounting date falls within the twelve months and it will also end if any of the following occurs:

(1) The company ceases to trade.

(2) The company begins or ceases to be resident in the United Kingdom.

(3) The company ceases to be within the charge to corporation tax altogether.

Where accounts are made up for a period of more than twelve months, the income will usually be apportioned on a time basis to the relevant accounting period. However, where a more appropriate basis of apportionment is available, the Inspector may apply that basis instead (*Marshall Hus & Partners Ltd v Bolton* [1981] STC 18). In some instances, the accounts year end may vary slightly for commercial reasons (for example where accounts are made up to the last Friday of a specified month). Provided the variation is not more than four days from the 'mean' date it will normally be acceptable to treat each period of account as if it were a twelve-month accounting period ending on the mean date.

24.2.2   The corporation tax rates
(TA 1988, s 6)

The rate of corporation tax is fixed for each financial year which, for these purposes, starts on 1 April. The rate of tax for the financial year 1994 (ie, 1 April 1994–31 March 1995) was announced in the November 1993 Budget. The current rate of corporation tax is 33 per cent and the following table shows the full corporation tax rate applicable for previous financial years.

Financial year	Rate
1986 to 1989	35 per cent
1990	34 per cent
1991	33 per cent
1992	33 per cent
1993	33 per cent

Before 16 March 1987, companies' chargeable gains were reduced so that although they were chargeable to corporation tax, they suffered the same average tax rate that individuals paid for CGT (at that time this was 30 per cent). Due to the general reduction in corporation tax rates, this adjustment was eliminated for accounting periods beginning after 16 March 1987 so that the whole of any chargeable gains arising are now included in profit chargeable to corporation tax.

24.2.3   Small companies rates and associated companies
(TA 1988, s 13)

A reduced rate of corporation tax (known as the 'small companies rate') applies to the profits of a company where those profits do not exceed a minimum level. The current rate of tax is 25 per cent and the current profit level below which the small companies rate applies is £300,000. The following table shows the small companies rate and maximum profit level for earlier financial years:

Financial year	Rate per cent	Max Profit Level
1987	27	£100,000
1988	25	£100,000
1989	25	£150,000
1990	25	£200,000
1991	25	£250,000
1992	25	£250,000
1993	25	£250,000

Where profits exceed the maximum profit limit for small companies rate purposes, an element of marginal relief is given for profits between £300,000 and £1,500,000. This relief operates on a tapered basis by charging the profits to the full corporation tax rate but gives an element of credit for the reduced corporation tax rate which would have been applicable to the initial tranche of profit.

The profit limits applicable to small companies relief are restricted, based upon the existence of any 'associated' companies which the company has during the accounting period concerned. A company is an associated company of another if they are under common control or one has control of the other. 'Control' for this purpose is defined as the ability to exercise direct or indirect control over the company's affairs and in particular:

(1)   the possession or entitlement to acquire more than 50 per cent of the share capital or voting rights in the company;
(2)   entitlement to receive the greater part of income distributed among the shareholders;
(3)   entitlement to receive the greater part of the assets of the company in the event of a winding up.

For example, if a company has one associated company, the small companies profit limits are divided by two, ie one plus the number of associated companies. However, an associated company which has not carried on any trade or business at any time during the accounting period concerned would be disregarded. Where a company's accounting period straddles more than one financial year and the marginal relief limits for each financial year differ, the twelve-month period is treated as separate accounting periods for the purpose of calculating marginal relief.

24.2.4   Payment of tax
(TA 1988, s 10)

Under the 'pay and file' rules (see 24.7) corporation tax for an accounting period ending after 30 September 1993 is automatically due and payable nine months from the end of the accounting period. For accounting periods ending on or before 30 September 1993, corporation tax is only due and payable thirty days after the date of issue of a Notice of Assessment to corporation tax if the assessment is not made until after eight months have elapsed since the end of the accounting period.

The pay and file system is dealt with in 24.7 below. The previous system of assessment and payment of corporation tax, which applied to accounting periods which ended on or before 30 September 1993, broadly worked in the following manner.

Normally, in the absence of accounts and tax computations the Revenue would issue an estimated assessment to corporation tax around seven months after the end of the accounting period. It was open to the taxpayer to lodge an appeal against the assessment although the full amount of tax charged was due and payable unless an application was made to postpone part or all of the tax assessed. Appeals had to be lodged in writing with the Inspector of Taxes within thirty days of the date of issue of the notice of assessment, together with an application to postpone part or all of the tax which had been assessed.

Once the Inspector of Taxes had agreed the tax computation and the actual liability to corporation tax for the accounting period, an amended assessment was issued to collect any balance of corporation tax due or repay any overpayment.

24.3   Companies' capital gains

24.3.1   Computation of gains

Capital gains made by companies are included in their chargeable profits and are subject to corporation tax. Capital gains tax therefore does not apply to companies, although chargeable gains and losses are computed in accordance with the detailed provisions of capital gains tax. The main differences between capital gains tax and corporation tax on chargeable gains for companies are, first, that provisions which clearly apply only to individuals (eg, annual exemption) have no application as far as companies are concerned, and second, that computations of chargeable gains are prepared on an accounting period basis rather than by income tax years of assessment. The total chargeable gains for an accounting period less a deduction for allowable losses are brought into charge to corporation tax in the same way as any other source of income.

Capital losses can only be offset against chargeable gains; they cannot be offset against trading or other income.

24.3.2   Roll-over relief
(TCGA 1992, ss 152–158 and 175)

Roll-over relief is available where the proceeds on the disposal of a qualifying asset are reinvested in further qualifying assets. It operates as a deferral of the corporation tax liability arising on the chargeable gain if the proceeds are fully reinvested in qualifying assets within a period of twelve months before and three years after the date of disposal.

Where the proceeds are only partly reinvested, a proportion of the gain is deferred or 'rolled over' and the balance (equivalent to the amount of proceeds not reinvested) is brought into charge. The element of gain deferred or rolled over is deducted from the base cost of the new asset for capital gains purposes. This, of course, will operate to increase the potential gain on the eventual sale of the new asset acquired, hence the term 'roll-over relief'.

Qualifying assets for this purpose are freehold and leasehold land and buildings, goodwill, ships, aircraft and hovercraft, fixed plant and machinery, satellite space stations and spacecraft and certain agricultural quotas.

24.4 Interest and other charges

24.4.1 Interest
(TA 1988, ss 74, 338 and 340)

For corporation tax purposes, interest payments can be classified as either overdraft and 'short interest' or annual interest.

Overdraft and 'short interest'

Overdraft interest will usually be treated as a business expense in arriving at the accounts profit and is normally treated as an allowable expense on an accruals basis. Short interest is defined as interest which is not annual interest or, in other words, interest on a loan or other obligation with a life span of less than twelve months. For example, interest charged by debtors on overdue debts would be regarded as short interest, and is dealt with, for tax purposes, in a similar manner to overdraft interest. Interest payable under HP agreements is also treated, in practice, as short interest on the basis that the payer will eventually become the owner of the property concerned and therefore the interest charged would be regarded in part, at least, as a rentcharge for the use of the asset. Annual interest paid to a UK bank may also be treated as short interest and claimed as an expense in computing chargeable profits of the trade on an accruals basis.

Much depends on the purpose to which the loan is put as to whether or not the interest charges will qualify for a trading deduction under TA 1988, s 74. There are circumstances where annual interest paid to a bank will not qualify as an expense of the business and therefore may be treated as a charge on income on a paid basis. Where an expense qualifies as a trading expense it will not be open to the company to treat the expense as a charge on income.

Discounts incurred on bills of exchange are generally treated as short interest and allowed as an expense of the trade.

Annual interest

Annual interest paid by a company to a person resident in the United Kingdom, but not carrying on a banking business in this country, is allowable only as a charge on income. A company must deduct basic rate income tax when making a payment of such annual interest.

Where interest is paid to an overseas lender, the following conditions must normally be satisfied in order for the interest to qualify as a charge on income:

(1)   It must be paid outside the United Kingdom wholly or mainly for the purposes of a trade carried on outside the United Kingdom.

(2)   It must be payable in a currency other than sterling and the liability should have been incurred for the purposes of a trade and the interest not paid to a connected person.

(3)   It must be paid under deduction of income tax at the basic rate unless permission from the Revenue has been obtained to withhold a lower rate of income tax under the terms of a double taxation agreement.

Where interest is payable to an overseas parent or group company, it will be treated as a distribution with the result that the payer will be required to account for advance corporation tax (see 24.5.3) as if it had paid a dividend, unless this requirement is overridden by the provisions of the double taxation agreement between the United Kingdom and the country of residence of the recipient.

24.4.2   Annual charges
(TA 1988, ss 338–339)

Apart from interest, a company may make annual payments in respect of annuities, royalties, covenanted payments etc, which are available for offset as charges on income against the chargeable profits of the company on a paid basis.

24.4.3   Income tax deduction at source

Companies must deduct and account to the Revenue for income tax on payments of annual interest and other charges on income, with the exception of annual interest paid to a UK bank. A return Form CT61 is required to be submitted on a quarterly basis detailing payments made and computing the income tax payable to the Revenue. In arriving at the income tax liability due, any income tax suffered on income received under deduction of tax may be offset. Where the income tax suffered on income received exceeds the income tax payable on annual charges, the surplus may be carried forward to the next quarterly return. If at the end of the accounting period it has not proved possible to obtain credit against income tax payable, credit may be obtained against the corporation tax liability for the accounting period (and if there is no or insufficient corporation tax liability to offset any income tax credit, a repayment may be obtained from the Revenue).

24.5 Dividends and advance corporation tax
(TA 1988, ss 238–241)

24.5.1 Taxation of company distributions

Company distributions are defined as any dividends, and any other distribution out of assets of the company, paid by a company in respect of shares in the company. The main exception to this is that any repayment of share capital is not regarded as a distribution of assets. When a company pays a dividend or makes some other qualifying distribution, there is a requirement to account for advance corporation tax (ACT). Most distributions will be regarded as qualifying distributions, the main exception being a bonus issue of redeemable share capital.

The current rate of ACT is 20/80 of the dividend, ie 20 per cent of the 'grossed up' amount. The rate of ACT for years up to 5 April 1993 was equal to the basic rate of income tax.

UK recipients of the distribution are entitled to a tax credit corresponding to the rate of ACT paid by the company. This aggregate amount is described as a 'franked' payment and, as far as individuals are concerned, represents the gross equivalent of the dividend received. This amount is taxable income, but the shareholder may set the tax credit against his tax liability on the 'grossed-up' amount.

Dividends received by a company from another UK company are termed franked investment income. This income is regarded as having already borne tax and does not form part of the chargeable profits of a company. However, in computing its ACT liability on distributions, a company is able to offset any franked investment income received against franked payments which it makes itself and the tax credit can therefore be utilised against the ACT liability arising on distributions made.

24.5.2   Surplus franked investment income
(TA 1988, ss 238 and 242)

Where a company incurs a loss in an accounting period and in the same period its franked investment income exceeds the franked payments made in that period, the tax credit attaching to the excess may be refunded to the company by means of a claim under TA 1988, s 242. This effectively treats the surplus franked investment income as an amount of profits chargeable to corporation tax for the purpose of obtaining relief against trading losses or charges on income in the period concerned. If relief cannot be obtained in this way, the surplus franked investment income is carried forward and treated as franked investment income received in the next accounting period for the purposes of franking distributions made by the company in that later period.

24.5.3   Advance corporation tax
(TA 1988, s 238)

A liability to account for ACT arises when a company makes a qualifying distribution to its shareholders. As its name suggests, ACT is treated as an advance payment of corporation tax and relief is obtained by deduction from the mainstream corporation tax liability payable on the profits for the accounting period in which the distribution has been made.

The collection of ACT on dividends and other distributions made by a company is undertaken on Inland Revenue Form CT61. There is a requirement for a company to submit this return on a quarterly basis to the Revenue in respect of the ACT liability arising on dividends and other distributions made during the three month period. ACT is due and payable fourteen days after the end of the quarterly period concerned.

24.5.4   Relief for payment of ACT
(TA 1988, s 239)

The maximum relief against mainstream corporation tax for ACT paid on distributions made in an accounting period is equivalent to the ACT which would be due on a franked payment equal to the profits chargeable to corporation tax. Where the ACT exceeds this maximum, relief can be obtained in the following ways:

(1)   It can be carried back to accounting periods beginning in the six years preceding the accounting period in which the surplus ACT arose, taking later years before earlier years. A claim must be lodged within two years of the end of the accounting period in which the surplus ACT arose.

(2)   It may be carried forward and treated as ACT payable in respect of the next accounting period. If it cannot be utilised in the next accounting period, it will be treated as surplus ACT in the following accounting period and carried forward indefinitely until utilised.

(3)   It can be surrendered to a 51 per cent subsidiary company resident in the United Kingdom. It is then treated as ACT paid by the subsidiary. A claim to surrender ACT must be made within six years of the end of the accounting period in which the ACT is paid and requires the consent of the subsidiary or subsidiaries concerned.

24.6   Losses

24.6.1   Losses arising in the accounting period
(TA 1988, s 393)

When a company makes a tax loss in respect of its trading activities for an accounting period, it may claim that the loss arising may be set off against other profits including chargeable gains arising in that accounting period. A tax loss is computed in the same manner as taxable profits, but is restricted to losses arising from trading activities carried out on a commercial basis and with a view to the realisation of profit.

24.6.2   Utilisation of loss relief

There are a number of ways in which a trading loss may be relieved for tax purposes apart from being offset against other profits arising in the accounting period. The loss can be carried forward and offset against trading profits arising in succeeding accounting periods. Losses can be carried forward indefinitely in this manner for as long as the company carries on the trading activity which generated the loss. A loss may also be carried back and offset against total profits for the period of three years which ended immediately before the period in which the losses were incurred (provided the company was carrying on the relevant trade in the earlier periods). Partial relief claims are not allowed, and relief is obtained for later years before earlier years. Relief must be obtained for the loss against other profits of the accounting period before computing the balance of the loss available for carry-back.

For accounting periods ending on or before 31 March 1991, the carry-back period was restricted to the period equal in length to the period in which the loss was incurred (ie normally twelve months) and ending immediately before the period in which the loss was incurred.

24.6.3   Capital losses

Capital losses, like capital gains, are computed in accordance with CGT rules although the net capital gains are subject to corporation tax as part of the overall chargeable profits for the accounting period. Capital losses may be offset against capital gains in computing net chargeable gains, and capital losses which cannot be relieved in this way may be carried forward and offset against gains arising in subsequent accounting periods without limit. The carry forward of capital losses is not dependent upon whether or not the company continues to carry on its trading activity, and may be offset against gains arising on trade and non-trade assets.

24.6.4   Surplus charges on income
(TA 1988, s 393(9))

Relief for charges on income is generally given as the last of all reliefs other than group relief (see 24.9). It is given against the total profits of the period in which the charges are paid. If profits are insufficient to absorb the charges, the amount of charges paid wholly and exclusively for the purposes of the company's trading activities may be carried forward to the next accounting period and treated as a trading loss to be offset against future trading income of the company. Non-trade charges on income may not be so carried forward and therefore relief will be lost.

24.6.5   Terminal losses
(TA 1988, ss 393A and 394)

For accounting periods ending after 31 March 1991, a trading loss arising in the accounting period in which the trade ceases may be carried back and offset against profits of the three years ending immediately before the commencement of the final period of trading. Charges on income paid wholly and exclusively for the purposes of the trade are treated as trading expenses for the purpose of computing the terminal loss available for carry-back.

For accounting periods ending on or before 31 March 1991, the trading loss incurred in the twelve months to the date of cessation may be carried back and offset against trading income arising in the thirty-six month period ending immediately before the final twelve months to cessation. Relief is given on a time basis and the income of accounting periods falling only partly within that thirty-six month period is apportioned accordingly.

24.6.6 Changes in company ownership
(TA 1988, s 768)

There are anti-avoidance provisions designed to ensure that trading losses carried forward can only be utilised against future trading income from the trading activity which generated the losses. Losses may not be carried forward if:

(1) within any period of three years there is a change in the ownership of the company preceded or followed by a major change in the nature or conduct of the trade carried on by the company; or

(2) there is a change in ownership of the company at any time after the scale of activities in a trade carried on by the company has become small or negligible, and before any considerable revival in the trade.

A 'change in ownership' means a change in more than 50 per cent of the ownership of the ordinary share capital in the company. A 'major change in the nature or conduct of a trade' includes a major change in the type of property dealt in, or the services or facilities provided in the trade, or in customers, outlets or markets. The Revenue have issued guidelines on some of the factors which will be relevant in determining whether or not there has been a major change in the nature or conduct of a trade or business (see Inland Revenue Statement of Practice SP10/91).

24.7 'Pay and file'
(TA 1988, ss 8 and 10; FA 1989, s 102 and FA 1990, ss 91–103 & Scheds 15–17)

24.7.1 Outline of the system

A new system of reporting profits and payment of corporation tax was introduced for accounting periods ending on or after 1 October 1993 which is known as the 'pay and file' system. A comprehensive return form (Form CT200–1) needs to be lodged in respect of each accounting period and this replaces the corporation tax computation previously required. The payment of corporation tax has also been streamlined with the aim of reducing the administrative costs of collection. Coupled with this is a more rigid system of penalties for delays in rendering a return form and in the assessment of interest on overdue tax and repayments of tax.

24.7.2 The pay and file return

The pay and file return is very comprehensive and requires full details of income from all sources during the accounting period, together with deductions and reliefs claimed. There is an alternative short return which may be completed if each entry on the return (including the company's *total* income) is less than £10 million. The return takes into account various deductions and credits such as ACT, double tax relief and tax payments made on account in arriving at the net corporation tax payable or repayable. A return is required to be submitted to the Revenue (together with accounts for the period and any other supporting information) within twelve months after the end of an accounting period. However, a company will only be required to file its return after it has received a notice to do so from the Inspector of Taxes. Such notices are expected to be issued approximately three months after the end of the accounting period. If a notice is issued more than twelve months after the end of its accounting period the return will be due within three months of the date of the notice.

24.7.3   Payment of corporation tax

Under the pay and file system, corporation tax for an accounting period is due and payable nine months from the end of the accounting period. It is not necessary for the Revenue to issue an assessment to collect corporation tax since the amount shown in the pay and file return as the corporation tax liability due for the period will be treated as tax charged under an assessment on the company. The Inspector of Taxes will only raise an assessment upon agreement of the final liability or if there is a contentious point which needs to be decided on appeal to the Commissioners.

24.7.4   Interest and penalties

Interest on unpaid tax automatically accrues from the due date, as will any interest on corporation tax which turns out to have been overpaid (but the rate of interest on overpayments is lower than that charged on tax which is paid late). The introduction of automatic penalties for late filing of the company's accounts and Form CT200 has considerably tightened the tax regime. Penalties will be calculated as shown below:

Period of delay from filing date	Penalty
Up to 3 months	£100
3 to 6 months	£200
Over 6 months	£200 plus 10 per cent of tax unpaid
Over 12 months	£200 plus 20 per cent of tax unpaid

Where there has been a delay for three consecutive accounting periods, the fixed £100 and £200 penalties for the third accounting period are increased to £500 and £1,000 respectively. There are provisions for waiving the penalty charges where the company can show a 'reasonable excuse' for its late filing but the scope to avoid penalties under this provision will be extremely limited.

It is anticipated that the pay and file system will considerably improve the collection of corporation tax and proprietors of companies would be well advised to verify that their reporting and information systems can ensure timely compliance with the new procedures.

24.8 Double taxation relief on foreign income
(TA 1988, ss 788–806)

24.8.1 The main reliefs

A UK-resident company may claim a credit for foreign tax paid on income or capital gains arising from any overseas source. Credit is available against the corporation tax liability payable on the same income or gains. Relief may be due either under the provisions of a double taxation agreement between the United Kingdom and the overseas country concerned, or under the general rules for 'unilateral relief' as provided in TA 1988, s 790.

Where credit is due under a double taxation agreement, the relevant agreement takes precedence over UK domestic legislation.

For most types of income and gains, the full amount is brought into charge for the purpose of computing the corporation tax liability on chargeable profits for the accounting period. Any overseas tax suffered is then offset by way of credit against the corporation tax liability. The amount of credit which is available is limited to the corporation tax liability on the source of income or gain which has suffered overseas tax. No relief is due for the excess foreign tax paid.

Further relief may be available in the case of dividends received. In addition to relief for withholding or other taxes suffered on payment of the dividend, relief may also be available for the foreign tax suffered on the profits out of which the dividend has been paid. This is known as 'underlying tax', for which relief is given automatically if the UK-recipient company controls, directly or indirectly, ten per cent or more of the voting share capital in the overseas company paying the dividend. The dividend taxable in the United Kingdom is grossed up at the rate of underlying tax applicable to the profits out of which the dividend has been paid. This, together with any withholding and other taxes suffered on payment of the dividend, can then be offset against the corporation tax liability arising on the grossed up equivalent of the dividend received (subject to the restriction that underlying tax relief cannot exceed the corporation tax liability on the same income).

Where double tax relief would be lost, (for example, where no corporation tax liability arises for the accounting period), it is possible to obtain relief for overseas tax paid by treating the tax as an expense in computing profits for the purposes of Schedule D Case I.

24.8.2 Interaction between corporation tax and ACT
(TA 1988, s 797)

Double tax relief for overseas taxes paid and underlying tax is given by way of credit against the corporation tax liability arising on the same income. In arriving at the corporation tax liability arising on the overseas income or gains, it is possible to take account of the following:

(1) Charges on income may be allocated against other sources of income in priority to overseas income and gains which have suffered overseas tax.

(2) Double tax relief is offset against the attributable corporation tax liability in priority to ACT.

If double taxation relief cannot be obtained by way of credit against the corporation tax liability arising on the same income or gains, it may be advisable to claim the tax paid as an expense deduction in computing the profit or loss arising for Schedule D Case I purposes.

24.8.3 Unremittable income

Where an overseas source of income is taxable on an arising basis but it is not possible to remit the income due to Government actions in the overseas territory, it is possible to make a claim to defer the corporation tax liability until such time as sufficient funds are remitted to the United Kingdom to satisfy the liability. A claim under these circumstances may be made to the Revenue at any time within six years of the end of the accounting period in which the income arises.

24.9 Groups of companies

24.9.1 Group relationships
(TA 1988, s 402)

There are special rules which apply to groups of companies. For corporation tax purposes, a group relationship exists between two companies if one company holds not less than 75 per cent of the ordinary share capital of the other, or if both companies are 75 per cent subsidiaries of a third company.

24.9.2 Use of losses
(TA 1988, s 402–413)

Where one company in a group makes a tax loss for an accounting period, it may 'surrender' that loss to a member of the group for offset against that company's taxable profits. For this purpose, losses available for surrender include charges on income to the extent that they exceed profits chargeable to corporation tax. Where the accounting periods of the surrendering and claimant companies do not coincide, the amount of loss to be surrendered is restricted on a time basis reflecting the length of the accounting periods common to both companies.

For group relief purposes, the requirement for a 75 per cent shareholding relationship is extended so that the company owning the shares must also be beneficially entitled to 75 per cent or more of the profits available for distribution to equity shareholders, and of assets available for distribution in a winding up.

24.9.3 ACT surrenders
(TA 1988, s 240)

Where a company pays ACT on a dividend distribution to shareholders, it may surrender the ACT to a 51 per cent subsidiary which is resident in the United Kingdom. The 51 per cent relationship refers to ordinary share capital and the shareholding relationship must subsist throughout the whole of the accounting period during which the dividend was paid. If a surrender of ACT is made, the subsidiary is treated as if it had itself paid both the dividend and the ACT. It may therefore offset the ACT against its own corporation tax liability for that accounting period, or carry it forward to subsequent accounting periods. It is not possible to carry back surrendered ACT, although for the purpose of determining the amount of surplus ACT to be carried forward or back, surrendered ACT is offset against the subsidiary's mainstream corporation tax liability before ACT paid by the subsidiary itself.

24.9.4 Transfers of assets between group companies
(TCGA 1992, ss 171–174)

Where a trading activity is transferred from one group company to another, relief is available under TA 1988, s 343 to ensure that the company transferring the trade does not suffer balancing charges on assets which have qualified for capital allowances. The successor company merely takes over the tax residue for capital allowances purposes relating to those assets. It is also possible to elect under CAA 1990, s 158 that properties may be transferred between group companies at tax written-down value for the purpose of industrial buildings allowances.

Section 343 can also apply where a trade is transferred to another company which is under common control, even though it is not a member of a group.

24.9.5   Payment of dividends and interest
(TA 1988, s 247)

The payment of dividends and interest by one company to another will normally require the payer to account for ACT on the dividend and income tax on the interest payment. Where the two companies concerned are members of the same group for tax purposes, relief is available from these procedures by lodging, with the Revenue, an election under TA 1988, s 247. This is effective for as long as both companies remain resident in the United Kingdom and one company beneficially owns more than 50 per cent of the ordinary share capital of the other. Dividends paid in these circumstances are termed 'group income' rather than franked investment income, and are not brought into charge to corporation tax in the hands of the recipient.

24.9.6   Capital gains
(TCGA 1992, s 171 and s 175)

For the purposes of capital gains, chargeable assets may be transferred from one group company to another without tax consequences. Such transfers are treated as if made at a 'no gain/no loss' price and the recipient company will take over the capital gains base cost of the asset concerned from the transferor company.

For assets held on 31 March 1982, it is possible for the principal company of a group (normally the holding company) to make an election on behalf of all companies in the group that assets held on 31 March 1982 should be subject to the general rebasing rule for capital gains purposes (see 14.3). Such an election is required within two years of the end of the accounting period in which the first disposal occurs after 5 April 1988 of an asset held on 31 March 1982 by a group company.

For roll-over relief purposes, all the trades carried on by group companies are treated as a single trade and therefore it is possible to roll over a gain made on qualifying assets by one member of a group against qualifying expenditure incurred by another member of the group within the appropriate timescale. Roll-over relief is generally available only for trading companies within a group although, concessionally, relief is also available for a property holding company where the properties concerned are used for trading purposes by the other members of the group.

24.10 Close and investment companies
(TA 1988, s 13A)

24.10.1 Close companies
(TA 1988, ss 414–415)

Companies which are under the control of five or fewer persons, or under the control of their directors, are known as 'close companies'. There are special provisions which are designed to ensure that such individuals cannot take undue advantage of corporation tax legislation by virtue of their positions of influence over a company's affairs.

A person controls a company if, in fact, he is able to exercise control directly or indirectly over its affairs by owning the greater part of its share capital, voting capital, or other capital giving entitlement to more than half the assets on a winding up. Shareholders and certain loan creditors in a close company are known as participators.

24.10.2 Loans to participators
(TA 1988, s 419)

Where a close company makes a loan or advances any money to a participator, or an associate of a participator, there is a liability to account for an amount of tax equal to the ACT liability which would arise if the loan or advance were treated as a dividend payment. The tax liability is due within fourteen days after the end of period for the purposes of interest on overdue tax. If the loan is repaid, the tax is repaid accordingly but if the loan is wholly or partly written off or released, the borrower is treated as receiving, as part of his total income, an amount equal to the amount so written off, grossed up at the lower rate of income tax. While no basic or lower rate tax liability arises, there may be a further liability to higher rate tax. No relief is available to the company for the ACT equivalent tax liability on the making of the loan or advance.

24.10.3   Investment companies
(TA 1988, ss 75 and 130)

An investment company is any company whose business consists wholly or mainly of the making of investments and the principal part of whose income arises as a result of that activity. The expenses of managing a UK-resident investment company are deductible in computing its total profits for corporation tax purposes. Where management expenses exceed the company's chargeable income and gains for an accounting period, the surplus may be carried forward and treated as management expenses incurred in the next succeeding accounting period, and may continue to be carried forward until relieved. Surplus management expenses may also be surrendered as group relief from one group company to another. Expenses brought forward from previous periods are not available for surrender as group relief. Unrelieved management expenses of an accounting period may also be set off against surplus franked investment income by a claim under TA 1988, s 242(2), for the purposes of claiming repayment of the tax credit attaching to it.

24.10.4   Close investment-holding companies
(TA 1988, s 13A)

A close investment-holding company means a close company carrying on specific investment-holding activities. For this purpose, investment-holding activities do not include the carrying on of a trade on a commercial basis, property holding, or holding shares in companies carrying on either of these activities.

For accounting periods beginning after 31 March 1989, a close investment-holding company does not qualify for the small companies rate of corporation tax. In addition, the Revenue has power to restrict repayment of tax credit to shareholders receiving dividends from a close investment-holding company where it appears that arrangements have been made in relation to the distribution of profits, the main purpose of which is to enable the individual shareholder to obtain the tax repayment.

24.11   Claims and elections

24.11.1   General

Throughout the Taxes Acts, there are various claims for relief from corporation tax which must be lodged with the Revenue and, in practice, are made to the Inspector of Taxes dealing with the company's affairs. Unless otherwise specified by legislation, claims must be made within six years of the end of the accounting period to which they relate. The most common claims and elections are set out below together with the time limit by which the claim or election must be made. The Inspector of Taxes does not generally have discretion to accept claims made after the time limit has expired for a particular claim unless the legislation (or Revenue practice) allows otherwise.

Relief may be claimed within the normal six year time limit against any over assessment to corporation tax due to an error or mistake in, or an omission from, any return or statement. No relief is due where the information was not used to form the basis of an assessment, or where the assessment was made in accordance with practice generally prevailing at the time of issue. An error or mistake claim under TMA 1970, s 33 should be made to the Revenue.

For accounting periods ended after 30 September 1993, group relief and capital allowances claims will no longer be made by submitting formal claims to the Inspector of Taxes. Such claims will be made in the pay and file return Form CT200, as will claims for repayment of tax deducted at source.

Claim	*Time Limit for Submission*	*Reference*
Trading losses carried forward	Six years	TA 1988, s 393
Trading losses offset against other income of accounting period	Two years	TA 1988, s 393A
Trading losses carried back	Two years	TA 1988, s 393A
Terminal loss relief	Two years	TA 1988, s 393A
Disclaimer of capital allowances	Two years	CAA 1990, s 24
Group relief	Two years	TA 1988, s 412
Surrender of ACT	Six years	TA 1988, s 240
Carry back of ACT	Two years	TA 1988, s 239
Surplus franked investment income	Two years (Six years for charges on income and management expenses)	TA 1988, s 242
Rollover relief	Six years	TCGA 1992, s 152
CGT rebasing at 31 March 1982	Two years after the end of the accounting period in which the first relevant disposal is made after 31 March 1988	TCGA 1992, s 35

24.12 Should you operate via a company?

There is no simple answer to the question 'should you operate via a company?' There are both advantages and disadvantages in carrying on business through a limited company rather than operating as an unincorporated business. Some of the considerations arise from commercial rather than tax aspects. Limited liability may be an important consideration, either for the proprietors of the business or in order to attract finance from an outside investor. However, the apparent protection given by limited liability is often illusory since banks or other lending institutions will normally require personal guarantees from directors in respect of any bank loans made to the company.

24.12.1 Tax considerations

Lower rate of tax on profits

Having a company means that a lower rate of tax will apply to retained profits.

The small companies rate of 25 per cent applies to profits up to £300,000 provided there are no associated companies. If there are associated companies, the threshold at which profits attract tax at either the normal 33 per cent rate or the marginal small companies rate will be reduced. If there are no associated companies, the small companies rate can produce a very substantial saving.

24.12.2 Example—Tax saving through incorporation

	£
Profits of an unincorporated business	400,000
Tax and NICs (assuming single personal allowance)	150,362
Profits of a company before director's remuneration	400,000
Less director's remuneration and NICs (say)	150,000
	250,000
Corporation tax at 25 per cent	62,500
Tax and NICs on director's remuneration	65,245
Total tax and NICs on profits of £400,000	127,745
Saving in tax through operating via a company	22,617

24.12.3 Other tax considerations

Timing difference

There is a useful timing difference where a business is carried on through a company in that remuneration can be deducted from the profits of the company even though it is not paid (and is not taxable income of the individuals until it is paid). Provided that the remuneration is actually paid within nine months of the company's year end, the company is normally entitled to a deduction in arriving at its profits.

24.12.4 Example—Timing of tax payments

If a company draws up accounts to 31 March 1994, it may secure a deduction for director's remuneration of £150,000 even though the remuneration is not paid until 31 December 1994 in which case PAYE tax does not have to be paid over until 14 January 1995.

Contrast this with an unincorporated business where tax needs to be paid over in two instalments, on 1 January during the tax year and on 1 July following the end of the tax year.

Preceding year basis not relevant

Some people would look at matters rather differently and, because an unincorporated business is taxed under the preceding year basis, would argue that there is often a longer gap between an unincorporated business' year end and the date at which tax is payable. However, this is misconceived in that it ignores the fact that tax is payable by an unincorporated business for each tax year. It is true that the measure of assessable profits may reflect profits of an earlier period under the preceding year basis, but the period of time during which tax has to be paid for a tax year is still shorter than that which is permitted where profits are reduced by directors' remuneration paid over near the end of the nine month period.

Pension contributions

Another aspect which favours having a company is that it is possible for a company to fund pensions for directors at a greater rate than the legislation permits them to make personal pension contributions. For example, if an individual is aged 44, the maximum personal pension contribution that he may make for the year is 20 per cent of his relevant earnings up to £76,800. In contrast, a company would normally be permitted by the Pension Schemes Office to fund a pension scheme for the benefit of the individual at the rate of 100 per cent of his remuneration up to the amount of the earnings cap (currently £76,800).

Payment of remuneration may prevent personal allowances going to waste

Where an unincorporated business operates at a loss, and the individuals have no other private income, the benefit of their personal allowances is lost forever. By trading through a company, it is possible to vote remuneration equal to the individuals' personal allowances and the remuneration voted in this way will increase the amount of the company's loss which can be carried forward and set against subsequent profits.

24.12.5   Possible disadvantages

Possible disadvantages of operating through a company include the following:

Extra administration

There are more statutory requirements concerning the keeping of books, filing of annual accounts, disclosure etc. An unincorporated business does not normally need to file annual accounts at all, whereas a company needs to file accounts with Companies House, and to make an annual return.

Admitting future partners

If profits are retained, this may make it increasingly difficult for individuals who come up through the business to become shareholder directors. For example, if a company has 100 £1 shares in issue and the company retains profits after tax of £15,000 per annum for ten years, each share will be worth £1,500 more at the end of the ten years than at the start of the period. In order for an individual to acquire a ten per cent shareholding, he must find sufficient finance to purchase shares which reflect this. The problem does not arise in the case of a partnership, since the normal procedure will be to allocate past profits to partners' capital accounts and then admit a new partner on the basis that he would share in future profits at a specified percentage.

Tax savings may only be a deferment

The traditional analysis has been that tax will generally become payable by the shareholders on their share of retained profits, either when the shareholders sell their shares and realise a capital gain, or as and when they extract retained profits by taking a dividend. On this analysis, the saving of tax on retained profits will often be little more than a deferment of tax. The validity of this way of looking at matters has been brought into question by the substantial increases in CGT retirement relief during recent years. The fact that, if a husband and wife both qualify for the maximum retirement relief, gains may be exempt up to £500,000 means that in many cases the traditional analysis is no longer valid since shareholder/directors are generally able to enjoy the full value of their shares on a sale or liquidation of the company.

Increased liability for national insurance contributions

A company is required to pay Class 1 NICs on all amounts paid as remuneration. There is no ceiling such as applies to the employees' own contributions. This can give rise to a substantially increased burden for a company as compared with an unincorporated business. Comparing an unincorporated business owned by four equal partners with a company which has four 25 per cent shareholders, (and it is assumed that in both cases the individuals will have income of £75,000 each), the national insurance bill for 1994–95 is as follows:

	Partnership £		Company £
Class 2	1,175.20	employees' Class 1	7,995.52
Class 4	4,634.04	employer's Class 1	30,600.00
	5,809.24		38,595.52

Whilst the benefits payable to employees are better than those received by the self-employed (a larger pension because of SERPS and entitlement to unemployment benefit) the higher NIC costs can be a very expensive way of financing such benefits.

Work in progress

Operating via a company may mean that work in progress has to be valued and brought into account in arriving at profits. In contrast, unincorporated businesses may draw up accounts on a cash basis. There is a further problem which is particularly acute for professional firms. In principle, a professional firm should not include partner time in arriving at the cost of work in progress. This means that the figure brought into account should be lower because of this. However, if a business is carried on by a company, time put in by a director should be included when valuing work in progress.

Treatment of wives' earnings

If a wife is a partner in an unincorporated business, it is most rare for the

Revenue to dispute the level of profits allocated to her. In this regard, unincorporated businesses are treated more favourably than companies where the Revenue regularly argue that a wife's remuneration is excessive and part of the remuneration should be disallowed in computing profits.

Potential double charge for capital gains

Where a valuable asset is held within a company, a tax liability may arise at two stages before the shareholders can enjoy the sale proceeds. For example, if a company acquired a property at a cost of £100,000, and five years later it is worth £550,000, there might be a gain for the company (after indexation) of £400,000. The company will pay tax on this capital gain either at the marginal small companies rate or at 33 per cent. If a tax charge at 33 per cent is assumed, the company will have net funds available after paying tax of £318,000 ie

	£
Gain	450,000
Less tax on gain	132,000
	318,000

If the company is then wound up, and the cash distributed to the shareholders, they are likely to have a personal CGT liability on the £318,000. If retirement relief is not available, the capital gains tax payable by them could be £127,200 (ie £318,000 at 40 per cent). This figure assumes that other assets and retained profits within the company are such that there would have been capital gains for the shareholders in any event, even if the company had not held the property concerned.

However, once again, the traditional analysis is open to question. If the company had paid a dividend in order to transmit the £318,000 cash to shareholders, their personal liability could not exceed £79,500. Furthermore, the ACT payable by the company on such a dividend could be offset against the company's chargeable gain, with any unrelieved ACT then being carried back against previous years' assessments. Consequently, whilst it is not generally good policy to have appreciating assets within a company, the extent of the extra tax payable is not as great as it was in the past. Furthermore, whilst some additional tax is likely to be payable if an appreciating asset is held within a company, this is not an argument in itself against a business operating through a company. Correctly analysed, the treatment of capital gains within a company is an argument in favour of shareholder/ directors holding such assets in their personal capacity rather than through a company. It should be borne in mind here that retirement relief is available to a full-time working director who disposes of a property which is used by his family company provided that a disposal is associated with a disposal of shares in the company (see 15.10).

24.12.6 Conclusion

The question of whether an individual should operate via a company is a complex question which needs professional advice.

25   Outline of VAT

by TIM BUSS

Value added tax was introduced by the Finance Act 1972 and became operational on 1 April 1973 when it replaced purchase tax and selective employment tax. In concept, it is a simple tax, although various exclusions from a VAT charge and the European Community influence, have resulted in a simple concept becoming one of the most complicated taxes of all time.

This chapter covers some of the detail of VAT under the following headings:

(1)   Introduction
(2)   Legal authorities
(3)   Liability to VAT
(4)   Practical implications
(5)   Anti-avoidance measures
(6)   Special schemes
(7)   Enforcement procedures
(8)   Fraud
(9)   Appeals.

25.1   Introduction

The introduction of VAT was a pre-condition of the acceptance of the United Kingdom into what was then known as the European Economic Community (EEC) which, as a result of the European Communities Act 1982, has now become the European Community (EC). Part of the EC philosophy is the harmonisation of taxing statutes, particularly those that affect cross-border trading activities. For example, customs duty is an EC tax and is payable when goods enter the EC and is charged at the same rate when or wherever the goods enter the Community.

Once customs duty is paid the goods are in free circulation and can move freely between member states without the payment of any further duty or being subject to Customs' controls. The legislative authority for customs duty is to be found in EC Regulations which, once agreed by the EC Commission, have immediate direct effect in each member state.

The harmonisation of VAT has been the subject of much discussion by the EC Commission in the recent past. This has resulted in the introduction of transitional rules with effect from 1 January 1993 and commonly referred to as The Single Market Legislation. These implement a degree of harmonisation on the VAT accounting requirements of the movement of goods between Member States. The ultimate legal authority for VAT is a number of EC VAT Directives, which must be reflected in the national legislation of each member state. To that extent, Directives have Direct effect. For example, if the national law is not in accordance with a directive and thereby disadvantages the taxpayer, it is possible for the taxpayer to argue his case, using the Directive, in the National Court, which must recognise the Directive and with the ultimate right of an appeal to the European Court of Justice.

The administration of VAT was given to HM Customs and Excise, which introduced a completely new system of tax enforcement to the majority of businesses and the accounting profession. Customs, which is steeped in the history of duty enforcement, brought with it its practical approach to controlling the taxpayer. For the first time, many businesses and their professional advisers had to justify, face to face with the enforcement agencies (the VAT control officer), what had been declared in the VAT return and the amounts shown in the annual accounts.

In principle, for the majority of businesses VAT is *not* a tax on profits. It is a tax on the consumer that is collected in stages throughout the business chain and is collected, eventually, by the business person supplying the consumer, whether that be an individual or a business which is not registered for VAT. If a business fails to charge and account for VAT correctly, it will have to account for both the VAT and any penalties from its own resources and thereby, by default, VAT becomes a charge on profits. Put simply, the business person is a tax collector.

25.2 Legal authorities

There is no single piece of legislation covering the administration and collection of VAT. The VAT legislation is described briefly below.

25.2.1 The VAT Act 1983 (VATA 1983)

This is a consolidation Act which brought together the Act that originally introduced VAT (Finance Act 1972) and subsequent Finance Acts amending the original legislation. VATA 1983 deals with the administration of the tax and provides for certain aspects to be dealt with by delegated legislation. Subsequent Finance Acts have amended VATA 1983 and it is possible there will be a further VAT consolidation Act in the foreseeable future.

25.2.2   Statutory instruments

There are various VAT Statutory Instruments which deal with particular aspects of VAT administration. The most notable is the VAT General Regulations 1985 (SI 1985/886) which deals with a wide range of administrative procedures which must be complied with, eg tax invoices, when they should be issued, the details required to be shown, the method of recovering VAT when a VAT registered person is not entitled to a full recovery of VAT paid to its suppliers and special VAT accounting procedures for particular transactions and many more. These regulations are overdue for consolidation and a draft consolidation Statutory Instrument was published in 1992, so it is possible that one will be introduced shortly.

25.2.3   Treasury orders

Certain Treasury orders describe amongst other things what is or is not chargeable to VAT and also give legal authority to certain organisations being able to recover VAT which would otherwise not be recoverable. Occasionally, Treasury orders are published only in the *London Gazette*.

25.2.4   Customs notices and leaflets

The general principle is that VAT public notices are not part of the law. Certain notices, however, are published pursuant to VATA 1983 and Statutory Instruments and, thereby, *are* part of the law. As such they have the same status as an Act of Parliament and are legally binding upon the taxpayer. For example, Notice 700 (General Guide) is principally Customs' interpretation of the law but the section that deals with the maintenance of accounting records is part of the law as is the Public Notice on the special VAT Retail Schemes (Notice 727).

Customs' leaflets are not strictly part of the law but certain leaflets, which explain the Commissioners' requirements for particular types of transactions are, in practical terms, legally binding. This applies to relatively few of the leaflets, the vast majority being simply the Commissioners' interpretation of the law.

25.2.5   EC Directives

All VAT law has its roots in the EC Sixth VAT Directive which has direct effect in the United Kingdom and other EC countries through their respective national laws. There are a number of other EC Directives that deal with specific aspects such as that which, on 1 January 1993, introduced VAT harmonisation in the Single Market and others which provide the right to recover VAT incurred in other countries.

25.3   Liability to VAT

The basic rule is that VAT is chargeable on the supply of any goods or services (for a consideration) in the United Kingdom when supplied 'in the course or furtherance of any business'.

25.3.1   Business
(VATA 1983, s 47)

Business has not been defined but has been interpreted to have a very wide meaning and covers all organisations that carry on an activity in a businesslike way. This has resulted in a number of organisations which do not consider themselves to be carrying on a business, (such as clubs and associations, charities etc), having to conform with the VAT legislation and, where appropriate, register and account for VAT on their business income. If it can be demonstrated that the activity is purely and simply a hobby, there will be no requirement to charge VAT on any resulting income. An employee's services to an employer in return for a salary meets the definition of a supply of services but the law specifically provides that such services are not in the course or furtherance of a business and, therefore, are outside the scope of VAT.

Charities

There is no automatic relief from VAT for supplies either to or made by charities. If a charity is carrying on a business activity it will be required to register and account for VAT on its business income the same as any commercial organisation.

There is relief from VAT by means of zero rating for certain supplies to charities but these are mainly in the health and welfare area and new commercial property which would otherwise be subject to a VAT charge and which is used wholly for charitable non-business activities. If a qualifying building is to be used for both non-business and business use the purchase price will be apportioned between the standard and zero-rated elements.

Clubs and associations
(VATA 1983, s 47 (2)(a))

Many local clubs and associations, usually formed by local residents, consider they are not carrying on a business, but this is not correct. The law specifically provides that the admission to premises for a consideration and the provision of benefits to members in return for a subscription or other payment is a business activity.

Similarly certain trade and professional organisations consider they are not in business or qualify for exemption as professional associations and there is no requirement to register for VAT. Such organisations generally provide other benefits to their members and, possibly, non-members which are not within the exemption and, therefore, there may be a liability to register for VAT.

Admission to premises
(VATA 1983, s 47 (2)(b))

The admission, for payment, of persons to any premises is a business activity. Any person carrying on such an activity will be required to register and account for VAT if such income exceeds the registration threshold. In order to avoid the risk of penalties all clubs, associations and similar organisations should review their activities to ensure that they meet their VAT obligations at the correct time.

25.3.2   Supplies

The application of VAT differs depending upon whether there is a supply of goods or a supply of services.

A supply of goods is where legal title to the property is, or is to be, transferred to another person. This includes, for example, the transfer of title in land by means of a freehold sale or a lease exceeding 21 years. In certain circumstances what appears to be a supply of services is, in fact, a supply of goods. A good example of this is where a person applies a process to another person's goods and the nature of the goods has changed, eg the making of a suit by a tailor from the cloth provided by his customer is a supply of goods and not a supply of tailoring services.

Anything which is not a supply of goods that is done for a consideration, is a supply of services and, therefore, subject to the VAT regime. A VAT charge will only arise where consideration is present and, accordingly, a free supply of services is outside the scope of VAT. Care is required, because what may appear to be free is not necessarily so in real terms and a hidden VAT liability could arise.

The VAT liability of supplies can fall into three main headings.

Taxable

These are supplies that are subject to VAT at either the zero or the standard (currently 17.5 per cent) rate. It is likely that multiple positive rates of VAT will be introduced in the foreseeable future.

Exempt

These are supplies that are exempt from VAT by statute, ie those that are listed in VATA 1983, Sched 6. Exemption and zero-rating must not be confused because the overall effect on a business is totally different. As will be seen later, zero-rating gives entitlement to recover VAT on underlying costs whereas exemption does not.

'Outside the scope'

Certain supplies or business activities are 'outside the scope' of VAT. This includes an employee's services to an employer but can also include what, on the face of it, are normal trading activities of the organisation. For example, the supply of goods that are situated outside the United Kingdom, although part of the UK business activities, are outside the scope of UK VAT. Similarly, with effect from 1 January 1993, certain services that are either physically performed or are to be received outside the UK are deemed to have been supplied outside the United Kingdom and, therefore, outside the scope of UK VAT.

Generally speaking, 'outside the scope' activities of an organisation do not permit the recovery of VAT on related costs. The exception to this general principle is where a VAT-registered person supplies goods or services outside the United Kingdom that would be subject to VAT if made in the United Kingdom. Supplies or income received by the business are known as outputs.

25.4 Practical implications

The administration of VAT is by a system of VAT registration, the submission of regular VAT returns and control verification visits by Customs.

25.4.1 VAT registration

Registration is required where a business or any other organisation makes taxable supplies over a pre-determined limit. The limits, which are based on gross turnover, are increased each year generally in line with inflation.

It is the person which is registered, not the business activity. Once registered, all business activities must be reflected in the VAT accounting records; for example a solicitor VAT-registered sole proprietor must also include his farming or writing income in his VAT accounts.

Currently registration is required when one of the following two conditions is satisfied:

(1)   When, at the end of any month, the gross taxable turnover during the previous 12 months, on a rolling basis, exceeds £45,000. Such a liability must be notified within 30 days and registration is effective from the first of the month following the month in which a liability to notify arose.

For example, where taxable turnover in the 12 months to 31 January was, say, £47,000, notification must be made within 30 days and registration is effective from 1 March. VAT will have to be accounted for on all income received after 1 March, whether or not it refers to invoices issued on or before 28 February.

There is no VAT liability for income received prior to the effective date of registration.

(2)   As soon as there are reasonable grounds to believe the value of taxable supplies to be made during the following 30 days will exceed £45,000. Registration is due immediately.

Before March 1990, different rules applied and a liability to register was then based, in general, on either a historic quarterly or annual turnover limit. These rules still apply when determining whether or not there is a past liability to register for VAT.

It is only *taxable* turnover (ie goods or services liable to VAT at either the zero or standard rate) that is taken into consideration when determining whether or not there is a liability to register for VAT. Income which is exempt and outside the scope of VAT is ignored.

Voluntary registration

There is an entitlement to register voluntarily for VAT even if the taxable turnover is below the VAT registration limits. This could be an advantage to an expanding or small business as VAT on costs would be recoverable and this, providing the charging of VAT on supplies does not reduce demand for the product, would increase profitability. Similarly businesses based in the United Kingdom which do not make any supplies in the United Kingdom but make what would be taxable supplies overseas are entitled to register and are thereby able to recover VAT on UK costs.

VAT groups

Incorporated companies under common control may register for VAT as a single unit—a VAT group. All supplies between the companies in the VAT group are disregarded for VAT purposes, ie no VAT or other consequence arises. One company is nominated as the representative member and is responsible for submitting the VAT returns and accounting for VAT on all supplies to or received from persons outside the VAT group. However, there is a joint and several liability on all companies within a VAT group for any VAT due to Customs.

25.4.2   VAT returns

Once a business is registered, VAT returns have to be submitted on a regular basis. Each VAT-registered person is allocated a three-monthly VAT accounting period, but it is possible to request a particular VAT period (for example to coincide with the business' financial year). It is also possible to request monthly returns if the business will be regularly recovering VAT from Customs and Excise.

VAT returns must be submitted with full payment by the end of the month following the end of the VAT accounting period. A failure to submit returns and make full payment by the due date is subject to penalties (see 25.7.2).

The VAT chargeable on supplies made during the period (known as output tax) must be declared on the VAT return (VAT 100) which is provided automatically each period by Customs.

Output VAT is due on all tax invoices issued during the period, irrespective of whether or not the invoices have been paid. There are special schemes available available to ease this particular requirement for certain classes of business as explained below. In addition, VAT is also due on all monies received for supplies made during the period and for which a tax invoice has not been issued, eg scrap sales, vending machine income, emptying telephone boxes, staff canteen sales, certain deductions from salaries for supplies to staff, etc.

For businesses which do not issue tax invoices, such as retailers, VAT is due on the gross taxable income received during the VAT period.

With effect from 1 January 1993, VAT on the value of goods which have been both supplied by other EC VAT registered persons and have been received from another EC country, must be declared as output tax in Box 2 of the VAT return.

25.4.3   VAT recovery

VAT-registered businesses may offset any VAT paid to suppliers (known as input tax) against the output tax declared, subject to the following conditions:

(1)   Goods/services have been *supplied to* and have been, or will be, used by the business to make taxable supplies.

(2)   Documentary evidence of the supply received, ie a tax invoice to the business by the supplier, is obtained and retained. If there is no tax invoice or other documentary evidence, the VAT officer will refuse claims for input tax.

However, Customs has discretion and may accept alternative evidence of VAT paid.

Supplies of zero-rated goods or services are taxable supplies with an entitlement to recover VAT on related costs whereas there is no such entitlement in respect of exempt supplies.

VAT on the purchase of a motor car or on business entertainment expenses is not recoverable as input tax (VAT(Cars) Order 1992 SI 1992/3122 and VAT (Input Tax) Order 1992 SI 1992/3222). In addition VAT on goods or services received by the VAT-registered person which are used for a non-business activity, certain outside-the-scope transactions or for private use, is not recoverable as input tax. Many people believe that because a VAT-registered business pays an invoice, there is an entitlement to recover the VAT shown on the invoice. This is not correct and to do so may give rise to penalties.

The recovery of VAT by businesses which make both taxable and exempt supplies is described below, under 'partial exemption'.

Bad debt relief

A claim for bad debt relief may be for any debt that is more than six months old whether or not the debtor has gone into formal bankruptcy, liquidation or winding up. Prior to 1 April 1989 there had to be a formal insolvency before VAT bad debt relief was available and these rules still apply to any supplies made before that date.

Once a debt is six months old and providing the VAT has previously been accounted for to Customs the debt may be written off by being entered in a Refund for Bad Debt Account (ie not written off in the accounting sense, as for corporation tax). The VAT is recovered by including the sum in the input tax recovered box of the VAT return (Box 4). Any payment received after the claim has been made is VAT inclusive and the VAT element must be repaid to Customs. VAT bad debt relief is not available for businesses which use either a retail or the cash accounting scheme, such relief is built into the scheme.

Payments on account

With effect from 1 October 1992, those businesses who normally pay more than £2 million annually to Customs are required to make monthly payments on account with a balancing payment when the three monthly VAT return is submitted.

Zero-rated supplies

The zero-rated supplies are exports of goods to places outside the EC (VATA 1983, s 16) and those listed in VATA 1983 Sched 5. There are some 16 groups in Sched 5:

(1) Food for human consumption
(2) Sewerage services and water (this does not include bottled water)
(3) Books and newspapers etc
(4) Talking books and wireless sets for the blind
(5) Fuel and power for domestic use up to 31 March 1994
(6) Construction of and sales of new dwellings
(7) Approved alteration of listed residential buildings
(8) International services (the services qualifying under this heading were greatly reduced on 1 January 1993)
(9) Transport
(10) Caravans and houseboats
(11) Gold
(12) Bank notes
(13) Drugs, medicines, aids for the handicapped etc
(14) Imports, exports etc
(15) Charities (certain supplies to or by charities)
(16) Clothing and footwear (protective).

25.4.4 Partial exemption

A business that makes both exempt and taxable supplies is known as partially exempt and will generally be unable to recover all VAT paid to its suppliers. However, if the VAT on costs relating, directly and indirectly, to the exempt activities (known as exempt input tax) is below prescribed limits, all the VAT is recoverable in full. The current limits are that the exempt input tax must not exceed £600 per month on average, in the VAT year (the VAT year ends March, April or May depending upon the business' VAT return period). This entitles a business to incur approximately £41,000 of costs, each year which relates to its exempt activities without having to restrict its recovery of input tax. Once the exempt input tax limit is exceeded in any VAT year, *all* the relevant VAT is irrecoverable ie the £600 per month is not an automatic entitlement.

There are other minor limits that apply in particular circumstances and certain exempt supplies may be ignored. The rules are complex and it is advisable to obtain professional advice. Full details may be found in the VAT General Regulations 1985 (SI 1985/886) regs 29–36 and Customs VAT Notice 706.

Goods and services which are exempt from VAT are listed in VATA 1983, Sched 6. The main headings are:

(1)   Land (with a number of exceptions)
(2)   Insurance
(3)   Postal services
(4)   Betting, gaming and lotteries
(5)   Finance
(6)   Education (when provided by schools, universities etc). This heading also includes supplies by youth clubs
(7)   Health and welfare
(8)   Burial and cremation
(9)   Trade unions and professional bodies
(10) Sports competitions
(11) Works of art etc (in limited circumstances)
(12) Fund raising events by charities and other qualifying bodies.

As the headings are a general description and the rules for exemption are extremely complicated, it is advisable to take professional advice before exempting a particular transaction.

25.5   Anti-avoidance measures

There are a number of anti-avoidance measures available to Customs.

25.5.1   Business splitting

Where a business activity has been divided amongst a number of legal entities (eg a series of partnerships with a partner common to all) and the reason for such a division is to avoid having to account for VAT, Customs may issue a direction informing all the businesses that they are registered as a single unit and that VAT must be accounted for on all taxable income. The direction can only be from a current or future date.

25.5.2   Sales to connected parties

Where a VAT registered business supplies goods or services at below market value to a connected party which is not entitled to a full recovery of input tax, Customs may direct, during the three years following the supply, that the open market value is used.

25.5.3 Self supplies etc

In certain circumstances, an output VAT charge will arise on normal business activities which are not supplies made to third parties ie a VAT charge arises on business expenditure (usually referred to as 'self supplies'). The value of such self supplies is taken into consideration when determining a liability to register for VAT; the more important ones are described below. The reasons behind such a liability are both anti-avoidance and to reduce possible trade distortion.

Buildings

Where a business constructs, or has constructed, on its own land a new commercial building of a value exceeding £100,000 and the building is used for exempt supplies (eg used as a head office of a partially exempt business, an exempt lease or as a doctor's surgery) there is an output VAT liability. The value is the total construction costs plus the value of the land.

Stationery

If an exempt, or partially exempt, business prints its own stationery there is an output VAT liability on the total printing cost (including all overheads). If the in-house printing costs of an otherwise exempt business exceed the VAT registration threshold there is a liability to register and account for VAT on such costs.

Reverse charges

Certain professional and intellectual services purchased from overseas persons give rise to an output tax liability on the recipient. The services are deemed to be both supplied by and received by the UK organisation ie there is an output tax liability and the VAT may also be recovered under the normal rules (restricted if partially exempt). The services include royalty and/or licence payments; financial, insurance advertising legal, accountancy, consultancy services and the hire of staff or equipment.

25.5.4 Transfer of a business

Where the assets of a business are transferred to another person, who intends to use the assets to carry on the same kind of business as the vendor, the transaction is not subject to a VAT charge. However, where a VAT group which is partially exempt (ie not entitled to a full recovery of input tax) acquires assets in these circumstances, there is a deemed taxable supply by the VAT group and output tax must be accounted for on the VAT group's return. The corresponding input tax will be restricted by whatever method has been agreed with the local VAT office.

25.6   Special schemes

There are a number of special schemes which are either designed to simplify accounting for VAT or reduce the VAT liability.

25.6.1   Retail schemes

These are special schemes for use by retailers, i.e. those in trade classification Group 24 (Retail Division) and Group 28 (Miscellaneous Services). Generally it is those who deal direct with the public on a cash basis and who do not normally issue tax invoices. The schemes are currently being reviewed. There are no major changes anticipated but a new scheme (D1) is being introduced which, it is claimed, will simplify dealing with multiple rates if they are ever re-introduced.

25.6.2   Secondhand schemes

There are a number of special secondhand schemes which provide for VAT to be charged on the profit, if any, as opposed to the full selling price. Currently schemes are available for:

(1)   Cars
(2)   Motor cycles
(3)   Caravans/motor caravans
(4)   Works of art, antiques and collector's items
(5)   Boats and outboard motors
(6)   Electronic organs
(7)   Aircraft
(8)   Firearms
(9)   Horses and ponies.

Special stock recording and records are required.

An EC Directive has been agreed which extends the scope of the second-hand schemes, eg to secondhand furniture and musical instruments. The implementation date for the directive has not yet been discussed.

25.6.3   Cash accounting

The general principle is that VAT must be accounted for on all tax invoices issued whether or not the customer/client has paid for the supply. Businesses that cannot use the retail scheme, and whose turnover is less than £350,000 (excluding VAT) annually, may apply and be authorised (in writing) by Customs to use the cash accounting scheme. Output VAT is not due until payment has been received but, similarly, input tax on purchases/expenses cannot be recovered until the supplier has been paid and a receipt obtained.

25.6.4   Annual accounting

To avoid having to submit returns quarterly, businesses with an annual turnover not exceeding £300,000 (excluding VAT) may be authorised, in writing, by Customs to use the annual accounting scheme. Nine payments, based on the previous year's VAT liability, are made by direct debit and a final, balancing payment, is made with the VAT return at the end of the second month following the allocated VAT year.

25.6.5   Tour operators' margin scheme

This scheme must be used by any VAT-registered business which supplies packaged travel/accommodation services. As the name implies, VAT is accountable on the margin, if any, on the taxable element of the package. Special record keeping and an annual calculation is required.

25.6.6   Agricultural flat rate scheme

This is a special scheme, introduced on 1 January 1993, under which farmers, and other agricultural businesses need not register and submit VAT returns in order to recover VAT on overhead expenses, etc. Instead, the farmer will charge VAT at a nominal four per cent on all his supplies which he will retain (in lieu of input tax) and the recipient will be entitled to recover as input tax under the normal rules. The scheme requires authorisation by Customs and is not applicable to all farmers. Farmers who would benefit by more than £3,000 compared to being VAT-registered are not entitled to join the scheme.

25.7   Enforcement procedures

25.7.1   VAT visits

Customs regularly visits VAT registered businesses to verify the returns submitted. Its powers are extensive and include the right to see any documents, accounts etc relating to the business activities and the right to inspect (but not search) the business premises. The frequency of visit depends upon a number of factors such the size of the business, types of business activity and compliance history. Visits can range from half a day every few years for the smaller business to several weeks a year for the multi-nationals.

Where errors are discovered, the visiting officer will raise an assessment for any VAT previously under-declared and, where appropriate, impose penalty and interest charges (see 25.7.2). It is advisable, therefore, to have all assessments independently reviewed. Customs collects over £1,000 m by the way of additional assessments from approximately 450,000 visits each year but most visits do not result in assessments being issued. If the accounting records have been well kept and have been independently reviewed regularly no problem should arise at the visit.

25.7.2   Penalties

There are a number of penalty provisions which Customs may impose automatically, and arbitrarily, for a failure to comply with the many complex VAT regulations. These were introduced with the view to improving compliance and reducing the amount of VAT outstanding at any one time.

Late registration
(FA 1985, s 15)

Failure to notify and register at the correct time (see 25.4.1) will result in Customs imposing a financial penalty. The penalty is a percentage of between 10 per cent and 30 per cent, (depending upon the length of the delay), of the net tax due between the date notification was required and the actual date of notification.

Late returns
(FA 1985, s 19)

With effect from 1 October 1993, if one payment is submitted late in any period of 12 months, Customs will notify the VAT registered person that payments submitted late during the following 12 months will be subject to a default surcharge. Prior to 1 October 1993, the business would be notified if two returns or payments were submitted late in any 12 months.

If a payment is submitted late during the 12 month surcharge period, a two per cent penalty is imposed and the surcharge period extended for a further 12 months. The surcharge rises for each successive late payment to five per cent and by increments of five per cent to a maximum of 15 per cent. If payments have been submitted by the due dates for 12 months, the business is removed from the default surcharge regime and the cycle starts again.

The surcharge is waived if it is below a minimum amount, ie £200.

Serious misdeclaration penalty
(FA 1985, s 14)

If a VAT officer discovers an under-declaration which exceeds specified limits, he will assess a serious misdeclaration penalty of 15 per cent of the additional VAT assessed. The penalty, which is based on each individual period, (ie it is not accumulative), is imposed where the additional VAT assessed exceeds the lesser of:

(1) £1m; and
(2) 30 per cent of the gross amount of tax due for the appropriate return period.

Interest
(FA 1985, s 18)

An interest charge will be imposed on all assessments for additional tax issued by VAT visiting officers. The rate of interest is the prescribed rate as enacted by Treasury order and is not deductible for income or corporation tax. There are a number of other penalty provisions such as failure to maintain or produce records, unauthorised issue of a tax invoice (by non-registered reasons), persistent incorrect returns etc. There are, in fact, over 60 regulatory offences which could give rise to a penalty.

25.8   Fraud

In VAT law there are two forms of fraud, civil and criminal.

25.8.1 Civil
(FA 1985, s 13)

If, after an investigation, Customs is satisfied there has been an element of dishonesty it may seek to impose a civil fraud penalty of 100 per cent of the tax involved. If there has been full co-operation by the taxpayer, Customs, or, (on appeal), a VAT Tribunal may reduce the penalty by whatever percentage is considered reasonable.

In a civil fraud investigation, Customs has only to prove on a balance of probabilities that a fraud had been committed in order to impose a penalty.

25.8.2 Criminal
(VATA 1983, s 39)

The more serious cases are dealt with under the criminal law with penalties of up to three times the VAT involved, or imprisonment or both. In these cases Customs must use the criminal rules of evidence etc and prove beyond reasonable doubt that a fraud has been committed deliberately.

25.9 Appeals

25.9.1 VAT tribunals

There is a right of an appeal to an independent VAT tribunal on a number of matters including:

(1) Assessments which are considered to be incorrect or not issued to the Commissioners' best judgement.
(2) Liability rulings by Customs in respect of a specified supply.
(3) Penalties, other than the interest charged for errors, if there is a reasonable excuse for the error. The law does not define reasonable excuse but does state the insufficiency of funds or the reliance on another is *not* a reasonable excuse.
(4) The amount of the reduction, if any, of a penalty for a civil fraud where the taxpayer considers he has provided full cooperation with the investigating officers.

The details of appeal procedures are outside the scope of this book. However, the procedure for lodging an appeal to a VAT tribunal, (which must be made within 30 days of the appealable event), is straightforward. It is prudent, however, to obtain professional advice before doing so and it is advisable to be represented at the tribunal hearing which in many ways resembles a court hearing although less formal.

A decision of the VAT tribunal may be appealed to a higher court on a point of law and, in limited circumstances, an appeal may be referred to the European Court of Justice for a ruling.

25.9.2 Departmental reviews

Many disputes are settled by negotiations with Customs by formally requesting a departmental review of the disputed ruling/assessment within the 30 day time limit. This allows discussions to continue without the loss of the right to appeal to an independent VAT tribunal. Commissioners, if requested, will usually review an assessment after the

30 days' limit has expired and will, where appropriate, reduce the amount assessed. In certain circumstances it is also possible to make an application to a VAT tribunal to hear a case that is out of time.

It is prudent to take professional advice before lodging an appeal.

26 Stamp duty

Stamp duty is a tax charged on the documents by which certain types of property are transferred to new owners—eg, it is charged on the conveyance of a freehold house. It is important to emphasise that stamp duty is not charged on the *sale* of the house, but on the *document* by which that house is conveyed to the purchaser.

The relevant document has to be submitted to an Inland Revenue Stamp Office with the appropriate payment. An official stamp is embossed onto the document—to confirm that duty has been paid—and it is then returned to the person presenting it for stamping. Documents are usually submitted by post, but a counter service is available in eleven major cities (Belfast, Birmingham, Bristol, Cardiff, Edinburgh, Leeds, Liverpool, London, Manchester, Newcastle and Nottingham).

This chapter looks at stamp duty under the following headings:

(1)   Documents liable to duty
(2)   Sanctions where duty is not paid
(3)   Avoiding or reducing duty

26.1   Documents liable to duty

Stamp duty was first introduced in 1694 and the law has not been redrafted since the Stamp Act of 1891. Numerous amendments have however been made (to block loopholes or to grant new reliefs) and the result is legislation which is archaic, exceptionally complex and difficult to follow, and in which the detailed exceptions are more important than the broad general rules. For example, the scheme of the legislation is not to impose duty on documents implementing the sale of certain types of property, but to impose duty on all documents implementing the sale of *any* type of property and then to provide a series of exceptions.

The practical effect of this legislation is to impose stamp duty on documents implementing:

(1) The sale of shares and other securities.
(2) The sale of freehold land and buildings and the grant or assignment of leases.
(3) The sale of certain types of business property, such as goodwill and patent rights.

This is *not* a comprehensive list but it does include all the charges likely to be incurred by an investor or business proprietor. (There is, for example, also a duty on life annuity policy documentation, but this will be paid by the assurance company and so is not of direct concern to the annuitant.)

Stamp duty is charged only on sales and not (since 1985) on gifts. Nor is any duty payable when assets are put into trust. However, a sale is defined to include the exchange of property for shares or securities, or the exchange of one block of shares for another.

Strictly speaking, a document should be stamped before it is executed (signed), though in practice the rule is that it must be presented for stamping within thirty days of execution. Late stamping attracts a substantial financial penalty (see 26.2).

26.1.1 Sale of shares or other securities

Stamp duty is charged on documents transferring ownership of shares (in both quoted and private companies), debentures, unit trust units and other securities. The rate of duty is one half of one per cent, rounded up to the next 50p (for example, the duty on a sale for £325 would be £2). British Government stocks ('gilts') and stocks issued by certain international bodies (such as the EC) are exempt from duty.

The stamp duty is borne by the purchaser and is shown as a disbursement on the broker's contract note. It counts as part of the cost of the holding for CGT purposes.

Where one block of shares is exchanged for another, the transaction is treated as two sales, so both participants must pay the usual duty.

In certain circumstances it is possible for shares to be sold without a stampable document being created. This most commonly happens where a block of shares, traded on the London Stock Exchange, changes hands several times in the space of a few days. In such circumstances, Stamp Duty Reserve Tax (SDRT) is charged on the transaction. The SDRT is equal in amount to the stamp duty that would otherwise have been paid and so, from the investor's point of view, it is immaterial which tax is paid.

In 1990 the Government announced that stamp duty on share transfers (and, indeed, on all transactions other than sales and leases of land) would be abolished once the London Stock Exchange had introduced 'paperless' share dealing under its TAURUS computer project. Unfortunately, in the Spring of 1993, the Stock Exchange announced that, because of technical difficulties, it was obliged to abandon TAURUS. It is not clear how this will affect the Government's plans to abolish stamp duty on share transfers.

26.1.2   Sale of land and buildings

Stamp duty is charged on the conveyance of freehold land or buildings at one per cent of the price paid, rounded up to the next whole pound. It is paid by the purchaser. Stamp duty is calculated in exactly the same way whether the property in question is residential or commercial. In both cases, where the sale price does not exceed £60,000, no duty is payable (ie if the sale price is £60,000, no duty is payable; but if the sale price is £60,250, the duty is £603.)

The threshold has changed from time to time, as follows:

13 March 1984 to 19 December 1991	£30,000
20 December 1991 to 19 August 1992	£250,000
20 August 1992 to 15 March 1993	£30,000
16 March 1993 onwards	£60,000

The relevant date is the date the conveyance was executed, not the date it was presented for stamping.

The stamp duty payable on an assignment of an existing lease is calculated in exactly the same way. It is the capital sum paid for the lease that determines the amount of stamp duty; the amount of rent payable under the lease is irrelevant.

However, when a *new* lease is granted, stamp duty is charged *both* on the premium *and* on the annual rent. The duty on the premium is one per cent of the premium paid. The premium will however be exempt if it does not exceed £60,000 *and* the annual rent does not exceed £600.

The duty on the rent depends on the length of the lease and (subject to minor rounding-up) is:

Length of lease	*Duty (as percentage of annual rent)*
Seven years or less	1 per cent[1]
Seven years and one day to thirty-five years	2 per cent
Thirty-five years and one day to one hundred years	12 per cent

More than 100 years   24 per cent

¹ Nil if the annual rent does not exceed £500. Also, if a dwelling is let furnished for less than a year, no stamp duty is payable if the total rent for the period of letting is less than £500. If it is £500 or more, a fixed duty of £1 applies.

26.1.3   Example—Stamp duty on a lease

A ten-year lease is granted at a premium of £50,000 and an annual rent of £1,000. Because the *rent* exceeds £600, the *premium* will not be exempt and the total duty payable is:

Duty on premium: 1 per cent of £50,000	£500
Duty on rent: 2 per cent of £1,000	£20
Total duty payable	£520

Sales and rentals of some commercial property may be subject to value added tax. In such cases, stamp duty is charged on the VAT-*inclusive* sale price, premium and/or rent. Moreover, in certain circumstances the landlord may have the right to add VAT to the rent at a later date: in such a case again the VAT-inclusive figure must be taken.

26.1.4   Sale of goodwill and other business assets

Land and buildings may of course be business assets and the rules explained above apply equally to commercial as to residential property.

Other types of property likely to be included in the value of a business for stamp duty purposes include goodwill, copyrights, patents and trade marks. Depending on the way in which the documentation is drafted, the value of plant and machinery, stock-in-trade and even book debts may have to be taken into account in calculating the stamp duty payable on the purchase of a business as a going concern. This is a complex area requiring the advice of a solicitor experienced in business transactions.

The rate of duty on goodwill, copyrights, patents and trade marks is the same as for land and buildings, ie one per cent rounded to the next whole pound. Exemption is available where the value of the transaction does not exceed £60,000, but the sale of a business as a going concern counts as a single transaction. Therefore, if a shopkeeper sells his shop premises for £50,000 and his goodwill for £20,000, the value of the transaction is £70,000 and exemption is not available.

Because the stamp duty definition of a sale includes an exchange of property for shares, the incorporation of a sole trader's or partnership business will be treated as a sale of that business in exchange for shares in the new company. Stamp duty will be charged according to the value of the shares received by the proprietor or the partners which will, effectively, be an amount equal to the value of the business as a going concern.

26.2   Sanctions where duty is not paid

As a general rule, the Revenue cannot enforce the payment of stamp duty by taking Court proceedings (though they can enforce the payment of SDRT).

Nevertheless, a number of effective sanctions do exist, which mean that in practice it is usually best to ensure that a stampable document is indeed stamped:

(1)   Although the Revenue cannot take civil proceedings to enforce payment of stamp duty, they can prosecute a purchaser or lessee who fails to produce for stamping a conveyance of freehold land, or the grant or transfer of a lease for seven years or more. The maximum fine is £1,000.

(2)   HM Land Registry will not accept any document which is not duly stamped and it is very unwise not to register a purchase of land at the Registry.

(3)   A transfer of shares or debentures cannot be registered unless the transfer document has been properly stamped. (Any purported registration by the company will simply not be valid in law.)

(4)   An unstamped document will not be accepted in any Court proceedings. An unstamped document required in Court could always be stamped, but there is a financial penalty where a document is presented for stamping outside the permitted thirty-day period of £10, plus interest at five per cent per annum from the time the document should have been stamped, plus a fine equal to the duty—ie a late stamper must pay double duty, plus interest, plus £10.

26.3   Avoiding or reducing duty

26.3.1   Sale of shares or other securities

The opportunities to avoid or mitigate duty are circumscribed by the rule that a company may not register a transfer of shares or debentures unless the transfer document has been duly stamped. Beneficial ownership may, of course, be transferred without any change in the registered owner of the shares (as where the shares are registered in the name of a nominee company) and beneficial ownership of shares in certain UK quoted companies, registered in the name of American banks, are traded free of stamp duty in the form of 'American Depositary Receipts' or ADRs. Practical difficulties mean, however, that ADRs are suitable only for institutions such as life assurance companies and pension funds and they are not normally held by private investors.

There is a limited statutory relief for the stamp duty payable on the documentation arising out of certain company reconstructions: this is an area in which proper professional advice is essential.

26.3.2 Sale of land and buildings

One widely used way of mitigating stamp duty was closed in the last Budget.

If two owners exchange houses, stamp duty is now payable on the market value of the properties as well as on any cash adjustment. Prior to 8 December 1993, stamp duty was payable only on the cash element in the consideration.

Stamp duty is not charged on that part of the agreed purchase price which is allocated to items such as carpets, curtains and domestic appliances which are to be left in the house. This is because ownership of such items is transferred, not by the conveyance, but by the vendor physically handing them over to the purchaser (the legal term is 'delivery'). However, do-it-yourself conveyancers should be warned that it is possible to transfer ownership of goods by conveyance rather than by delivery, so that if the documentation is faulty, stamp duty can be charged on the price paid for the carpets and other house contents.

In order to reduce duty, purchasers are sometimes tempted to apportion an unrealistically high percentage of the agreed overall price to the contents—especially where this will bring the price allocated to the house itself below the threshold and so avoid duty altogether. The Stamp Offices are, of course, alive to this temptation and will refuse to stamp a conveyance if the valuations used cannot be justified.

A suggestion sometimes put forward is that a purchaser wishing to buy a brand new house should buy the site and then contract separately with the builder for the construction of the required dwelling. Certainly, if the buyer buys a building plot and then contracts with an unrelated third party for the construction of a house, stamp duty is payable only on the 'site value' price actually paid. A recent Court case suggests that the same holds true if the buyer buys a plot from the builder and then commissions him to build a house on that site *provided that the site is conveyed to the purchaser before a substantial start is made on the building work.*

At first sight, this means that all developers should sell bare sites coupled with agreements to build houses, but in practice there would be problems. The developer probably would not want to convey the site until he had received the full price for the completed house, but at the same time the purchaser would not be willing to pay for a house that had yet to be built. Moreover, if (as would usually be the case) the purchaser needed a mortgage to buy the house, he would almost certainly find that the building society would not make the money available until the house was at least virtually complete. Solutions to these difficulties could no doubt be found, but would probably cost more than the stamp duty saving.

Finally, where a long lease at a substantial rent is proposed, it is sometimes possible to save duty by splitting the period between two shorter leases eg instead of a fifty-year lease with stamp duty of 12 per cent of the annual rent (see 26.1.2) at the outset sign two leases, one for twenty years and the second for thirty years (commencing on the expiry of the first) with the duty on each lease then being only two per cent of the annual rent.

For legal reasons, the first lease must be for less than twenty-one years and so counts as a short lease which cannot be registered at the Land Registry.

26.3.3   Sale of goodwill and other business assets

The assets of a business sold as a going concern will typically include buildings, goodwill, plant and machinery and stock-in-trade. As for house contents, duty can be saved if the vendor transfers ownership of plant, machinery and stock-in-trade to the purchaser by physical delivery rather than by conveyance.

Generally speaking, the ownership of buildings and goodwill can only be transferred by a written document and so duty has to be paid. There are however three ways of avoiding or reducing duty, though all three are usually only practicable where vendor and purchaser trust each other completely.

(1)   Stamp duty is payable on a *conveyance* of freehold land although the *contract* is sufficient to transfer ownership to the purchaser. Therefore, if vendor and purchaser sign and exchange contracts, but never 'complete' by conveyance, no duty is payable. This was upheld by the Courts as long ago as 1889 and the Government has never blocked the loophole. The drawback is that, without a stamped conveyance, the purchase cannot be registered at the Land Registry, which is why this device is only to be recommended where vendor and purchaser trust each other completely.

(2) The second method is simply not to stamp the documentation. Though failing to stamp a conveyance or the grant or assignment of a lease is a punishable offence (see section 26.2 above), the only sanction against failure to stamp a transfer of goodwill is the double charge if it later needs to be stamped out of time.

(3) Where substantial amounts of money are at stake, advantage may be taken of the rule that a document executed (signed) outside the United Kingdom need not be stamped until it is brought into the United Kingdom. (The document may be stamped without interest or penalty provided it is presented at a Stamp Office within thirty days of being brought to the United Kingdom.) The usual procedure is to take a day trip to Jersey or Guernsey, sign the documents, and leave them in a local safe deposit or bank vault.

Stamp duty is payable where a sole trader's or partnership business is incorporated, because the trader or the partnership is treated as having sold the business in exchange for shares in the new company (see 26.1.4). Where the successor company is a limited company, its proprietors must produce to the Registrar of Companies a properly stamped copy of the contract by which the business was sold to the company. It is therefore necessary to pay stamp duty, not only on the value of the goodwill, but also on that of the plant, machinery and stock-in-trade. No stamped contract is however required where a business is transferred to an unlimited company and it is possible to transfer a business to an unlimited company by means of an unstamped contract (for example, one kept outside the United Kingdom) and then to re-register that company as a limited company.

Statutory exemption from stamp duty applies, subject to conditions, where property is transferred from one member of a group of companies to another. For this purpose, a 'group' consists of a holding company and its 90 per cent subsidiaries.

27 Tax tables

27.1 Income tax

Table 27.1—Rates of tax

1994–95	Rate	Taxable Income £	Cumulative Tax £
Lower rate	20%	0–3,000	600
Basic rate	25%	3,001–23,700	5,175
Higher rate	40%	over 23,700	
1993–94			
Lower rate	20%	0–2,500	500
Basic rate	25%	2,501–23,700	5,800
Higher Rate	40%	over 23,700	
1992–93			
Lower rate	20%	0–2,000	400
Basic rate	25%	2,001–23,700	5,825
Higher rate	40%	over 23,700	
1991–92			
Basic rate	25%	0–23,700	5,925
Higher rate	40%	over 23,700	
1990–91 and 1989–90			
Basic rate	25%	0–20,700	5,175
Higher rate	40%	over 20,700	
1988–89			
Basic rate	25%	0–19,300	4,825
Higher rate	40%	over 19,300	

Table 27.2—Personal allowances and reliefs

Allowances (£s)	1988–89	1989–90	1990–91	1991–92	1992–93	1993–94	1994–95
Single person—under 65	2,605	2,785	3,005	3,295	3,445	3,445	3,445
– 65 plus	3,180	3,400	3,670	4,020	4,200	4,200	4,200
– 75 plus	–	3,540	3,820	4,180	4,370	4,370	4,370
– 80 plus	3,310	–	–	–	–	–	–
Married man—under 65	4,095	4,375	–	–	–	–	–
– either spouse 65 plus	5,035	5,385	–	–	–	–	–
– either spouse 75 plus	–	5,565	–	–	–	–	–
– either spouse 80 plus	5,205	–	–	–	–	–	–
Wife's earned income—up to	2,605	2,785	–	–	–	–	–
Married couple's allowance:							
– under 65	–	–	1,720	1,720	1,720	1,720	1,720*
– either spouse 65 plus	–	–	2,145	2,355	2,465	2,465	2,665*
– either spouse 75 plus	–	–	2,185	2,395	2,505	2,505	2,705*
Age allowances—reduced by:							
– £2 in £3 for income over	10,600	11,400	–	–	–	–	–
– £1 in £2 for income over	–	–	12,300	13,500	14,200	14,200	14,200
Additional personal allowance	1,490	1,590	1,720	1,720	1,720	1,720	1,720*
Widow's bereavement allowance	1,490	1,590	1,720	1,720	1,720	1,720	1,720*
Blind person's allowance	540	540	1,080	1,080	1,080	1,080	1,200

*Allowance where relief is restricted to 20% in 1994–95.

Table 27.3—'Official rate' of interest for beneficial loans

From	To	Rate
6 April 1993	5 January 1994	7.75%
6 January 1994	5 April 1994	7.50%
Averate rate for 1993–94		7.687%

Table 27.4—Personal pension schemes maximum contributions by individuals 1989–90 to 1994–95

Age at the beginning of the Tax Year	*Percentage of net relevant earnings*
up to 35	17.5
36–45	20
46–50	25
51–55	30
56–60	35
61 or more	40

Note—there is a 'cap' on relevant earnings as follows:

	£
1994–95	76,800
1993–94	75,000
1992–93	75,000
1991–92	71,400
1990–91	64,800
1989–90	60,000

1988–89

Age at 6 April 1988	*Percentage of net relevant earnings*
up to 50	17.5
51–55	20
56–60	22.5
61 or more	27.5

There was no earnings cap for this year.

Table 27.5—Retirement annuity premiums

1994–95	
Age at 6 April 1994	*Percentage of net relevant earnings*
Up to 50	17.5
51–55	20
56–60	22.5
61 or more	27.5
1987–88 to 1993–94	
Age at beginning of tax year	
Up to 50	17.5
51–55	20
56–60	22.5
61 or more	27.5

27.2   Capital gains tax

Table 27.6—Rates of tax

	1992–93 to 1994–95	1991–92	1990–91	1989–90	1988–89
Annual Exemptions					
Individuals	5,800	5,500	5,000	5,000	5,000
Trusts	2,900	2,750	2,500	2,500	2,500
Rates of Tax					
Individuals					
1987–88: All gains 30%					
For years thereafter gains effectively taxed on top slice of taxable income:					
Gain less than lower rate limit	20%				
Gain less than basic rate limit (1992–93 only) greater than lower rate limit	25%	25%	25%	25%	25%
Gain greater than basic rate limit	40%	40%	40%	40%	40%
Trusts					
Discretionary (including Accumulation and Maintenance)	35%	35%	35%	35%	35%
Interest in possession	25%	25%	25%	25%	25%
Settlor (or settlor's spouse) retain an interest	Chargeable on settlor at his personal rate (see Individuals, above)				

Table 27.7—Capital gains tax indexation allowance

RETAIL PRICE INDEX FIGURES

	1982	1983	1984	1985	1986	1987
January		325.9	342.6	359.8	379.7	394.5/100.0[1]
February		327.3	344.0	362.9	381.1	100.4
March	313.4	327.9	345.1	366.1	381.6	100.6
April	319.7	332.5	349.7	373.9	385.3	101.8
May	322.0	333.9	351.0	375.6	386.0	101.9
June	322.9	334.7	351.9	376.4	385.8	101.9
July	320.0	336.5	351.5	375.5	384.7	101.8
August	323.1	338.0	354.8	376.7	385.9	102.1
September	322.9	339.5	355.5	376.5	387.8	102.4
October	324.5	340.7	357.7	377.1	388.4	102.9
November	326.1	341.9	358.8	378.4	391.7	103.4
December	325.5	342.8	358.5	378.9	393.0	103.3

	1988	1989	1990	1991	1992	1993	1994
January	103.3	111.0	119.5	130.2	135.6	137.9	141.3
February	103.7	111.8	120.2	130.9	136.3	138.8	142.1
March	104.1	112.3	121.4	131.4	136.7	139.3	142.5
April	105.8	114.3	125.1	133.1	138.8	140.6	
May	106.2	115.0	126.2	133.5	139.3	141.1	
June	106.6	115.4	126.7	134.1	139.3	141.0	
July	106.7	115.5	126.8	133.8	138.8	140.7	
August	107.9	115.8	128.1	134.1	138.9	141.3	
September	108.4	116.6	129.3	134.6	139.4	141.9	
October	109.5	117.5	130.3	135.1	139.9	141.8	
November	110.0	118.5	130.0	135.6	139.7	141.6	
December	110.3	118.8	129.9	135.7	139.2	141.9	

[1] *Note*: At January 1987 the index base was changed to 100.0. This means that an adjustment must be made where an asset was acquired before 1987 and sold after 31 Dec 1986. Thus where an asset was acquired in January 1986 and sold in January 1989, RD will be 394.5 x $\frac{111}{100}$

Table 27.8—Rates of interest on overdue tax/repayment supplement

6 April 1987 to 5 June 1987	9%
6 June 1987 to 5 September 1987	8.25%
6 Sept 1987 to 5 December 1987	9%
6 Dec 1987 to 5 May 1988	8.25%
6 May 1988 to 5 August 1988	7.75%
6 August 1988 to 5 October 1988	9.75%
6 October 1988 to 5 January 1989	10.75%
6 January 1989 to 5 July 1989	11.5%
6 July 1989 to 5 November 1989	12.25%
6 November 1989 to 5 November 1990	13%
6 November 1990 to 5 March 1991	12.25%
6 March 1991 to 5 May 1991	11.5%
6 May 1991 to 5 July 1991	10.75%
6 July 1991 to 5 October 1991	10%
6 October 1991 to 5 November 1992	9.25%
6 November 1992 to 5 December 1992	7.75%
6 December 1992 to 5 March 1993	7%
6 March 1993 to 5 January 1994	6.25%
6 January 1994 onwards	5.5%

27.3   Inheritance tax

Table 27.9—Rates of Tax

	TRANSFERS ON DEATH			GROSS	LIFETIME TRANSFERS			GROSS
Cumulative chargeable transfers net £	Rate on gross % age	Rate on net fraction £	Cumulative tax £	Cumulative chargeable transfers £	Rate on gross % age	Rate on net fraction	Cumulative tax £	Cumulative chargeable transfers £
from 17 March 1987 to 14 March 1988								
0–90,000	nil	nil	nil	0–90,000	nil	nil	nil	0–90,000
90,001–125,000	30	3/7	15,000	90,000–140,000	15	3/17	7,500	90,001–132,500
125,001–173,000	40	2/3	47,000	140,000–220,000	20	1/4	23,500	132,501–196,500
173,001–228,000	50	1	102,000	220,000–330,000	25	1/3	51,000	196,501–279,000
over 228,000	60	3/2	–	over 330,000	30	3/7	–	over 279,000
from 15 March 1988 to 5 April 1989								
0–110,000	nil	nil	nil	0–110,000	nil	nil	nil	0–110,000
over 118,000	40	2/3	–	over 110,000	20	1/4	–	over 110,000
from 6 April 1989 to 5 April 1990								
0–118,000	nil	nil	nil	0–118,000	nil	nil	nil	0–118,000
over 118,000	40	2/3	–	over 118,000	20	1/4	–	over 118,000
from 6 April 1990 to 5 April 1991								
0–128,000	nil	nil	nil	0–128,000	nil	nil	nil	0–128,000
over 128,000	40	2/3	–	over 128,000	20	1/4	–	over 128,000
from 6 April 1991 to 5 April 1992								
0–140,000	nil	nil	nil	0–140,000	nil	nil	nil	0–140,000
over 140,000	40	2/3	–	over 140,000	20	1/4	–	over 140,000
from 6 April 1992								
0–150,000	nil	nil	nil	0–150,000	nil	nil	nil	0–150,000
over 150,000	40	2/3	–	over 150,000	20	1/4	–	over 150,000

27.4   Corporation tax

Table 27.10—Rates of tax

Financial year commencing 1 April	*1988*	*1989*	*1990*	*1991*	*1992 & 1993*	*1994*
Full rate	35%	35%	34%	33%	33%	33%
Small companies rate	25%	25%	25%	25%	25%	25%
Small companies rate —profit limit	£100,000	£150,000	£200,000	£250,000	£250,000	£300,000
Small companies marginal relief profit limit	£500,000	£750,000	£1,000.000	£1,250,000	£1,250,000	£1,500,000

Index

Other titles in the Allied Dunbar Library

- Allied Dunbar Capital Taxes and Estate Planning Guide — WI Sinclair & PD Silke

- Allied Dunbar Expatriate Tax and Investment Guide — David Phillips

- Allied Dunbar Investment and Savings Handbook 1994–95 — General Editor: Harry Littlefair

- Allied Dunbar Retirement Planning Handbook 1994–95 — David Vessey

- Allied Dunbar Pensions Handbook 1994–95 — AM Reardon

All of these titles in the Allied Dunbar Library are available from leading bookshops

For more information please contact: Longman Law, Tax and Finance, 21–27 Lamb's Conduit St, London WC1N 3NJ Tel: (071) 242 2548